PHILIP'S

G000297609

STREE'
Herefordshire
Monmouthshire

First published 2003 by

Philip's, a division of
Octopus Publishing Group Ltd
2-4 Heron Quays, London E14 4JP

First edition 2003
First impression 2003

ISBN 0-540-08491-3 (pocket)

© Philip's 2003

 Ordnance Survey®

This product includes mapping data licensed from
Ordnance Survey® with the permission of the
Controller of Her Majesty's Stationery Office.
© Crown copyright 2003. All rights reserved.
Licence number 100011710.

Printed and bound in Spain
by Cayfosa-Quebecor

Contents

Inside front cover
Administrative and Postcode boundaries

II **Key to map pages**

IV **Route planning**

VIII **Key to map symbols**

2 **Street maps** at 1⅓ inches to 1 mile

79 **Street maps** at 2⅔ inches to 1 mile

136 **Street maps of centres of Hereford and Monmouth** at 5⅓ inches to 1 mile

138 **Index** of towns and villages

140 **Index** of streets, hospitals, industrial estates, railway stations, schools, shopping centres, universities and places of interest

Digital Data

The exceptionally high-quality mapping found in this atlas is available as digital data in TIFF format, which is easily convertible to other bitmapped (raster) image formats.

The index is also available in digital form as a standard database table. It contains all the details found in the printed index together with the National Grid reference for the map square in which each entry is named.

For further information and to discuss your requirements, please contact Philip's on 020 7644 6932 or james.mann@philips-maps.co.uk

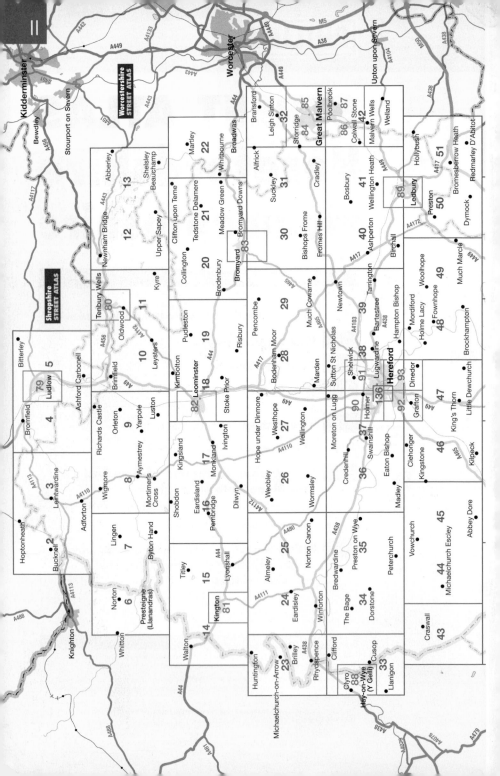

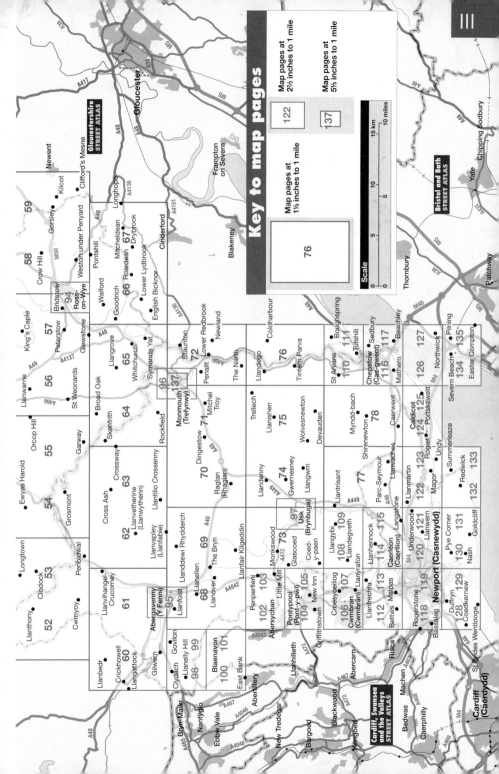

III

Key to map pages

Map pages at 2⅓ inches to 1 mile

122

Map pages at 5⅓ inches to 1 mile

137

Map pages at 1⅓ inches to 1 mile

76

Scale

0	5	10	15 km
0	5	10 miles	

Gloucestershire STREET ATLAS

Bristol and Bath STREET ATLAS

Cardiff, Swansea and the Valleys STREET ATLAS

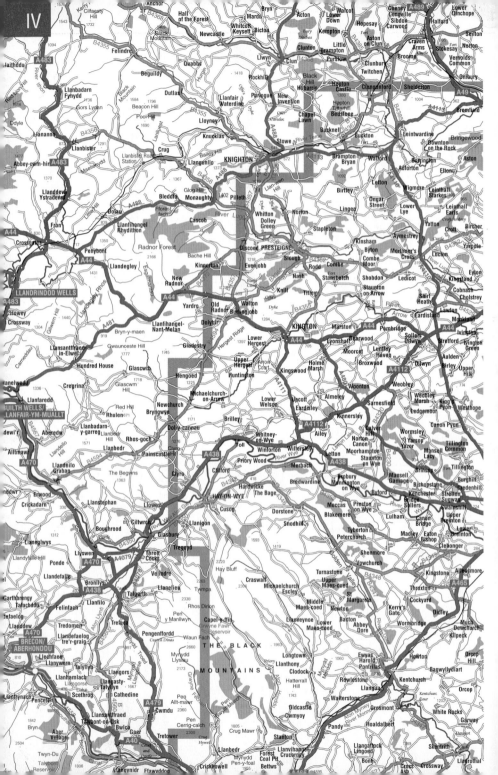

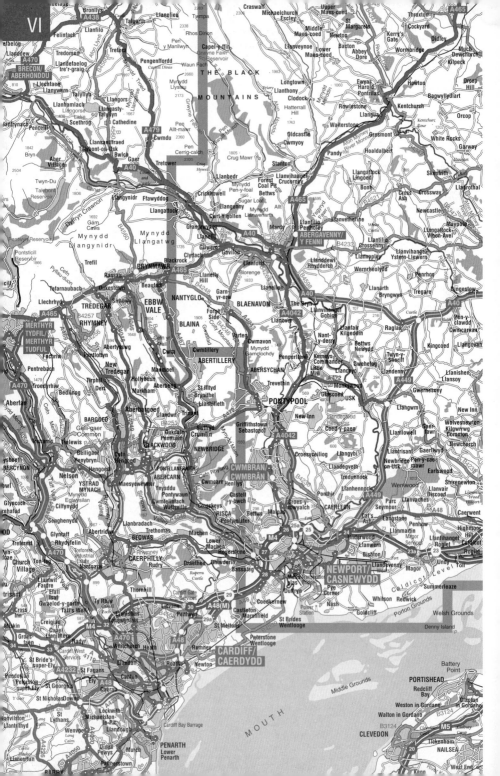

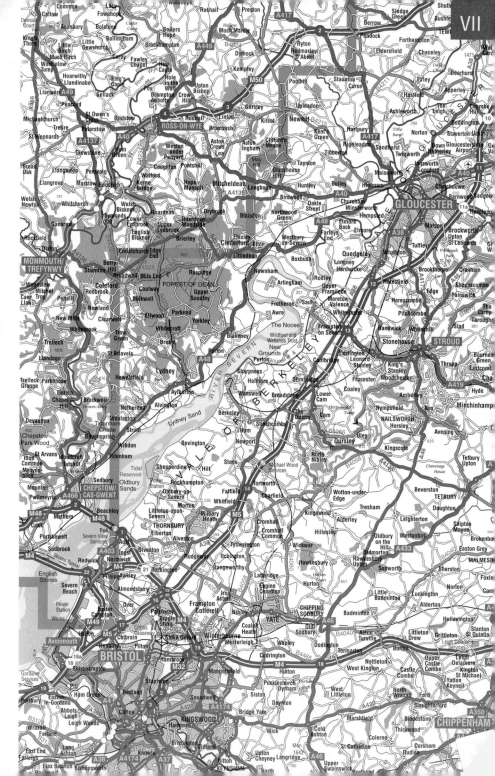

Allwedd i symbolau'r map

Trafford gyda rhif y gyffordd

Prif dramwyfeydd – ffordd ddeuol/un lôn

Ffordd A – ffordd ddeuol/un lôn

Ffordd B – ffordd ddeuol/un lôn

Ffyrdd bychan – ffordd ddeuol/un lôn

Ffyrdd bychan eraill – ffordd ddeuol/un lôn

Ffordd yn cael ei hadeiladu

Twnnel, ffordd dan orchudd

Trac gwledig, ffordd breifat, neu ffordd mewn ardal ddinesig

Llidiart neu rhwystr i draffig (gall fod cyfyngiadau ddim yn ddilys ar gyfer bob amser neu i bob drafnidiaeth)

Llwybr, llwybr march, cilffordd yn agored i bob trafnidiaeth, ffordd a ddefnyddir yn lwybr cyhoeddus

Mân cerddwyr

DY7   Ffiniau codau-post

Ffiniau Sir ac awdurdod unedol

Rheilffordd, twnnel, rheilffordd yn cael ei hadeiladu

Tramffordd, tramffordd yn cael ei hadeiladu

Rheilffordd ar raddfa fychan

Walsall   Gorsaf rheilffordd

Gorsaf rheilffordd breifat

South Shields   Gorsaf metro

Atalfa tram, atalfa tram yn cael ei hadeiladu

Gorsaf fysiau

♦   Gorsaf ambiwlans

♦   Gorsaf gwylwyr y glannau

♦   Gorsaf Dân

♦   Swyddfa'r heddlu

✚   Mynedfa damwain ac argyfwng i'r ysbyty

H   Ysbyty

✛   Lle o addoliad

i   Canolfan gwybodaeth (a'r agor drwy'r flwyddyn)

P   Parcio

P&R   Parcio a chludo

PO   Swyddfa'r post

⅄   Safle gwersylla

⏗   Safle carafan

▶   Cwrs golff

✕   Safle picnic

Prim Sch   Adeiladau pwysig, ysgolion, colegau, prifysgolion ac ysbytai

River Medway   Enw dŵr

Afon, cored, nant

Camlas, loc, twnnel

Dŵr

Dŵr llanw

Coed

Ardal adeiledig

Acad	Academi	IRB Sta	Gorsaf bad	Pal	Palas brenhinol	Church	**Hynafiaeth anrhufeinig**
Allot Gdns	Gerddi ar osod		achub y glannau	PH	Tŷ tafarn		
Cemy	Mynwent	Inst	Institiwt	Recn Gd	Maes chwaraeon	ROMAN FORT	**Hynafiaeth rhufeinig**
C Ctr	Canolfan	Ct	Llys cyfraith	Resr	Cronfa ddŵr		
	ddinesig	L Ctr	Canolfan	Ret Pk	Parc adwerthu	**87**	**Arwyddion dalennau cyfagos a bandiau gorymylon**
CH	Tŷ Clwb		hamdden	Sch	Ysgol		Y mae lliw a'r saeth â'r band yn dynodi gradd y ddalen gyfagos â'r ddalen gorymyl (gwelwch y graddau islaw)
Coll	Coleg	LC	Croesfan	Sh Ctr	Canolfan Siopa	**228**	
Crem	Amlosgfa		wastad	TH	Neuadd y dref		
Ent	Menter	Liby	Llyfrgell	Trad Est	Ystad Fasnachol		
Ex H	Neuadd	Mkt	Marchnad	Univ	Prifysgol		
	Arddangos	Meml	Coffa	W Twr	Tŵrddwr		■ Y mae'r rhifau bach o gwmpas ochrau'r mapiau yn dynodi llinelli grid cenedlaethol 1 cilomedr
Ind Est	Ystad	Mon	Cofgolofn	Wks	Gwaith		■ Mae'r ffin llwyd tywyll ar ochr fewn rhai tudalennau yn dynodi nad yw'r mapio yn canlyn ymlaen i'r tudalen gyffiniol
	ddiwydiannol	Mus	Amgueddfa	YH	Hostel ieuenctid		
		Obsy	Arsylffa				

Gradd y mapiau ar y dalennau gyda rhifau glas yw 4.2 cm i 1 km • 2⅔ modfedd i 1 filltir • 1: 23810	0 ¼ ½ ¾ 1 milltir 0 250m 500m 750m 1 km
Gradd y mapiau ar y dalennau gyda rhifau gwyrdd yw is 2.1 i to 1 km • 1⅓ modfedd i 1 filltir • 1: 47620	0 ¼ ½ ¾ 1 milltir 0 250m 500m 750m 1 km
Gradd y mapiau ar y dalennau gyda rhifau coch yw is 8.4 i to 1 km • 5⅓ modfedd i 1 filltir • 1: 11900	0 220 yards 440 yards 660 yards ½ milltir 0 125m 250m 375m ½ km

	Motorway with junction number
	Primary route – dual/single carriageway
	A road – dual/single carriageway
	B road – dual/single carriageway
	Minor road – dual/single carriageway
	Other minor road – dual/single carriageway
	Road under construction
	Tunnel, covered road
	Rural track, private road or narrow road in urban area
	Gate or obstruction to traffic (restrictions may not apply at all times or to all vehicles)
	Path, bridleway, byway open to all traffic, road used as a public path
	Pedestrianised area
DY7	**Postcode boundaries**
	County and unitary authority boundaries
	Railway, tunnel, railway under construction
	Tramway, tramway under construction
	Miniature railway
Walsall	**Railway station**
	Private railway station
South Shields	**Metro station**
	Tram stop, tram stop under construction
	Bus, coach station

◆	**Ambulance station**
◆	**Coastguard station**
◆	**Fire station**
◆	**Police station**
✚	**Accident and Emergency entrance to hospital**
H	**Hospital**
+	**Place of worship**
i	**Information Centre** (open all year)
P	**Parking**
P&R	**Park and Ride**
PO	**Post Office**
Ⓧ	**Camping site**
⊕	**Caravan site**
►	**Golf course**
✕	**Picnic site**
Prim Sch	**Important buildings, schools, colleges, universities and hospitals**
River Medway	**Water name**
	River, weir, stream
	Canal, lock, tunnel
	Water
	Tidal water
	Woods
	Built up area
Church	**Non-Roman antiquity**
ROMAN FORT	**Roman antiquity**
87	**Adjoining page indicators and overlap bands** The colour of the arrow and the band indicates the scale of the adjoining or overlapping page (see scales below)
228	

Acad	**Academy**	Inst	**Institute**	Recn Gd	**Recreation**		
Allot Gdns	**Allotments**	Ct	**Law Court**		**Ground**		
Cemy	**Cemetery**	L Ctr	**Leisure Centre**	Resr	**Reservoir**		
C Ctr	**Civic Centre**	LC	**Level Crossing**	Ret Pk	**Retail Park**		
CH	**Club House**	Liby	**Library**	Sch	**School**		
Coll	**College**	Mkt	**Market**	Sh Ctr	**Shopping Centre**		
Crem	**Crematorium**	Meml	**Memorial**	TH	**Town Hall/House**		
Ent	**Enterprise**	Mon	**Monument**	Trad Est	**Trading Estate**		
Ex H	**Exhibition Hall**	Mus	**Museum**	Univ	**University**		
Ind Est	**Industrial Estate**	Obsy	**Observatory**	W Twr	**Water Tower**		
IRB Sta	**Inshore Rescue**	Pal	**Royal Palace**	Wks	**Works**		
	Boat Station	PH	**Public House**	YH	**Youth Hostel**		

■ The small numbers around the edges of the maps identify the 1 kilometre National Grid lines

■ The dark grey border on the inside edge of some pages indicates that the mapping does not continue onto the adjacent page

The scale of the maps on the pages numbered in blue is 4.2 cm to 1 km • 2⅔ inches to 1 mile • 1: 23810	0 ¼ ½ ¾ 1 mile
	0 250m 500m 750m 1 kilometre

The scale of the maps on pages numbered in green is 2.1 cm to 1 km • 1⅓ inches to 1 mile • 1: 47620	0 ¼ ½ ¾ 1 mile
	0 250m 500m 750m 1 kilometre

The scale of the maps on pages numbered in red is 8.4 cm to 1 km • 5⅓ inches to 1 mile • 1: 11900	0 220 yards 440 yards 660 yards ½ mile
	0 125m 250m 375m ½ kilometre

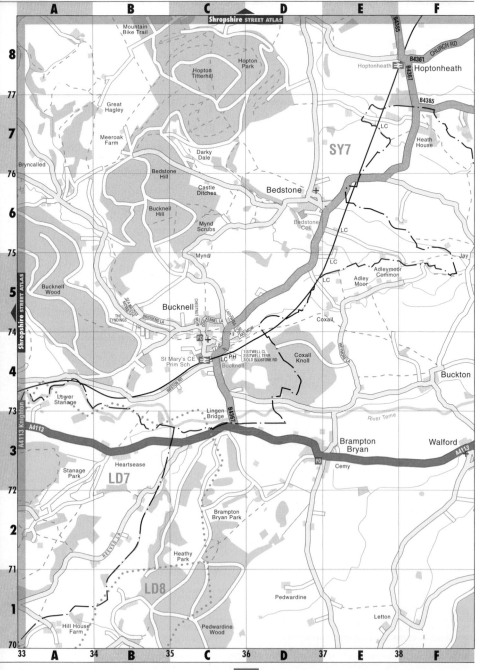

Scale: 1½ inches to 1 mile

0   ¼   ½ mile
0   250m 500m 750m 1 km

Mountain
Bike Trail

Hopton
Titterhill

Hopton
Park

CHURCH RD

B4385

Hoptonheath

B4361

B4367

Hoptonheath

Great
Hagley

B4385

LC

Heath
House

SY7

Meeroak
Farm

Darky
Dale

Bryncalled

Bedstone
Hill

Castle
Ditches

Bedstone

Bedstone
Coll

Bucknell
Hill

LC

Mynd
Scrubs

LC

Jay

Myrnd

LC

Adleymoor
Common

Bucknell
Wood

LC

Adley
Moor

THE
TYNDINGS

SKYBORRY
LANDING

Bucknell

CHESTNUT VIEW

KEMEL LA

BRIDGEND LA

MILL MDW

Coxall

WEYMOORE LA

St Mary's CE
Prim Sch

PH

LC

1 SITWELL CL
2 SITWELL TERR
3 OLD BEDSTONE RD

Coxall
Knoll

Buckton

Bucknell

WESTON RD

B4367

Lower
Stanage

Lingen
Bridge

River Teme

A4113 Knighton

A4113

Brampton
Bryan

Walford

A4113

Stanage
Park

Heartsease

LD7

Cemy

PO

HEAVES LA

Brampton
Bryan Park

Heathy
Park

LD8

Pedwardine

Hill House
Farm

Pedwardine
Wood

Letton

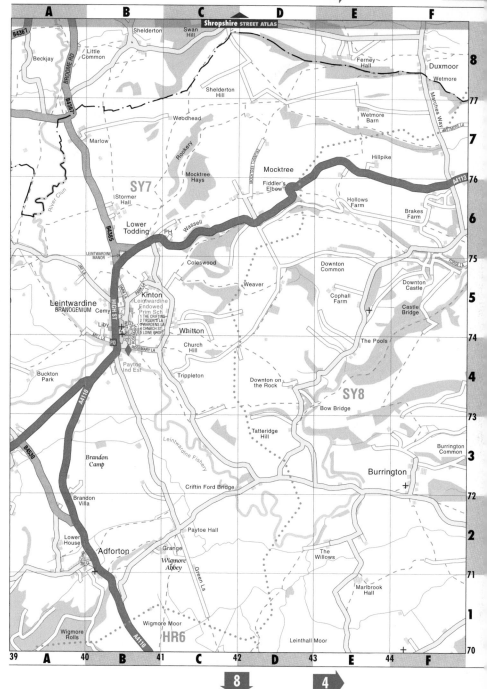

Shropshire STREET ATLAS

4

A   B   C   D   E   F

8
Beckjay
Little
Common
Shelderton
Swan
Hill
Ferney
Hall
Duxmoor
Wetmore

77
Shelderton
Hill
Wetmore
Barn
WETMORE LA

B4361
BROOME RD
B4361

Woodhead

7
Marlow
Rookery
Mocktree
Mocktree
Hays
Hillpike
A4113

SY7
Fiddler's
Elbow
Mocktree
MOCKTREE TURN PIKE

76
iStormer
Hall
Hollows
Farm
Brakes
Farm

6
River Clun
Lower
Todding
PH
Wassell
Downton
Common
Downton
Castle
FORGE LA

75
LEINTWARDINE
MANOR
Coleswood
Weaver
Cophall
Farm
Castle
Bridge

5
Leintwardine
BRANOGENIUM
Cemy
Kinton
Leintwardine
Endowed
Prim Sch
1 THE CRUFTS
2 TIPSON'S LA
3 WARDENS LA
4 CHURCH ST
5 LOWE GROFT
HIGH ST
B4350
Whitton
The Pools

74
Liby
MILL LA
PO
ROSEMARY LA
Church
Hill

4
Buckton
Park
A4110
Paytoe
Ind Est
Trippleton
Downton on
the Rock
SY8
Bow Bridge

73
B4530
Leintwardine Fishery
Tatteridge
Hill
Burrington
Common

3
Brandon
Camp
Criftin Ford Bridge
Burrington

72
Brandon
Villa

2
Lower
House
Adforton
Paytoe Hall
Grange
Wigmore
Abbey
The
Willows
Green La

71
Marlbrook
Hall

1
Wigmore
Rolls
Wigmore Moor
A4110
HR6
Leinthall Moor

70
39   A   40   B   41   C   42   D   43   E   44   F

8   **4**

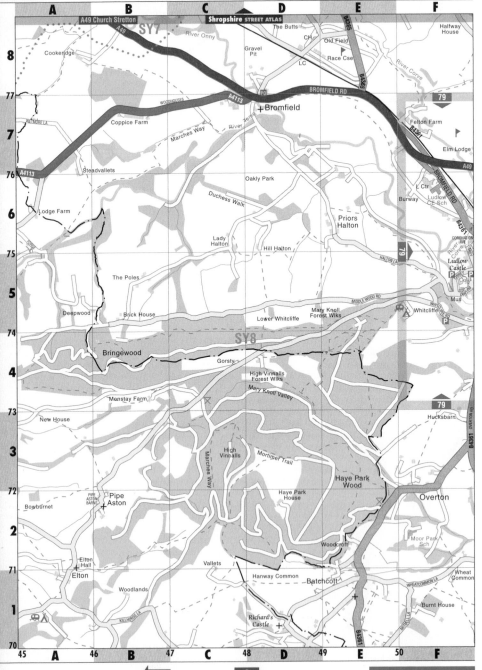

Shropshire STREET ATLAS

A49 Church Stretton

A   B   C   D   E   F

SY7

The Butts

CH
Old Field
Race Cse

Halfway
House

8

Cookeridge

River Onny

Gravel
Pit

LC

River Corve

79

77

WOODHOUSES

A4113

BROMFIELD RD

PO

+ Bromfield

Felton Farm

Coppice Farm

B4361

Marches Way

River Teme

7

Elm Lodge

A49

WIGMORE LA

Steadvallets

BROMFIELD RD

76

A4113

Oakly Park

Duchess Walk

L Ctr
Burway

Ludlow
CE Sch

6

Lodge Farm

Priors
Halton

B4361

CORONATION
AVE

75

Lady
Halton

Hill Halton

HALTON LA

A49

Ludlow
Castle
P

Mus

5

The Poles

MIDDLE WOOD RD

Deepwood

Brick House

Mary Knoll
Forest Wlks

Whitcliffe

74

Lower Whitcliffe

SY8

P

Bringewood

Gorsty

4

Monstay Farm

High Vinnalls
Forest Wlks

Mary Knoll Valley

73

New House

Hucksbarn

B4361

OVERTON RD

3

High
Vinnalls

Marches Way

Mortimer Trail

Haye Park
Wood

Overton

72

Bowburnet

PIPE
ASTON
BARNS

Pipe
Aston

Haye Park
House

Moor Park
Sch

2

Woodcroft

Elton
Hall

Vallets

Wheat
Common

71

Elton

Hanway Common

Batchcoft

WHEATCOMMON LA

KILLHORSE LA

Woodlands

Burnt House

B4361

MILL LA

1

Richard's
Castle

70

45   A   46   B   47   C   48   D   49   E   50   F

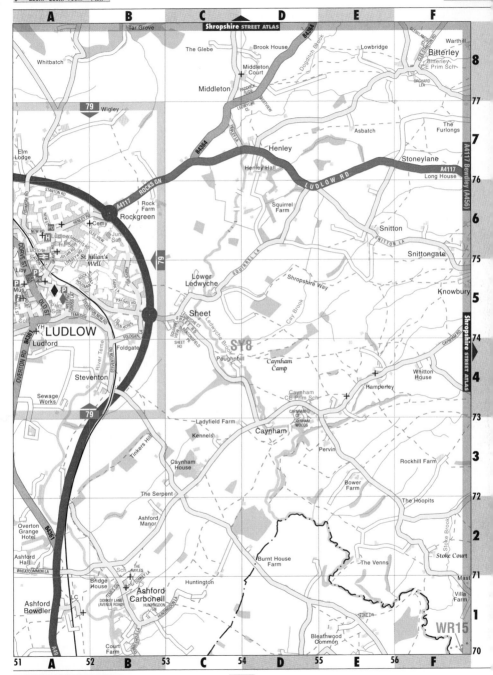

Scale: 1½ inches to 1 mile

0   ¼   ½ mile
0   250m 500m 750m 1 km

Shropshire STREET ATLAS

Whitbatch

The Glebe

Brook House

Oaditch Brook

Lowbridge

Warthill

Bitterley

Bitterley
CE Prim Sch

8

Middleton
Court

77

Wigley

Middleton

The Furlongs

7

Elm
Lodge

Henley

Asbatch

Stoneylane

Long House

A4117 Bewdley (A456)

Rockgreen

Rock
Farm

Henley Hall

LUDLOW RD

Squirrel
Farm

76

Cemy

St Julian's
Well

Snitton

Snittongate

6

75

LUDLOW

Ludford

Lower
Ledwyche

Sheet

Shropshire Way

Cay Brook

Knowbury

5

SY8

Caynham
Camp

Whitton
House

74

Foldgate

Poughnhill

4

Steventon

Sewage
Works

Caynham
CE Prim Sch

Hamperley

79

Ladyfield Farm

Caynham
of
CAYNHAM
WOODS

73

Kennels

Caynham

Pervin

Rockhill Farm

3

Tinkers Hill

Caynham
House

Bower
Farm

The Hoopits

72

The Serpent

Overton
Grange
Hotel

Ashford
Manor

Stoke Brook

Ashford
Hall

WHEATCOMMON LA

Burnt House
Farm

The Venns

Stoke Court

2

Mast

Villa
Farm

71

Bridge
House

THE
HAYLES

Huntington

Ashford
Bowdler

Ashford
Carbonell

DONKEY LANE
(AVENUE ROAD)

STOKE DR

WR15

1

Court
Farm

Bleathwood
Common

70

For full street detail of the
highlighted area see page 79.

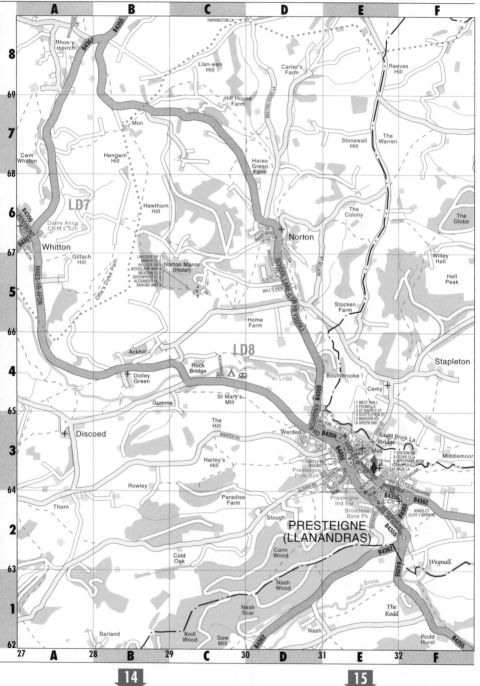

A   B   C   D   E   F

8

FARRINGTON LA

Rhos-y-meirch

WOODHOUSE LA

B4357

B4355

Llan-wen Hill

Carter's Farm

Reeves Hill

69

Hill House Farm

MEETING HOUSE LA

7

Mon

Cwm Whitton

Hengwm Hill

Stonewall Hill

The Warren

68

Hares Green Farm

LD7

Hawthorn Hill

The Colony

The Globe

6

B4356

Dame Anna Child's Sch

MAES-YR-AFON

Whitton

Gilfach Hill

Offa's Dyke Path

OFFA'S DYKE

OLD MILL RD

GRAVEL HILL

OFFICE ON MANS OFFA'S

B4356

MYND RD

SCHOOL LANE (LON YR YSGOL)

Norton

NEWTON LA

Willey Hall

Hell Peak

67

LAKESIDE DR 1
MANOR CL 2
HILLSIDE DR 3
WOODLAND WAY 4
MEADOW CL 5
GREENPRICE CL 6
ALEXANDER CL 7
BARONS WAY 8

Norton Manor (Hotel)

MILBROOK EST

CAEFFLUS

WILL'S VIEW

Stocken Farm

5

Home Farm

66

Ackhill

LD8

Rock Bridge

HOOKMORE

River Lugg

Boultibrooke

Stapleton

4

Dolley Green

St Mary's Mill

KINSHAM RD

B4355

Cemy

Middlemoor

65

Gumma

The Hill

Warden

WILSON

B4356

MILL ST

HIGH ST

Lugg Brink La

Bridge

1 WEST WALL
2 POUND LA
3 ST DAVID'S ST
4 SCOTTLETON ST
5 WARDEN RD
6 GREEN END

7 STATION RD
8 CEDAR CL
9 APPLETREE MDW
10 HARPER'S LA
11 BACK LA

Discoed

WARDEN RD

3

Harley's Hill

B4355

Mus

Liby

P

THE PLANTATION

KINGS CT (LLYS Y BRENIN)

64

Thorn

Rowley

Paradise Farm

Presteigne Prim Sch

CASTLE RD BGLWS

SLOUGH RD

Presteigne Ind Est

Broadaxe Bsns Pk

L Ctr

B4356

BROADAXE

B4362

Wegnall

2

Slough

Cold Oak

Cann Wood

PRESTEIGNE (LLANANDRAS)

B4362

B4355

63

Nash Wood

Hindwell Brook

The Rodd

1

Barland

Knill Wood

Nash Scar

Saw Mill

Nash

B4362

Rodd Hurst

B4355

62

27   A   28   B   29   C   30   D   31   E   32   F

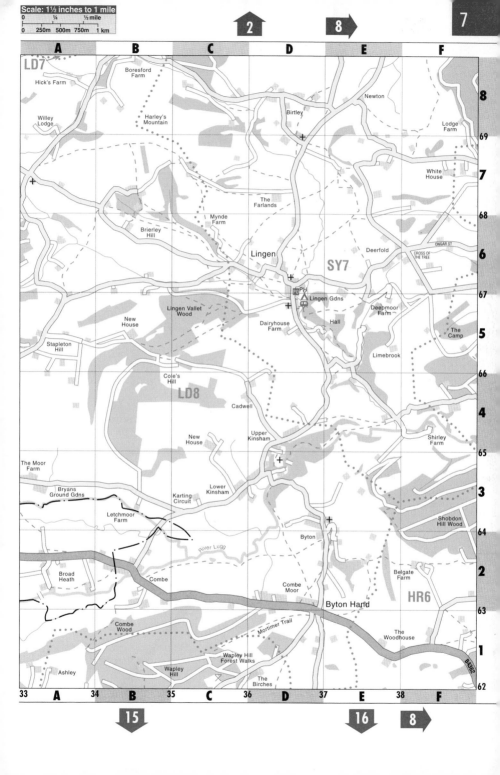

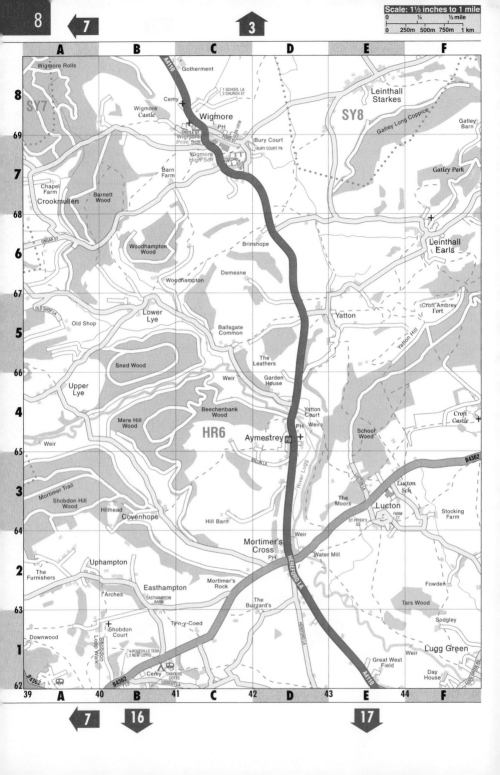

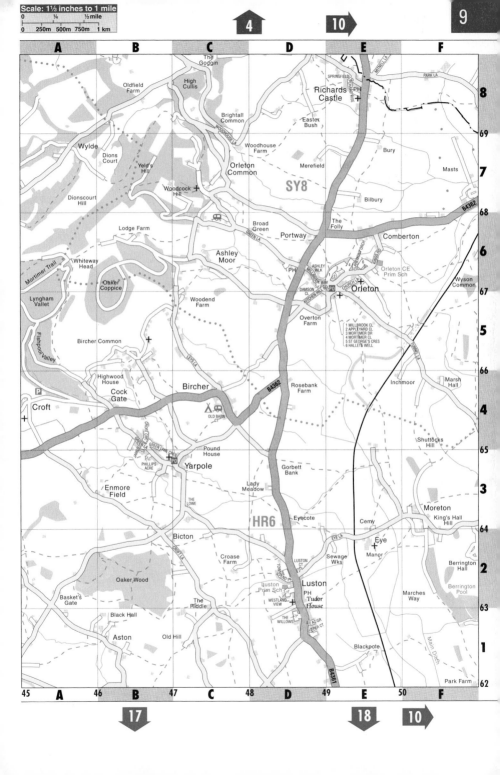

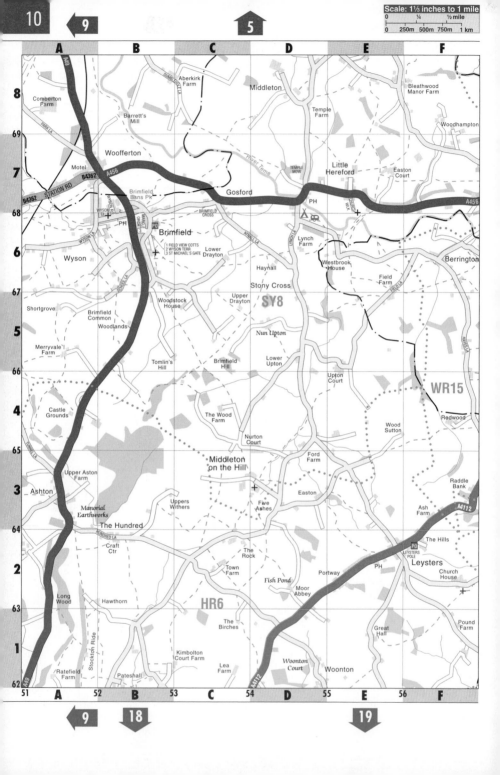

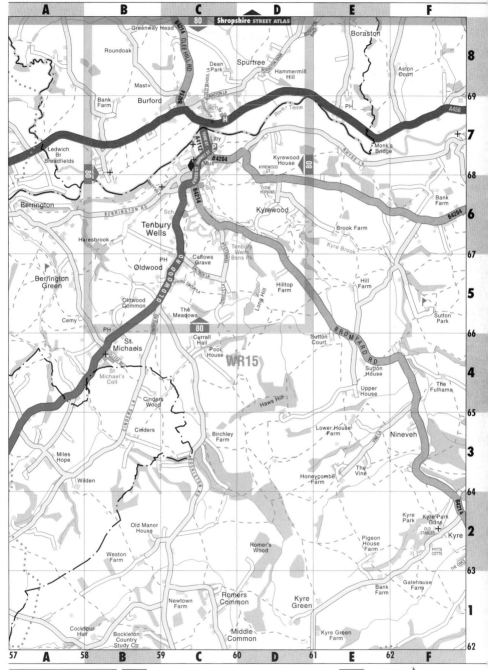

A **B** **C** **D** **E** **F**

8

Greenway Head

Roundoak

Boraston

Dean Park

Spurtree

Hammermill Hill

Aston Court

Mast

Burford

69

Bank Farm

Sch

River Teme

PH

A456

H

7

Liby

Trink St

Monk's Bridge

Ledwich Br
Broadfields

P

A4112

Mus

Kyrewood House

BRYSE LA

Sch

B4204

KYREWOOD CT

68

80

B4214

THE HOPKINS

Bank Farm

Berrington

BERRINGTON RD

Sch

Kyrewood

B4204

6

Haresbrook

Tenbury Wells

Brook Farm

Kyre Brook

67

PH

Callows Grave

Tenbury Wells Bsns Pk

Hill Farm

Oldwood

OLDWOOD RD

Berrington Green

SPRING GROVE LA

Hilltop Farm

5

Oldwood Common

Long Hill

Sutton Park

Cemy

The Meadows

80

Sutton Court

66

PH

Currall Hall

Pool House

WR15

Sutton House

St Michaels

Upper House

The Fulhams

4

St Michael's Coll

Cinders Wood

Haws Hill

65

CINDERS LA

Cinders

Lower House Farm

Nineveh

BROMYARD RD

3

Miles Hope

BOCKLETON RD

Birchley Farm

The Vine

Honeycombe Farm

64

Wilden

B4214

Kyre Park

Kyre Park Gdns

OLD STABLES

Kyre

2

Old Manor House

Pigeon House Farm

PYTTS COTTS

Weston Farm

Romer's Wood

THE OAKS

63

Gatehouse Farm

Cockspur Hall

Newtown Farm

Romers Common

Kyre Green

Bank Farm

1

Bockleton Country Study Ctr

Middle Common

Kyre Green Farm

62

A **B** **C** **D** **E** **F**

57 58 59 60 61 62

For full street detail of the highlighted area see page 80

19

20

12

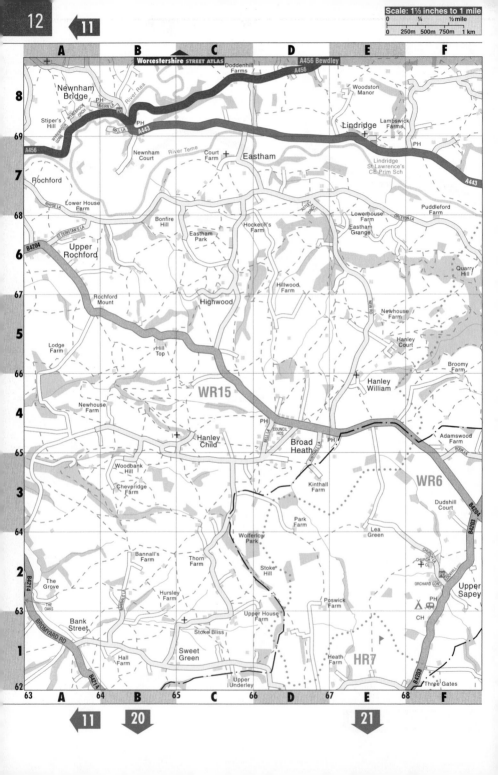

Worcestershire STREET ATLAS

A456 Bewdley

8

Newnham
Bridge

Doddenhill
Farms

A456

Woodston
Manor

PH
TAVERN LA
WITHINGTON LA
RD

Stiper's
Hill

WINDMILL
HILL
GRANGE

PH
MILE LA

PH
A443

River Rea

Lindridge

Lambswick
Farms

69

A456

River Teme

Newnham
Court

Court
Farm

Eastham

PH

Lindridge
St Lawrence's
CE Prim Sch

A443

7

Rochford

RHYSE LA

Lower House
Farm

Bonfire
Hill

Eastham
Park

Hockerill's
Farm

ASTLEY
DRIVE

Lowerhouse
Farm

Eastham
Grange

ORLETON LA

Puddleford
Farm

68

ST DUNSTAN'S LA

B4204

Upper
Rochford

Rochford
Mount

Highwood

Hillwood
Farm

NEW RD

Newhouse
Farm

Quarry
Hill

6

67

Lodge
Farm

Hill
Top

Hanley
Court

Broomy
Farm

5

66

WR15

Hanley
William

4

Newhouse
Farm

Hanley
Child

PH
BELL LA
COUNCIL
HOS

Broad
Heath

PH

Adamswood
Farm

DICK LA

WR6

65

Woodbank
Hill

Cheveridge
Farm

Kinthall
Farm

Dudshill
Court

B4204

3

64

B4214

Bannall's
Farm

Thorn
Farm

Wolferlow
Park

Park
Farm

Stoke
Hill

Lea
Green

CHURCH
CL
CHURCH
LA
PO

Upper
Sapey

2

The
Grove

THE OAKS

BARNALL'S LA

Hursley
Farm

ORCHARD GDNS

PH
CH

63

BROMYARD RD

Bank
Street

Stoke Bliss

Upper House
Farm

Poswick
Farm

1

B4214

Hall
Farm

Sweet
Green

Heath
Farm

HR7

B4203

62

Upper
Underley

Three
Gates

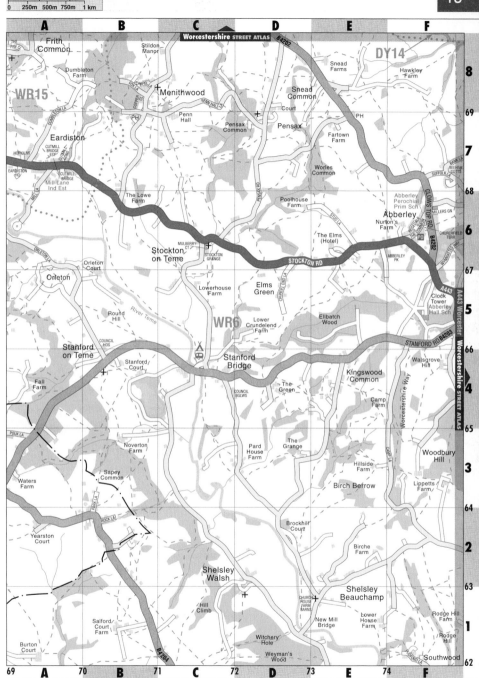

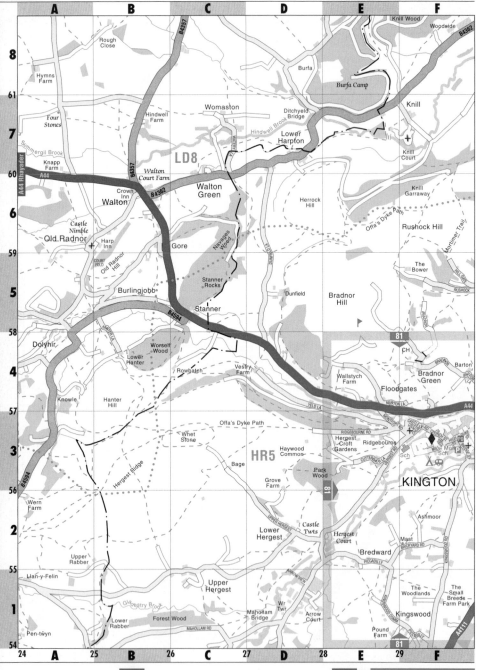

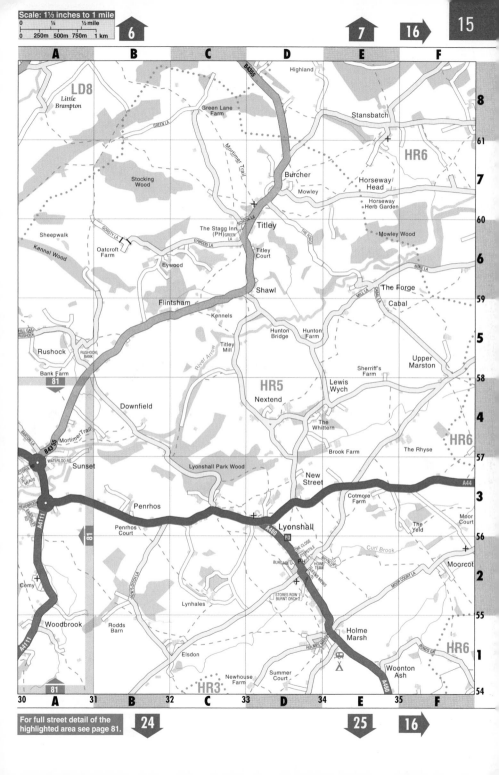

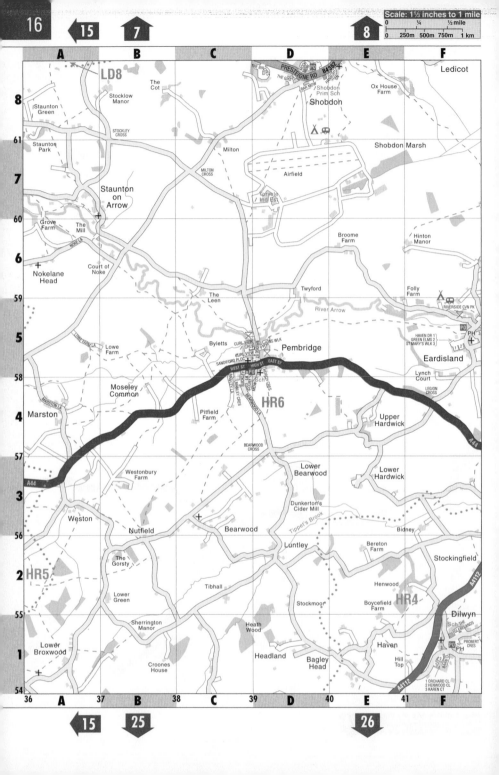

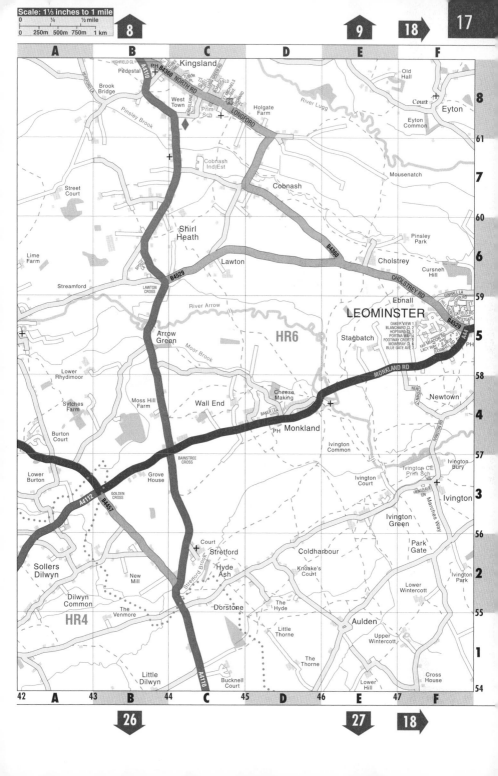

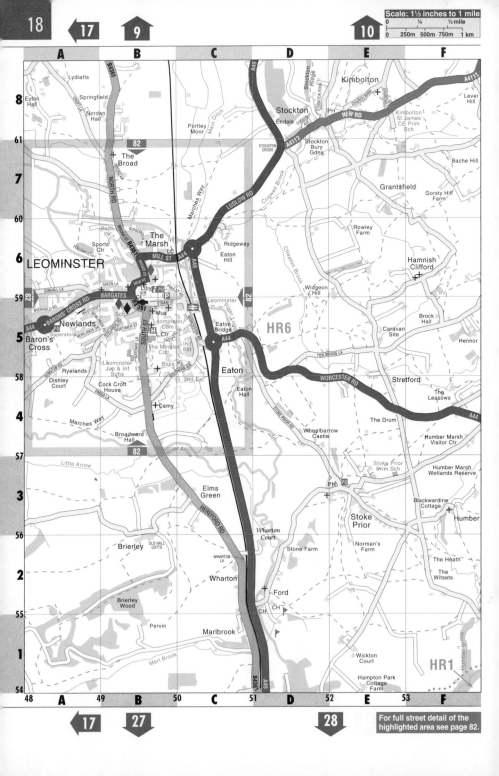

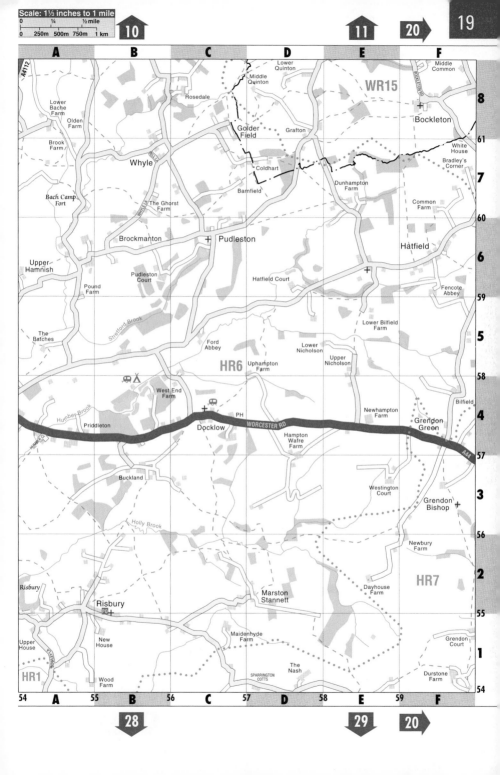

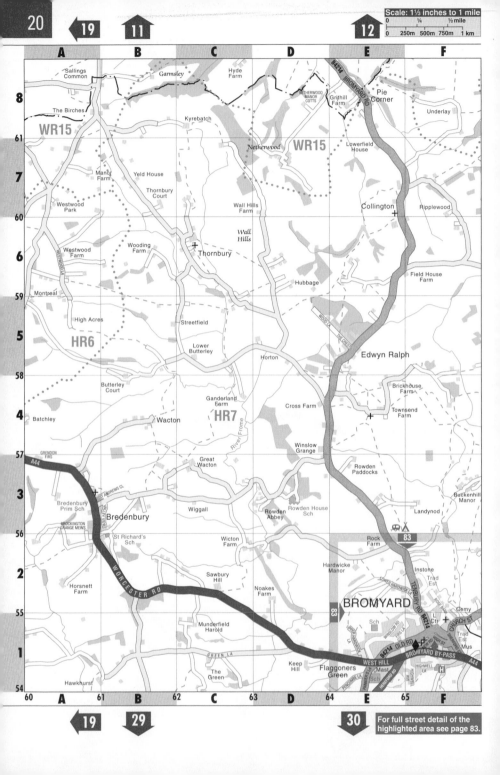

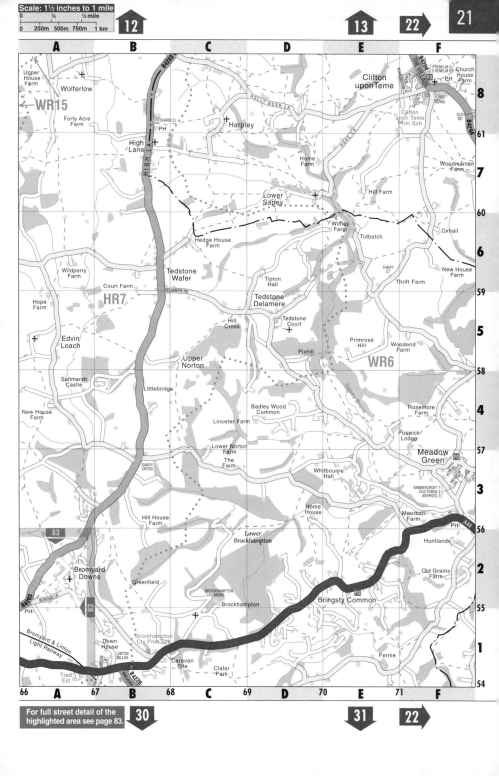

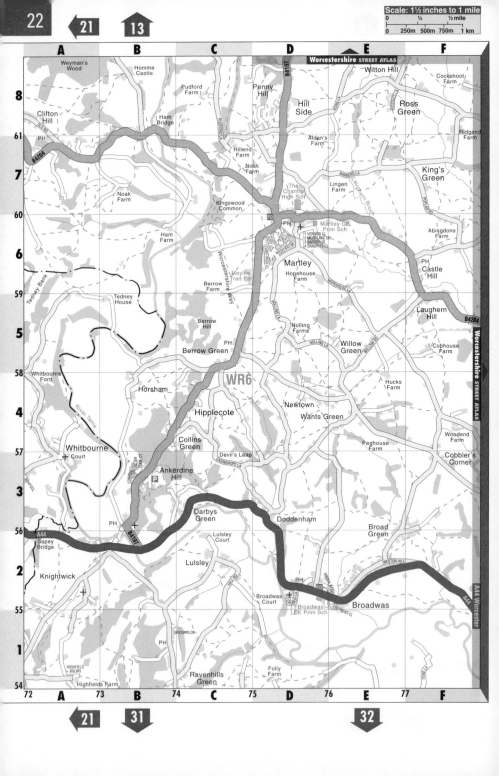

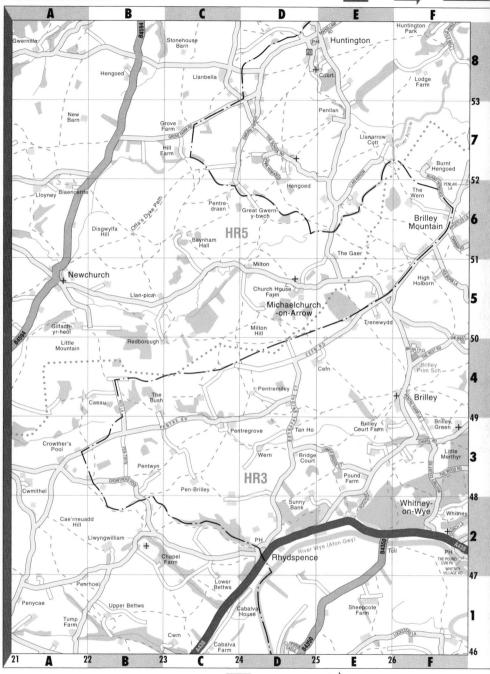

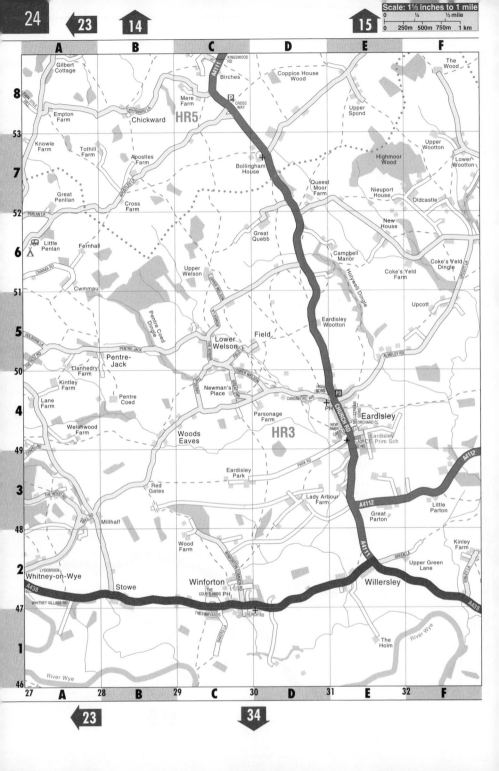

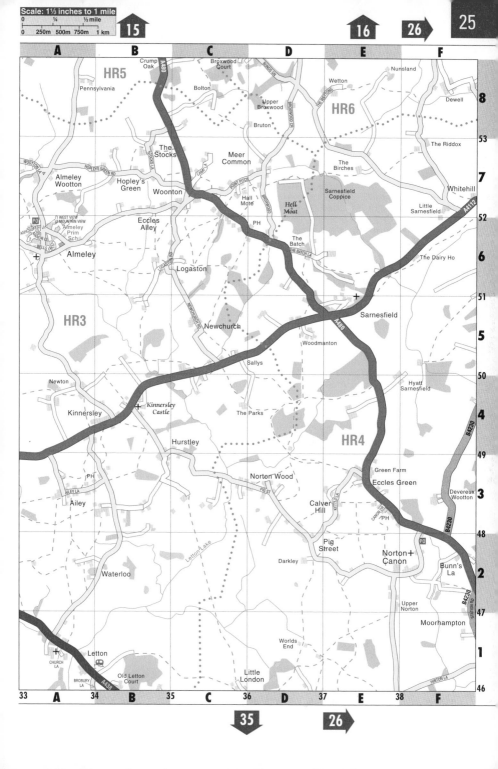

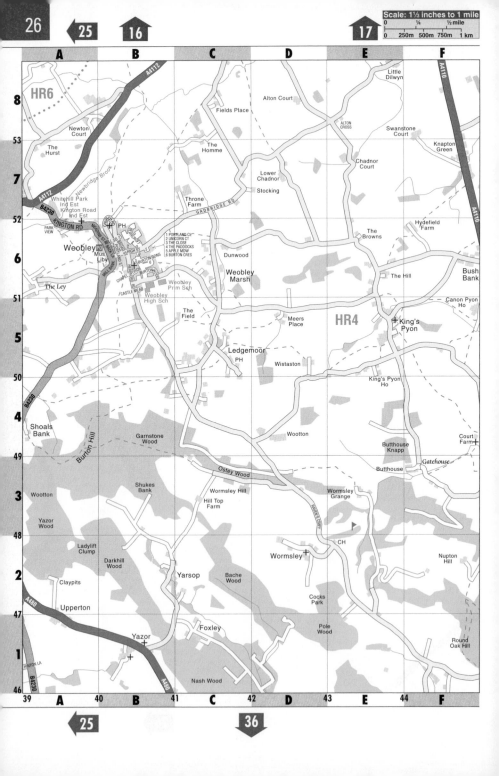

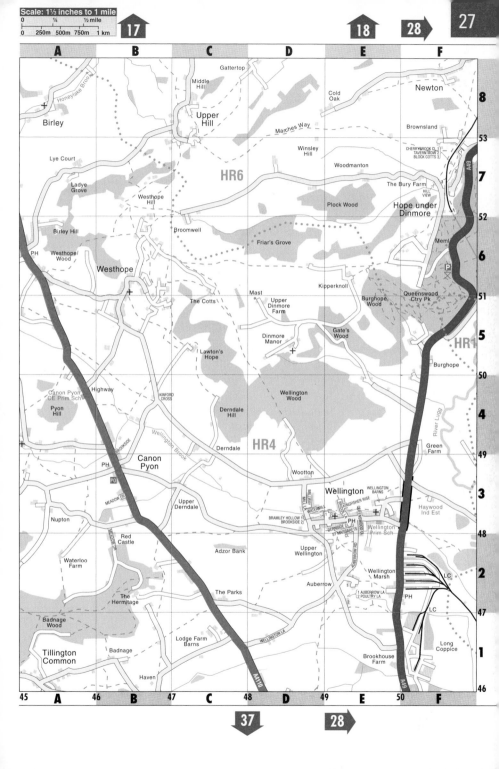

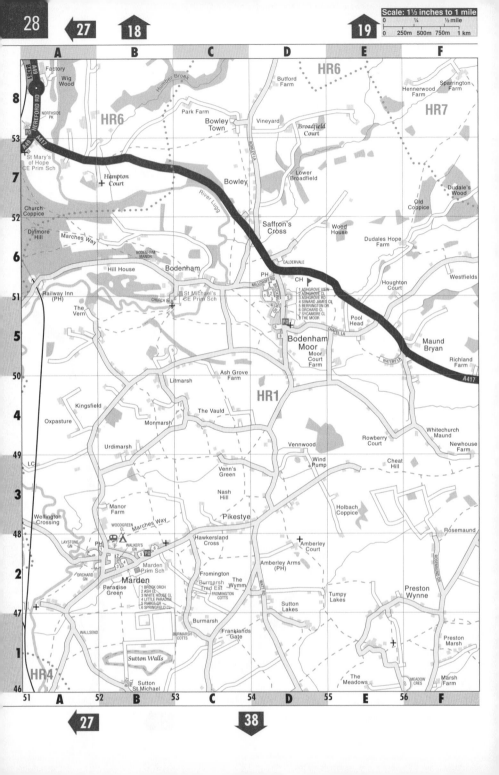

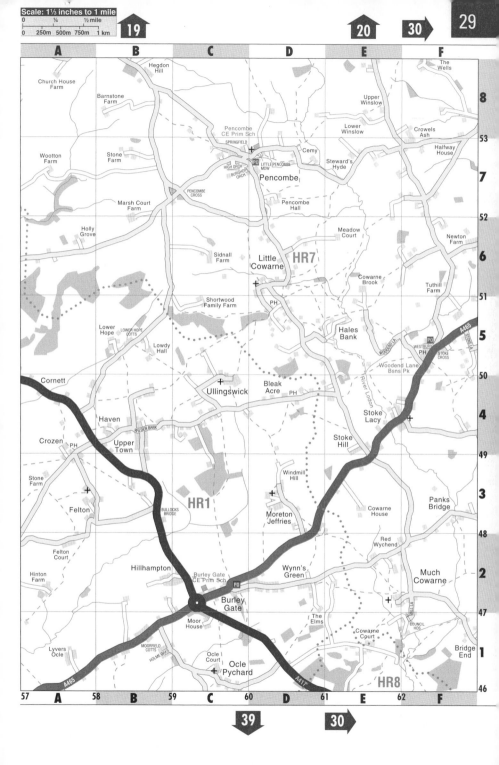

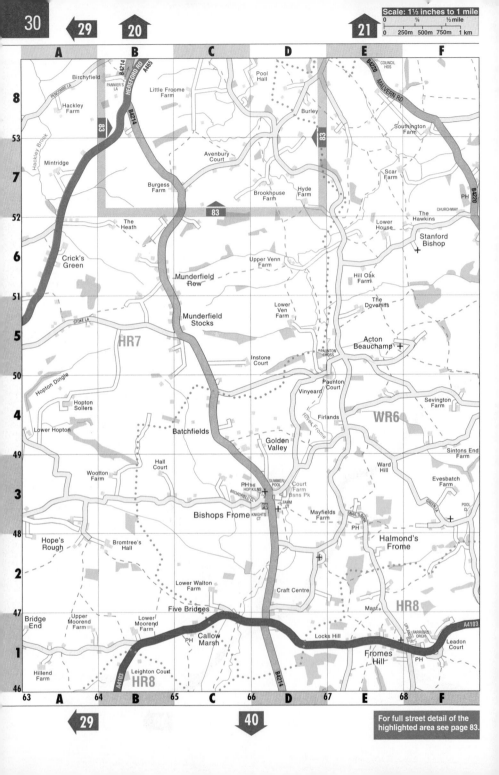

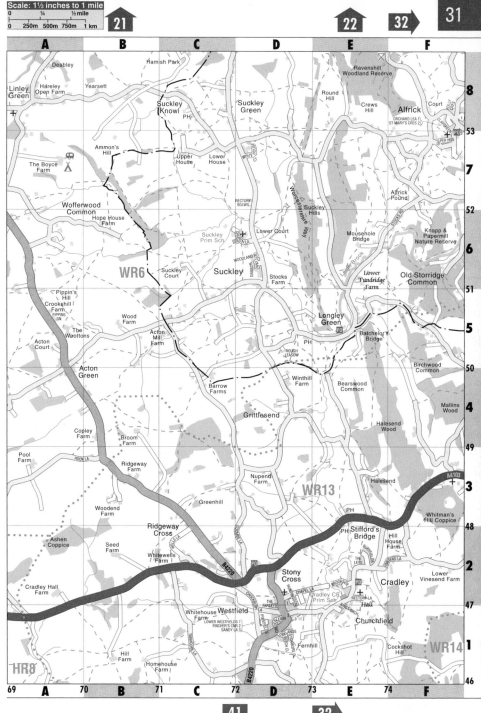

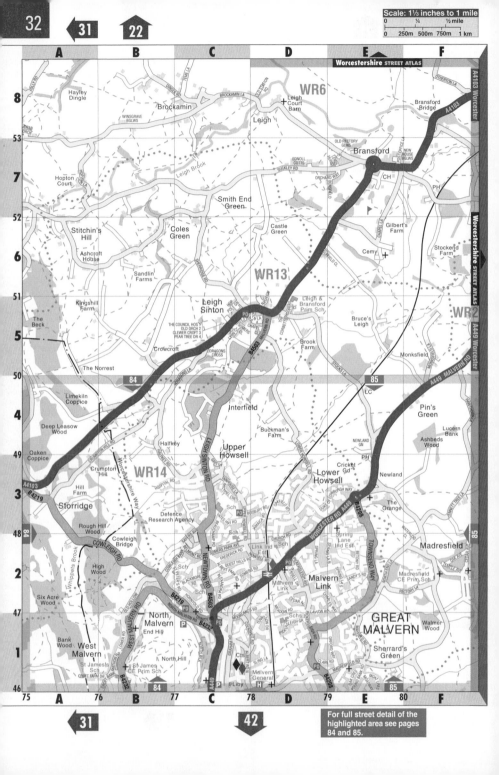

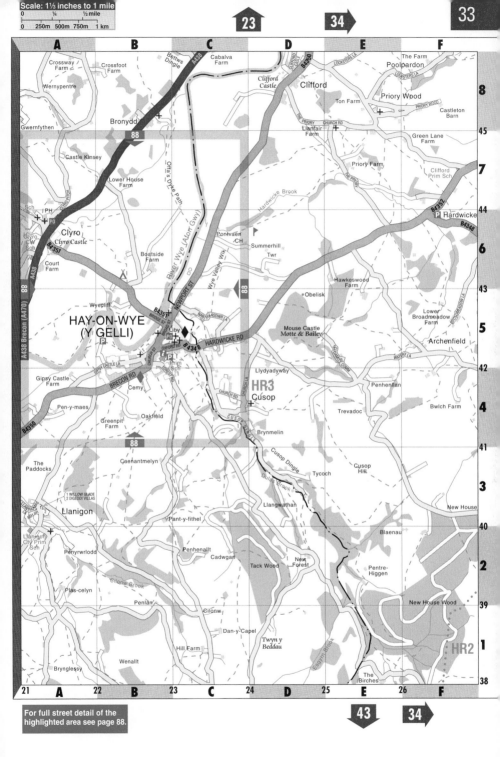

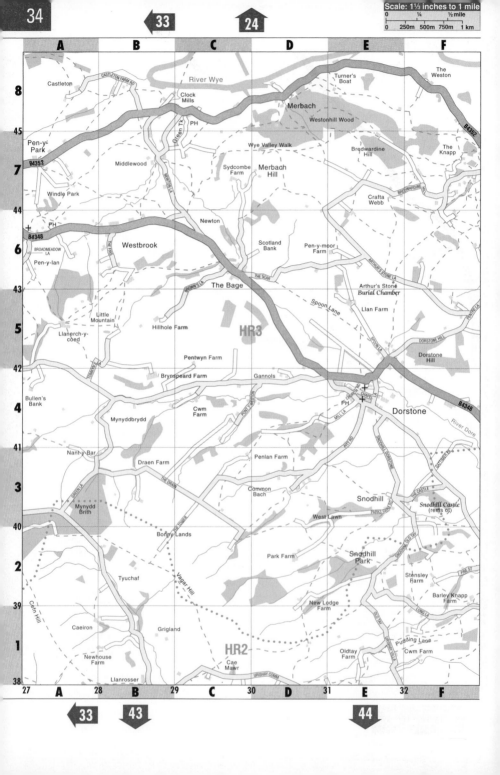

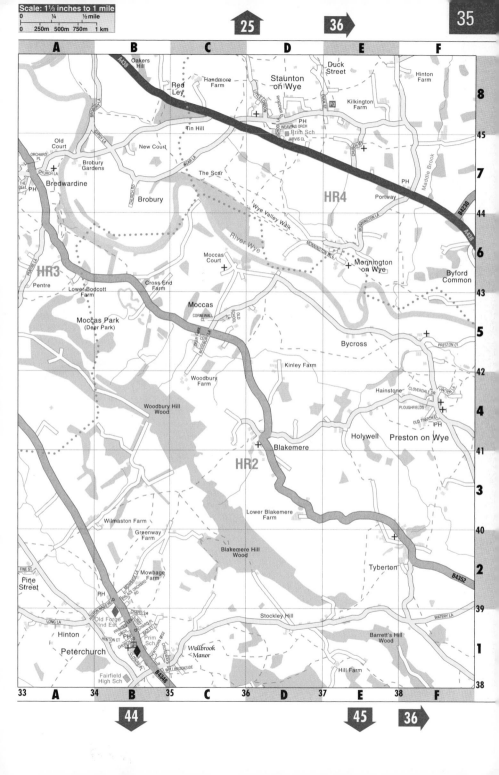

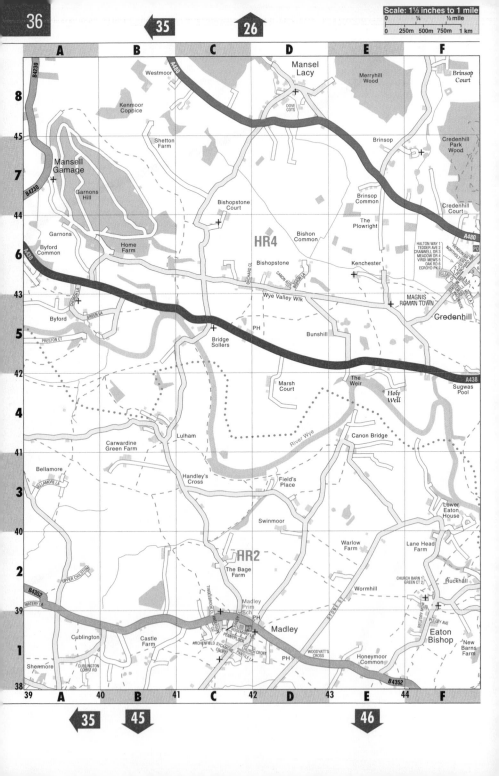

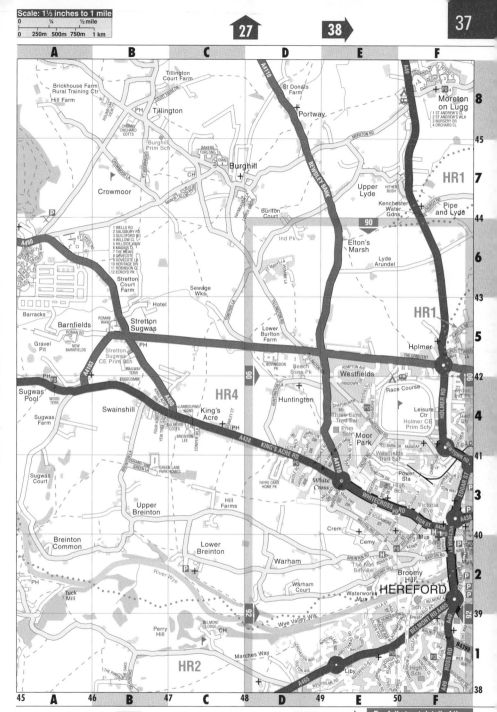

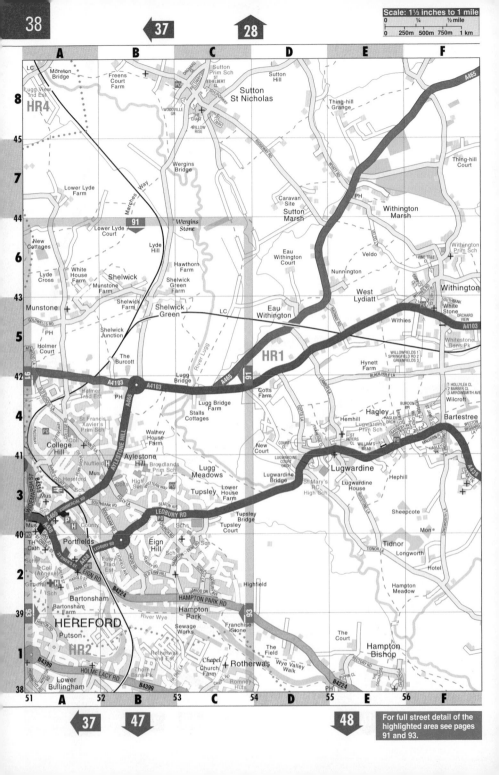

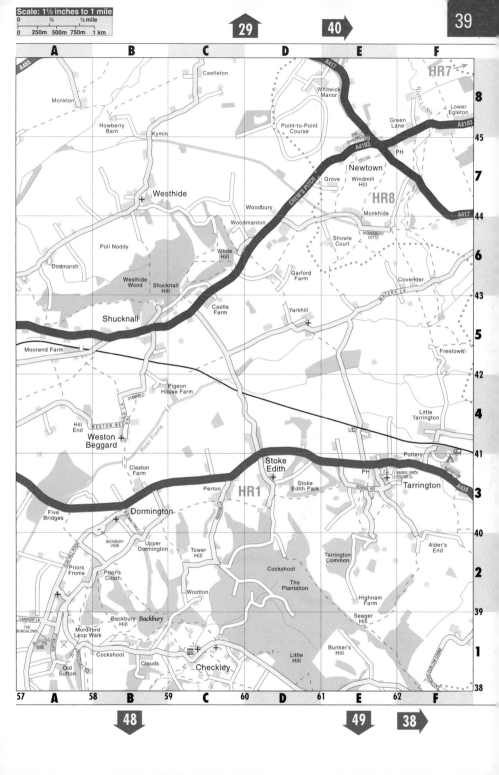

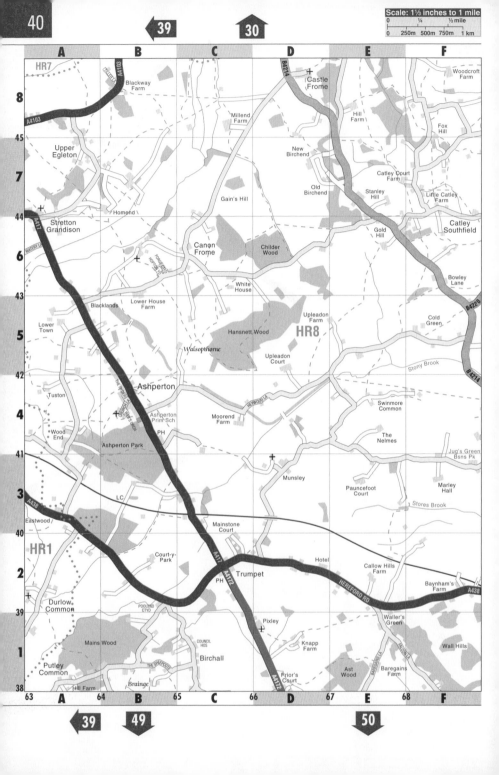

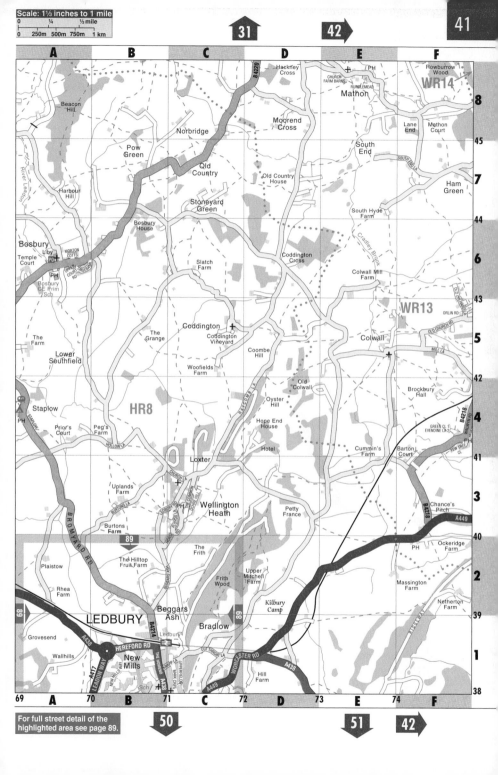

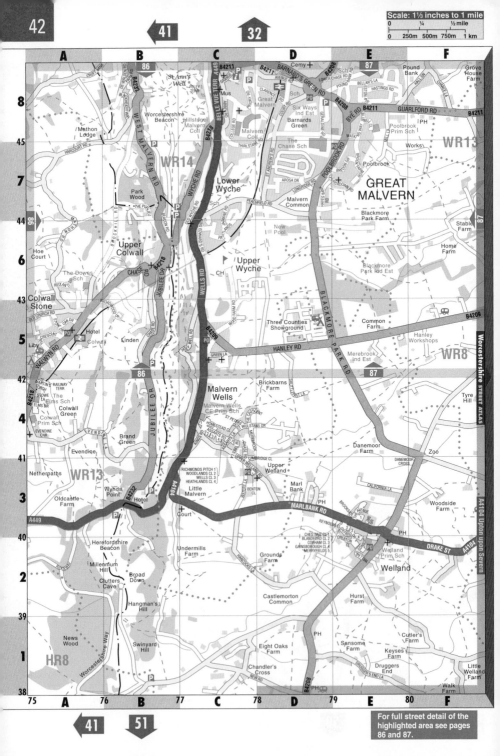

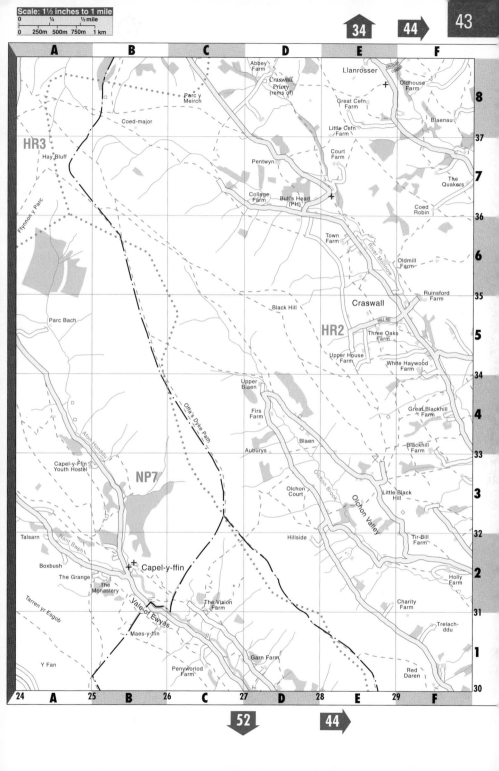

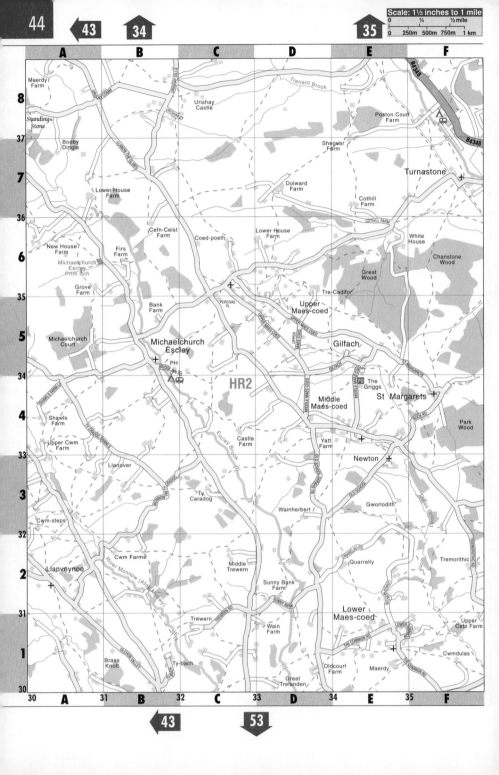

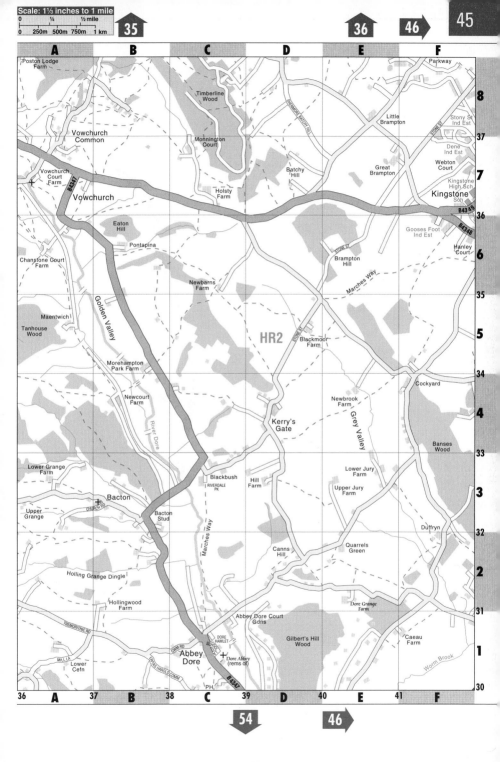

A   B   C   D   E   F

Poston Lodge Farm

Timberline Wood

Parkway

8

Vowchurch Common

Monnington Court

Little Brampton

Stony St Ind Est

37

Vowchurch Court Farm

Batchy Hill

Great Brampton

Dene Ind Est

Webton Court

Kingstone High Sch

7

B4347

Vowchurch

Holsty Farm

Kingstone

Sch

B4349

36

Eaton Hill

B4348

Pontapina

Stone St

Gooses Foot Ind Est

Hanley Court

6

Chanstone Court Farm

Newbarns Farm

Brampton Hill

Marches Way

35

Golden Valley

Maentwich

HR2

Blackmoor Farm

5

Tanhouse Wood

Stone St

34

Morehampton Park Farm

Cockyard

Newcourt Farm

Newbrook Farm

Grey Valley

4

River Dore

Kerry's Gate

Banses Wood

33

Lower Grange Farm

Blackbush

RIVERDALE PK

Hill Farm

Lower Jury Farm

Upper Jury Farm

3

Bacton

CHURCH RD

Upper Grange

Bacton Stud

Marches Way

Duffryn

32

Holling Grange Dingle

Canns Hill

Quarrels Green

2

Hollingwood Farm

Dore Grange Farm

31

TREMORITHIC RD

Abbey Dore Court Gdns

Caeau Farm

1

MILL LA

CRM RD

DORE HAMLET

Gilbert's Hill Wood

Lower Cefn

B4347

ST KEVELIN HAROLD COMM

Abbey Dore

Dore Abbey (rems of)

B4347

Worm Brook

PH

30

36   A   37   B   38   C   39   D   40   E   41   F

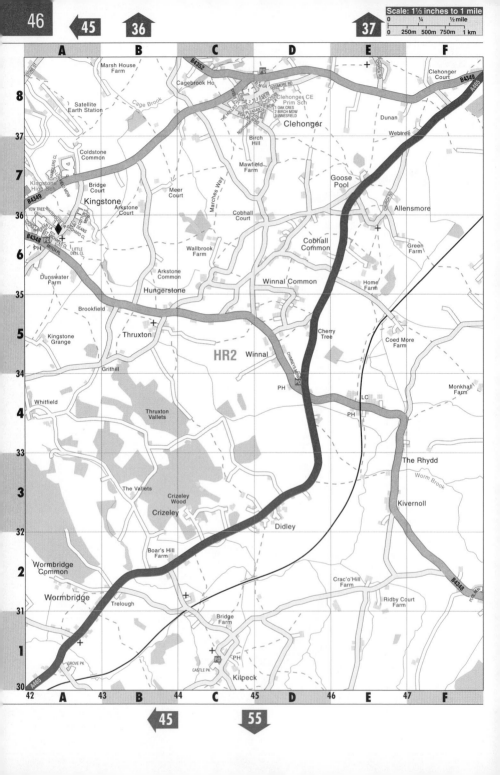

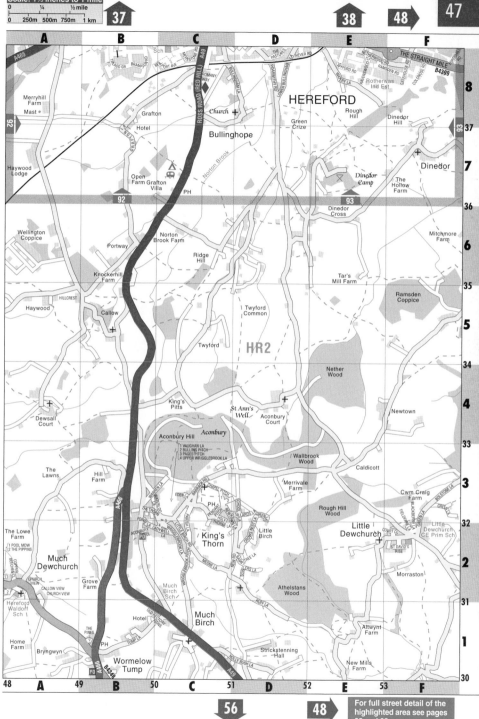

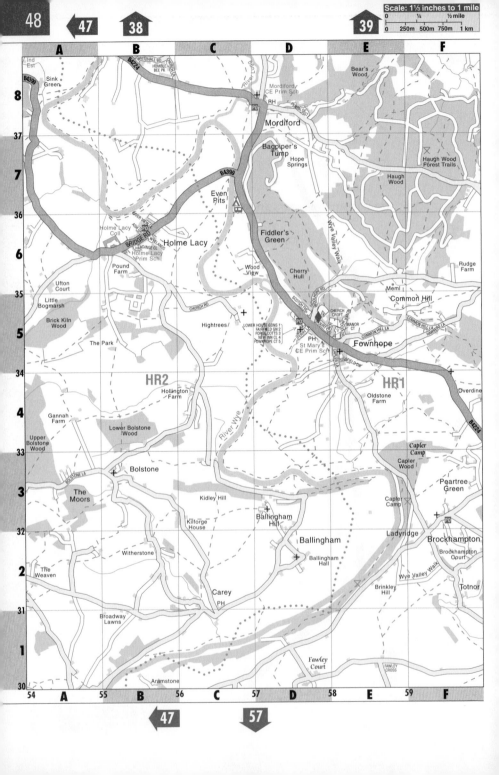

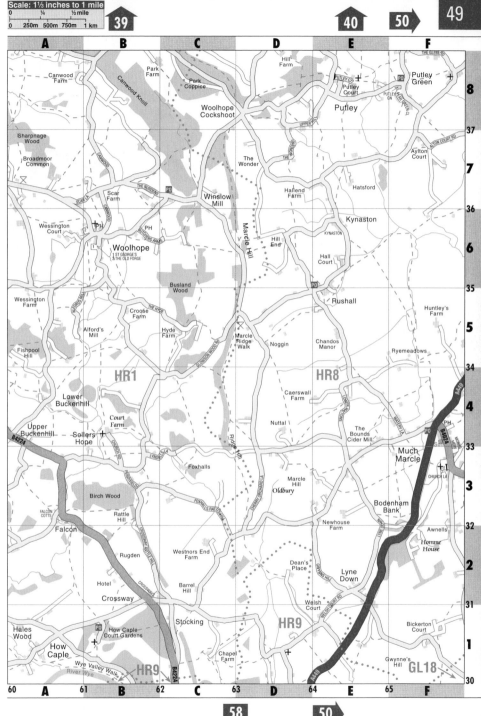

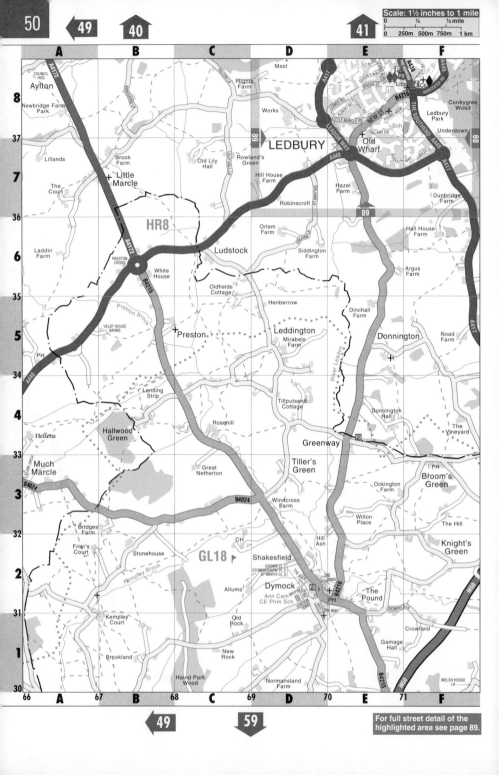

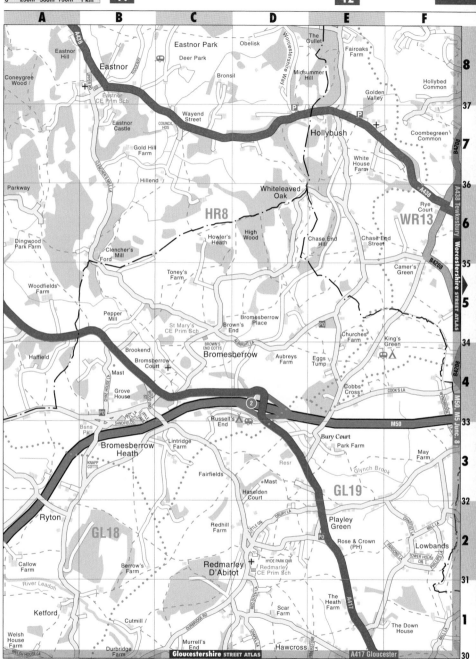

Scale: 1⅓ inches to 1 mile

0 ¼ ½ mile
0 250m 500m 750m 1 km

41 42

| A | B | C | D | E | F |

Coneygree Wood

Eastnor Hill

Eastnor

Eastnor Park

Deer Park

Obelisk

Eastnor CE Prim Sch

Wayend Street

Eastnor Castle

COUNCIL HOS

Gold Hill Farm

Hillend

Parkway

Dingwood Park Farm

Clencher's Mill Ford

Woodfields Farm

Pepper Mill

Haffield

Brookend

Bromsberrow Court

Grove House

Bsns Pk

Bromesberrow Heath

Lintridge Farm

KNAPP COTTS

Ryton

GL18

Callow Farm

Berrow's Farm

River Leadon

Ketford

Cutmill

Welsh House Farm

Durbridge Farm

Murrell's End

Redmarley D'Abitot

Redmarley CE Prim Sch

Scar Farm

Hawcross

Bronsil

Midsummer Hill

The Gullet

Fairoaks Farm

Hollybed Common

Golden Valley

Hollybush

Coombegreen Common

White House Farm

Whiteleaved Oak

HR8

Howler's Heath

High Wood

Toney's Farm

Brown's End

Bromesberrow Place

St Mary's CE Prim Sch

Bromesberrow

Aubreys Farm

Eggs Tump

Chase End Hill

Chase End Street

Camer's Green

Churches Farm

King's Green

Cobbs Cross

Rye Court

WR13

COOK'S LA

M50

Russell's End

Bury Court

Park Farm

May Farm

Fairfields

Resr

Mast

Haselden Court

Glynch Brook

GL19

Redhill Farm

Playley Green

Rose & Crown (PH)

Lowbands

The Heath Farm

The Down House

8

37

7

36

6

35

5

34

4

33

3

32

2

31

1

30

Gloucestershire STREET ATLAS

| 72 | A | 73 | B | 74 | C | 75 | D | 76 | E | 77 | F |

A438 Tewkesbury Worcestershire STREET ATLAS

M50, M5 Junc. 8

A417 Gloucester

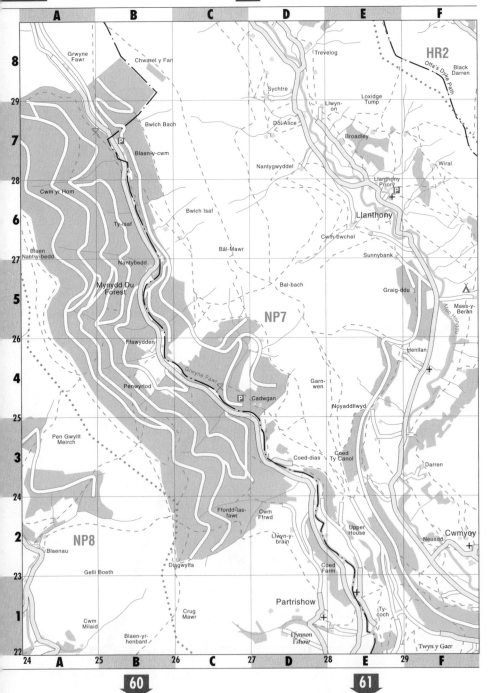

Scale: 1½ inches to 1 mile
0   ¼   ½ mile
0 250m 500m 750m 1 km

A **B** **C** **D** **E** **F**

8

Grwyne Fawr

Chwarel y Fan

HR2

Offa's Dyke Path

Black Darren

Trevelog

29

Sychtre

Loxidge Tump

Llwyn-on

Bwlch Bach

7

Dôl Alice

Broadley

Blaen-y-cwm

Wiral

Nantygwyddel

28

Llanthony Priory

Cwm yr Hom

Bwlch Isaf

Llanthony

Ty-isaf

6

Cwm-bwchel

Bâl-Mawr

Blaen
Nant-y-bedd

27

Sunnybank

Nantybedd

Graig-ddu

Mynydd Du
Forest

5

Bal-bach

NP7

Maes-y-
Beran

Afon Honddu

26

Ffawydden

Henllan

Penwyrlod

Grwyne Fawr

4

Garn-
wen

Cadwgan

Noyaddllwyd

25

Pen Gwyllt
Meirch

Coed
Ty Canol

Darren

3

Coed-dias

24

Ffordd-las-
fawr

Cwm
Ffrwd

Upper
House

Cwmyoy

2

NP8

Llwyn-y-
brain

Neuadd

Blaenau

Coed
Farm

Gelli Boeth

Dugwylfa

23

Crug
Mawr

Partrishow

Ty-
coch

1

Cwm
Milaid

Blaen-yr-
henbant

Ffynnon
I'show

Twyn y Gaer

22

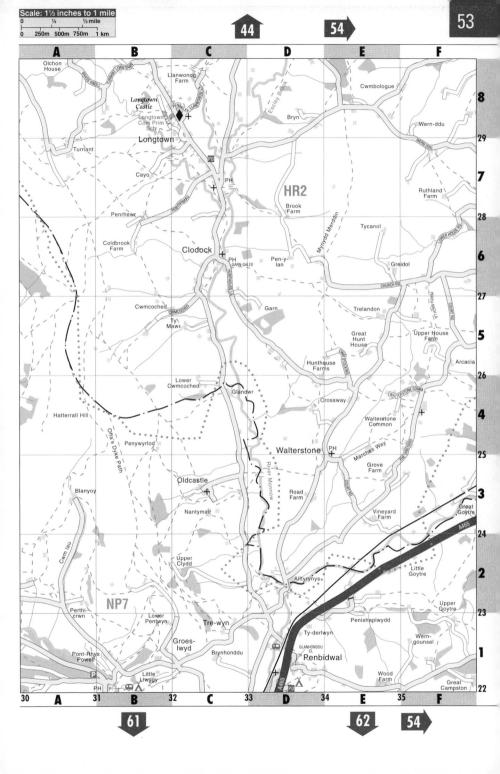

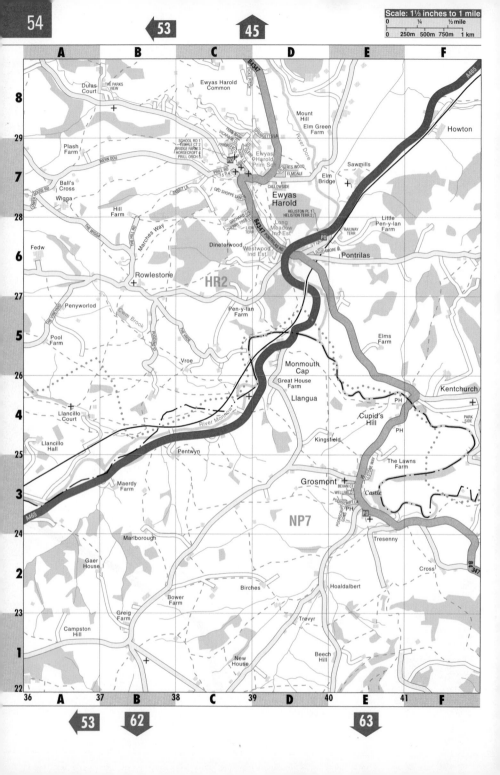

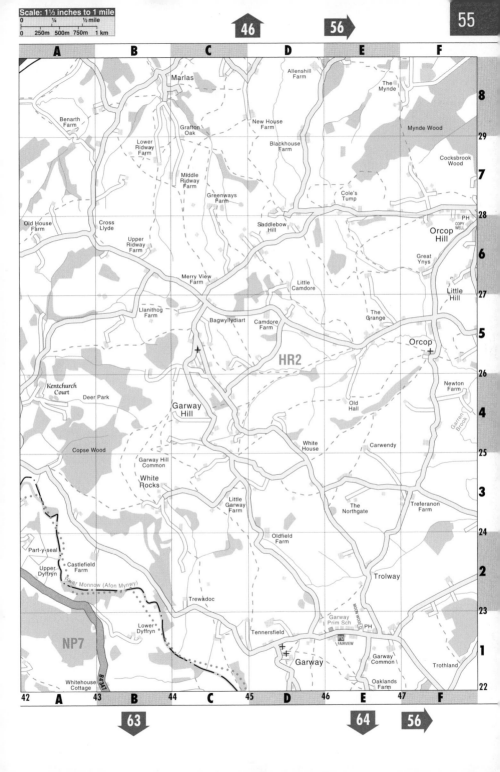

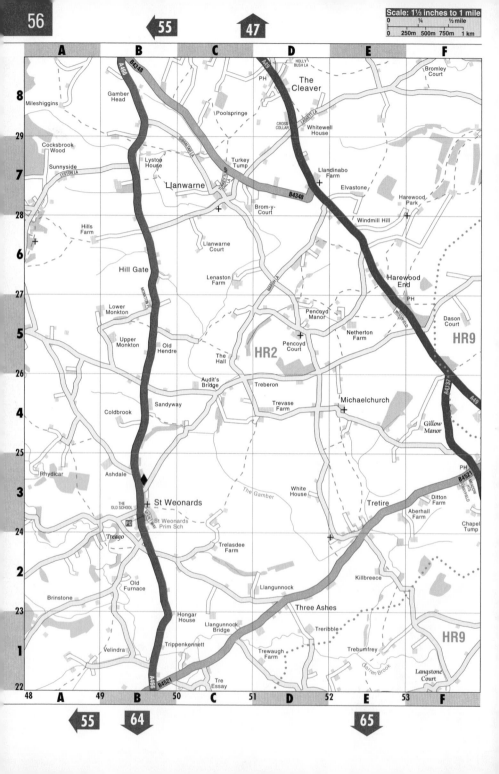

55
47

Scale: 1½ inches to 1 mile

0   ¼   ½ mile
0 250m 500m 750m 1 km

A **B** **C** **D** **E** **F**

8

Mileshiggins

Bromley
Court

HOLLY
BUSH LA

PH

The
Cleaver

Gamber
Head

Poolspringe

CROSS
COLLAR

Whitewell
House

29

Cocksbrook
Wood

Lyston
House

Turkey
Tump

Llandinabo
Farm

Elvastone

Harewood
Park

Sunnyside

LYSTON LA

Llanwarne

B4348

28

Hills
Farm

Brom-y-
Court

Windmill Hill

7

Llanwarne
Court

6

Hill Gate

Lenaston
Farm

Harewood
End

PH

27

Lower
Monkton

Pencoyd
Manor

Netherton
Farm

Dason
Court

5

Upper
Monkton

Old
Hendre

The
Hall

HR2

Pencoyd
Court

HR9

26

Audit's
Bridge

Treberon

Coldbrook

Sandyway

Trevase
Farm

Michaelchurch

4

Gillow
Manor

25

Rhydicar

Ashdale

White
House

PH

B4521

3

THE
OLD SCHOOL

St Weonards

The Gamber

Tretire

Aberhall
Farm

Ditton
Farm

PO

St Weonards
Prim Sch

Chapel
Tump

Treago

24

Trelasdee
Farm

2

Old
Furnace

Killbreece

23

Brinstone

Llangunnock

Three Ashes

HR9

Hongar
House

Treribble

Llangunnock
Bridge

Trebumfrey

1

Velindra

Trippenkennett

Trewaugh
Farm

Garren Brook

Langstone
Court

Tre
Essay

22

A4521

A **B** **C** **D** **E** **F**

48   49   50   51   52   53

55
64
65

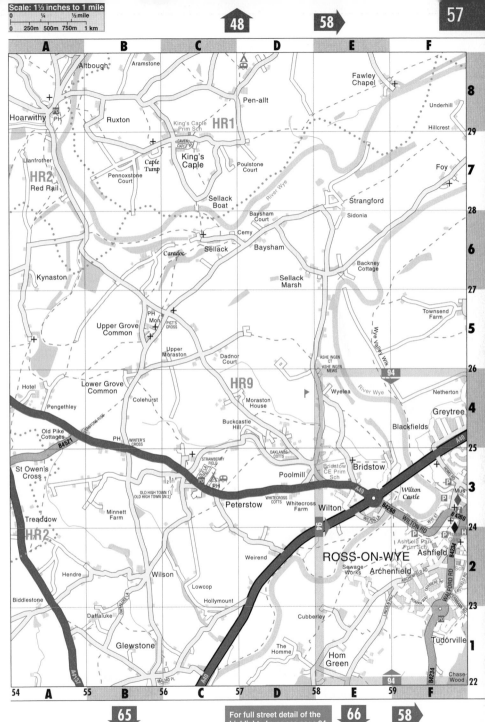

Scale: 1⅓ inches to 1 mile

| 0 | ¼ | ½ mile |
| 0 | 250m 500m 750m | 1 km |

8
29
7
28
6
27
5
26
4
25
3
24
2
23
1
22

Altbough
Aramstone
Pen-allt
Fawley Chapel
Underhill
Hillcrest
PO
PH
Hoarwithy
Ruxton
King's Caple Prim Sch
HR1
Llanfrother
HR2
Red Rail
Caple Tump
King's Caple
Poulstone Court
Pennoxstone Court
Foy
Sellack Boat
River Wye
Strangford
Sidonia
Kynaston
Caradoc
Cemy
Sellack
Baysham
Baysham Court
Sellack Marsh
Backney Cottage
Townsend Farm
PH
Mon
PICT'S CROSS
Upper Grove Common
Upper Moraston
Dadnor Court
ASHE INGEN CT
ASHE INGEN MEWS
94
Hotel
Lower Grove Common
Colehurst
HR9
Moraston House
Wyelea
River Wye
Netherton
Pengethley
Old Pike Cottages
B4521
BRIDSTONE RISE
PH
WINTER'S CROSS
Buckcastle Hill
OAKLANDS COTTS
Greytree
Blackfields
A40
St Owen's Cross
STRAWBERRY FIELD
PO
PH
OLD HIGH TOWN 1
OLD HIGH TOWN GN 2
WHITECROSS COTTS
Bridstow CE Prim Sch
Bridstow
Wilton Castle
P
Mus
Treaddow
HR2
Minnett Farm
Peterstow
Whitecross Farm
Wilton
A49
94
WILTON LA
B4260
WILTON RD
WYE ST
B 4260
Ashfield
P
H
Hendre
Wilson
Weirend
Sewage Works
ROSS-ON-WYE
Archenfield
Ashfield Park Prim Sch
ARCHENFIELD RD
OVERROSS RD
WALFORD RD
Biddlestone
Daffaluke
Lowcop
Hollymount
Cubberley
LINCOLN HILL
PO
Tudorville
Glewstone
The Homme
Hom Green
94
B4234
Chase Wood
A4137
MALMO PL
A40

For full street detail of the highlighted area see page 94.

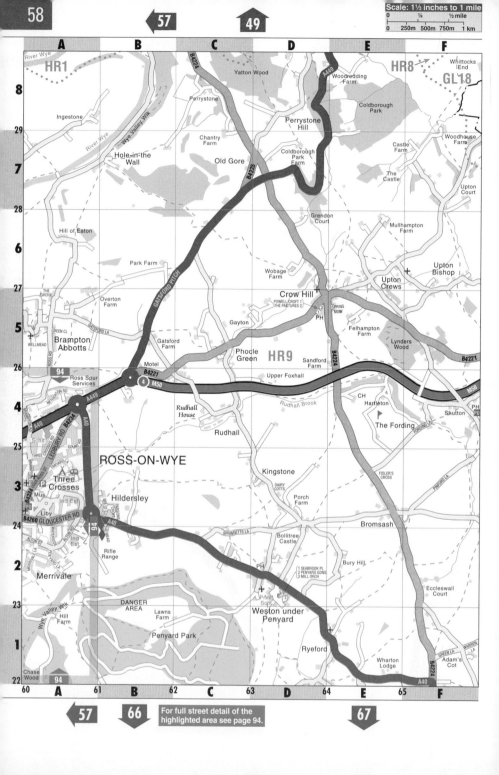

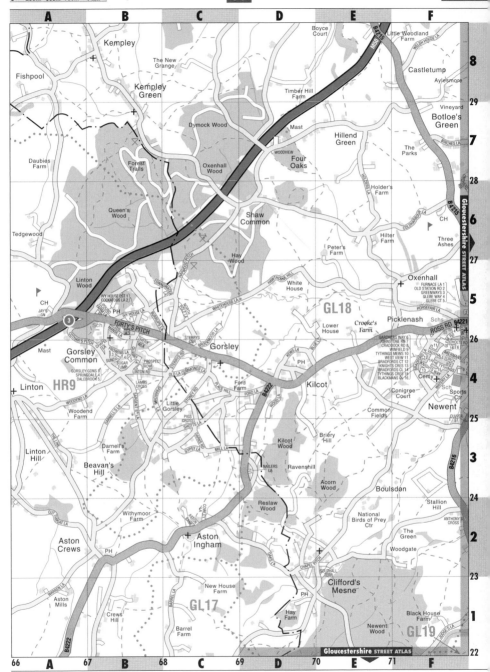

Gloucestershire STREET ATLAS

A **B** **C** **D** **E** **F**

Boyce Court
Little Woodland Farm
WELSH HOUSE LA
Kempley
The New Grange
Castletump
Aylesmore
8
Kempley Green
Timber Hill Farm
29
Fishpool
Dymock Wood
Mast
Hillend Green
Vineyard
Botloe's Green
BIRCHES LA
7
The Parks
Daubies Farm
Forest Trails
Oxenhall Wood
WOODVIEW
Four Oaks
28
Queen's Wood
Holder's Farm
Oxenhall
CH
6
Tedgewood
Hay Wood
Shaw Common
White House
Hilter Farm
Three Ashes
HOLDERS LA
FURNACE LA 1
OLD STATION RD 2
GREENWAYS 3
GLEBE WAY 4
GLEBE CT 5
HORSEFAIR LA
27
Linton Wood
HARDWICK DITCH
HARTHORNE HILL
Peter's Farm
Crooke's Farm
Picklenash
Schs
ROSS RD B4221
5
CH
JAY'S GN
WHITEHOUSE LA
GL18
Lower House
GARDNERS WAY 6
JOHNSTONE RD 7
CRADDOCK RD 8
WINFIELD 9
TYTHINGS MEWS 10
WEST VIEW 11
BRADFORDS CT 12
KNIGHTS CRES 13
BRADFORDS CL 14
TYTHINGS CRES 15
BLACKMANS CL 16
IVY HOUSE EST 1
COCKATOOS LA 2
PH
Sch
IVY HOUSE LA
FORTY'S PITCH
3
Mast
Gorsley
Kilcot
26
Gorsley Common
SUGAR JUMP
PROSPECT ROW
Newent
Cemy
Sch
Sports Ctr
HR9
GORSLEY GDNS 1
SPRINGDALE 4
DALEBROOK 5
LINTON RD
PH
4
Linton
LAMBS CROSS
OLD LA (COMMONS LA)
Ford Farm
B4222
Conigree Court
CULVER ST
25
Woodend Farm
Little Gorsley
PIGS CROSS
SHOTS LA
Common Fields
Linton Hill
Darnell's Farm
GYPSY LA
MILL LA
Kilcot Wood
Briery Hill
3
NAILERS LA
Ravenshill
Boulsdon
24
Beavan's Hill
Reslaw Wood
Acorn Wood
Stallion Hill
ANTHONY'S CROSS
Withymoor Farm
National Birds of Prey Ctr
The Green
2
Aston Crews
PH
Aston Ingham
OAKS LA
Woodgate
23
CHAPEL PITCH
SOUTHALL TERR
Clifford's Mesne
Aston Mills
New House Farm
PH
Black House Farm
1
Crews Hill
GL17
Hay Farm
Newent Wood
GL19
Barrel Farm
B4222
BRIDGES LA
22

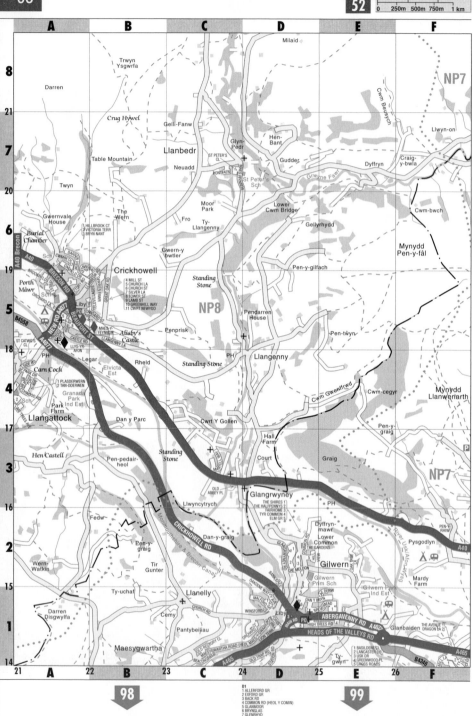

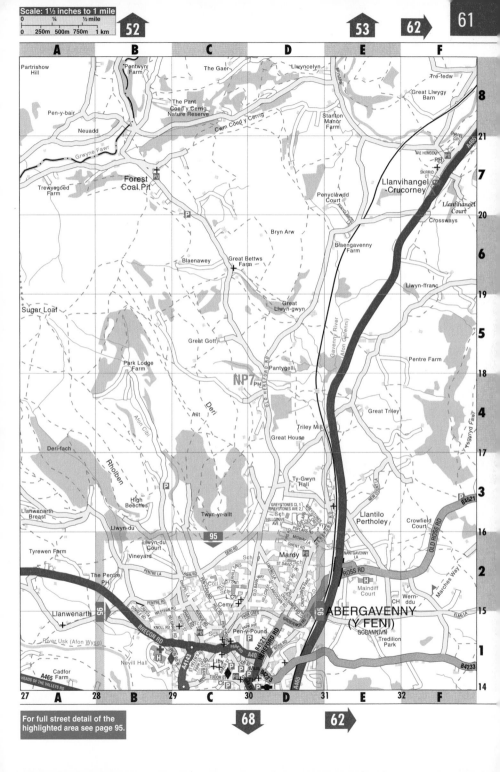

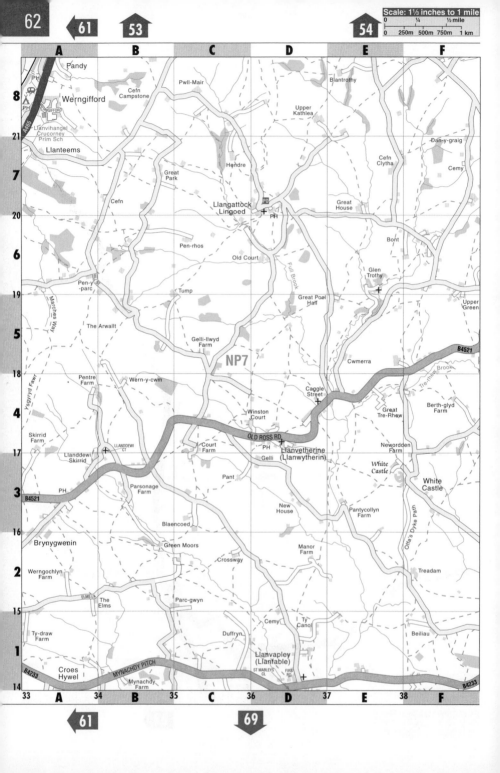

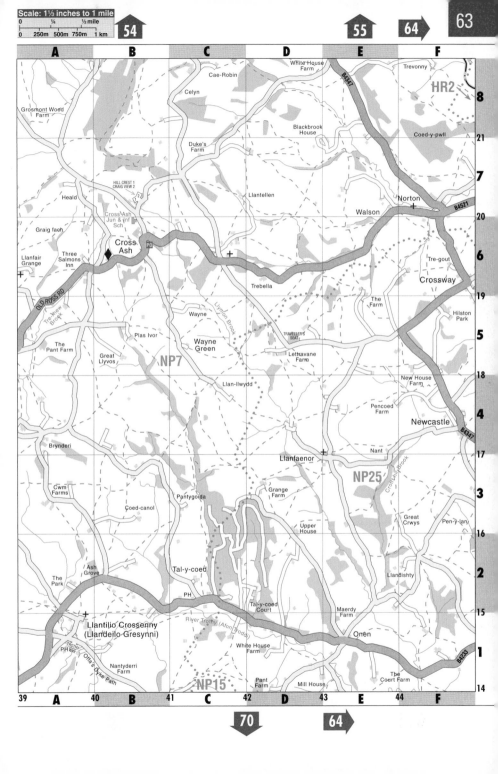

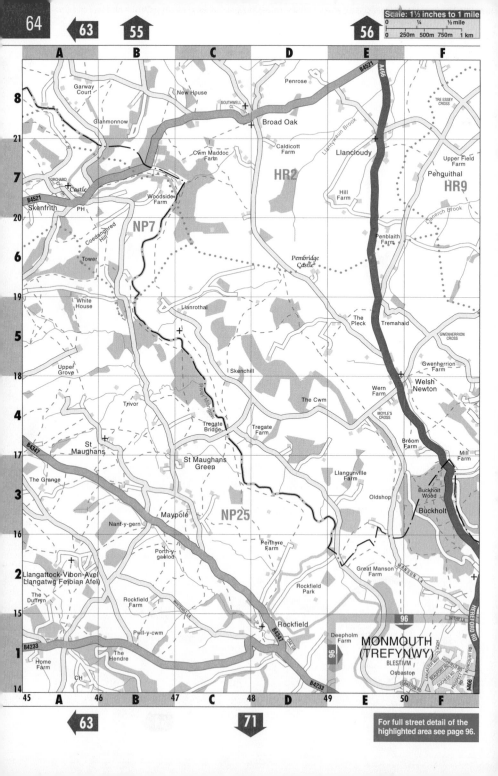

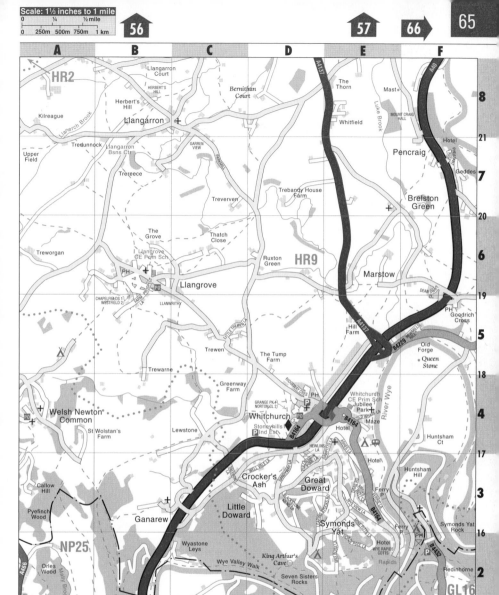

For full street detail of the
highlighted area see page 96.

72 66

HR2

Kilreague

Upper
Field

Tredunnock

Llanarch Brook

Llangarron

Llangarron
Court

Herbert's
Hill

Bernithan
Court

The
Thorn

Whitfield

Mast

MOUNT CRAIG
HALL

LUKE Brook

Hotel

Pencraig

Geddes

Herbert's
Hill

Llangarron
Bsns Ctr

Trereece

GARREN
VIEW

21

7

Treworgan

Treverven

Trebandy House
Farm

Brelston
Green

20

The
Grove

Thatch
Close

Ruxton
Green

HR9

Marstow

6

Llangrove
CE Prim Sch

PH

SPO

Llangrove

CHAPELFIELDS 1
WESTFIELD 2

LLANWRITHY

DEAN SWIFT
CL.

PH

Goodrich
Cross

19

Trewen

Little Trevella

The Tump
Farm

Hill
Farm

A4137

B4229

Old
Forge

Queen
Stone

5

Trewarne

Greenway
Farm

ROCKFIELD CES

The Tump
Farm

PH

Whitchurch
CE Prim Sch

Jubilee
Park

River Wye

18

Welsh Newton
Common

St Wolstan's
Farm

Lewstone

GRANGE PK 1
NORTON CL 2

Stoneyhills
Ind Est

Whitchurch

B4164

PO

Hotel

B4164

Maze

Huntsham
Ct

4

17

Callow
Hill

Pyefinch
Wood

Crocker's
Ash

Great
Doward

Hotel

Ferry
P

Huntsham
Hill

3

Ganarew

Little
Doward

Symonds
Yat

Ferry
P

Symonds Yat
Rock

16

NP25

Wyastone
Leys

King Arthur's
Cave

Hotel

WYE RAPIDS
COTTS

Rapids

B4432

Redinhorne

GL16

2

Orles
Wood

Manly Brook

Wye Valley Walk

Seven Sisters
Rocks

Lord's
Wood

Holly
Barn

15

Cannes
Farm

96

Far Hearkening
Rock

Lady Park
Wood

The
Biblins

The Slaughter

1

Hayes
Coppice

Hadnock
Court

Suck
Stone

GL16

Mailscot
Wood

PH

14

Priory
Farm

THE
RICKFIELD

Newton
Court

A40

A466

A4137

A40

51 52 53 54 55 56
A   B   C   D   E   F

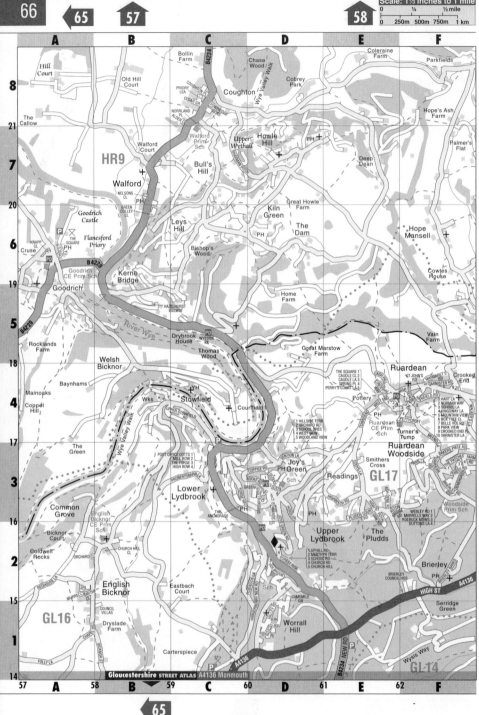

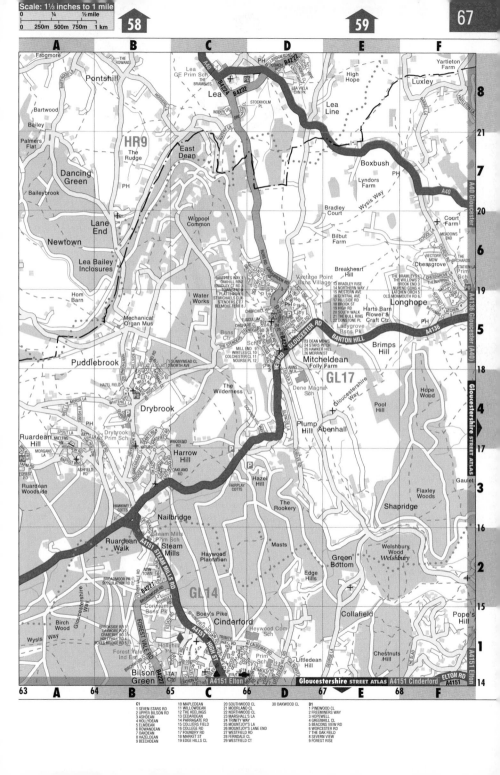

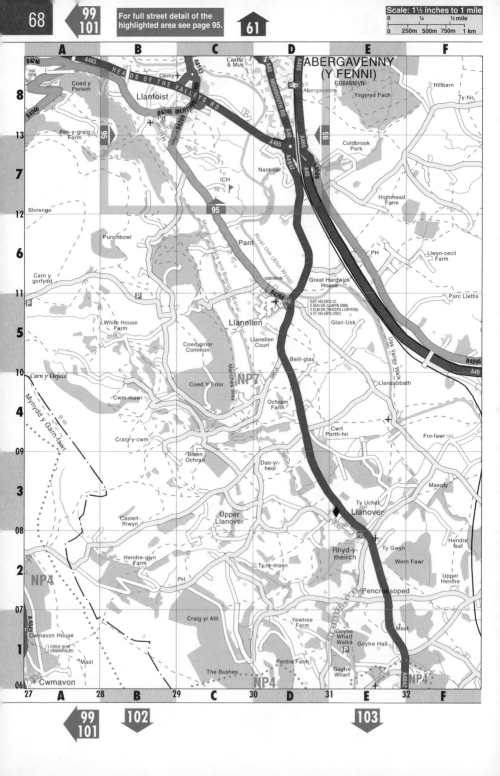

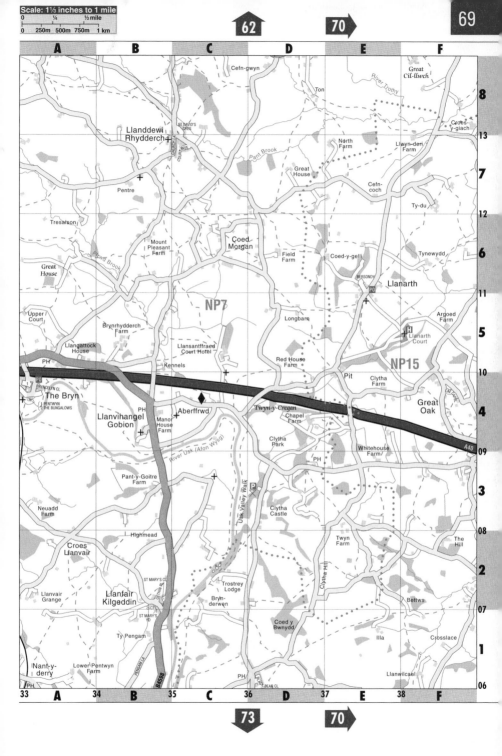

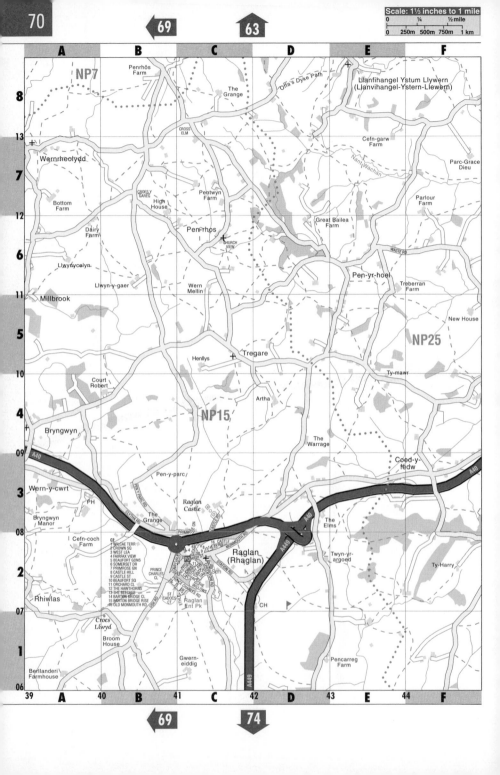

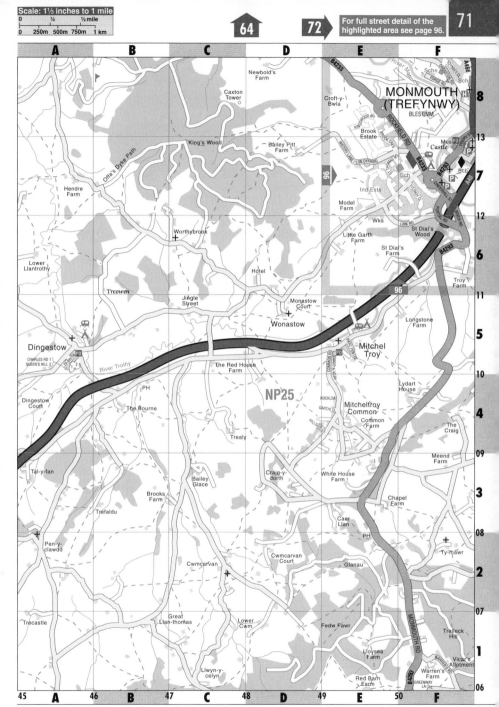

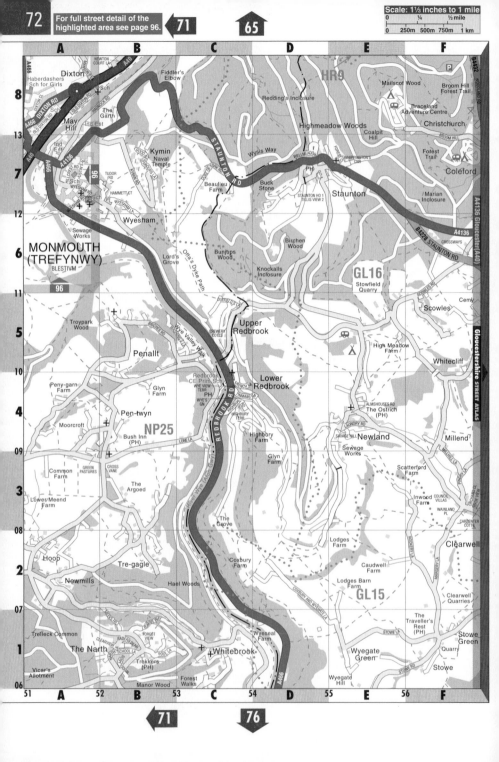

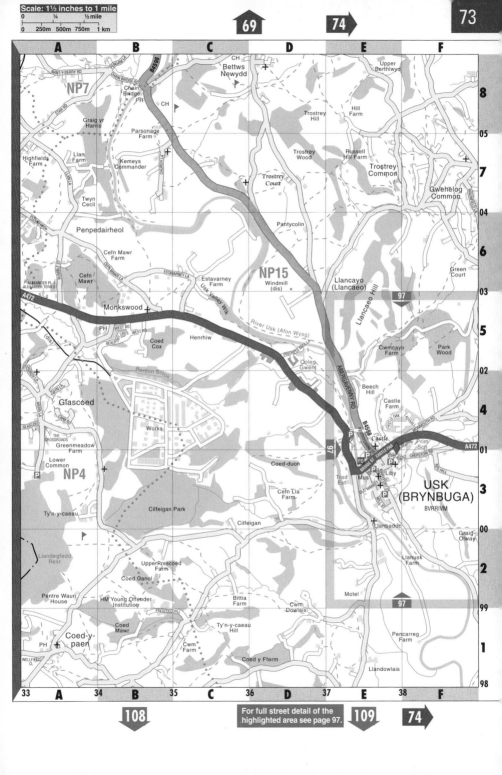

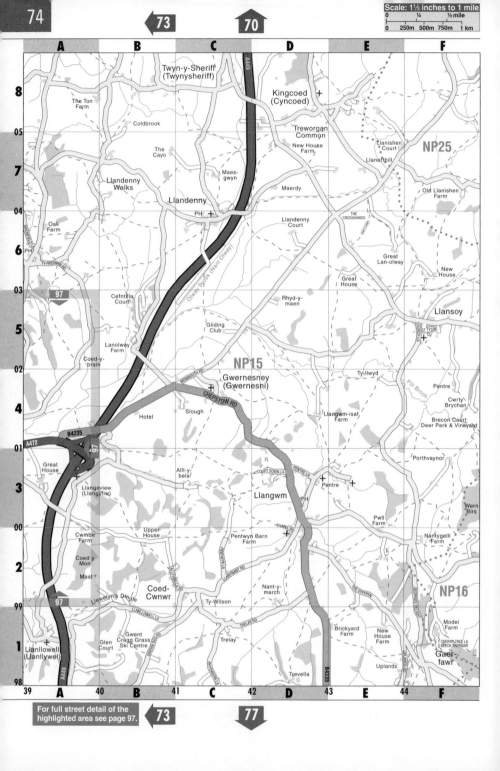

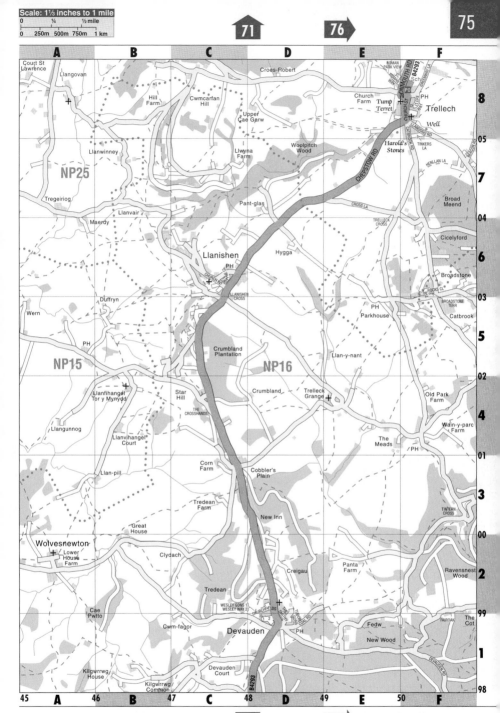

A   B   C   D   E   F

Court St Lawrence

Llangovan

Croes-Robert

ROMAN PARK VIEW

Church Farm   Tump Terret   Trellech

MONMOUTH RD   B4293

Sch

PH

Well   8

Hill Farm

Cwmcarfan Hill

Upper Cae Garw

Llwyna Farm

Woolpitch Wood

Harold's Stones

TINKERS LA

HENLLAN LA

BRIDGE RD

05

Llanwinney

CHEPSTOW RD

Broad Meend

7

NP25

Tregeiriog

Pant-glas

CROSS LA

TRELLECK CROSS

Cicelyford

04

Llanvair

Maerdy

Llanishen   PH   Hygga

CHURCH RD   PONTYR

Broadstone

ROCKS CL   BROADSTONE TERR   Catbrook

6

Duffryn

LLANISHEN CROSS

03

Wern

PH

PH   Parkhouse

5

NP15

Crumbland Plantation

NP16

Llan-y-nant

02

Llanfihangel Tor y Mynydd

Star Hill

THE CROSSHANDS

Crumbland

Trelleck Grange

Old Park Farm

4

Llangunnog

Llanvihangel Court

Llan-pill

Corn Farm

Cobbler's Plain

The Meads

PH

Wain-y-parc Farm

01

Tredean Farm

New Inn

TINTERN CROSS

3

Great House

Wolvesnewton   Lower House Farm

Clydach

Creigau

Panta Farm

Ravensnest Wood

00

Tredean

2

Cae Pwtto

Cwm-fagor

WESLEY GDNS   WESLEY WAY

Devauden

CHURCHFIELD

PH

DEVAUCHEN RD

Fedw

New Wood

FAIROAK

The Cot

99

Kilgwrrwg House

Devauden Court

B4293

Kilgwrrwg Common

1

98

45   A   46   B   47   C   48   D   49   E   50   F

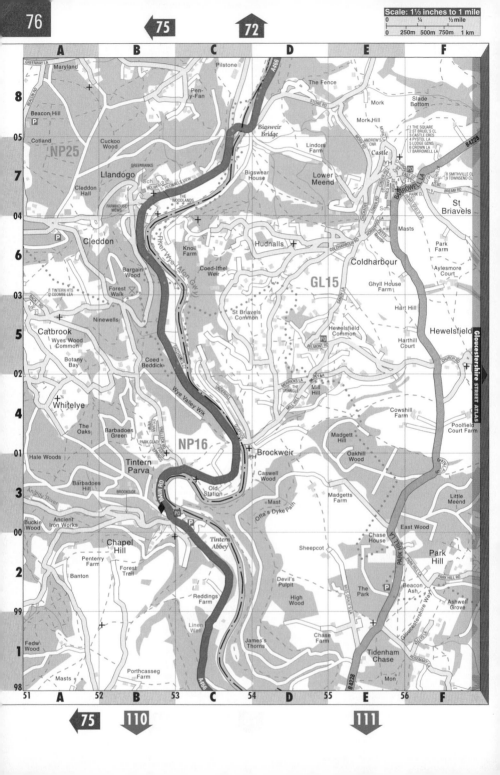

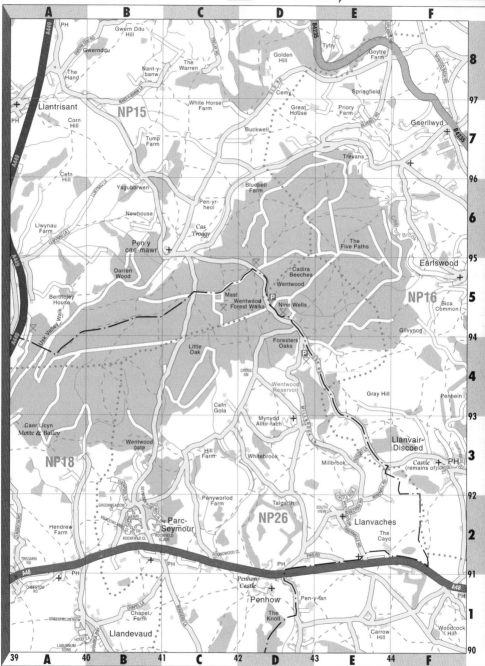

A   B   C   D   E   F

PH
Gwern Ddu Hill
Gwernddu
Nant-y-banw
The Warren
Golden Hill
Tyfry
Goytre Farm

8

The Hand
White Horse Farm
Cemy
Springfield

97

Llantrisant
NP15
Great House
Priory Farm
Gaerllwyd

PH
Corn Hill
Buckwell

7

Tump Farm
Trevans

Cefn Hill
Bluebell Farm

96

Ysguborwen
Pen-yr-heol

6

Newhouse
Cas Troggy

Llwynau Farm
The Five Paths

Pen y cae-mawr
Earlswood

95

Darren Wood
Cadira Beeches
Wentwood
NP16

Berthon
House
Mast
Wentwood Forest Walks
P
Nine Wells
Bica Common

5

Usk Valley Walk
Little Oak
Foresters Oaks
P
Gilvynog

94

CROSS GN
Wentwood Reservoir
Gray Hill
Penhein

4

Caer Licyn Motte & Bailey
Cefn Gola
Mynydd Alltir-fach
Llanvair-Discoed

93

Wentwood gate
Hill Farm
Whitebrook
Millbrook
Castle (remains of)
PH

NP18
Penyworlod Farm
Talgarth
SOUTH VIEW

3

Hendrew Farm
GREENMEADOW
MEADOW LANE
Parc-Seymour
NP26
Llanvaches
The Cayo

92

ROCKFIELD CL
ROCKFIELD GLADE
ROUNDWOOD CL
PH
PIKE RD

2

TREGARN RD
A48
PH
PH
Penhow Castle
A48
PH

91

CHEPSTOW RD
GREENFIELDS VIEW
Chapel Farm
Penhow
Pen-y-fan
The Knoll

1

HOLLY LA
BRAMBLE DRIVE
LABURNUM GDNS
Llandevaud
Carrow Hill
Woodcock Hill

90

39   A   40   B   41   C   42   D   43   E   44   F

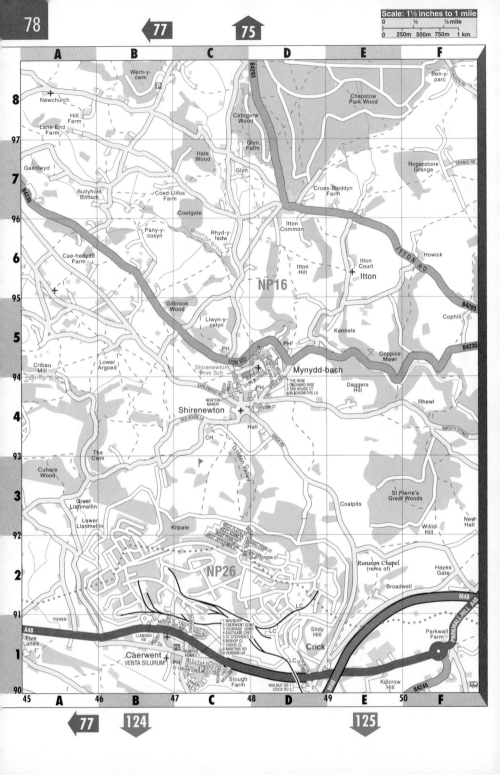

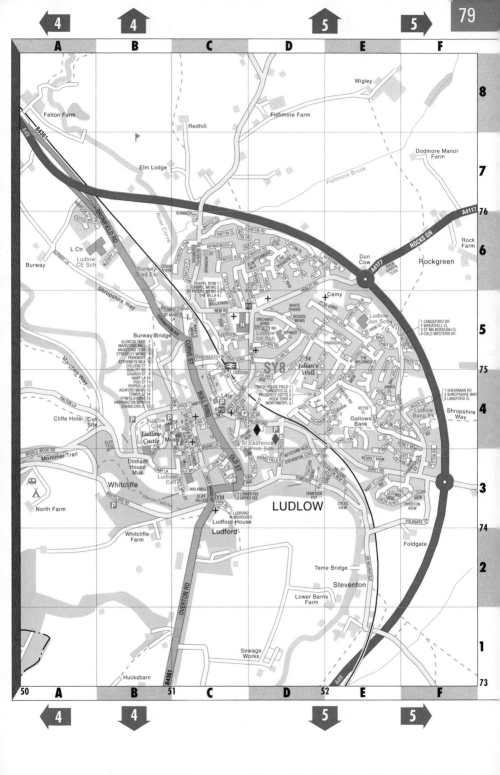

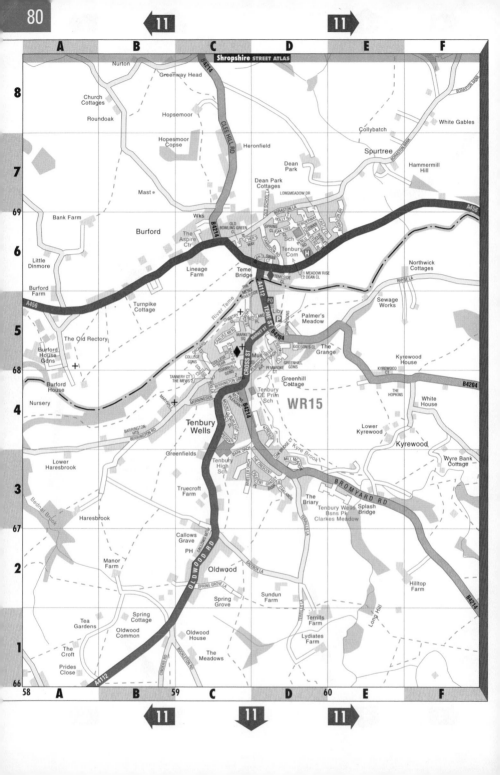

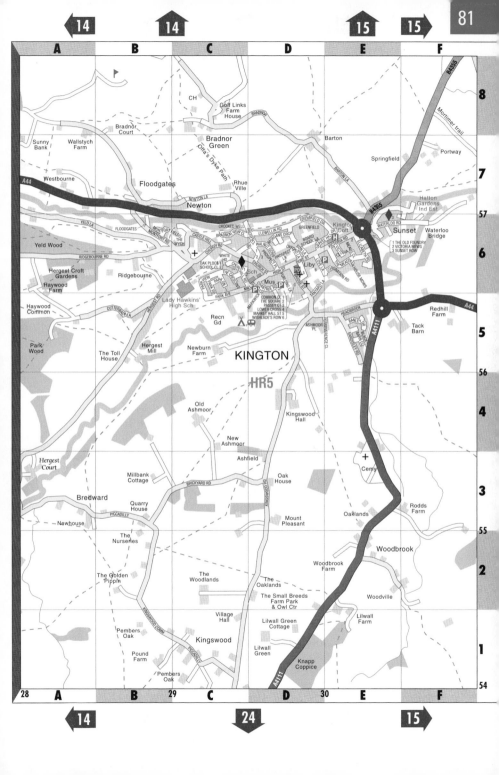

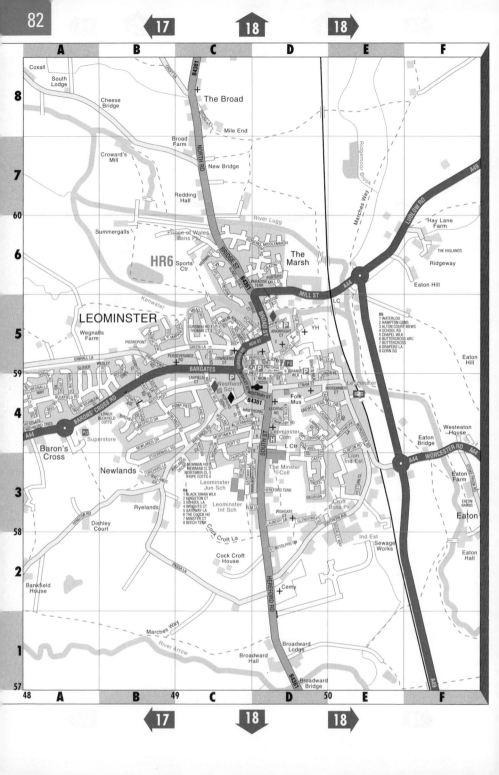

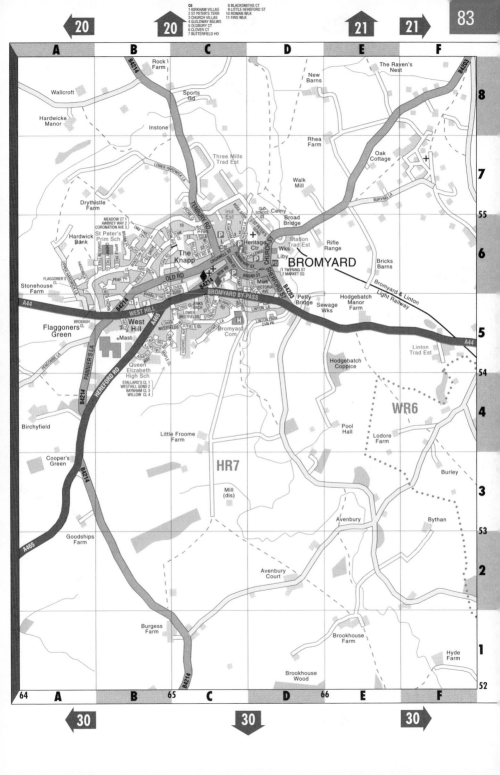

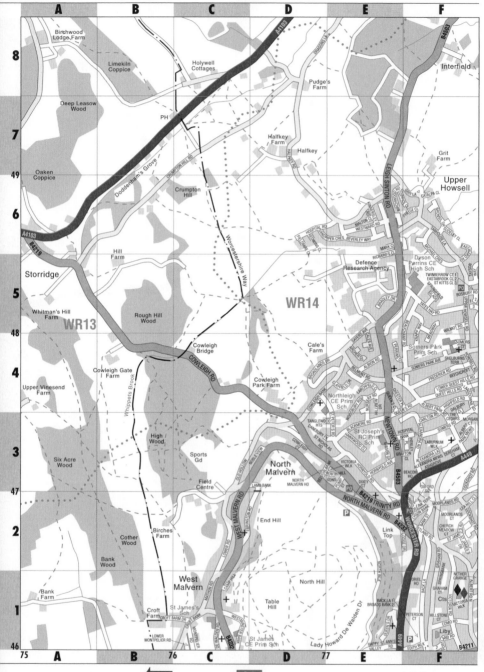

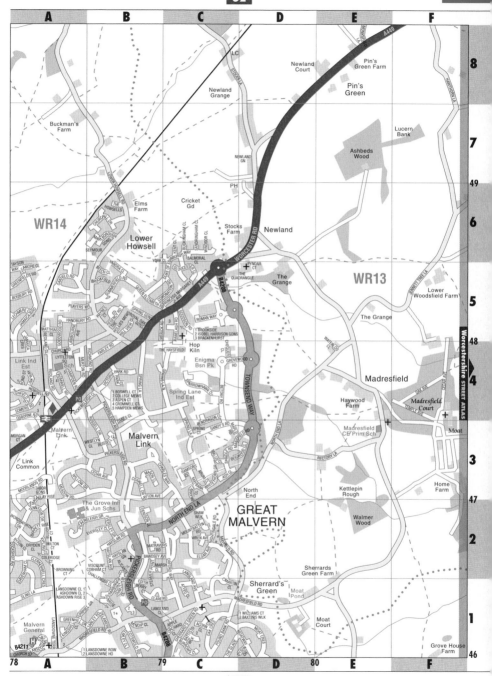

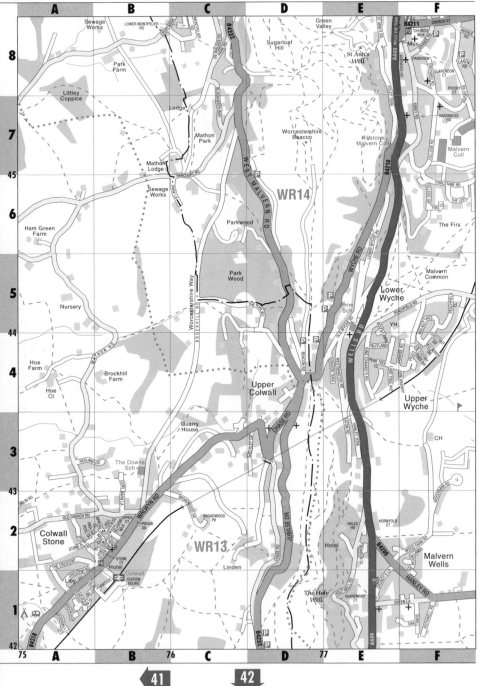

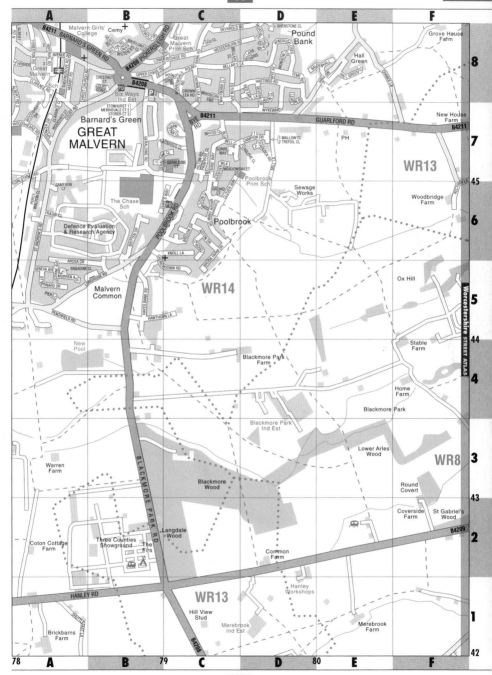

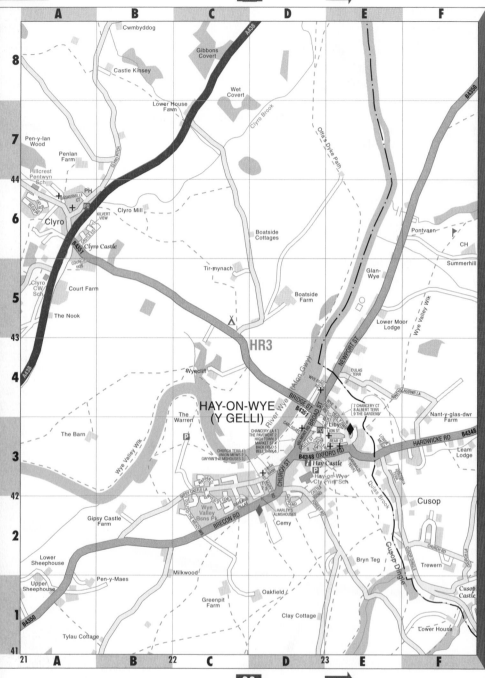

HAY-ON-WYE
(Y GELLI)

HR3

Clyro

Cusop

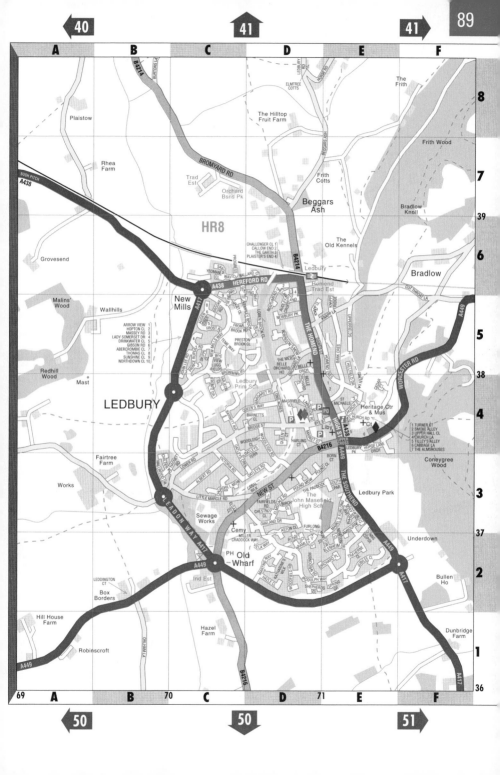

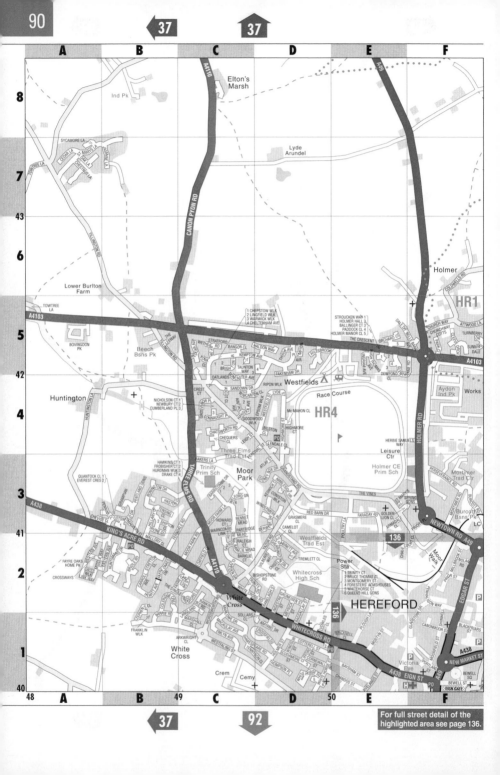

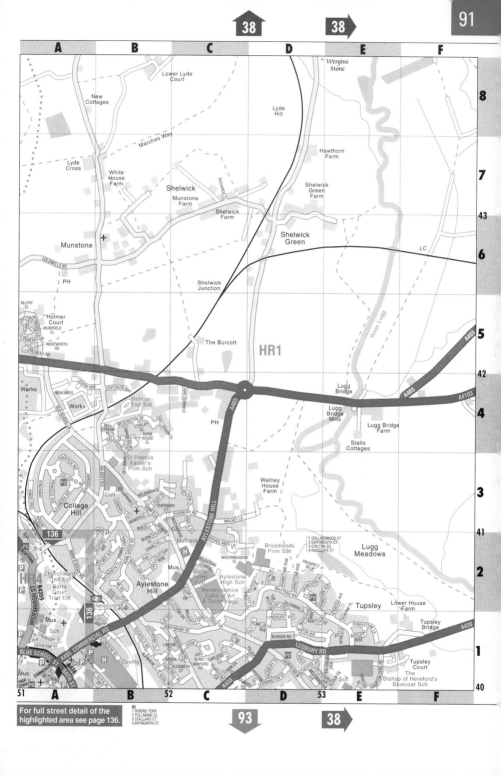

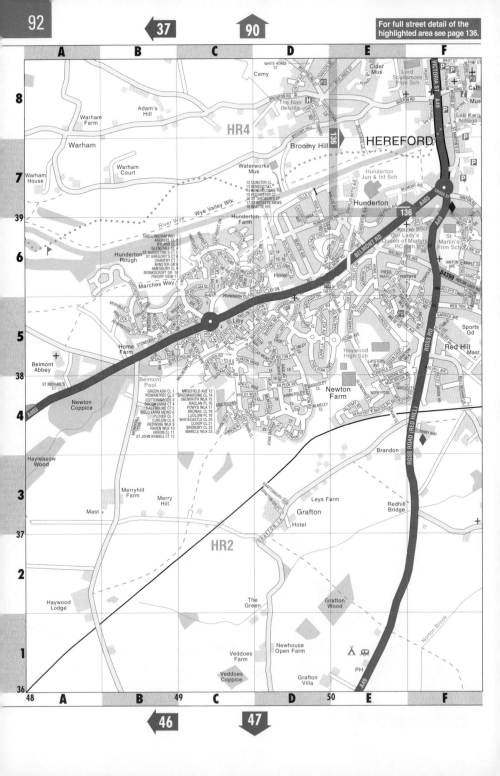

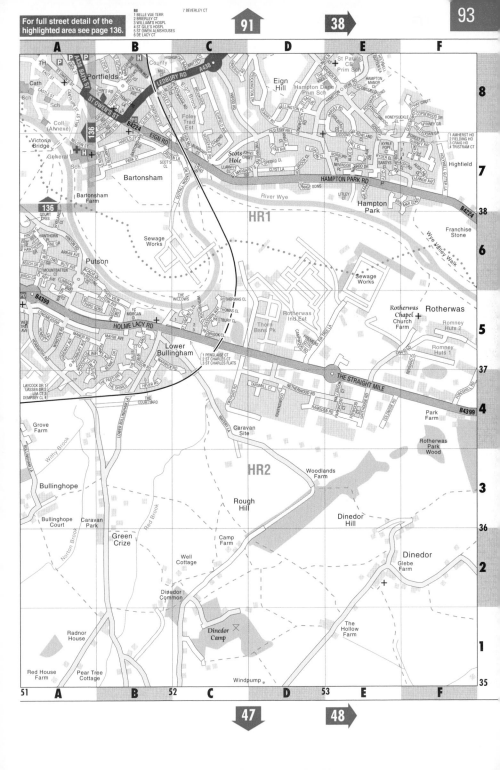

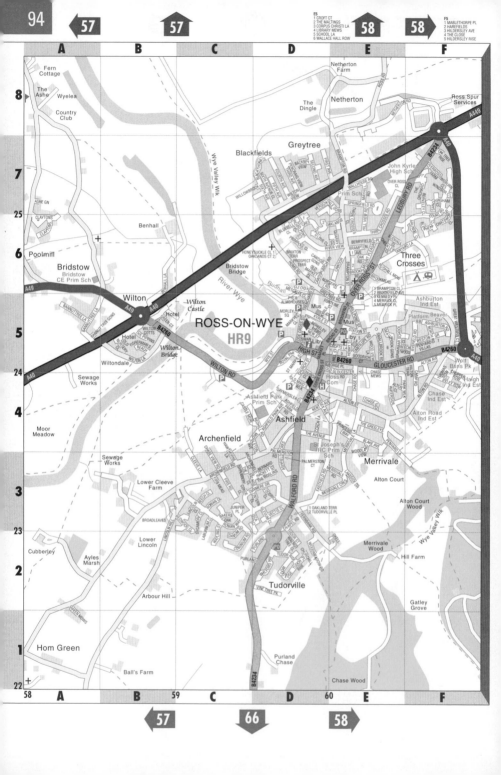

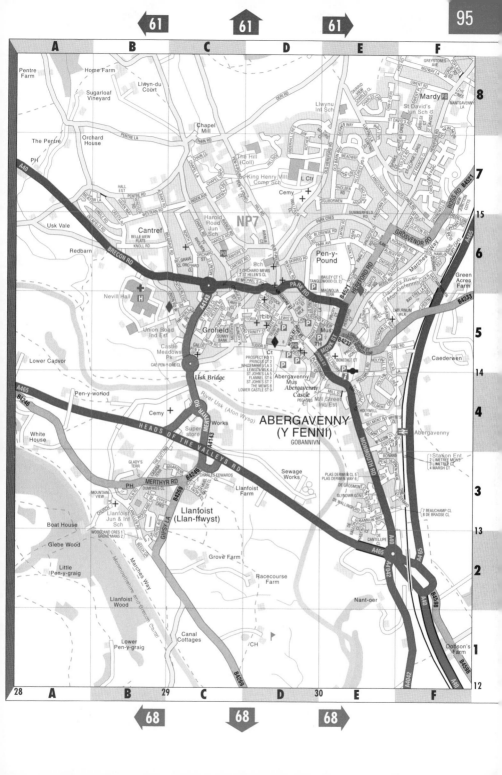

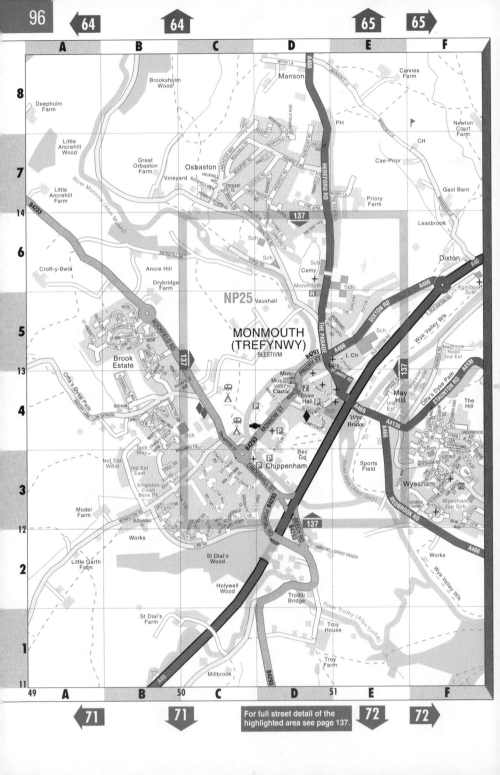

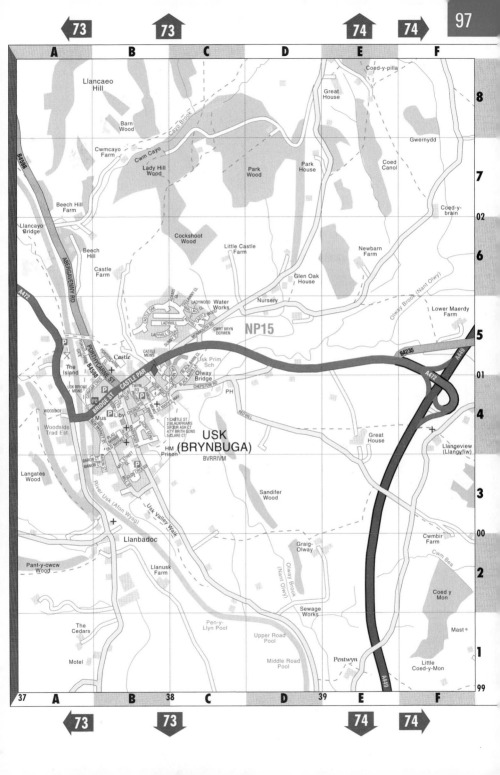

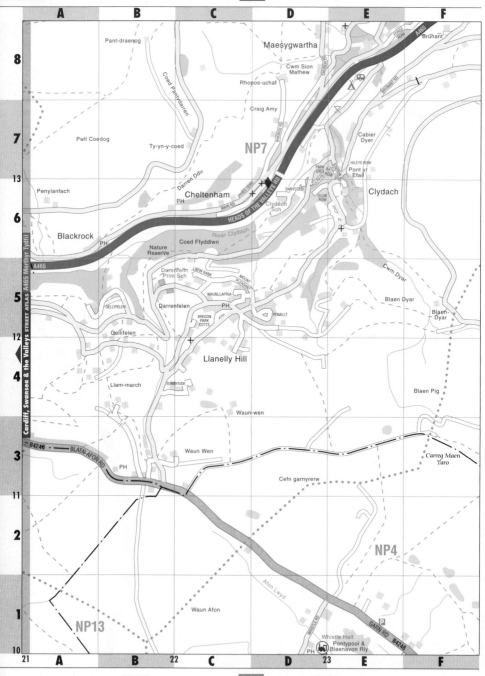

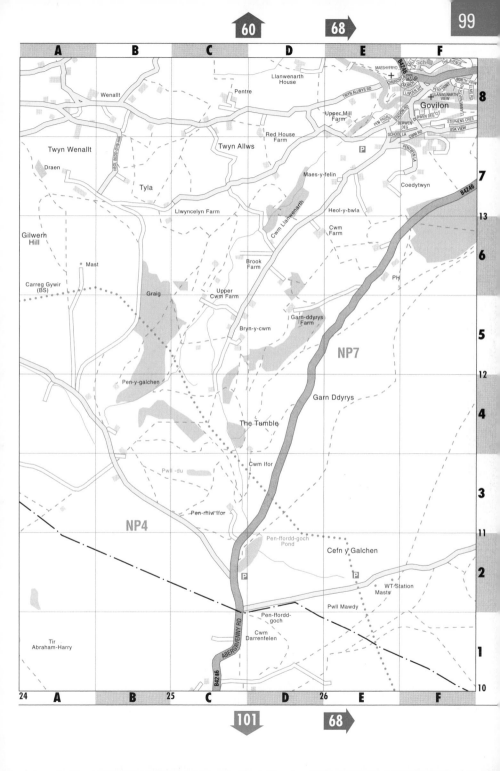

98

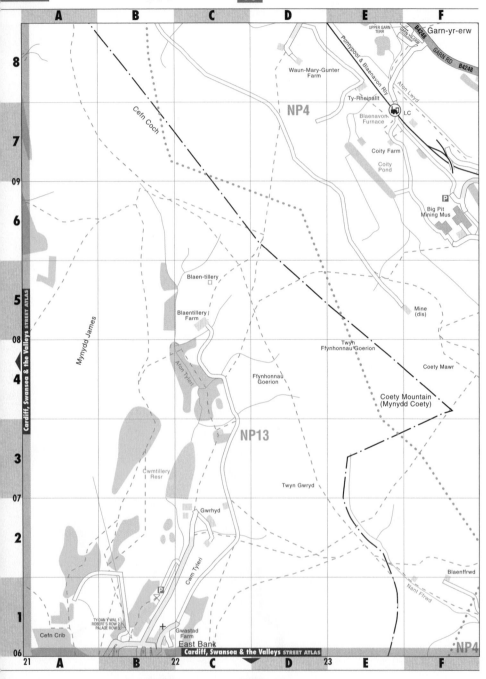

Garn-yr-erw

UPPER GARN TERR

Waun-Mary-Gunter Farm

NP4

Ty-Rheipallt

Pontypool & Blaenavon Rly

Afon Lwyd

LC

Blaenavon Furnace

Coity Farm

Coity Pond

Big Pit Mining Mus

P

Cefn Coch

Mine (dis)

Blaen-tillery

Blaentillery Farm

Twyn Ffynhonnau Goerion

Coety Mawr

Afon Tyleri

Ffynhonnau Goerion

Mynydd James

Coety Mountain (Mynydd Coety)

NP13

Cwmtillery Resr

Twyn Gwryd

Gwrhyd

Blaenffrwd

Nant Ffrwd

NP4

P

Cwm Tyleri

TY-DAN Y WAL 1 ROBERT'S ROW 2 PALACE ROW 3

Cefn Crib

Gwastad Farm

East Bank

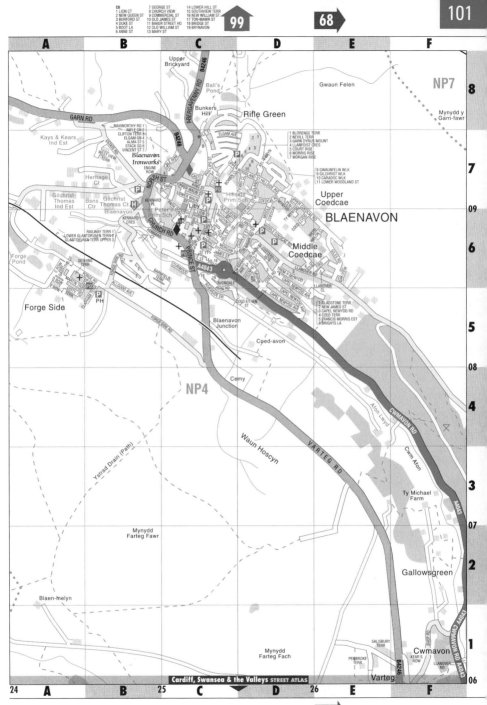

C6
1 LION CT
2 NEW QUEEN ST
3 BURFORD ST
4 DUKE ST
5 BOOT LA
6 ANNE ST

7 GEORGE ST
8 CHURCH VIEW
9 COMMERCIAL ST
10 OLD JAMES ST
11 BAKER STREET HO
12 OLD WILLIAM ST
13 MARY ST

14 LOWER HILL ST
15 SOUTHVIEW TERR
16 NEW WILLIAM ST
17 TON-MAWR ST
18 BRIDGE ST
19 BRYNAVON

NP7

Upper
Brickyard

Ball's
Pond

Gwaun Felen

Mynydd y
Garn-fawr

GARN RD

Bunkers
Hill'

Rifle Green

Kays & Kears
Ind Est

MAXWORTHY RD 1
RIFLE DR 2
CLIFTON TERR 9
ELGAM GN 4
ALMA ST 5
STACK SQ 6
VINCENT ST 7

Blaenavon
Ironworks

ENGINE
ROW

ELGAM AVE

1 BLORENGE TERR
2 NEVILL TERR
3 GARN DYRUS MOUNT
4 LLANFOIST CRES
5 COURT RISE
6 MORRIS RISE
7 MORGAN RISE

WEST VIEW
TERR

Heritage
Ct

8 GWAUNFELIN WLK
9 GILCHRIST WLK
10 CARADOC WLK
11 LOWER WOODLAND ST

Gilchrist-
Thomas
Ind Est

Bsns
Ctr

Gilchrist
Thomas Ct
Blaenavon

Liby

Hillside
Prim Sch

Upper
Coedcae

BLAENAVON

KENNARD
PL

St Peter's
Prim Sch

09

KENNARD
CRES

Middle
Coedcae

Forge
Pond

GETHING
TERR

RAILWAY TERR 1
LOWER GLANTORVAEN TERR 2
GLANTORVAEN TERR UPPER 3

JAMES ST

6

A4043

Forge Side

AVONDALE

1 GLADSTONE TERR
2 NEW JAMES ST
3 CAPEL NEWYDD RD
4 COED TERR
5 FRANCIS MORRIS EST
6 BRIGHTS LA

RIVERSIDE DR

LLANOVER

Blaenavon
Junction

COED EITHEN
ST

CAPEL NEWYDD AVE

5

Coed-avon

08

Cemy

FORGE SIDE RD

NP4

CWMAVON RD

Afon Lwyd

4

Waun Hoscyn

VARTEG RD

Cwm Afon

Ty Michael
Farm

3

Ystrad Drain (Path)

07

Mynydd
Farteg Fawr

A4043

2

Gallowsgreen

Blaen-melyn

Mynydd
Farteg Fach

SALISBURY
TERR

KEAR'S
ROW

CWMAVON RD A4043

1

PEMBROKE
TERR

SHOP RD

Cwmavon

B4246

LLANOVER
RD

Varteg

06

24

25

26

68

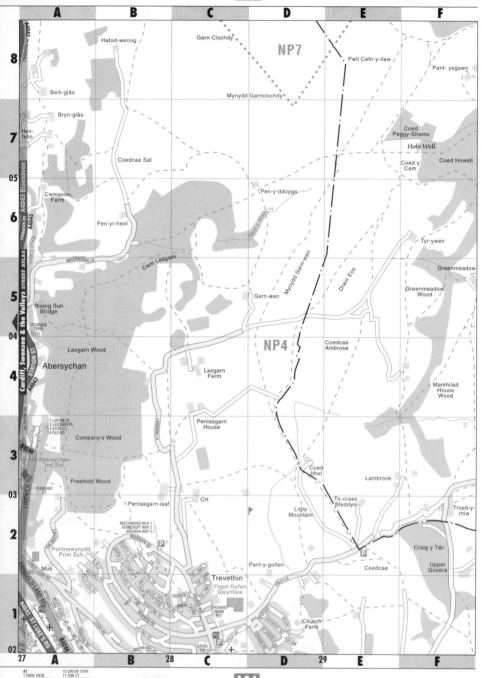

A1
1 PARK VIEW
2 TORFAEN TERR
3 MACHINE MDW
4 MITCHELL TERR
5 ROCHDALE CT
6 PARK TERR
7 CHURCH TERR
8 GROVESIDE VILLAS
9 COLLEGE TERR
10 GROVE TERR
11 OAK CT
12 NEWLANDS CT
13 BELLE VIEW CT
14 BELGRAVE CT
15 CAPEL CT
16 WEST BANK CT
17 HARDY CT
18 PARKSIDE CT

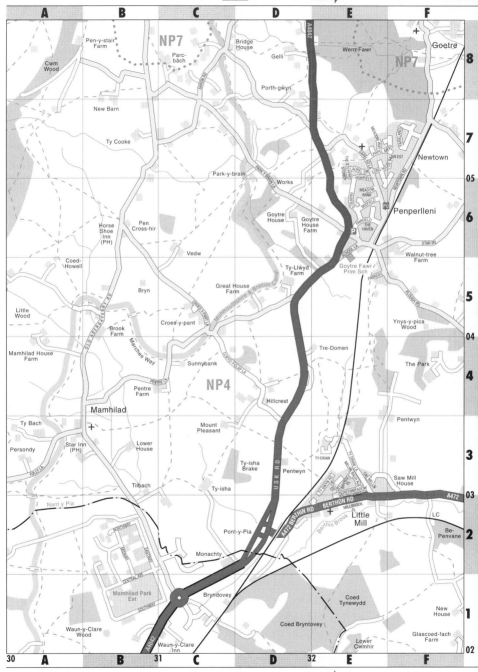

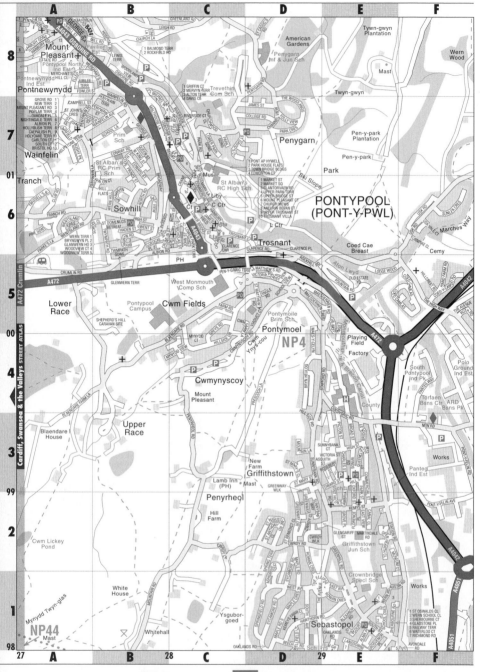

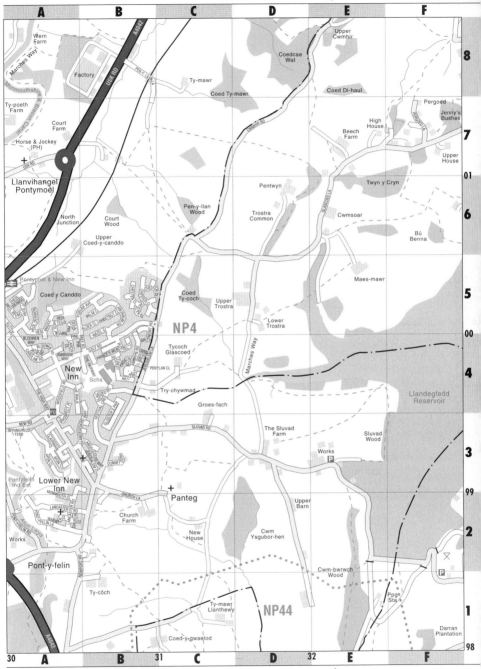

C6
1 TY TRAPPA PL
2 DINGLE LA
3 GWYNLLYW
4 CALYN CT
5 CADOC RD

104

E5
1 RICHMOND ST
2 BROOKLAND HO
3 STATION TERR
4 RUSSELL ST
5 COMMERCIAL PL
6 HAROLD ST
7 STANLEY PL
8 PADARN PL
9 CROMWELL PL
10 PLAS TROSNANT

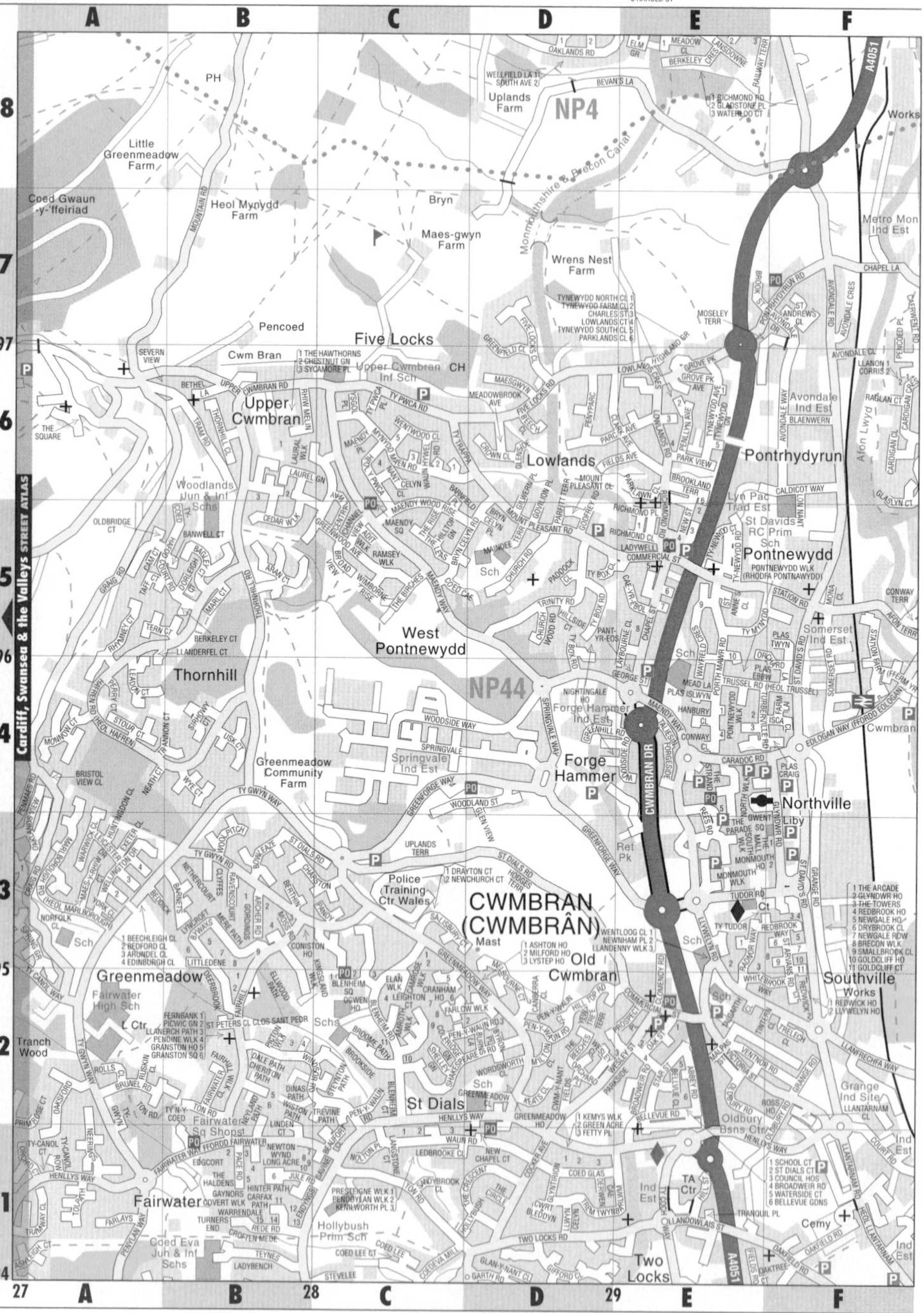

NP4
NP44
Upper Cwmbran
Five Locks
Lowlands
Pontrhydyrun
Pontnewydd
West Pontnewydd
Thornhill
Forge Hammer
Northville
CWMBRAN (CWMBRÂN)
Old Cwmbran
Greenmeadow
Southville
St Dials
Fairwater
Two Locks
Little Greenmeadow Farm
Coed Gwaun -y-ffeiriad
Heol Mynydd Farm
Uplands Farm
Maes-gwyn Farm
Wrens Nest Farm
Pencoed
Bryn
Monmouthshire & Brecon Canal
Metro Mon Ind Est
Avondale Ind Est
Somerset Ind Est
Greenmeadow Community Farm
Springvale Ind Est
Police Training Ctr Wales
Grange Ind Site
Oldbury Bsns Ctr
Tranch Wood
Cwmbran
A4051
CWMBRAN DR

Cardiff, Swansea & the Valleys STREET ATLAS

B1
1 ROWAN HO
2 HAYSWAYN
3 WALKDENS
4 MAYNES
5 HASSOCKS LEA
6 MOLESCOMBE
7 FIELDINGS
8 POSTERN
9 BETWYNS
10 KINGSLEA
11 FALLOWFIELD
12 TEWENDS
13 INGLES
14 THE WADES
15 MINORIES

B3
1 MARLOSS PATH
2 PENNYFIELDS
3 CROFTS CNR
4 BADGERS MEDE
5 EARLSMEDE
6 THE TWININGS
7 THE COURTLANDS
8 HOLMDALE
9 MAYBURY HO

C2
1 RANNOCH HO
2 BELA HO
3 DERWENT HO
4 CHARWOOD HO
5 OAKDALE PATH
6 GILESTON WLK
7 SHAWLEY CT
8 HANLEY PATH
9 ROMSLEY CT
10 NORBURY HO
11 THORNCLIFF CT

112

E4
1 LONG HOLLOW
2 ST WOOLOS GN
3 LLANDAFF GN
4 GRANGE LA
5 GENERAL REES SQ

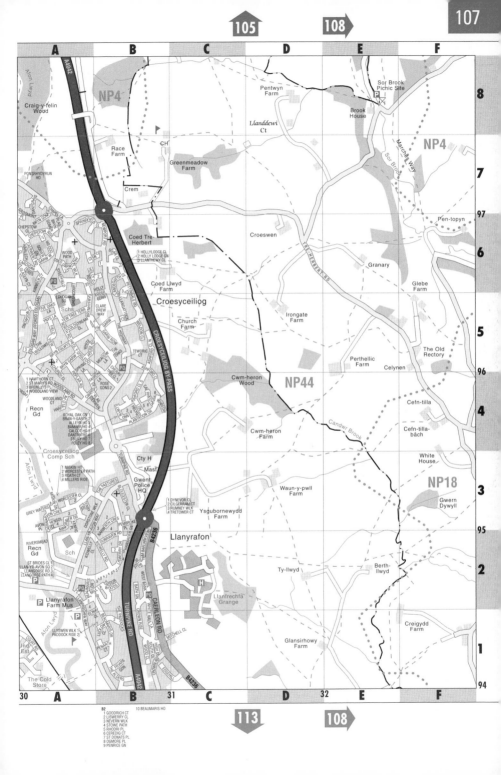

105
108
113
108

A B C D E F

8
7
97
6
5
96
4
95
3
2
94
1

NP4

Craig-y-felin Wood
PONTRHYDYRUN HO

NP4

Pentwyn Farm
Sor Brook Picnic Site
Brook House
Llanddewi Ct

Race Farm
CH
Greenmeadow Farm
Crem
Croeswen

Marches Way

Pen-topyn

Coed Tre-Herbert
1 HOLLYLODGE CL
2 HOLLY LODGE GN
3 LLANTHEWY CL

Granary

Glebe Farm

Coed Llwyd Farm
Croesyceiliog

Church Farm

Irongate Farm

The Old Rectory

CROESYCEILIOG BY-PASS

Cwm-heron Wood

NP44

Perthellic Farm
Celynen

Cefn-tilla

Recn Gd

1 HAWTHORN CT
2 ST MARY'S RD
3 BRONLLYS PL
4 WOODLAND VIEW

ROYAL OAK CN 1
BRAN-Y-GARTH 2
ALLEYN HO 3
BAMBER HO 4
CALGOT HO 5
DANTHY HO 6
ERI-JH HO 7
FOLEY HO 8

Cwm-heron Farm

Cefn-tilla-bâch

White House

NP18

Croesyceiliog Comp Sch

1 MISKIN HO
2 WORCESTER PATH
3 ROATH CT
4 MILLERS RIDE

Cty H
Mast
Gwent Police HQ

Waun-y-pwll Farm

Gwern Dywyll

1 DYNEVOR CL
2 CILGERRAN CT
3 RUMNEY WLK
4 TRETOWER CT

Ysgubornewydd Farm

Berth-llwyd

Recn Gd
Sch

Llanyrafon

1 GREY WATERS CT
2 AVON CRES

ST BRIDES CL 1
LLAN-YR-AVON SQ 2
LLANGOOSE RD 3
LLANGORSE PATH 4

RIVERSMEAD

Ty-llwyd

R
Llanfrechfa Grange

Creigydd Farm

Llanyrafon Farm Mus

1 LLYSWEN WLK 1
PADDOCK RISE 2

Glansirhowy Farm

B4236

CAERLEON RD

TURNPIKE RD

A4042

The Cold Store

30 A B 31 C D 32 E F

B2
1 GOODRICH CT
2 LISWERRY CL
3 NEVERN WLK
4 STOWE PATH
5 RHODRI PL
6 CEREDIG CT
7 ST DONATS PL
8 OGMORE PL
9 PENRICE GN

10 BEAUMARIS HO

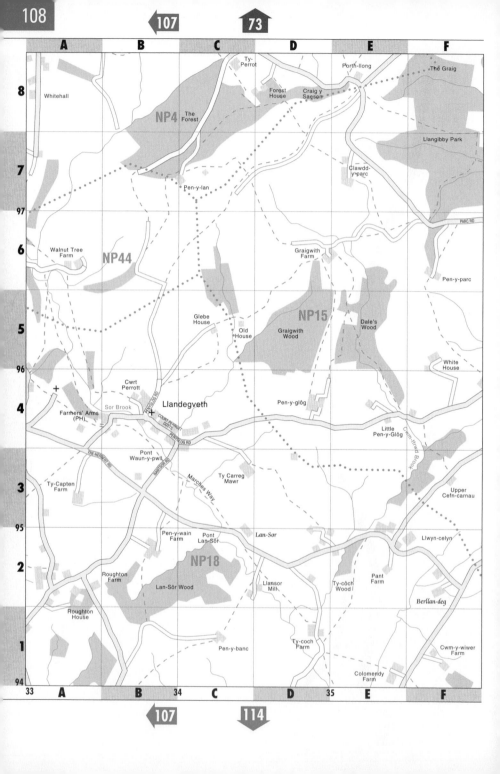

78
76

A B C D E F

8

Wet
Wood

Gaer
Hill

Gaer Hill
Farm

Minepit
Wood

A466

Liveoaks
Grove

Livox
Cottages

7

Wyndcliffe
Court

PENTERRY LA

Wet
Wood

Wynd Cliff

Moss
Cottage

Lower Wyndcliff
Wood

Liveoaks
Brake

Livox
Farm

Mill
Farm

P

Nature
Trail

97

DINGATES RD

WOODLANDS C

GRANGE RD

St Arvans

Lower Martridge
Wood

Lover's
Leap

Ban-y-gor Wood

LANCAUT LA

6

The
New Temple
Barn

PORT CLIFFE
COURT GDNS
MANOR VIEW
THE ROW

Lancaut

SYCAMORE
CT

Cave
Wood

River Wye (Afon Gwy)

PIERCEFIELD
TERR

PH

Giant's
Cave

5

Sewage
Works

96

Oakgrove

Wye Valley Walk

Piercefield Cliffs

NP16

Stables

4

Stables

Piercefield

Pierce Wood

Piercefield
Park

Chepstow
Race Course

Longhope Reach

Offa's Dyke Path

B4228

3

Fryth Wood

Rossfield

95

Chapelhouse
Wood

GOWER
COTTS

COLEFORD RD

B4228

B4293

ITTON RD

Sandy
Way

Goldenhill
Farm

MOPLA RD

CASTLEFORD HILL

CASTLEFORD GDNS

B4228

PO

2

Crossway
Green

Chepstow
Comp Sch

St John's-on-the-hill
Sch

CAMDA L

ROCK VILLA

B4235

Cockshoot Wood

B4293

St LAWRENCE RD

THE ROMANS

Ctr

1 SOMERSET COTTS
2 RIVERSIDE MILL
3 ORCHARD GDNS
4 KENDALL SQ
5 CHURCH ROW

1

Great Barnets Woods

Bishop's
Barnets Wood

TURNPIKE CL 1
TUDOR DR 2
ST JOHN'S GDNS 3
RANOVER CL 4

PIERCEFIELD AVE

PARK VIEW

WELSH ST

The Dell
Prim Sch

Chepstow
Castle

Mus

P

B4235

A466

WALLGATE
BARNETS
WOOD

STUART CL

MOUNT WAY

B4293

DAVIS

94

51 A B 52 C D 53 E F

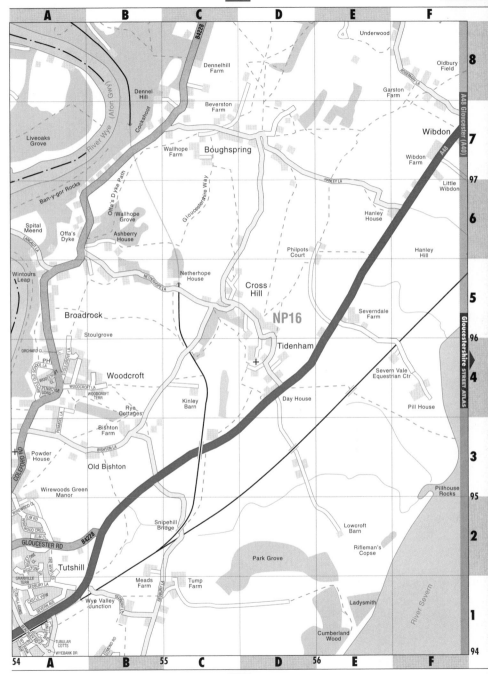

A B C D E F

8

Underwood

Oldbury
Field

Dennelhill
Farm

Dennel
Hill

Beverston
Farm

Garston
Farm

Wibdon

7

Liveoaks
Grove

Cockshoot

Wallpope
Farm

Boughspring

Wibdon
Farm

Little
Wibdon

97

Ban-y-gor Rocks

Offa's Dyke Path

Gloucestershire Way

HANLEY LA

Hanley
House

6

Spital
Meend

Wallhope
Grove

Ashberry
House

Offa's
Dyke

Netherhope
House

Philpots
Court

Hanley
Hill

Wintours
Leap

NETHERHOPE LA

Cross
Hill

5

Broadrock

Stoulgrove

NP16

Severndale
Farm

96

PH

ORCHARD CL

STOULGROVE LA

Woodcroft

WOODCROFT LA

WOODCROFT
TERR

Kinley
Barn

Tidenham

Day House

Severn Vale
Equestrian Ctr

Pill House

4

SCHOOL CL

PENMOYLE
GDNS

PENMOYLE LA

Rye
Cottages

Bishton
Farm

BISHTON LA

COLEFORD RD

Powder
House

Old Bishton

Wirewoods Green
Manor

Pillhouse
Rocks

3

95

WHIDDON CRES

ELM RD

ELM CL

GLOUCESTER RD

B4228

Snipehill
Bridge

Lowcroft
Barn

Rifleman's
Copse

2

STONE

GRANVILLE
TERR

CASTLE VIEW

SEDBURY LA

Tutshill

Wye Valley
Junction

SEDBURY LA

Meads
Farm

Tump
Farm

Park Grove

Ladysmith

River Severn

1

TUBULAR
COTTS

WYEBANK DR

Cumberland
Wood

54 A B 55 C D 56 E F 94

A48 Gloucester (A40)

A48

Gloucestershire STREET ATLAS

106

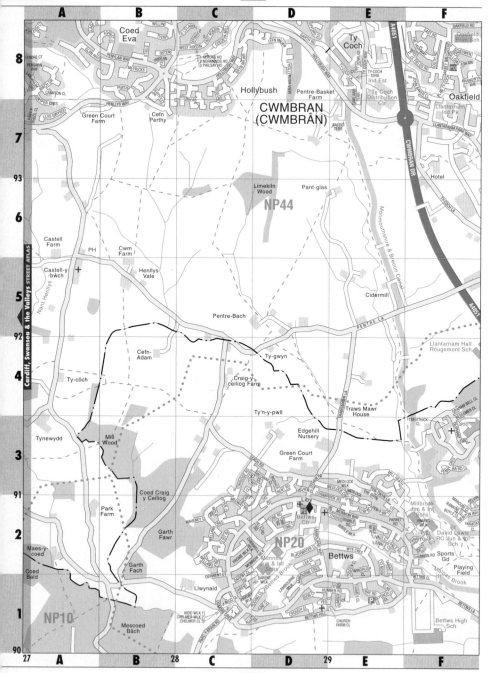

118

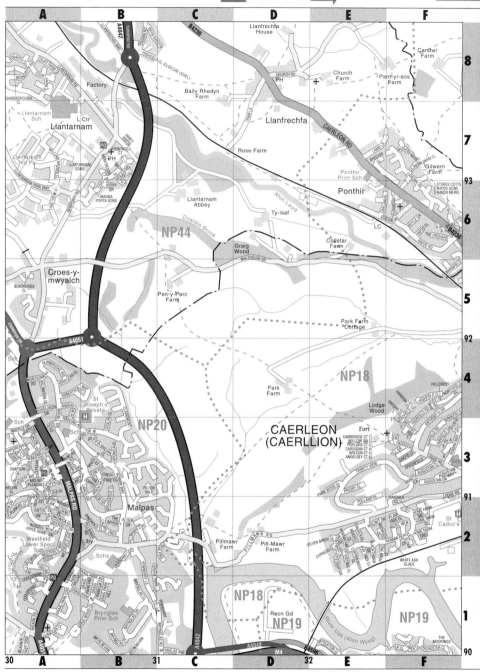

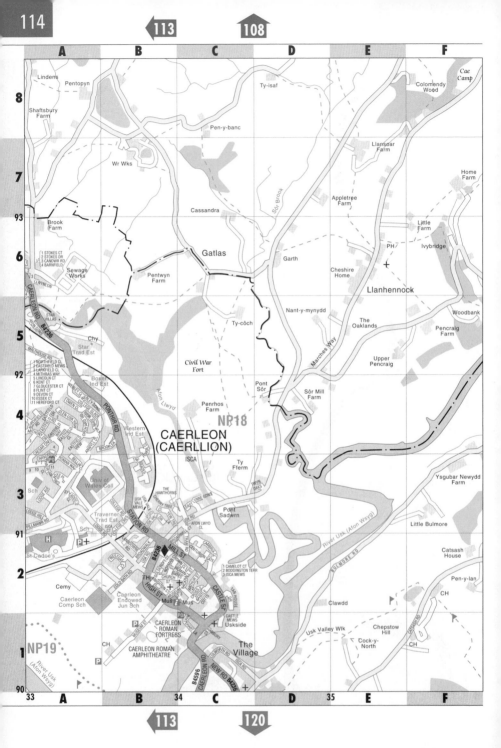

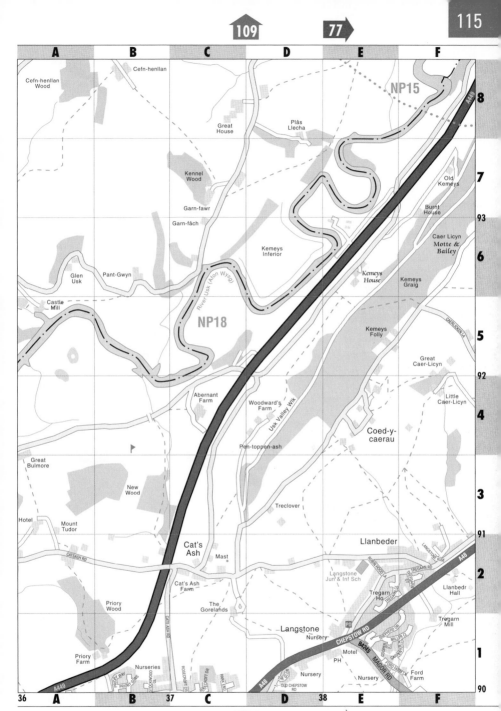

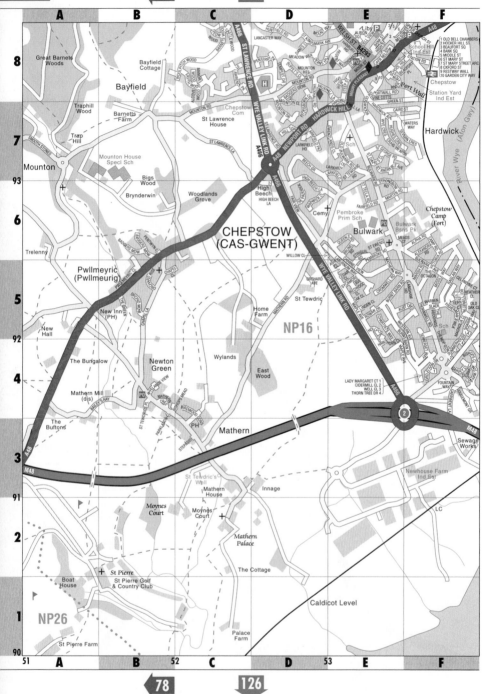

Offa's Dyke Path

Mast
ST EDMUNDS
GRAHAME CLOSE
Sedbury Bend
Badams Court

Sch
THE HAYES

WYECLIFF CRES
NEWTON DR
HANOVER CT
WYEBANK WAY
WYEBANK RISE
TALLARD'S
PL
LYNDA
MADOCKE
RD
PH
PO

Sedbury

Baker's Wood

Hitchen's Grove

Sewage Works

WYNDCLIFFE HO 1
WYE VIEW HO 2
OFFA'S CL
MERCIAN WAY
BUTTINGTON HILL
BEACHLEY WAY
PACK WAY

THE BELFREY

Sedbury Park

Pennsylvania Farm

CLIFF VIEW
ORCHARD DENE
BRIDGET DR

Offa's Dyke Path

The Combe

Sedbury Cliffs

Buttington Trump

BUTTINGTON TERR

Buttington Farm

NP16

INNER LOOP RD
LOOP RD

Warren Slade

Park Redding

River Wye

Works

Slime Road

Slimeroad Sand

River Severn

DRIBDIN CLOSE
EDGEWOOD CL
OVELL CL
MARINERS WAY
VALENTINE
HIGHLAND

ST GEORGES WAY

BEACHLEY RD
PITTERS CROFT
MUTTON HO

APPRENTICE CL

1 PHOENIX DR
2 CLARENDON CL
3 ALMA DR
4 BRITON CL

River Wye (Afon Gwy)

Whirls End

Beachley Barracks

Beachley

OLD COACH RD
OLD COACH CL

LC

Hen And Chickens

Hunger Pill

PAVILION RD

The Old Ferry Hotel
IRB Sta

Leary Rock

Sports Gd
P

Severn Road Bridge

Upper Bench

Beachley Point

M48

Aust Rock

112

F4
1 WEST PARK LA
2 WATKINS LA
3 PROSSER LA
4 HOMEVALLEY HO
5 BRYNGWYN RD
6 CLEWER CT
7 CLEWER COURT MEWS
8 SOUTHVILLE RD
9 WESTVILLE RD
10 CHAPMAN CT

A B C D E F

Cardiff, Swansea & the Valleys STREET ATLAS A468 Caerphilly A467 Crumlin

Mescoed Mawr

Coed Kemeys

Gwern-y-Ceffyla

Llwyni Wood

Rogerstone

Coed Garw

Gwastad Mawr

1 ROBERTS CL
2 WATERSIDE CL
3 PAXTON WLK

Croesllanfro Farm

Coed y Nant

Ynysfro Farm

Wern-ddu Wood

Wern-ddu

1 LANDSEFFED CL
2 LLYN CELYN CL
3 LLYN BERWYN CL

Cwm Farm

Ynysfro Resrs

Strawberry Farm

Marshes Way

Fourteen Locks Canal Ctr

Monmouthshire & Brecon Canal

Alteryn Wood

CEFN RD

S V Walk

Pensarn Farm

Graig Ddifaith

Mast

Univ of Wales Coll

1 STEVENSON CT
2 GALFA WLK
3 WATERSIDE WLK W
4 GRINOLE WLK
5 LITTLE OAKS VIEW
6 ROYCE WLK
7 SCOTT WLK

Cefn

HIGHCROSS RD

Cefn Wood

Cwrt-y-mwnws Farm

Ridgeway

NP10

High Cross Jun & Inf Sch

The Woodlands

RISCA RD

Caerau Park

Cefn Wood Jun & Inf Sch

1 HUBERT RISE
2 LEWIS VIEW
3 LYNDON WAY
4 HUBERT RISE

L Ctr

Coed-Melyn Park

Ridgeway

Nant Coch House
Rougemont Sch

High Cross

GLASLLWCH CRES

St Woollos Cemy

NP20

Stelvio Park

Tregwilym Ind Est

Greenfield Stores

Glasllwch Jun & Inf Sch

Glasllwch

Stelvio

Thornbury Park

Basil Stores

Parklands

Pye Corner

Bassaleg

CAERPHILLY RD

A468

Bassaleg Comp Sch

Ebbw River (Afon Ebwy)

Gaer Jun & Inf Sch

Gaer

Ffynon-oer

Court Wood

Dyffryn Court

FORGE RD

Simhowy Valley Walk

1 HILLVIEW
2 FORTIE

Coed Ffynnon-oer

MACAULAY GDNS
MARLOWE GDNS
VANBRUGH GDNS
JANE AUSTEN CL

St David's RC Jun & Inf Sch

CARDIFF RD

A48

Sports Gd

128

F1
1 MAESGLAS GR
2 MAESGLAS CRES
3 MAESGLAS ST

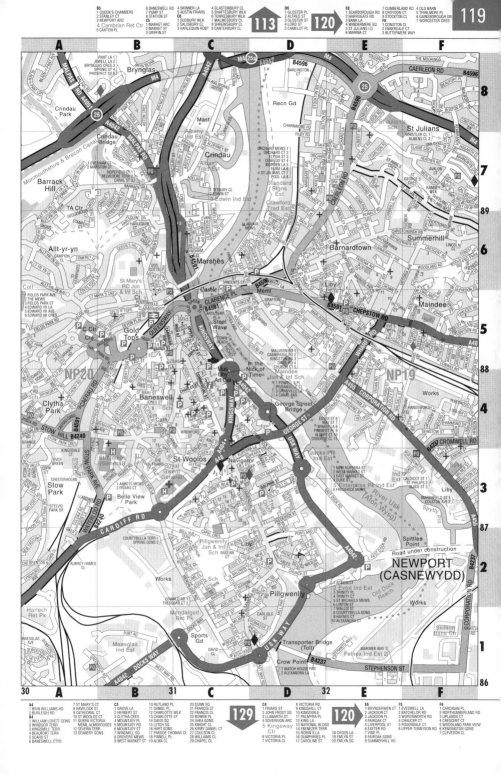

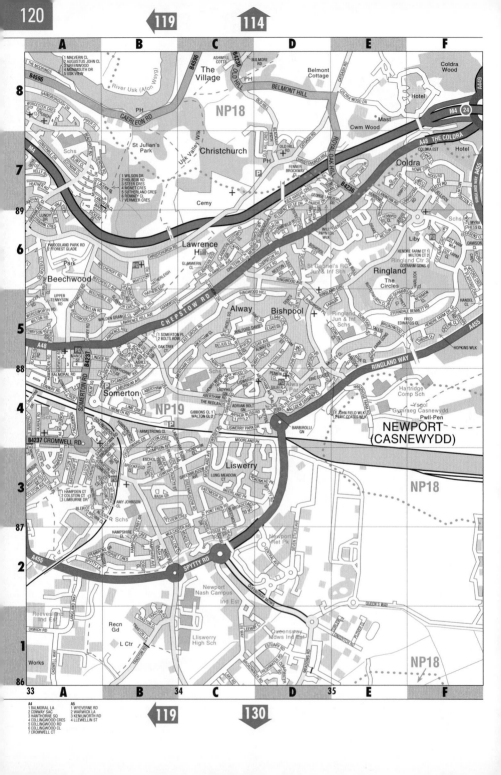

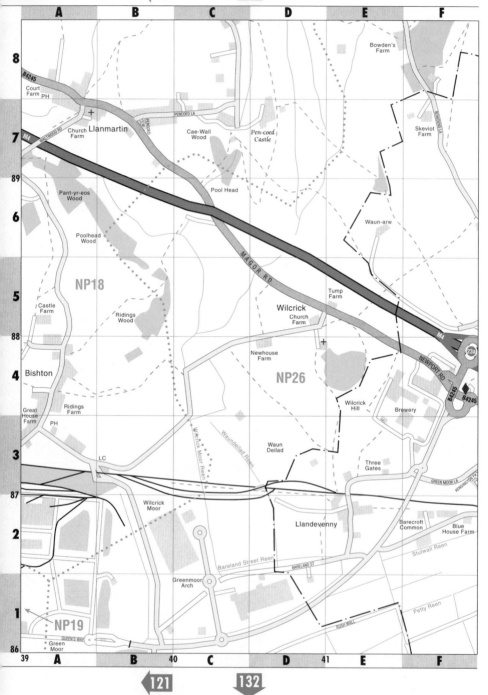

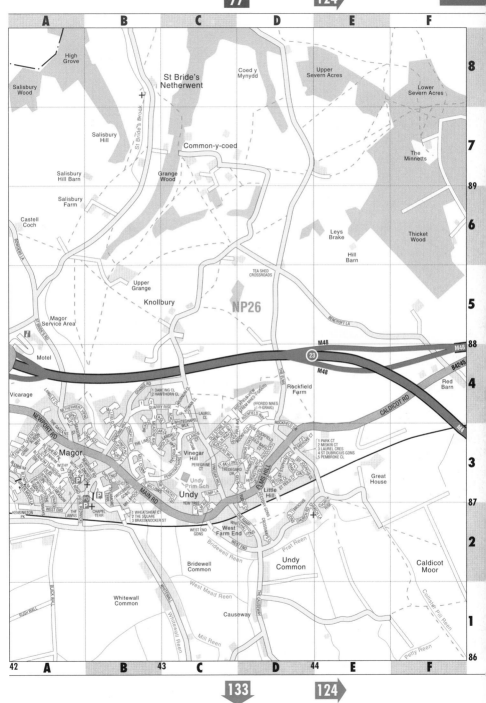

123
78

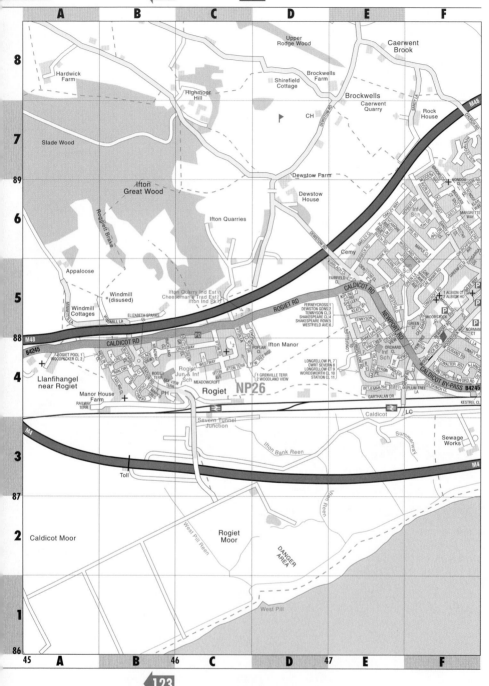

123

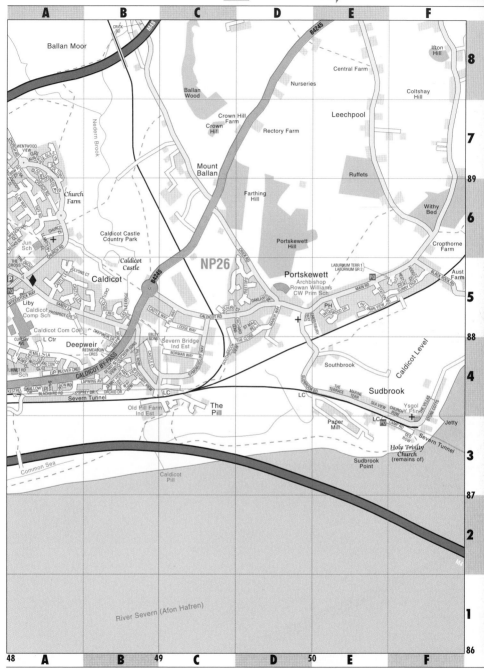

Ballan Moor

Crick Rd

M48

Central Farm

Ifton Hill

8

Nurseries

Coltshay Hill

Ballan Wood

Crown Hill Farm

Leechpool

7

Crown Hill

Rectory Farm

89

Nedern Brook

Mount Ballan

Ruffets

Farthing Hill

Withy Bed

6

Church Farm

Caldicot Castle Country Park

Portskewett Hill

Cropthorne Farm

Jun Sch

Caldicot Castle

NP26

Portskewett

LABURNUM TERR 1
LABURNUM GR 2

Aust Farm

THE CROSS

Archbishop Rowan Williams CW Prim Sch

5

P

Caldicot

Black Rock Rd

Liby

Caldicot Comp Sch

PH

Sunny Croft

Caldicot Com Coll

L Ctr

Oaklands

Main Rd

88

Deepweir

Southbrook

Caldicot Level

CALDICOT BY-PASS

Severn Bridge Ind Est

Norman Way

Southbrook

Sudbrook

4

Kestrel Rd

Lapwing Ave

LC

LC

THE TERRACE

MARINE TERR

Ysgol Ffin

Severn Tunnel

Old Pill Farm Ind Est

The Pill

Paper Mill

SEA VIEW

CHURCH ROW

LC

Severn Tunnel

Jetty

3

Common Sea

Holy Trinity Church (remains of)

Sudbrook Point

87

Caldicot Pill

2

M48

River Severn (Afon Hafren)

1

86

48 A B 49 C D 50 E F

125
116

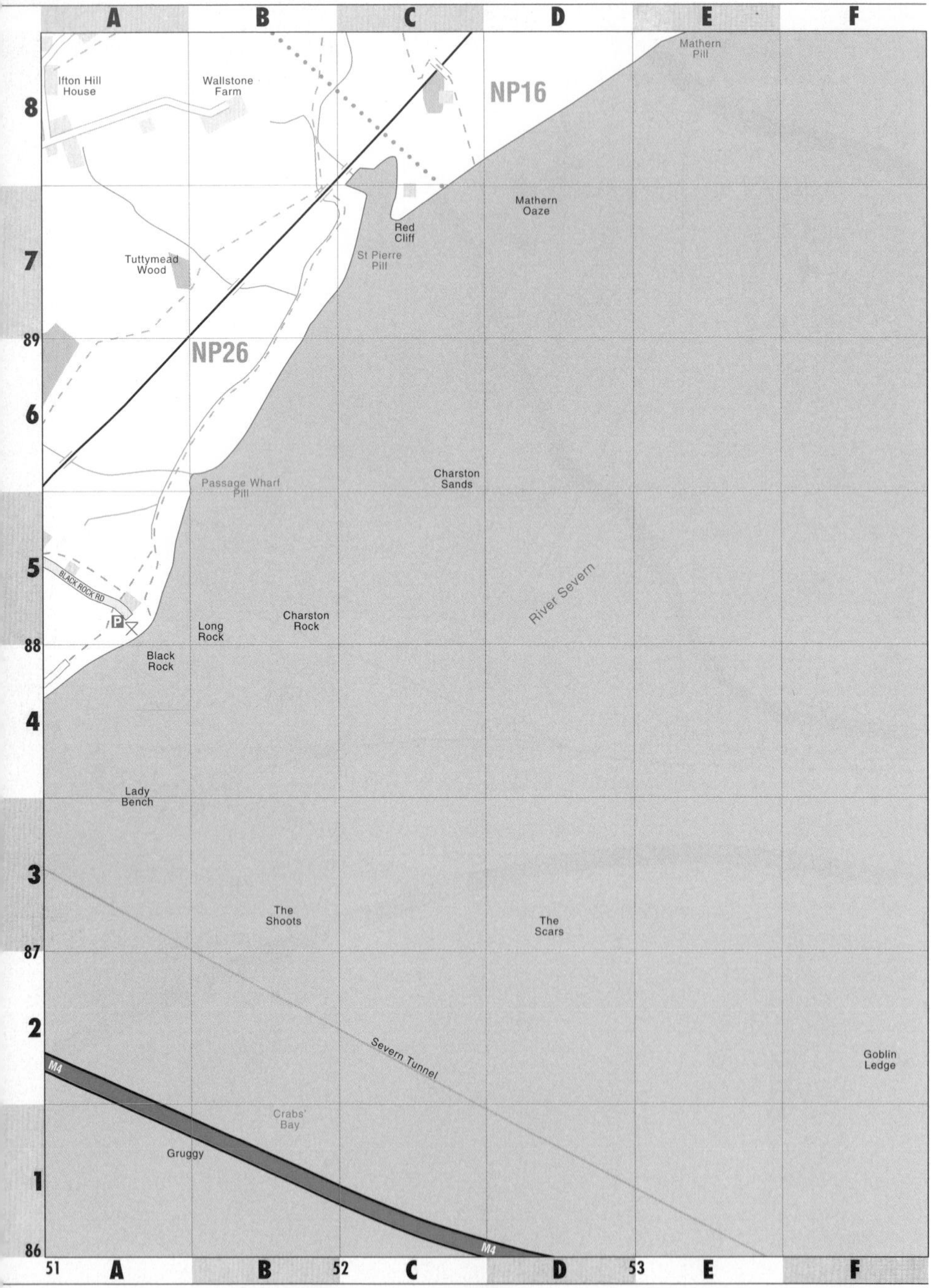

A B C D E F

8

NP16

Mathern
Pill

Ifton Hill
House

Wallstone
Farm

Red
Cliff

Mathern
Oaze

7

St Pierre
Pill

Tuttymead
Wood

89

NP26

6

Passage Wharf
Pill

Charston
Sands

5

River Severn

BLACK ROCK RD

P

Long
Rock

Charston
Rock

88

Black
Rock

4

Lady
Bench

3

The
Shoots

The
Scars

87

2

Severn Tunnel

Goblin
Ledge

M4

Crabs'
Bay

1

Gruggy

86

M4

51 A B 52 C D 53 E F

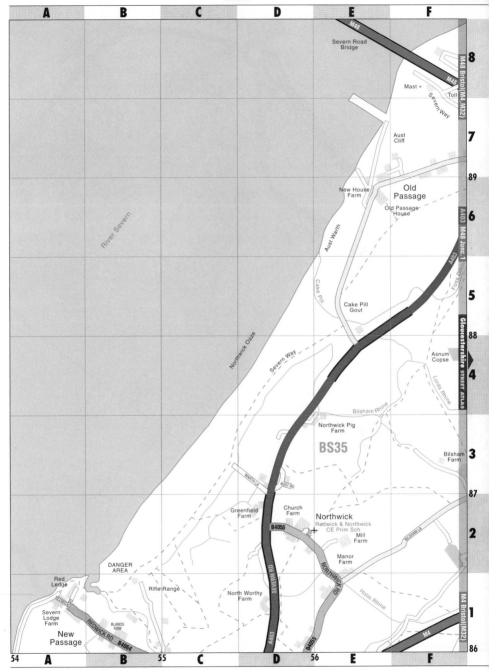

M48

Severn Road Bridge

M48

M48 Bristol (M4, M32)

8

Mast

Toll

Severn Way

Aust Cliff

7

89

New House Farm

Old Passage

A403 M48 Junc. 1 M48 (M4)

6

Old Passage House

Aust Warth

A403

Cake Pill

5

Cake Pill Gout

88

Gloucestershire STREET ATLAS

Asnum Copse

4

Northwick Oaze

Severn Way

Lords Rhine

Bilsham Rhine

Northwick Pig Farm

BS35

Bilsham Farm

3

WARTH LA

AUST RD

87

BELSHAM LA

Greenfield Farm

Church Farm

Northwick

Redwick & Northwick CE Prim Sch

Mill Farm

2

B4055

SEVERN RD

NORTHWICK RD

Manor Farm

M4 Bristol (M32)

DANGER AREA

Red Ledge

Rifle Range

North Worthy Farm

Holm Rhine

REDWICK RD

Severn Lodge Farm

BLANDS ROW

A403

B4055

M4

1

New Passage

B4064

86

54

A

B

55

C

D

56

E

F

118

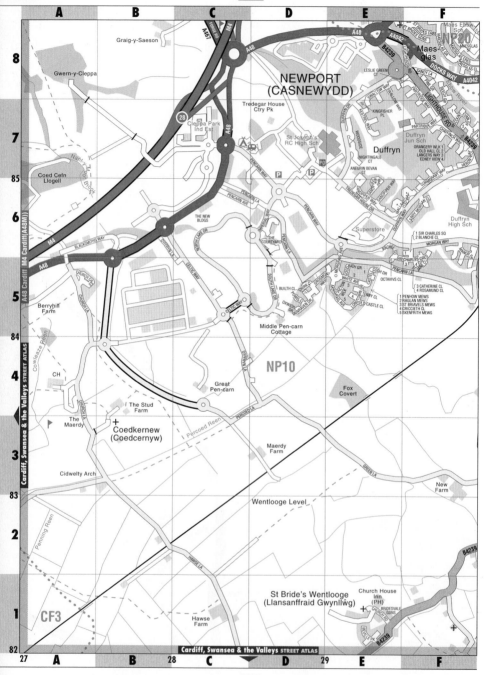

NEWPORT
(CASNEWYDD)

Graig-y-Saeson

Gwern-y-Cleppa

Coed Cefn
Llogell

Tredegar House
Ctry Pk

St Joseph's
RC High Sch

Cleppa Park
Ind Est

THE NEW
BLDGS

Duffryn

Leslie Green
CT

Kingfisher
PL

NIGHTINGALE
CT

ANEURIN BEVAN
CT

Duffryn
Jun Sch

ORANGERY WLK 1
OLD HALL CL 2
LANCERS WAY 3
EDNEY VIEW 4

Maes Ebbw
Sch

NP20

Maes-
glas

Duffryn
High Sch

Superstore

Duffryn

Berryhill
Farm

Middle Pen-carn
Cottage

THE
COURTYARD

1 SIR CHARLES SQ
2 BLANCHE CL

MORGAN WAY

SIR CHARLES CRES

BUILTH CL

3 CATHERINE CL
4 ROSAMUND CL

1 PENHOW MEWS
2 RAGLAN MEWS
3 ST BRIAVELS MEWS
4 CRICCIETH CL
5 SKENFRITH MEWS

NP10

Great
Pen-carn

Fox
Covert

CH

The Stud
Farm

The
Maerdy

Coedkernew
(Coedcernyw)

Maerdy
Farm

New
Farm

Cidwelty Arch

Percoed Reen

Wentlooge Level

Penning Reen

CF3

St Bride's Wentlooge
(Llansanffraid Gwynllwg)

Church House
Inn
(PH)

BRIDESVALE
GDNS

Hawse
Farm

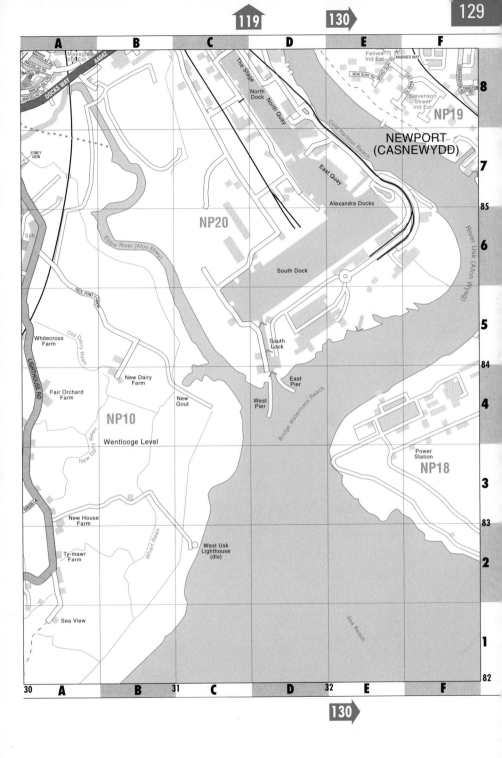

119
130

A **B** **C** **D** **E** **F**

Maesglas Ind Est
MAESGLAS RD
MAESGLAS RD
A4042
Sch
MAESGLAS CRES
DOCKS WAY
Felnex Ind Est
MARINER WAY
NEW QUAY RD
BROAD ST
EAST BANK RD
CORPORATION RD
TRASTON RD

8

Stevenson Street Ind Est

NP19

EDNEY VIEW

The Stage
North Dock
North Quay
Cold Harbour Reach

NEWPORT
(CASNEWYDD)

7

Sch

East Quay

85

NP20

Alexandra Docks

Ebbw River (Afon Ebwy)

River Usk (Afon Wysg)

6

Whitecross Farm

HEOL PONT-Y-CWM

Old Dairy Reen

South Dock

5

New Dairy Farm

84

South Lock

LIGHTHOUSE RD

Fair Orchard Farm

New Gout

East Pier

West Pier

4

NP10

New Dairy Reen

Wentlooge Level

Bridge Watermans Reach

Power Station

NP18

3

Wharf Reen

New House Farm

83

GREEN LA

Ty-mawr Farm

West Usk Lighthouse (dis)

2

Sea View

Sea Reach

1

82

30 **A** **B** 31 **C** **D** 32 **E** **F**

130

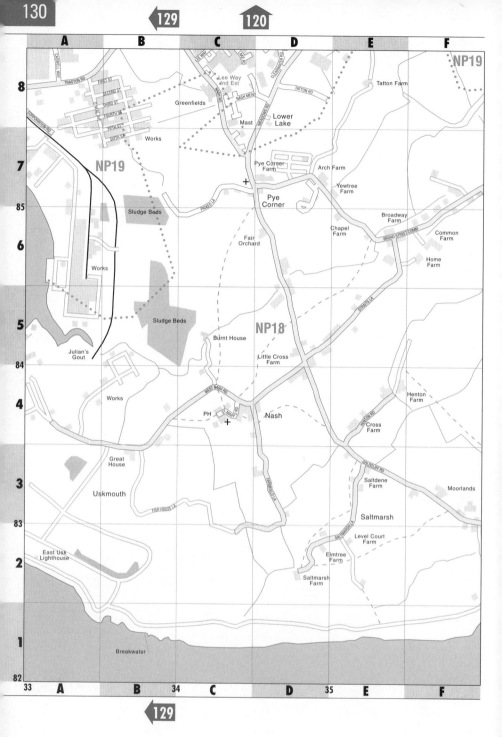

129
120

NP19

A   B   C   D   E   F

8

CASTELL WAY
TRASTON RD
DUKE'S WAY
FIRST ST
SECOND ST
THIRD ST
FOURTH ST
FIFTH ST
SIXTH ST
Works

LEE WAY
LAKE RD
CLEPPWATER RD
Lee Way
2nd Est
Greenfields
NASH RD
NASH MEAD
MORDENS RD
TATTON RD
Tatton Farm
Mast
Lower
Lake

7

NP19

CORPORATION RD

Pye Corner
Farm
Arch Farm
Yewtree
Farm

85

Sludge Beds

PICKED LA.

Pye
Corner

Broadway
Farm
BROAD STREET COMM
Common
Farm

6

Works

Fair
Orchard

Chapel
Farm

Home
Farm

5

Sludge Beds

Burnt House

NP18

Little Cross
Farm

STRAITS LA.

84

Julian's
Gout

Works

WEST NASH RD
ST. MARY'S RD

PH

Nash

HENTON RD

Henton
Farm

Cross
Farm

4

Great
House

FARM FIELD LA.

GOLDCLIFF RD

Saltdene
Farm

Moorlands

3

Uskmouth

FISH HOUSE LA.

SALTMARSH LA.

Saltmarsh

Level Court
Farm

83

East Usk
Lighthouse

Elmtree
Farm

Saltmarsh
Farm

2

1

Breakwater

82

33   A   B   34   C   D   35   E   F

129

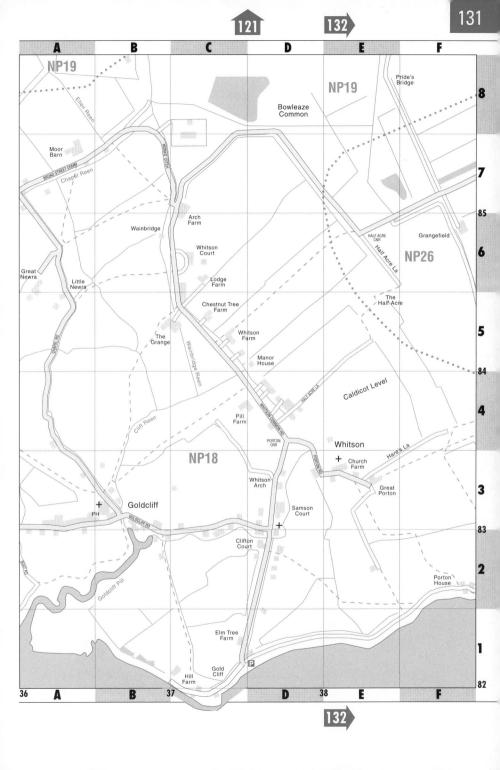

NP19

NP19

Pride's Bridge

Bowleaze Common

Moor Barn

BROAD STREET COMM

Chapel Reen

Ellen Reen

MONKS DITCH

Arch Farm

Wainbridge

Whitson Court

HALF ACRE CNR

Grangefield

Half Acre La

NP26

Great Newra

Little Newra

Lodge Farm

Chestnut Tree Farm

The Grange

Wainbridge Reen

Whitson Farm

Manor House

The Half Acre

CHAPEL RD

Cliff Reen

Pill Farm

PORTON CNR

Caldicot Level

HALF ACRE LA

WHITSON COMMON RD

Hare's La

Whitson

NP18

+ Church Farm

Goldcliff

+ PH

GOLDCLIFF RD

Whitson Arch

PORTON RD

Great Porton

Samson Court

Clifton Court

Porton House

BOAT RD

Goldcliff Pill

Elm Tree Farm

Hill Farm

Gold Cliff

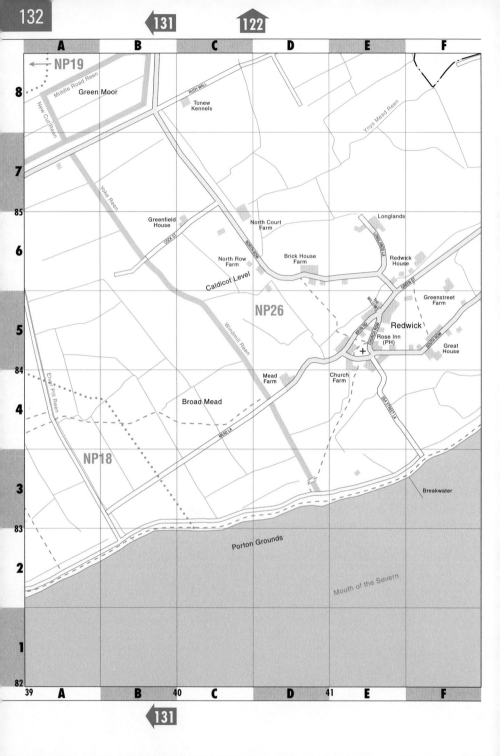

131

122

NP19

Green Moor

Middle Road Reen

New Cut Reen

Tonew Kennels

RUSH WALL

Yoke Reen

Ynys Mead Reen

Greenfield House

LOCK ST

North Court Farm

NORTH ROW

North Row Farm

Brick House Farm

Longlands

LONGLANDS LA

Redwick House

Caldicot Level

NP26

Greenstreet Farm

THE WILLOWS

BRYN RD

GREEN ST

Redwick

Rose Inn (PH)

CHURCH ROW

SOUTH ROW

Great House

Windmill Reen

Elwg Pill Reen

Broad Mead

MEAD LA

Mead Farm

Church Farm

SEA STREET LA

NP18

Breakwater

Porton Grounds

Mouth of the Severn

8

7

85

6

5

84

4

3

83

2

1

82

39   A   B   40   C   D   41   E   F

A   B   C   D   E   F

131

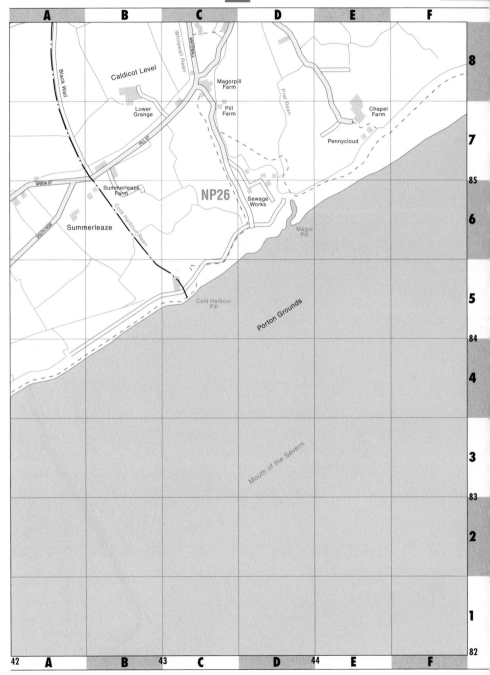

Black Wall

Caldicot Level

Whitewall Reen

WHITEHALL

Magorpill
Farm

Pill
Farm

Pral Reen

Chapel
Farm

Pennycloud

Lower
Grange

PILL ST

GREEN ST

85

Summerleaze
Farm

NP26

Sewage
Works

Cold Harbour Reen

SOUTH ROW

Summerleaze

Magor
Pill

Cold Harbour
Pill

Porton Grounds

Mouth of the Severn

8

7

6

5

84

4

3

83

2

1

82

42

43

44

A   B   C   D   E   F

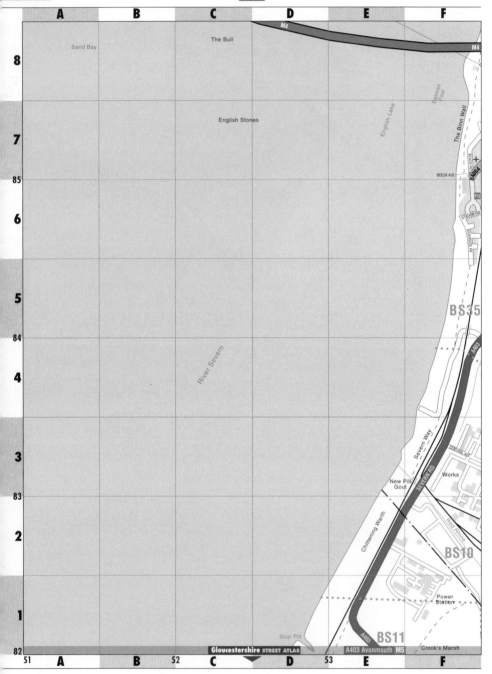

Sand Bay

The Bull

M4

M4

English Stones

Salmon Pool

English Lake

The Binn Wall

BEECH AVE

BEECH AVE

STATION RD

River Severn

BS35

A403

Severn Way

CENTRAL AVE

SEVERN RD

New Pill
Gout

Works

Chittening Warth

Red Rhine

BS10

Power
Station

Stup Pill

BS11

A403

A403 Avonmouth M5

Crook's Marsh

51 A   B 52 C   D 53 E   F

82 83 84 85

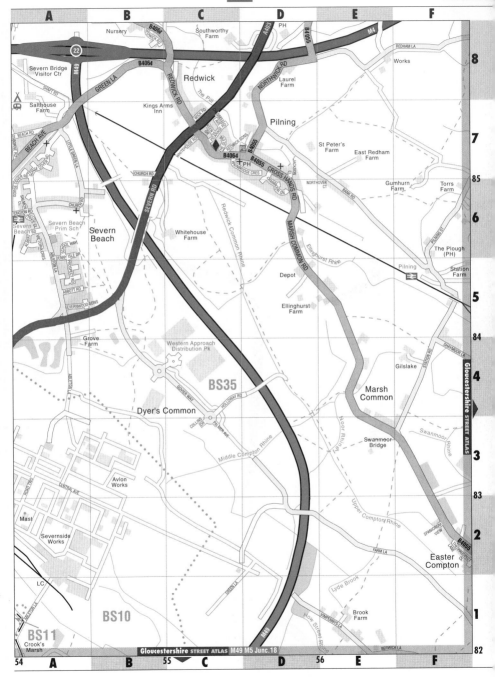

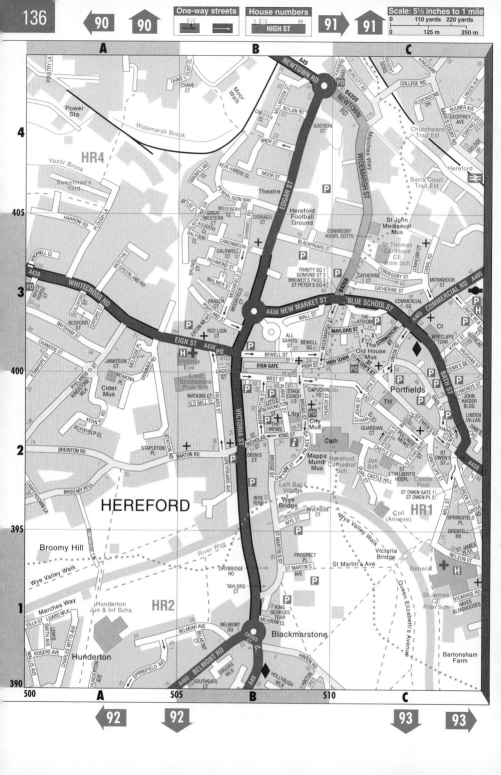

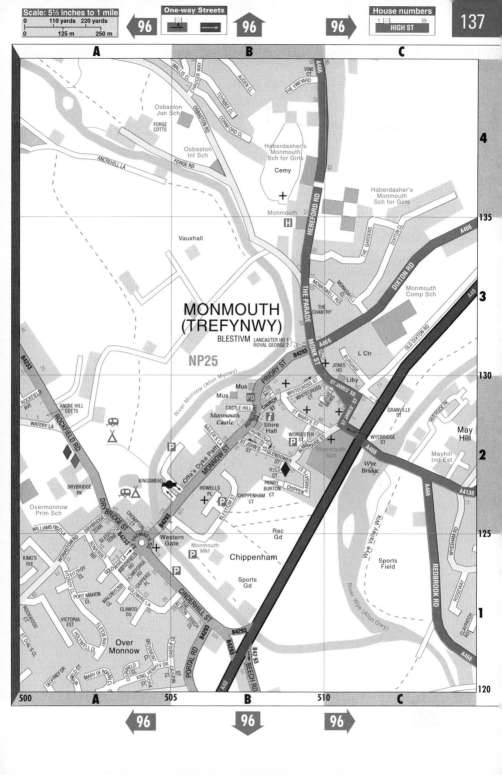

Index

Church Rd **6** Beckenham BR2.......... **53** C6

Place name	Location number	Locality, town or village	Postcode	Page and
May be abbreviated on the map	Present when a number indicates the place's position in a crowded area of mapping	Shown when more than one place has the same name	**district** District for the indexed place	**grid square** Page number and grid reference for the standard mapping

Public and commercial buildings are highlighted in magenta. Places of interest are highlighted in blue with a star★

Abbreviations used in the index

Acad	Academy	Comm	Common	Gd	Ground	L	Leisure	Prom	Promenade
App	Approach	Cott	Cottage	Gdn	Garden	La	Lane	Rd	Road
Arc	Arcade	Cres	Crescent	Gn	Green	Liby	Library	Recn	Recreation
Ave	Avenue	Cswy	Causeway	Gr	Grove	Mdw	Meadow	Ret	Retail
Bglw	Bungalow	Ct	Court	H	Hall	Meml	Memorial	Sh	Shopping
Bldg	Building	Ctr	Centre	Ho	House	Mkt	Market	Sq	Square
Bsns, Bus	Business	Ctry	Country	Hospl	Hospital	Mus	Museum	St	Street
Bvd	Boulevard	Cty	County	HQ	Headquarters	Orch	Orchard	Sta	Station
Cath	Cathedral	Dr	Drive	Hts	Heights	Pal	Palace	Terr	Terrace
Cir	Circus	Dro	Drove	Ind	Industrial	Par	Parade	TH	Town Hall
Cl	Close	Ed	Education	Inst	Institute	Pas	Passage	Univ	University
Cnr	Corner	Emb	Embankment	Int	International	Pk	Park	Wk, Wlk	Walk
Coll	College	Est	Estate	Intc	Interchange	Pl	Place	Wr	Water
Com	Community	Ex	Exhibition	Junc	Junction	Prec	Precinct	Yd	Yard

Index of localities, towns and villages

A

Abberley 13 F6
Abbey Dore 45 C1
Abergavenny 95 D4
Abersychan 102 A4
Adforton 3 B2
Alfrick 31 F8
Almeley 25 A6
Ashford Carbonell 5 B1
Ashperton 40 B4

B

Bartestree 38 F4
Bassaleg 118 A2
Beachley 117 C3
Bettws 112 E2
Bettws Newydd 69 C8
Birchall 40 C1
Bircher 9 C4
Bishops Frome 30 C3
Bishton 121 F3
Bitterley 5 F8
Blaenavon 101 E6
Bodenham Moor 28 D5
Bosbury 41 A6
Boughspring 111 C7
Brampton Abbotts ...58 A5
Bransford 32 E7
Bredenbury 20 B3
Bredwardine 35 A7
Bridstow 94 A6
Brierley 66 F2
Brilley 23 F4
Brilley Mountain 23 F6
Brimfield 10 B6
Broadheath 12 D4
Broad Oak 64 D8
Broadwas 22 E2
Brockhampton 48 F2
Bromesberrow Heath ..51 B3
Bromyard 83 D6
Bryn The 69 A4
Bucknell 2 C5
Burghill 37 C7
Byton Hand 7 E2

C

Caerleon 114 C4
Caerwent 78 B1
Caldicot 125 B5
Canon Pyon 27 B3
Cheltenham 98 C6
Chepstow 116 D6
Cinderford 67 C1
Clearwell 72 F2
Clehonger 46 D8
Clifford 33 D8
Clifford's Mesne 59 E1
Clifton upon Teme ...21 E8
Clodock 53 C6
Clydach 98 E6
Clyro 88 A6
Coed-Cwnwr 74 B2
Coedkernew 128 B3
Coed-y-paen 73 A1
Coldharbour 76 E6
Coleford 72 F7
Colwall 86 D4
Colwall Stone 86 A2
Cradley 31 F2
Craswall 43 E5
Credenhill 36 F5
Crickhowell 60 B5
Croesyceiliog 107 C5
Cross Ash 63 B6
Crossway 63 F6
Crow Hill 58 D5
Cusop 88 F2
Cwmavon 101 F1
Cwmbran 106 D3

D

Devauden 75 D1
Dilwyn 16 F1
Dingestow 71 A5
Dormington 39 B3
Dorstone 34 E4
Drybrook 67 B4
Dymock 50 D2

E

Eardisland 16 F5
Eardisley 24 E4
Eardiston 13 A7
East Bank 100 C1
Easter Compton 135 F1
Eastnor 51 B8
Eaton Bishop 36 F1
English Bicknor 66 B2
Ewyas Harold 54 D7

F

Forge Side 101 A5
Fownhope 48 E5
Fromes Hill 30 E1

G

Gaer-fawr 74 F1
Garway 55 D1
Gilfach 44 E5
Gilwern 60 E2
Glascoed 73 A4
Glewstone 57 B1
Goldcliff 131 B3
Goodrich 66 A5
Gorsley 59 C4
Govilon 99 F8
Great Oak 69 F4
Grosmont 54 E3
Gwernesney 74 C4

H

Hampton Bishop 38 E1
Harrow Hill 67 C3
Hay-on-Wye 88 C4
Hewelsfield 76 F5
Holme Lacy 48 B6
Hom Green 94 A1
Hope under Dinmore ..27 F7
Hoptonheath 2 F8
How Caple 49 A1
Huntington 23 E8

I

Ivington 17 F3

J

Joy's Green 66 D3

K

Kilcot 59 D4
Kimbolton 18 E8
King's Caple 57 C7
Kingsland 17 C8
King's Thorn 47 C2
Kingstone 46 A7
Kington 81 D5
Knowbury 5 F5

L

Langstone 115 D1
Lea 67 C8
Ledbury 89 B4
Leigh 32 D8
Leigh Sinton 32 C5
Leintwardine 3 A5
Leominster 82 B5
Letton 25 A1
Lindridge 12 E8
Lingen 7 D6
Little Cowarne 29 D6
Little Dewchurch ...47 E2
Little Hereford 10 E7
Llanarth 69 E6
Llanbedr 60 C7
Llanddewi Rhydderch ..69 B8
Llandegveth 108 B4
Llandevaud 77 B1
Llandogo 76 B7
Llanellen 68 C5
Llanelly Hill 98 C4
Llanfair Kilgeddin ..69 B2
Llanfoist 95 C3
Llanfrechfa 113 D7
Llangarron 65 B8
Llangattock 60 A4
Llangrove 65 C6
Llangwm 74 D3
Llangybi 109 B6
Llanigon 33 A3
Llanishen 75 C6
Llanmartin 122 B7
Llanover 68 E3
Llansoy 74 F5
Llanthony 52 E6
Llantilio Crossenny ..63 B1
Llantrisant 77 A7
Llanvaches 77 E2
Llanvapley 62 D1
Llanveynoe 44 A2
Llanvihangel-Crucorney .61 F7
Llanwarne 56 C7
Llanwern 121 B5
Llanyrafon 107 C2
Longhope 67 F5
Longtown 53 B7
Lowbands 51 F2
Lower Lydbrook 66 C3
Lower Maes-coed 44 E1
Lower Redbrook 72 D4
Lucton 8 E3
Ludlow 79 D3
Lugg Green 8 F1
Lugwardine 38 E3
Luston 9 D2

M

Madley 36 D1
Madresfield 85 E4
Maesygwartha 98 D8
Magor 123 A3
Malvern 85 D2
Malvern Wells 42 C4
Marden 28 D2
Marston 64 A4
Martley 22 D6
Menithwood 13 C8
Michaelchurch Escley ..44 B5
Michaelchurch-on
  -Arrow 23 D5
Middle Maes-coed ...44 D4
Middleton 5 C8
Middleton on the Hill ..10 C3
Mitcheldean 67 D5
Mitchel Troy 71 E5
Moccas 35 C5
Monkland 17 D4
Monkswood 73 B5
Monmouth 96 D5
Monnington on Wye ..35 E6
Moorhampton 25 F1

Mordiford 48 D8
Moreton-On-Lugg ...37 F8
Mortimer's Cross 8 D2
Much Birch 47 C1
Much Cowarne 29 F2
Much Dewchurch 47 A2
Much Marcle 49 F3

N

Narth The 72 A1
Nash 130 D4
Newent 59 F4
Newland 72 E4
Newport 119 F2
Newtown 39 E7
Norton 6 D6
Norton Canon 25 E2

O

Ocle Pychard 29 C1
Oldwood 80 C2
Orcop Hill 55 F6
Orleton 9 E6

P

Pembridge 16 D5
Penallt 72 B5
Penbidwal 53 D1
Pencombe 29 D7
Penperlleni 103 F6
Pen-y-Park 34 A7
Peterchurch 35 A1
Peterstow 57 C3
Pilning 135 D7
Ponthir 113 E6
Pontshill 67 B8
Pontypool 104 E6
Portskewett 125 D5
Presteigne 6 E2
Preston on Wye 35 E4
Preston Wynne 28 F2
Pudleston 19 C6
Putley 49 E8
Pye Corner 130 D7

R

Raglan 70 C2
Ravenhills Green ...22 C1
Redmarley D'Abitot ..51 D2
Redwick 132 E5
Rhydspence 23 D2
Richards Castle 9 E8
Risbury 19 B2
Rockfield 64 D1
Rogerstone 118 A8
Rogiet 124 C4
Ross-on-Wye 94 C5
Ruardean 66 F4
Ruardean Hill 67 A4
Ruardean Woodside ..66 F3

S

St Arvans 110 B6
St Briavels 76 F7
St Brides Wentlooge .128 D1
St Weonards 56 B3
Saltmarsh 130 E3
Sedbury 117 B8
Severn Beach 135 B6
Sheet 5 C5
Shelsley Beauchamp ..13 E1
Shirenewton 78 C4
Shirl Heath 17 C6
Shobdon 16 D8
Skenfrith 64 A7

Snitton 5 E6
Snodhill 34 E3
Staunton 72 E7
Staunton on Arrow ..16 B7
Staunton-On-Wye ...35 D8
Stockton on Teme ...13 C6
Stoke Edith 39 D3
Stoke Prior 18 E3
Storridge 84 A5
Stretton Sugwas ...37 B5
Suckley 31 C6
Sudbrook 125 E4
Summerleaze 133 A6
Sutton St Nicholas ..38 C8
Swainshill 37 B4
Symonds Yat 65 E3

T

Tarrington 39 F3
Tedstone Delamere ..21 D5
Tenbury Wells 12 B7
The Bage 34 C6
Tidenham 111 D4
Tidenham Chase 76 E1
Tillington 37 B8
Tintern Parva 76 B3
Trellech 75 F8
Tutshill 111 A2
Tyberton 35 E2

U

Ullingswick 29 C4
Undy 123 C3
Upper Lydbrook 66 C2
Upper Redbrook 72 C5
Upper Sapey 12 F2
Usk 97 C4
Uskmouth 130 B3

V

Varteg 101 E1

W

Walford 66 B7
Walterstone 53 D4
Walton 14 B6
Welland 42 C3
Wellington 27 E3
Wellington Heath ...41 C3
Welsh Newton 64 F4
Weobley 26 A6
Weston Beggard 39 B4
Weston under Penyard .58 D1
Whitbourne 22 A3
Whitchurch 65 D4
Whitney-on-Wye 23 F2
Whitson 131 E4
Whitton 6 A6
Wigmore 8 C8
Wilton 94 B5
Winforton 24 C2
Withington 38 F6
Woodcroft 111 B4
Woofferton 10 B7
Woolhope 49 B6
Wormbridge 46 A2
Wormelow 47 B1

Y

Yarpole 9 C3

A

A R D Bsns Pk NP4 ....104 F4
Abberley Hall Sch WR6 ....13 F5
Abberley Perochial Prim Sch
  WR6 ....13 F6
Abberley Pk WR6 ....13 F6
Abbey Cotts NP44 ....113 B7
Abbey Dore Court Gdns*
  HR2 ....45 C1
Abbey Gn NP4 ....112 F8
Abbey Gr NP44 ....113 B6
Abbey Rd Cwmbran NP44 ...106 E2
  Newport NP19 ....120 D6
Abbey Tintern Furnace*
  NP16 ....76 A3
Abbeyfield Ho NP25 ....137 A1
Abbots Mews NP20 ....119 B3
Abbotsmead Rd HR2 ....92 C6
Abbots Rd BS35 ....135 A5
Abercrombie Cl HR8 ....89 C5
Abergavenny Castle*
  NP7 ....95 D4
Abergavenny Mus* NP7 95 D4
Abergavenny Rd
  Blaenavon NP4 ....101 C8
  Gilwern NP7 ....60 E1
  Usk NP15 ....97 A6
Abergavenny Sta NP7 .....95 F4
Aberystwyn Ind Est
  NP4 ....102 A3
Aberthaw Ave NP19 ....120 D4
Aberthaw Circ NP19 ....120 C5
Aberthaw Cl NP19 ....120 C5
Aberthaw Dr NP19 ....120 B4
Aberthaw Rd NP19 ....120 C4
Abingdon Dr HR2 ....92 B5
Ableton La BS35 ....135 A5
Acacia Ave
  Newport NP19 ....120 B5
  Undy NP26 ....123 C4
Acacia Cl NP4 ....93 A6
Acacia Sq NP19 ....120 B5
Aconbury Ave HR2 ....93 A5
Aconbury Cl HR2 ....47 B2
Acorn Cl Colwall WR13 ....86 B2
  Malvern WR14 ....85 C1
Acorns The NP18 ....121 E7
Acreage WR6 ....21 F3
Adams Cl NP15 ....97 C5
Addison Ct HR4 ....136 B4
Adelaide St NP20 ....119 C7
Adeline St NP20 ....119 C2
Adit Wlk NP44 ....106 C5
Admirals Cl HR1 ....91 B3
Adrian Bolt Gn NP19 ......120 C4
Adrian Cl HR2 ....92 E4
Ael-y-Bryn NP4 ....101 D7
Aerons Ho NP44 ....112 C8
Afon Cl NP4 ....105 A3
Afon Ct NP4 ....102 A3
Afon Gdns NP18 ....114 A5
Afon Llwyd Terr NP4 ......102 A2
Afon Lwyd Cl NP18 ....114 C3
Afon Terr NP44 ....106 F5
Agincourt Rd NP25 ....96 D7
Agincourt Sch NP25 ....96 F6
Agincourt Sq NP25 ....137 B2
Agincourt St
  Monmouth NP25 ....137 B2
  Newport NP20 ....119 B7
Ailesbury St NP20 ....119 C7
Ailey La HR3 ....25 A3
Ainslie Cl HR1 ....91 C3
Aintree Ave HR4 ....90 C4
Akermans Orch GL18 ......59 F4
Alan Cl NP10 ....118 B4
Alanbrooke Ave NP20 ....113 A4
Albany Ind Est NP20 .....119 C7
Albany Rd NP7 ....95 B7
Albany St NP20 ....119 C7
Albany Trad Est NP20 .....119 C7
Albert Ave NP19 ....119 E5
Albert Ct NP19 ....119 E5
Albert Park Mews WR14 ...84 F3
Albert Park Rd WR14 ......84 F4
Albert Rd
  Abergavenny NP7 ....95 F6
  Colwall WR13 ....86 A1
  Ledbury HR8 ....89 C3
  Severn Beach BS35 ....135 A6
Albert Rd N WR14 ....84 F3
Albert Rd S WR14 ....87 A8
Albert St NP20 ....119 C3
Albert Terr Hay-on-W HR3 ..88 E3
  Newport NP20 ....119 C3
Albion Cl Caldicot NP26 ...124 F5
  Newport NP20 ....119 D2
Albion Ho NP20 ....124 F5
Albion Pl NP4 ....104 A8
Albion Rd Cinderford GL14 ..67 C1
  Malvern WR14 ....84 E4
  Pontypool NP4 ....104 A8
Albion Sq NP16 ....116 E8
Albion St NP20 ....119 C2
Albion The NP25 ....137 B1
Albion Way NP26 ....123 A3
Albright La HR8 ....51 D4
Alcock Cl NP19 ....120 B3
Alcove Wood NP16 ....116 C8
Alder Cl Pontypool NP4 ...105 B5

Alder Cl continued
  Walford HR9 ....66 C8
Alder Gr NP20 ....113 B2
Aldermans Mdw HR6 ....82 C4
Alderney St NP20 ....119 C7
Alders The NP44 ....107 B1
Alexander Cl LD8 ....6 C5
Alexander Pl NP15 ....73 A5
Alexander Terr NP15 ......73 A5
Alexandra Ave HR1 ....91 A3
Alexandra Ct NP20 ....119 D2
Alexandra La
  Malvern WR14 ....84 F3
  Newport NP20 ....119 C7
Alexandra Mews WR14 ....84 F3
Alexandra Rd
  Abergavenny NP7 ....95 E6
  Chepstow NP16 ....116 F6
  Malvern WR14 ....84 F3
  Newport NP20 ....119 C2
Alfords Mill HR1 ....49 A5
Alfred St 2 NP19 ....119 D6
Alianore Rd NP26 ....124 F4
Alicante Cl WR14 ....85 B2
Alice Cl HR1 ....93 E7
Alice Cres NP19 ....117 A4
Alice St NP20 ....119 C1
All Saints St HR4 ....136 B3
Allan Cl NP20 ....112 C1
Allerford Gr NP7 ....60 D1
Alleyn Ho NP44 ....107 B4
Allgood Ave NP44 ....101 B6
Allt-yr-Yn Ave NP20 ......118 F5
Allt-yr-Yn Cl NP20 ....119 A6
Allt-yr-Yn Cres NP20 .....119 A7
Allt-yr-Yn Hts NP20 ....118 F6
Allt-yr-Yn Rd NP20 ....119 A6
Allt-yr-Yn View NP20 .....118 F6
Allt-yr-Yn Way NP20 ......119 A7
Alltybella Rd NP15 ....74 B2
Alma Cl 2 NP20 ....119 C3
Alma Dr NP10 ....117 A4
Alma Pl NP4 ....104 E1
Alma St Blaenavon NP4 ...101 C7
  Newport NP20 ....119 C3
Almeley Cl HR2 ....92 D4
Almeley Prim Sch HR3 ....25 A6
Almond Cl NP10 ....113 A3
Almond Dr NP20 ....113 B3
Almshouse St NP25 ....137 B2
Almshouses Rd GL16 .....72 E4
Almshouses The HR8 ......89 E4
Alpha Rd NP16 ....116 F6
Alton Ave HR9 ....94 E4
Alton Cl HR9 ....94 E4
Alton Court Mews 3
  HR6 ....82 D5
Alton Court Rd HR8 ....49 F7
Alton Cross HR4 ....26 E8
Alton Rd HR9 ....94 F4
Alton Road Ind Est HR9 ...94 F5
Alton Terr NP4 ....104 B7
Alway Cl NP19 ....120 D5
Alway Cres NP19 ....120 D5
Alway Inf Sch NP19 ....120 C4
Alway Jun Sch NP19 ......120 C4
Alway Par NP19 ....120 D4
Alwyn Cl NP10 ....118 A7
Amazing Hedge Puzzle The
  (Jubilee Maze)* HR9 ....65 E4
Ambleside Dr HR4 ....90 D3
Ambrose Way NP4 ....105 A4
Ambryn Rd NP4 ....105 B4
Amesbury Cl HR2 ....92 C6
Amherst Ho HR1 ....93 F7
Amroth Wlk NP44 ....106 C2
Amy Johnson Cl NP19 ....119 B3
Amyand Dr HR4 ....90 D1
Anchorage The GL17 ......66 C3
Ancient Rd GL16 ....65 F1
Ancre Hill Cotts NP25 ...137 A2
Ancrehill La NP25 ....96 B6
Anderson Pl NP20 ....113 A4
Andrew's Cnr GL15 ....76 E7
Anethony's Cross GL18 ...59 F2
Aneurin Bevan Ct
  Newport NP10 ....128 E2
  Pontypool NP4 ....104 C6
Angela Ct HR1 ....93 D7
Angelsey Ct NP18 ....113 F3
Angiddy Ct NP26 ....125 A7
Ann Cam CE Prim Sch
  GL18 ....50 D2
Anne St 6 NP4 ....101 C6
Annesley Rd NP19 ....119 E6
Ann's Wlk GL17 ....67 D4
Anson Gn NP19 ....120 E7
Anthony Dr NP18 ....113 F4
Anwyll Cl NP18 ....114 A4
Apex Bsns Ctr NP25 ......96 B3
Apostles La HR5 ....24 B7
Apple Ave NP26 ....123 C3
Apple Mdw HR4 ....90 C3
Apple Orchard Cl WR14 ...85 C1
Appletree Mdw LD8 ....6 E3
Appleyard Cl SY8 ....9 F6
Apprentice Cl NP10 ......117 B4
Aragon Ho NP20 ....119 C7
Aragon St NP20 ....119 C2
Aramstone Rise HR4 ......91 D2
Aran Ct NP44 ....106 B5
Arcade The NP44 ....106 F3

Arcadia Way NP4 ....102 B2
Archbishop Rowan Williams
  CW Prim Sch NP26 .....125 D5
Archenfield Rd HR2 ....36 C1
Archenfield Ct HR9 ....94 D3
Archenfield Rd HR9 ....94 C3
Archer Cl WR14 ....84 E4
Archer Rd NP44 ....106 B3
Archer's Way WR15 ....80 C6
Archfield St NP19 ....119 A5
Arden Ct HR1 ....91 C1
Argyle St NP20 ....119 C2
Argyll Rise HR2 ....92 C4
Arkwright Cl
  Hereford HR4 ....90 C2
  Leominster HR6 ....82 D5
Arkwright Ct NP44 ....82 D5
Arlington Cl
  Newport NP20 ....113 A4
  Undy NP26 ....123 D3
Armadale Ct HR4 ....90 E3
Armstrong Cl NP19 ....120 B4
Arne Cl NP19 ....120 E5
Arnold Cl NP20 ....118 F2
Arosa Dr WR14 ....44 A5
Arran Ave HR2 ....93 A6
Arrow View Kington HR5 ...14 D1
  Ledbury HR8 ....89 C5
Arrowsmith Ave HR1 ......38 F4
Arthur Bliss Rd NP19 ....120 C4
Arthur Cl NP20 ....119 C2
Arthur St Caerleon NP18 ..114 C7
  Newport NP20 ....119 C2
Arthur's Stone* HR3 ......34 E6
Arthur's Stone La HR3 ....34 E6
Arthurs Ct NP26 ....125 C5
Artillery Pl NP19 ....119 C5
Arum Cl WR14 ....85 C3
Arundel Cl
  Cwmbran NP44 ....106 A3
  Hereford HR2 ....92 C6
  Ross-on-W HR9 ....94 F6
Arundel Rd NP19 ....119 F5
Ascot Cl HR4 ....90 C4
Ash Ave HR2 ....93 A6
Ash Cl Chepstow NP16 ...116 E5
  Ludlow SY8 ....79 E3
  Malvern WR14 ....88 B2
  Marden HR1 ....92 F7
Ash Cres HR7 ....83 B5
Ash Dene Rd GL17 ....66 E3
Ash Gn NP44 ....112 F8
Ash Gr Caldicot NP26 ....124 F6
  Holme Lacy HR2 ....48 B6
  Llanigon HR3 ....33 A3
  Llanmarlin GL18 ....121 E6
  Mitcheldean GL17 ....67 D6
  Pontypool NP4 ....119 C2
Ash Grove (Llwyn Onn)
  NP7 ....68 D5
Ash La NP25 ....96 B4
Ash Tree Rd NP26 ....78 C1
Ashburton Ind Est HR9 ...94 F5
Ashburton Rd HR9 ....94 F5
Ashcroft HR3 ....94 A6
Ashdean 3 GL14 ....67 C1
Ashdown Cl WR14 ....85 B1
Ashdown Rise WR14 ......85 B1
Ashe Gn HR4 ....94 A7
Ashe Ingen Mews HR9 ...57 E5
Ashe La HR9 ....94 D7
Ashfield Cres HR9 ....94 D3
Ashfield La HR6 ....82 B4
Ashfield Park Ave HR9 ...94 D4
Ashfield Park Prim Sch
  HR9 ....94 D4
Ashfield Park Rd HR9 ....94 D4
Ashfield Rd GL17 ....67 A3
Ashfield Way HR7 ....83 B5
Ashford Carbonell CE Prim
  Sch SY8 ....? F4
Ashford Cl WR14 ....107 B5
Ashford Cl N NP44 ....107 B5
Ashford Cl S NP44 ....107 B4
Ashford Ho HR1 ....91 C1
Ashford Mews SY8 ....79 C4
Ashgrove WR14 ....84 F3
Ashgrove Cl
  Bodenham Moor HR1 .....28 D6
  Pontypool NP4 ....104 D1
Ashgrove Rd HR1 ....28 D5
Ashgrove View HR1 ....28 D5
Ashleigh Ct NP44 ....106 A1
Ashley Rd NP19 ....120 B5
Ashley Wlk SY8 ....92 B7
Ashmoor Ph HR5 ....81 D5
Ashperton Prim Sch HR8 ..48 B4
Ashpool WR6 ....22 A3
Ashton Ho NP44 ....106 C3
Ashwell Cotts NP18 ......120 C8
Aspen Ct WR14 ....85 A4
Aspen Way NP20 ....113 A3
Aspley Gr HR2 ....36 B8
Asquith Cl NP44 ....104 F3
Asquith St NP4 ....104 E3
Assarts La WR14 ....42 C4
Assarts Rd WR14 ....42 C4
Astley Orch WR15 ....12 D7
Aston Bank HR9 ....59 C2
Aston Bridge Rd GL17 ....66 E3
Aston Cl HR8 ....49 F8
Aston Cres NP20 ....119 B8
Atherstone Cl HR2 ....92 B5
Atlay St NP4 ....90 D3
Atrium The HR1 ....136 C3

Attlee Cl HR4 ....136 B4
Attorneys Wlk SY8 ....79 C4
Attwood La HR1 ....91 A5
Atyed Cl WR14 ....85 C1
Auberrow La HR4 ....27 E2
Auberrow Rd HR4 ....27 E2
Aubrey Hames Cl NP20 ...119 A2
Aubrey St HR4 ....136 B2
Auckland Cl HR1 ....93 F7
Auckland Rd NP44 ....106 A4
Auden Cl NP25 ....137 B4
Auden Cres HR8 ....89 C5
Audley Cres HR1 ....91 B2
Audley Croft HR8 ....89 D5
Augustan Cl NP18 ....113 F3
Augustan Dr NP18 ....113 F3
Augustan Way NP18 ......113 F3
Augustus John Cl NP20 ..118 A8
Aust Cres NP16 ....116 F5
Aust Rd BS35 ....127 D3
Austin Friars 5 ....119 C5
Austin Rd HR4 ....104 F1
Avalon Cl Newport NP19 ..119 F7
  Pontypool NP4 ....104 B6
Avalon Dr NP19 ....119 F7
Avenue Cres NP7 ....95 C7
Avenue Ct NP7 ....95 C6
Avenue Rd
  Abergavenny NP7 ....95 C6
  Malvern WR14 ....87 A8
Avenue The
  Caldicot NP26 ....124 E4
  Pontypool NP4 ....104 F5
  Pontypool, Sebastopol
  NP4 ....104 D1
  Ross-on-W HR9 ....94 D4
  Welland WR13 ....42 E3
Avon Cl Bettws NP20 .....112 E2
  Caldicot NP26 ....124 F6
  Malvern WR14 ....87 D8
Avon Pl NP44 ....107 A3
Avon Rd NP4 ....119 A5
Avondale Cl NP44 ....106 F6
Avondale Cres NP44 ......106 F6
Avondale Ct NP44 ....106 F7
Avondale Dr NP44 ....106 F7
Avondale Ind Est NP44 ...106 F6
Avondale Rd
  Cwmbran NP44 ....106 F7
  Newport NP20 ....104 F1
Avondale Way NP44 ......106 F6
Awbrey Way HR7 ....83 B6
Aydon Ind Pk HR4 ....90 F4
Aylesbrook HR4 ....90 D5
Aylestone Dr HR1 ....91 C2
Aylestone Grange HR1 ...91 C2
Aylestone High Sch HR1 ..91 C2
Aylestone Hill HR1 ....91 C3
Aynall La SY8 ....10 D6

B

Back Fold HR3 ....88 D3
Back La Drybrook GL17 ....67 B4
  Malvern WR14 ....84 F1
  Prestenope LD8 ....6 E3
  Weobley HR4 ....26 B6
Back Rd Gilwern NP7 ......60 D1
  Tintern Parva NP16 ....76 A5
Back The NP16 ....110 F1
Backbury Rd HR1 ....39 B3
Backhall St NP18 ....114 C2
Backney View HR9 ....94 D7
Bacon La HR6 ....8 D3
Bacon Pl NP20 ....113 A3
Bailey Brook Rd HR2 .....39 B3
Bailey Cl HR2 ....36 C1
Bailey La NP7 ....95 E5
Bailey St NP20 ....119 B4
Bailey's Hay NP16 ....116 B4
Bainstree Cross HR6 .....17 C3
Baird Cl NP20 ....112 F3
Baker Cl SY8 ....79 F6
Baker Lea HR6 ....17 D4
Baker St NP20 ....119 C5
Baker Street Ho 11 NP4 .101 C6
Bakers Furlong HR4 ....37 C7
Bakers La Eardisley HR3 ..24 C1
  Hereford HR4 ....90 D1
Bakers Oak HR9 ....94 C3
Bakers Piece Rd GL17 ....66 F1
Bala Dr NP10 ....118 B7
Baldenhall WR14 ....87 E8
Baldwin Cl NP20 ....119 C3
Baldwin St NP20 ....119 C2
Balfe Rd NP19 ....120 D4
Balfour Cl WR14 ....84 E2
Ballard Cl Colwall WR13 ..86 B2
  Ledbury HR8 ....89 D5
  Ludlow SY8 ....79 E4
Ballhurst Rd HR4 ....83 C6
Ballinger Cl HR4 ....90 E5
Balmond Terr NP4 ....104 B8
Balmoral Cl WR14 ....85 C4

Balmoral La 1 NP19 .....120 A4
Balmoral Rd NP19 ....120 A4
Baltic Terr NP44 ....112 E7
Bamber Ho NP44 ....107 B4
Baneswell Ctyd 6 NP20 ..119 C4
Baneswell Rd 6 NP20 ....119 B5
Bangor Cl HR4 ....90 C5
Bank Cres Gilwern NP7 ...60 D2
  Ledbury HR8 ....89 E5
Bank La Abberley WR6 ....13 F7
  Gilwern NP7 ....60 D1
  8 Newport NP20 ....119 E8
Bank Rd BS35 ....135 E6
Bank Sq NP16 ....116 E8
Bank St Chepstow NP16 ..116 E8
  Malvern WR14 ....84 F2
  Newport NP19 ....119 D4
Bankside HR8 ....89 E6
Banley Dr HR5 ....81 E5
Bannals La WR15 ....12 B2
Bannercroft HR6 ....21 F3
Bannut Tree HR7 ....83 B5
Bannut Tree Gdns HR9 ...94 A5
Bannutree La HR2 ....47 D2
Banntree La HR9 ....94 A5
Bantock Cl NP19 ....120 E5
Banwell Ct NP44 ....106 B5
Baptist Way GL17 ....67 B4
Bar Mdw HR4 ....16 D8
Barber Cl HR1 ....38 F4
Barbers La WR6 ....22 E7
Barbirolli Gn NP19 ....120 D4
Bardolph Ct HR2 ....92 E4
Bardsy Cl NP19 ....119 F7
Baregains La HR8 ....50 B8
Bareland Rd NP20 ....122 D2
Bargates HR6 ....82 C5
Barkle Ct HR4 ....90 C2
Barklie Mead HR4 ....90 C2
Barn Cl Dilwyn HR4 ....16 F1
Barn La GL17 ....66 F3
Barn Owl Rd NP26 ....124 B4
Barnard St NP19 ....119 D6
Barnard's Green Rd
  WR14 ....87 B8
Barnards Cl WR14 ....87 C7
Barneby Ave HR1 ....38 E4
Barnets NP44 ....106 B3
Barnets Wood NP16 ......116 C8
Barnett Ave HR8 ....89 F4
Barnetts Cl HR8 ....89 D4
Barnfield HR8 ....113 F5
Barnfield Cl NP15 ....109 C4
Barnfield Pl NP44 ....106 C5
Barnfield Terr NP44 ......101 B6
Barns Cl NP25 ....97 B3
Barons Cl NP25 ....123 D3
Barons Mead HR2 ....92 D5
Barons Way LD8 ....6 C5
Barr's Court Rd HR1 ......116 C4
Barrack Hill
  King's Thorn HR2 ....47 C3
  Newport NP20 ....119 B2
Barrat La GL17 ....67 F8
Barrett Rise WR14 ....85 A2
Barricombe Dr HR4 ....90 C3
Barrie Gdns NP20 ....112 E1
Barrie Rd HR4 ....90 B1
Barrington Hts WR15 .....80 B4
Barroll St HR1 ....136 C2
Barrots Cl GL15 ....76 F7
Barrs Court Ho HR1 ......91 B2
Barrs Court Trad Est
  HR1 ....136 C4
Barrs Orch HR9 ....39 E3
Barry Wlk NP10 ....119 A3
Barthropp St NP19 ....120 A3
Barton Bridge 15
  ....70 C2
Barton Bridge Rise 16
  NP15 ....70 C2
Barton Hill GL17 ....67 E5
Barton La HR5 ....81 E7
Barton Rd HR4 ....136 B2
Bartonsham Rd HR1 ......93 B7
Bartwood La HR9 ....67 A8
Basildene Cl NP7 ....92 C4
Baskerville Cl HR3 ....88 A6
Bassaleg Comp Sch
  NP10 ....118 A2
Bassaleg Rd NP20 ....118 E3
Batch La The HR4 ....25 D6
Batchelor Rd 2 NP19 ....119 F5
Bath Gn NP44 ....107 B2
Bath Row NP7 ....98 E7
Bath St Hereford HR1 ...136 C2
  Newport NP19 ....119 D4
Bathams Cl GL17 ....67 F5
Battisto Wlk HR4 ....85 C1
Battlebridge Cl HR6 ......82 D4
Batts La GL17 ....67 A4
Bawdsey Ave WR14 ......85 C1
Bay Cl WR14 ....85 A2
Bay Tree Cl NP18 ....113 E2
Bay Tree La NP7 ....95 F6
Bayfield Gdns GL18 ......50 D2
Baynham Cl NP4 ....83 B5
Baynham Rd GL17 ....67 D5
Baysham St HR4 ....136 A3
Beach Ave BS35 ....135 A7
Beach Rd BS35 ....135 E6
Beachley Rd
  Beachley NP16 ....117 B4
  Tutshill NP16 ....111 A1
Beacon Ho WR14 ....84 F3

Beacon Rd Llandogo NP25 .76 A8
Malvern WR14 ....86 D4
Trellech NP25 ....75 F7
Beacons Cl NP10 ....118 A7
Beacons View Rd [5]
　GL14 ....67 D1
Beaconsfield NP7 ....60 C1
Beaconsfield Pk SY8 ....5 C5
Bear St HR3 ....88 E3
Bearcroft HR4 ....26 B6
Bearwood Cross HR6 ....16 D4
Bearwood La HR6 ......16 D4
Beattie Ave HR2 ....92 D6
Beattie Ho HR2 ....92 D6
Beatty Rd NP19 ....120 F7
Beauchamp Cl NP7 .....95 E3
Beauchamp Rd WR14 ...84 F4
Beaufort Ave
　Hereford HR2 ....92 E4
　Llangattock NP8 ....60 A4
Beaufort Cl NP44 ....106 C1
Beaufort Cres NP15 ....73 B5
Beaufort Gdns [5] NP15 .70 C2
Beaufort Pl
　Chepstow NP16 ....116 E8
　Newport NP19 ....119 F8
Beaufort Rd
　Monmouth NP25 ....96 C7
　Newport NP7 ....120 A7
Beaufort Sq
　Chepstow NP16 ....116 E8
　[10] Raglan NP15 .....70 C2
Beaufort St [8] NP4 ....60 A5
Beaufort Terr [4] NP20 .119 B4
Beaumaris Dr NP44 ....90 C2
Beaumaris Ho [16] NP44 .107 B2
Beaupreau Pl NP7 ......95 F5
Beaver Ctr HR9 ....94 F5
Beavers Wlk NP10 ......118 B4
Beddick NP44 ....106 A3
Bedford Cl NP44 ....106 A3
Bedford Dr NP19 ....119 D5
Bedford St HR4 ....136 A3
Bedstone Coll SY7 .....22 B6
Beech Bsns Pk HR4 ....90 B5
Beech Gr Chepstow NP16 .116 D7
　Hereford HR2 ....93 A6
　Llanfoist NP7 ....95 B2
　Newport NP18 ....128 F8
Beech Rd Caldicot NP26 .124 E6
　Monmouth NP25 ....96 D2
　Pontypool NP4 ....104 D1
Beech Terr [8] HR4 ....54 A2
Beech Tree Cnr NP15 ..74 F1
Beechcroft WR14 ....84 F4
Beechcroft Rd NP19 ...120 B6
Beechdale Rd NP19 ....120 A5
Beechen [9] GL14 ....67 C1
Beeches Rd NP44 ......102 B1
Beeches The
　Cwmbran NP44 ....106 C2
　Pontypool NP4 ....102 A2
　[18] Raglan NP15 .....70 C2
Beechfield Ave NP19 ...120 B6
Beechleigh Cl NP44 ....106 A3
Beechwood HR9 ....94 E5
Beechwood Cres NP19 .120 A5
Beechwood Ct NP19 ...91 C3
Beechwood Rd
　Llangattock NP8 ......60 A4
　Newport NP19 ....120 A5
Beechwood Wlk NP4 ..102 B2
Beehive Cotts WR6 ....13 F7
Beggars Ash HR8 ......89 E7
Begwyns Bluff HR3 ....88 A6
Beili Priory NP7 ....95 E5
Bela Ho [2] NP44 ......106 C2
Belfrey The NP16 ......117 C7
Belfry Cl HR1 ....91 A5
Bellamore La HR2 .....36 A3
Bellar's La WR14 ......87 C8
Bellars Cl WR14 ....87 C8
Bellars Gdns WR14 ...87 B8
Bell Bank HR3 ....92 C5
Bella Bank Ave HR4 ...90 F5
Belle Orch Ledbury HR8 .89 E8
　Tenbury Wells WR15 ..80 D5
Belle Orchard Cl HR8 ..89 D4
Belle Orchard Ho HR8 .09 D5
Belle View Ct [18] NP4 .102 A1
Belle View Flats NP7 ..95 D6
Belle Vue Cl NP4 ......102 A1
Belle Vue La NP20 ....119 B3
Belle Vue Rd GL17 ....66 F4
Belle Vue Terr
　[1] Hereford HR1 .....93 B8
　Ludlow SY8 ....79 C5
　Malvern WR14 ....86 F8

Bellevue Gdns NP44 ...106 E2
Bellevue Rd NP44 .....106 E2
Bellin Cl NP18 ....114 A3
Bells Orch HR3 ....25 A6
Bellvue Cl NP44 ....106 C2
Belmont Abbey* HR2 ..92 A5
Belmont Ave NP44 ....136 B1
Belmont Cl NP7 ....95 E4
Belmont Cres NP7 ....95 E4
Belmont Ct HR2 ....136 B1
Belmont Hill NP18 ....120 D8
Belmont Lodge HR2 ...37 C1
Belmont Rd
　Abergavenny NP7 .....95 E4
　Hay-on-W HR3 ....88 D3
　Hereford HR2 ....92 E6
　Hewelsfield GL15 .....76 D5
　Malvern WR14 ....84 E4
Belmont Sq HR2 ....136 B1
Belmont Terr GL17 ....67 C5
Belvedere La HR4 .....136 A2
Belvedere Terr NP7 ...11 B7
Belvoir Bank WR14 ....84 D3
Belvoir Ct HR2 ....92 C6
Ben Jonson Way NP20 .118 E2
Benbow Cl WR14 ......86 E2
Benbow Rd NP19 ......120 E7
Bencroft La NP26 .....123 E5
Benedict Cl HR2 ......92 D6
Benedict Ct NP7 ......95 E5
Benhall La HR4 ....94 B6
Bennet Mead HR4 ....90 C3
Bennett Dr HR2 ....93 B5
Bensfield WR6 ....32 E7
Benson Ave NP10 ....118 B4
Bentley Cl NP10 ......118 B4
Benton Cl WR14 ......42 C3
Beresford Rd NP19 ...119 D5
Berkeley Cl HR1 ......94 F7
Berkeley Cres NP44 ..106 E8
Berkeley Ct NP44 ....106 B5
Berkeley Mews HR4 ..94 D3
Bernard Hackett Ct HR9 .94 D3
Berrington Dr HR1 ...28 D5
Berrington Gdns WR15 .80 C4
Berrington Hall* HR6 .9 F2
Berrington Rd WR15 ..80 B4
Berrington St HR4 ....136 B2
Berryfield Cl NP25 ...96 D8
Berryfield Pk NP25 ...96 D7
Berryfield Pl HR9 ....94 E6
Berryfield Rise NP25 .96 D7
Bersandy NP15 ....69 E6
Bert Evans Ct HR4 ...92 C4
Berthin NP44 ....106 B3
Berthin Rd NP44 .....103 D2
Berthon Rd NP20 ....103 F4
Bessemer Cl NP20 ...112 F4
Bethel La WR14 ......118 A6
Bethesda Cl NP10 ...118 A6
Bethesda Pl NP10 ...118 A6
Betjeman Ave NP26 .124 E4
Betony Rd WR14 .....85 C4
Bettws Cl NP20 ......112 F1
Bettws Ctr NP20 .....112 D2
Bettws High Sch NP20 .112 F1
Bettws Hill NP20 .....112 D2
Bettws La NP20 ......112 F1
Bettws [5] NP20 .....106 B1
Bevan Ct NP7 ....54 E3
Bevan's La NP4,NP44 .106 D8
Beverley Ct [7] HR1 ..93 B8
Beverley Way WR14 ..84 E6
Bewdley Bank HR4 ...37 D7
Bewell Sq WR14 .....136 B3
Bewell St HR4 ....136 B3
Bicentennial Ave NP26 .78 C2
Biddulph Rise HR1 ...91 E1
Biddulph Way HR1 ...89 D2
Bideford Cl NP20 ....119 A1
Bideford Rd NP20 ....119 A1
Big Pit Mining Mus*
　NP4 ....100 F6
Bigham Close / Clos Bigham
　NP25 ....96 B4
Bigstone Cl NP16 ....111 A2
Bigstone Gr NP16 ....111 A2
Bilsham La BS35 .....127 F2
Bilson GL14 ....67 C1
Bilston Cl HR4 ....90 D4
Bilston St NP19 ......119 C4
Birbeck Rd NP26 .....124 E6
Birch Cl Ledbury HR8 .89 D3
　Undy NP26 ....123 C3
Birch Gr Cwmbran NP44 .112 A8
　Hereford HR2 ....93 A6
Birch Hill NP20 ......113 B3
Birch Hill Rd HR2 ....46 D8
Birch Mdw HR2 ......46 D8
Birch Rd NP18 ....121 F7
Birch Trees NP10 ....118 B2
Birch Wlk HR7 ....82 B4
Bircher Comm* HR6 .9 A5
Birches La GL18 .....59 F7
Birches Rd NP25 .....72 B5
Birches The
　Cwmbran NP44 ......106 C5
　Shabdon HR6 ....16 D8
Birchgrove Cl NP10 .113 B2
Birchwood [2] WR14 .87 A8
Birchwood Cl GL14 ..67 B1
Birchwood Rd HR14 .84 E6
Birdwood Gdns NP10 .116 C4
Birwick La BS35 .....135 E1
Bishon La HR4 ....36 C6
Bishop Cl NP26 ......78 C1
Bishop Cres NP7 ....95 E7

Bishop of Hereford's
　Bluecoat Sch The HR1 .91 E1
Bishop St NP19 ......119 D6
Bishops Cl NP16 .....116 F4
Bishops Mead HR1 ..95 E4
Bishopstone Rd HR4 .90 C2
Bishpool Est NP19 ...120 D6
Bishpool La NP19 ....120 D6
Bishton La NP16 .....111 B3
Bishton Rd NP18 ....121 B5
Bishton St NP19 .....119 C5
Bitterley Cl SY8 .....79 F5
Black Barn Cl Kington HR5 .81 E5
　Usk NP15 ....97 C5
Black Barn La NP15 .97 C4
Black Bear La NP15 .69 D1
Black Hole La HR1 ...38 E5
Black Rock Rd NP26 .125 F5
Black Stone Kilns La
　HR8 ....65 D3
Black Swan Wlk [1] HR6 .82 D4
Black Wall NP26 .....123 A1
Blackash Path NP18 .120 D7
Blackberry La HR2 ..47 F2
Blackbird Cl NP10 ..118 C3
Blackbird Rd NP26 ..125 A4
Blackbirds Cl NP44 .113 A5
Blackett Ave NP10 ..101 C7
Blackfriars HR5 .....97 B4
Blackfriars St HR4 ..136 B3
Blackheath Way WR14 .86 C7
Blackmans Cl GL18 .59 F4
Blackmarston Rd HR2 .92 E6
Blackmarston Sch HR2 .92 F6
Blackmore Park Ind Est
　WR8 ....87 D3
Blackmore Park Rd
　WR14,WR13 ....87 B2
Blackmore Rd WR14 .84 E3
Blacksmiths Cl [6] HR7 .83 C6
Blacksmiths La HR7 .78 C4
Blacksmiths Way NP10 .128 A6
Blackthorn Cl
　Hereford HR2 ....92 C5
　Ross-on-W HR9 ......94 D7
Blackthorn Gr NP18 .113 E2
Blackwater Cl NP20 .112 D2
Bladon Cres HR1 ....91 B1
Blaen-Afon-Rd NP4,NP7 .98 A3
Blaen-y-Pant Ave NP20 .119 A8
Blaen-y-Pant Cres
　NP20 ....119 A8
Blaen-y-Pant Pl NP20 .119 A8
Blaenavon Furnace Sta
　NP4 ....100 E7
Blaenavon Hospl NP4 .101 B7
Blaenavon Ironworks*
　NP4 ....101 B7
Blaendare Farm La NP44 .104 A4
Blaendare Rd NP44 ..104 C5
Blaenwern NP44 .....106 F6
Blake Ave WR9 ......94 E4
Blake Rd NP19 ......120 B3
Blake St NP25 ....96 F4
Blakemore Cl HR4 ..92 D4
Blanchard Cl NP4 ...17 F5
Blandford Cl WR13 .42 E3
Blands Row BS35 ...127 B1
Blashfield Rd SY8 ...79 F4
Blenheim Ave NP26 .123 A3
Blenheim Cl Hereford HR1 .91 B1
　Magor NP26 ....123 A3
　Ross-on-W HR9 ......94 F6
Blenheim Ct
　Cwmbran NP44 ......106 C2
　Magor NP26 ....123 A3
Blenheim Dr Ledbury HR8 .89 E2
　Magor NP26 ....123 A3
Blenheim Gdns NP26 .123 A3
Blenheim Pk NP26 ..123 A3
Blenheim Rd
　Cwmbran NP44 ......106 C2
　Newport NP20 ....120 A5
Blenheim Sq HR4 ...106 C2
Bleriot Cl NP20 .....120 A3
Blestium St NP25 ...137 B2
Blethyn Cl NP10 ....78 D5
Blewitt St NP20 .....119 B4
Block Cotts HR6 ....27 F7
Blodwen Rd NP4 ....105 A6
Blodwen Way NP4 ..105 A4
Blorenge Rd NP7 ....95 E6
Blorenge Terr NP4 ..101 D7
Blossom Cl NP18 ....121 B8
Blue Bell Cl WR14 ..87 C7
Blue Gate Ave HR1 .17 F5
Blue La GL18 ....59 D4
Bluebell Cl NP20 ....113 A4
Bluebell Cl HR9 .....94 D6
Bluebell Dr NP16 ...116 F5
Bluebell Rd NP4 ....77 E7
Board School La HR5 .81 D6
Boarsfield HR4 ......17 E8
Boat Rd NP18 ....131 A2
Bockleton Rd
　Oldwood WR15 ......80 C1
　Pudleston WR15 ....19 F8
　Tenbury Wells WR15 .11 C3
Boddington Terr NP18 .114 C2
Bodenham Manor HR1 .28 B6
Bodenham Rd HR1 ..91 C1
Bodmin Cl NP20 .....92 C5
Bog La WR15 ....80 C4
Bolstone La HR2 ....48 A3
Bolt Cl NP20 ....119 D3
Bolt St NP20 ....119 D3
Bolton Rd NP20 .....119 A4

Bolts Row NP19 .....120 B5
Bond St Malvern WR14 .85 A4
　Newport NP19 ......119 C6
Bonds Gn HR5,HR6 ..11 F1
Bonington Dr HR4 ..90 B3
Book End GL17 .....67 F5
Boot La [5] NP4 ....101 C6
Boraston Bank WR15 .80 E7
Boraston Dr WR15 ..80 D7
Boraston La WR15 ..80 D7
Borderway WR15 ...80 D6
Bosbury CE Prim Sch
　HR8 ....41 A6
Bosbury Rd WR14 ..85 A5
Boswell Cl NP20 ....118 F2
Boswell Ct NP15 ....85 A4
Bosworth Dr NP20 .119 A7
Bounds Cider Mill Rd The*
　HR8 ....49 E4
Bovingdon Pk HR4 .90 A5
Bowdens La
　Llandevaud NP18 ...77 C1
　Llanmartin NP26 ...122 F7
　Magor NP26 ....123 A6
Bowdler Cl SY8 .....79 E4
Bowen Cl NP25 .....96 C6
Bowen Pl [26] NP20 .119 C3
Bower La HR3 ......24 C5
Bower The HR3 .....24 C5
Bowleaze NP44 .....106 B3
Bowlers La HR7 ....92 C6
Bowley La
　Bodenham Moor HR1 .28 D7
　Risbury HR1,HR6 ..19 A1
Box Tree Cl GL17 ..66 F4
Boxer Ind Est NP18 .114 A4
Boxgrove HR2 ......92 C6
Boxtree Cl NP18 ...113 E2
Boycott Rd HR2 ....92 E2
Boyle Cl NP20 .....112 F2
Brackenhurst HR2 ..92 C5
Bradbury Cl HR2 ...92 F5
Brades The NP18 ..114 B3
Bradfords Cl GL18 .59 F4
Bradfords Ct GL18 .59 F4
Bradfords La GL18 .59 F4
Bradley Court Rd GL17 .67 D6
Bradley Dr HR4 .....92 C4
Bradley Rise GL17 ..67 D6
Bradnor HR5 ....81 C6
Bradnor View Cl HR5 .81 C6
Braemar Gdns HR1 ..93 F7
Brain Cl NP19 ......121 A6
Bramble Cl WR14 ..85 C3
Bramble Way NP18 .77 B1
Brambles The HR9 ..67 C8
Bramlea Cl HR6 ....82 A4
Bramley Cl
　Langstone NP18 ....121 C8
　Ledbury HR8 ....89 D2
Bramley Ct HR4 ....37 C4
Bramley Hollow HR4 .43 C4
Bramley Orchs HR7 .83 B6
Bramleys The GL17 .67 F5
Brampton Abbots CE Prim
　Sch HR9 ....94 E7
Brampton Ave HR9 .94 E7
Brampton Cl HR9 ..94 E6
Brampton Rd
　Hereford HR2 ....92 D4
　Ross-on-W HR9 ....94 E6
Brampton St HR9 ..94 E6
Bran y-Garth NP44 .107 B4
Branch The GL17 ..67 F5
Brand La SY8 ......79 D4
Brangwyn Ave NP44 .113 A8
Brangwyn Cres NP19 .119 F7
Brass Knoll HR2 ...53 A8
Brassknocker St NP26 .123 B3
Bray Ave HR9 ......89 E3
Bream Rd GL15 ....76 F7
Brechfa Cl NP18 ...113 E7
Brecon Court Deer Park &
　Vineyard* HR15 ...74 F4
Brecon Pk NP18 ...113 F3
Brecon Park Cotts NP7 .98 C5
Brecon Rd
　Abergavenny NP7 ..95 B6
　Crickhowell NP8 ...60 A5
　Hay-on-W HR3 .....88 C2
　Newport NP15 .....119 F7
Brecon Wlk NP44 ..106 F3
Bredenbury Prim Sch
　HR7 ....20 A3
Bredon Gr WR14 ..87 C6
Bredwardine Cl HR2 .92 C5
Bredwardine Hill HR3 .34 F7
Breinton Ave HR4 ...92 D8
Breinton La HR4 ....37 B3
Breinton Lee HR4 ...92 D7
Breinton Rd HR4 ...92 D8
Brewer's Pass HR1 .136 C3
Brewery Cotts NP25 .72 C5
Briar Cl NP20 ......123 B4
Briardene NP7 .....95 C3
Briars The HR2 ....123 A3
Bricknell Cl HR4 ...136 A3
Brickyard Rd HR5 ..81 C3
Bridesvale Rd HR8 ..49 E4
Bridewell Gdns NP26 .123 D2
Bridge Ct HR2 .....92 C6
Bridge Farm HR2 ..54 C7
Bridge Inn Rd HR4 .37 D6
Bridge La HR4 .....27 E3
Bridge Rd
　Harrow Hill GL17 ..67 B3

Bridge Rd continued
　Holme Lacy HR2 ....48 B6
Bridge St
　[18] Blaenavon NP4 .101 C6
　Chepstow NP16 ....110 F1
　Crickhowell NP8 ...60 A5
　Hay-on-W HR3 .....88 D4
　Hereford HR4 ......136 B2
　Kington HR5 ....81 B6
　Ledbury HR8 ....89 D4
　Leominster HR6 ....82 C6
　Newport NP20 .....119 B5
　Pembridge HR6 ....16 D5
　Pontypool NP4 .....104 E3
　Usk NP15 ....97 B4
Bridgend La SY7 ...2 B5
Bridget Dr NP16 ...117 A7
Bridgford Cl NP4 ..90 C2
Bridle Rd HR4 .....90 B2
Bridstow CE Prim Sch
　HR9 ....94 A6
Brierley Banks GL17 .66 F2
Brierley Council Hos
　GL17 ....66 F2
Brierley Cl [3] HR7 .93 B8
Brierley Rd GL17 ..66 F1
Brierley Way HR6 .82 E3
Brighton Gr HR4 ..90 C5
Brights La NP4 ....101 C6
Brilley Prim Sch HR3 .23 F4
Brimfield Bsns Pk SY8 .10 B7
Brimfield Cross SY8 .10 C7
Brin Williams Ho [1]
　NP20 ....119 A4
Bringewood Cl SY8 .79 C6
Bringewood Rd SY8 .79 C6
Bringewood Rise SY8 .79 C6
Bristol Ho HR4 ....104 A8
Bristol Packet Wharf
　NP20 ....119 C5
Bristol St NP19 ....119 E6
Bristol View Cl NP44 .106 A4
Briton Cl NP16 ....117 A4
Britten Cl Hereford HR1 .93 C8
　Newport NP19 .....120 D4
Britten Dr WR14 ..87 B6
Brixton Terr HR9 ..94 D6
Broad Leys Cres HR4 .42 D7
Broad Quay Rd NP19 .129 E8
Broad St Blaenavon NP4 .101 B7
　Bromyard HR7 .....83 D6
　Hay-on-W HR3 .....88 D4
　Hereford HR4 ......136 B2
　Leominster HR6 ....82 D5
　Ludlow SY8 ....79 C4
　Pontypool NP4 ....104 E3
　Presteigne LD8 ....6 E3
　Ross-on-W HR9 ....94 E5
　Weobley HR4 ......26 B6
Broad Street Comm
　NP18 ....130 E6
　Whitson NP18 .....131 A7
Broad View NP44 ..106 C5
Broadacre LD8 .....6 C5
Broadaxe Bsns Pk LD8 .26 C3
Broadcommon Cl NP19 .120 C3
Broadfield Cl WR15 .80 D6
Broadfield Garden &
　Vineyard* HR1 ....28 D8
Broadholme Rd HR2 .92 C6
Broadlands Cl NP26 .123 C3
Broadlands Dr WR14 .84 D4
Broadlands La HR1 .91 C2
Broadlands Prim Sch
　HR1 ....91 D2
Broadleaves HR9 ..94 B3
Broadmead NP7 ...60 E1
Broadmeadow La HR3 .88 A3
Broadmoor Comm* HR1 .49 A7
Broadmoor Pk GL14 .67 B2
Broadmoor Rd GL14 .67 D2
Broads Bank HR9 ..72 C5
Broadwalk NP18 ...116 C3
Broadwas CE Prim Sch
　WR6 ....22 D2
Broadwater Rd NP17 .92 C3
Broadway NP44 ....104 B6
Broadweir Rd NP44 .116 B2
Broadwell Ct NP18 .114 B2
Broadwell Rd NP18 .114 E2
Brobury Gdns* HR3 .35 A7
Brobury La HR3 ...35 B8
Brockamin La WR6 .32 C8
Brockhampton Cty Prim Sch
　WR6 ....21 B1
Brockhampton Mews
　HR7 ....91 B2
Brockhill Rd WR13 .86 C5
Brockington Dr HR1 .93 D8
Brockington Grange Mews
　HR7 ....28 D5
Brockington Rd HR1 .28 D5
Brockmoor La HR9 .59 C4
Bromfield Rd Ludlow SY8 .79 B4
　Ludlow, Bromfield SY8 .4 E8
Bromley Rd SY8 ..79 C5
Bromyard By-Pass HR7 .83 C5

Bromyard Com Hospl
HR7 .....83 C5
Bromyard Heritage Ctr*
HR7 .....83 C6
Bromyard Rd
Bromyard WR15 .....12 A1
Bromyard, Pie Corner WR6 ..20 E3
Ledbury HR8 .....89 C7
Tenbury Wells WR15 .....11 E4
Tenbury Wells WR15 .....80 E3
Bronail Cl HR2 .....92 D4
Bronllys Pl NP44 .....107 A5
Bronsil Dr WR14 .....84 F6
Bronte Dr HR8 .....89 C4
Bronte Gr NP20 .....118 E2
Brook Bank WR6 .....22 E2
Brook Crescent NP25 .....96 B5
Brook Farm Ct HR2 .....92 C5
Brook Farm Dr WR14 .....87 C6
Brook Orch HR1 .....28 B2
Brook St Cwmbran NP44 ..106 E7
Hay-on-W HR3 .....88 E3
Mitcheldean GL17 .....67 D5
Brooke Rd HR8 .....89 C5
Brookend St HR9 .....94 E5
Brookfield WR14 .....85 B5
Brookfield Ave HR9 .....94 E6
Brookfield Cl NP19 .....120 B3
Brookfield Prim Sch
NP44 .....106 E3
Brookfield Rd HR9 .....94 E6
Brookfields NP8 .....60 A5
Brookland Ho 2 NP44 ..106 E5
Brookland Terr NP44 .....106 E6
Brooklea NP18 .....114 B4
Brookmead HR9 .....94 E6
Brookmill Cl WR13 .....86 A1
Brookside Bettws NP20 ..112 E2
Caldicot NP26 .....124 F6
Canon Pyon HR4 .....27 B4
Colwall WR13 .....86 A1
Cradley WR13 .....31 E2
Cwmbran NP44 .....106 C2
Hereford HR1 .....93 C8
Malvern WR14 .....85 C5
Tintern Parva NP16 .....76 B3
Welland WR13 .....42 E3
Wellington HR4 .....27 E3
Brookside Rd GL14 .....67 B1
Broom Hill GL16 .....72 F7
Broom Hill Forest Trial*
GL16 .....72 F8
Broome Path NP44 .....106 C2
Broome Rd SY7 .....3 A8
Broomfield Cl NP19 .....120 D6
Broomy Hill HR4 .....92 D8
Brown Cl NP19 .....120 A3
Brown's End Cotts HR8 ..51 C4
Brown's La HR3 .....34 C6
Browning Cl NP20 .....118 F2
Browning Ct WR14 .....85 A2
Browning Rd HR8 .....89 C5
Broxash Cl HR7 .....83 A5
Broxash Dr HR2 .....92 E5
Broxwood HR3 .....25 D7
Broxwood Cr HR3,HR6 .....25 D8
Bruce Thomas Cl HR4 .....90 D1
Brunant Rd NP7 .....98 E8
Brunel Ave NP10 .....118 B6
Brunel Ct HR4 .....136 B3
Brunel Rd
Chepstow NP16 .....116 E6
Cwmbran NP44 .....106 A2
Brunel St NP20 .....119 D1
Brunley Cl HR3 .....23 F4
Bryans Ground Gdns*
LD8 .....7 A3
Bryn Bevan NP20 .....119 B8
Bryn Celyn Pl NP44 .....106 D5
Bryn Celyn Rd NP44 .....106 C5
Bryn Eglwys NP44 .....107 A5
Bryn Garw NP44 .....107 A5
Bryn Gomer NP44 .....107 A6
Bryn Heulog NP4 .....104 D4
Bryn Milwr NP44 .....112 C8
Bryn Nant NP8 .....60 A5
Bryn Rd NP26 .....132 E5
Bryn Rhedyn NP44 .....113 B8
Bryn The NP20 .....112 E3
Bryn-Welon Cl NP4 .....101 E6
Brynafal Bridge Ct HR3 ..23 D3
Brynarw NP7 .....61 E8
Brynavon 19 NP4 .....101 C6
Bryncelyn Cl NP7 .....69 A4
Bryncurl HR5 .....15 E2
Brynderwen Ct 1 NP19 .119 E6
Brynderwen Gr NP19 ....119 E6
Brynderwen Rd NP19 ....119 E6
Brynglas Cwmbran NP44 .112 C8
Gilwern NP7 .....60 D1
Brynglas Ave NP20 .....119 C8
Brynglas Cl NP20 .....113 B1
Brynglas Cres NP20 .....119 B8
Brynglas Ct NP20 .....113 B1
Brynglas Dr NP20 .....113 B1
Brynglas Prim Sch
NP20 .....113 B1
Brynglas Rd NP20 .....119 B8
Bryngwyn Cl HR1 .....91 B2
Bryngwyn Ct 4 HR1 .....91 B2
Bryngwyn Pl NP4 .....104 B6
Bryngwyn Rd
Newport NP20 .....119 A4
Pontypool NP4 .....104 B6
Brynhyfryd NP44 .....107 A5
Brynhyfryd Ave NP20 .....119 B4
Brynhyfryd Rd NP20 .....119 A4
Brynteg Pl NP4 .....103 E3
Brynwern NP4 .....104 B6
Buchan Cl NP20 .....118 F2
Buchanan Cl NP25 .....96 B3
Buckfast Cl HR2 .....92 C6
Buckfield Rd HR6 .....82 A4
Buckholt View NP25 .....96 C7
Buckingham Cl WR14 .....85 C6
Buckingham Cres NP19 .119 F6
Buckingham Pl NP19 .....119 F6
Buckland Cl NP26 .....124 B4
Bucknell Sta SY7 .....2 C4
Budden Cres NP26 .....124 F6
Builth Cl NP10 .....128 D5
Bull Ring SY8 .....79 C4
Bull Ring The GL17 .....67 D5
Bulling Pitch HR2 .....47 C3
Bullingham La HR2 .....93 A3
Bullocks Bridge HR1 .....29 B3
Bullrush Cl HR1 .....93 B8
Bulmer Ave HR1 .....91 B2
Bulmers Cotts HR4 .....37 C4
Bulmore Rd NP18 .....114 E2
Bulwark Ave NP16 .....116 F5
Bulwark Bsns Pk NP16 ..116 E6
Bulwark Rd NP16 .....116 E7
Bungalows The
Bryn The NP7 .....69 A4
Mordiford HR1 .....39 A1
Burcott Bsns Pk HR4 .....90 F3
Burcott Rd HR4 .....136 C4
Burden Rd HR1 .....91 D1
Burdon Dr HR1 .....38 F4
Burford CE Prim Sch
WR15 .....80 D6
Burford House Gdns*
WR15 .....80 A5
Burford St 3 NP4 .....101 C6
Burgage NP25 .....137 C3
Burgage Cl HR5 .....15 D2
Burgess St HR6 .....82 D5
Burghill Prim Sch HR4 ...37 B8
Burghope Orch HR7 .....29 C7
Burleigh Cl WR15 .....80 C4
Burleigh Rd 2 NP20 .....119 A4
Burley Gate CE Prim Sch
HR1 .....29 C2
Burmarsh Cotts HR1 .....28 C1
Burmarsh Trad Est HR1 ....28 C2
Burnfort Rd NP20 .....118 F3
Burns Cl NP20 .....118 E1
Burns Cres NP26 .....124 E4
Burns La NP44 .....106 D2
Burnt Barn Rd NP16 .....116 F4
Burnt Hengoed HR3 .....23 F6
Burnt Orch HR5 .....15 D2
Burrington SY8 .....3 F3
Burrows Cl WR14 .....85 C1
Burrows Ct HR1 .....93 C7
Burrups La HR9 .....59 B5
Burton Cres HR4 .....26 B6
Burton Ct* HR6 .....17 A4
Burton Gdns HR4 .....26 B6
Burton Homes
Caerwent NP26 .....78 C1
Newport NP20 .....119 B3
Burton Rd NP19 .....119 F8
Burtons La HR8 .....41 B3
Burtonwood HR4 .....26 B6
Burway Cl SY8 .....79 B6
Burway La SY8 .....79 A6
Burway Trad Est SY8 .....79 B6
Burwood Cl HR1 .....91 B2
Bury Court Pk HR6 .....8 C7
Buryfields WR13 .....31 E2
Burying La HR7 .....83 E7
Bush Pitch HR8 .....89 A7
Bushy Pk NP4 .....104 A7
Busy Hill HR1 .....28 B1
Butchers Arms HR1 .....49 B6
Butchers Row Mus The*
HR8 .....89 E4
Bute Ave HR2 .....93 A6
Buttercross 7 HR6 .....82 D5
Buttercross Arc 6 HR6 ..82 D5
Butterfield Ho 7 HR7 ...83 C6
Buttermere Way 3
NP19 .....119 F8
Butterworth Cl NP19 .....120 E5
Buttington Hill NP16 .....117 B7
Buttington Rd NP16 .....117 A7
Buttington Terr NP16 .....117 B6
Button Mus* HR9 .....94 D5
Buxton Cl NP20 .....118 F1
Buzzard Cl NP26 .....124 B4
Bye Rd WR14 .....87 C7
Bye St HR8 .....89 D4
Byland Cl HR2 .....92 C6
Byrde Cl NP19 .....120 C5
Byron Cl WR14 .....85 A2
Byron Pl Caldicot NP26 ..124 E4
Cwmbran NP44 .....106 D2
Byron Rd NP20 .....118 F2
Bythway Rd NP4 .....102 B1
Byways NP44 .....106 B3

C

C Row NP4 .....101 A6
Cabal La HR5 .....15 E6
Caban Cl NP10 .....118 B7
Cabbage La HR8 .....89 E4
Cadoc Cl NP26 .....78 C1
Cadoc Rd 5 NP44 .....106 C6
Cae Brynton Rd NP20 ...119 A2
Cae Capel NP15 .....69 F4
Cae Derw NP7 .....60 E1
Cae Derwen NP44 .....106 D1
Cae Mawr Ave NP26 .....124 F5
Cae Mawr Gr NP26 .....124 F5
Cae Mawr Rd NP26 .....124 F5
Cae Meldon NP7 .....60 D2
Cae Melln NP4 .....103 E3
Cae Pen Y Dre NP7 .....95 C5
Cae Pen-y-Dre Cl NP7 ...95 C5
Cae Perllan Rd NP20 .....119 A3
Cae Rhedyn NP44 .....107 B4
Cae-Yr-Ebol NP44 .....106 E5
Caefelyn LD8 .....6 D5
Caenbrook Mdw LD8 .....6 E3
Caepalish Pl NP4 .....104 A8
Caepound HR3 .....88 D2
Caerau Cres NP20 .....119 A4
Caerau Rd NP20 .....119 A4
Caerleon (Lodge Hill) Inf Sch
NP18 .....114 A3
Caerleon (Lodge Hill) Jun
Sch NP18 .....113 F3
Caerleon Comp Sch
NP18 .....114 A2
Caerleon Endowed Jun Sch
NP18 .....114 A2
Caerleon Rd
Caerleon NP18 .....114 A5
Newport NP19 .....119 E7
Ponthir NP18, NP44 .....113 E7
Caerleon Roman
Amphitheatre* NP18 114 B1
Caerleon Roman Fortress*
NP18 .....114 B1
Caerlicken La NP18 .....77 A2
Caernarvon Cres NP44 .107 A3
Caerphilly Rd NP10 .....118 A2
Caerwent Gdns NP26 .....78 C1
Caerwent La NP16 .....116 F4
Caerwent Rd
Croesyceiliog NP44 .....107 A6
Pontypool NP4 .....102 D1
Caesar Cres NP18 .....114 A4
Caestory Ave NP15 .....70 C2
Caestory Cres NP15 .....70 C2
Cagebrook Ave HR2 .....92 D7
Caird St NP16 .....116 E7
Calcot Ho NP44 .....107 B4
Caldervale HR1 .....28 D6
Caldicot By-Pass NP26 ..125 B4
Caldicot Castle* NP26 125 B5
Caldicot Castle Country Pk*
NP26 .....125 B6
Caldicot Com Coll NP26 .125 A5
Caldicot Comp Sch
NP26 .....125 A5
Caldicot Green Lane Jun Sch
NP26 .....124 F5
Caldicot Rd
Caldicot NP26 .....124 E5
Portskewett NP26 .....125 C5
Rogiet NP26 .....124 B4
Undy NP26 .....123 F4
Caldicot Sandy Lane Inf Sch
NP26 .....124 F6
Caldicot St NP19 .....119 F4
Caldicot St Mary's Jun Sch
NP26 .....125 A6
Caldicot Sta NP26 .....124 E4
Caldicot Way NP44 .....106 F6
Caldicot West End Inf Sch
NP26 .....124 E4
Caldwell Ct HR4 .....136 B3
Caldy Cl NP19 .....119 F7
Cales Ave WR14 .....84 E4
California La WR13 .....42 E3
Callow End HR8 .....89 D6
Callow View HR2 .....47 A2
Callows Mdw WR15 .....80 C2
Callowside HR2 .....54 D7
Calyn Ct 4 NP44 .....106 C6
Cam Ct NP44 .....106 A5
Cambria Cl NP18 .....114 C2
Cambria St NP4 .....104 E2
Cambrian Ret Ctr 4
NP20 .....119 B5
Cambridge Cl WR14 .....42 C3
Cambridge Ct NP18 .....113 F3
Cambridge Rd NP19 .....119 D5
Camelot Cl HR4 .....90 D2
Camelot Ct NP18 .....114 C2
Camelot Pl 5 NP19 .....119 D6
Cameron Ct WR14 .....87 A6
Camomile Gn GL17 .....66 D2
Camp Hill WR14 .....84 C1
Camp La Almeley HR3 .....25 C7
Ludlow SY8 .....79 B3
Shelsley Beachamp WR6 .....13 F3
Camp Rd Chepstow NP16 .116 F6
Ross-on-W HR9 .....94 F4
Sudbrook NP26 .....125 F3
Campbell St NP4 .....104 A7
Camperdown La HR4 .....136 A2
Camperdown Rd NP19 ..120 B3
Campion Cl
Cwmbran NP44 .....112 A8
Newport NP20 .....119 A6
Campion Dr WR14 .....87 D7
Campwood Rd HR2 .....93 D5
Camrose Wlk NP44 .....106 C2
Canal Cl NP4 .....104 E2
Canal Par NP20 .....119 D4
Canal Rd HR1 .....136 C3
Canal St NP20 .....119 B7
Canal Terr NP20 .....119 D3
Canal Wlk HR8 .....89 D3
Canberra Cl NP44 .....106 D2
Canberra Cres NP20 .....118 E4
Candwr Pk NP18 .....113 F7
Candwr Rd NP18 .....114 A6
Canford Cl NP4 .....102 B2
Cangeford Dr SY8 .....79 F5
Cannon La NP26 .....78 C1
Canon Dr HR4 .....25 E3
Canon Pyon CE Prim Sch
HR4 .....27 A4
Canon Pyon Rd HR4 .....90 C7
Canon Rise HR4 .....36 D6
Canon St NP19 .....119 D6
Canonford Ave HR3 .....24 D4
Canonmoor St HR4 .....136 B3
Canterbury Ave HR1 .....91 D1
Canterbury Cl 9 NP20 ..119 C6
Canterbury Way NP26 ..125 D5
Cantilupe Rd HR9 .....94 E5
Cantilupe St HR1 .....136 C2
Cantref Cl NP10 .....118 B7
Cantref Rd NP7 .....95 C6
Canwood HR1 .....49 B7
Capel Cres NP20 .....119 C2
Capel Ct 15 NP4 .....102 A1
Capel Ed La NP4 .....103 E7
Capel Newydd Ave NP4 .101 D5
Capel Newydd Rd NP4 ..101 D6
Capel St NP4 .....104 C6
Caple Ave HR1 .....57 C7
Capler Camp* HR1 .....48 E3
Capler La HR1 .....48 E5
Cappers' Pl NP25 .....137 A1
Capuchin Yd HR4 .....136 B2
Caradoc Dr HR6 .....82 D3
Caradoc Rd NP44 .....106 E4
Caradoc Wlk NP4 .....101 D7
Caradog Cl NP18 .....114 A3
Carbonne Cl NP25 .....96 B3
Cardiff Rd NP20 .....119 B3
Cardigan Cl NP44 .....106 F6
Cardigan Cres NP44 .....106 F6
Cardigan Ct NP18 .....113 F3
Cardigan Pl 1 NP19 .....119 F6
Carey Rd NP19 .....120 A5
Carfax Path NP44 .....106 B1
Carisbrook Rd GL17 .....67 D6
Carisbrooke Rd NP19 ...119 F5
Carless Cl HR1 .....91 C1
Carlisle St NP20 .....119 D2
Carlsgate HR3 .....88 D3
Carlton Ct NP4 .....104 A8
Carlton Rd Malvern WR14 ..84 F3
Newport NP19 .....119 E7
Caroline Rd NP4 .....105 A4
Caroline St 17 NP20 .....119 C4
Carpenter Cl NP18 .....115 F1
Carpenter Cotts GL16 .....72 F3
Carr La HR2 .....92 D5
Carroll Ave HR4 .....90 B2
Carter Gr HR1 .....91 C2
Cartwright Gn NP20 .....113 A2
Carwardine Gn HR2 .....92 D5
Cas Troggy NP26 .....124 F6
Casaba Terr NP7 .....95 B3
Cash Hill GL17 .....66 E4
Castell Coch Dr NP10 ...128 E5
Castle Cl Eardisley HR3 ....24 E4
Monmouth NP25 .....137 B1
Rogerstone NP10 .....118 B4
Tenbury Wells WR15 .....80 D6
Castle Cres GL15 .....76 F7
Castle Ct Caldicot NP26 ..125 B4
Usk NP15 .....97 B4
Castle Est HR3 .....88 A6
Castle Gdns
Caldicot NP26 .....124 F6
Chepstow NP16 .....110 D1
Hay-on-W HR3 .....88 D3
Castle Hill Hereford HR1 .136 C2
Kington HR5 .....81 C6
Monmouth NP25 .....137 B2
8 Raglan NP15 .....70 C2
Castle La Goodrich HR9 ...66 A6
Hay-on-W HR3 .....88 D3
Castle Lea NP26 .....125 A5
Castle Lodge Cl NP26 ...125 B5
Castle Lodge Cres NP26 .125 B5
Castle Mdw HR9 .....94 D4
Castle Mead HR4 .....26 B6
Castle Meadows Pk NP7 .95 C5
Castle Mews
Caerleon NP18 .....114 C1
Usk NP15 .....97 B5
Castle Oak NP15 .....97 B5
Castle Par NP15 .....97 B4
Castle Park Cl NP20 .....118 D3
Castle Park Rd NP20 ....118 D3
Castle Pk HR2 .....46 C1
Castle Rd Crickhowell NP8 .60 A5
Presteigne LD8 .....6 E3
Raglan NP15 .....70 C2
Castle Rd Bglws LD8 .....6 E3
Castle Rise NP26 .....77 E2
Castle Sq SY8 .....79 C4
Castle St Abergavenny NP7 .95 D5
Blaenavon NP4 .....101 C7
Caerleon NP18 .....114 C2
Hay-on-W HR3 .....88 D3
Hereford HR1 .....136 C2
Ludlow SY8 .....79 C4
Newport NP20 .....119 D2
9 Raglan NP15 .....70 C2
Usk NP15 .....97 B4
Wigmore HR6 .....8 C8
Castle The HR3 .....34 F3
Castle View NP16 .....111 A1
Castle View Terr SY8 .....79 C5
Castle Way NP26 .....125 C5
Castle Wood
Chepstow NP16 .....116 C8
Usk NP15 .....97 C5
Castlefields HR6 .....82 D3
Castleford Gdns NP16 ...110 F2
Castleford Hill NP16 .....110 E2
Castleford Rd SY8 .....79 A6
Castleton Farm Rd HR3 ..34 B8
Caswell Cres HR6 .....82 E4
Caswell Rd HR6 .....82 D4
Caswell Terr HR6 .....82 D4
Caswell Way NP19 .....120 A1
Catalpa Cl Malvern WR14 ..84 F6
Newport NP20 .....113 B3
Catbrook Rd NP25 .....75 F8
Catchmays Ct NP16,NP25 .76 C5
Cathedral Ct 9 NP20 .....119 B4
Catherine Cl NP10 .....128 F5
Catherine Ct HR1 .....136 C3
Catherine St HR1 .....136 C3
Catsash Rd NP18 .....114 F1
Caudle Cl GL17 .....66 E4
Caudle La GL17 .....66 E4
Causeway Rd GL14 .....67 D1
Causeway The NP26 .....123 D1
Caven HR1 .....57 C7
Cawdor HR9 .....94 E6
Cawdor Arch Rd HR9 .....94 D6
Cawdor Gdns HR9 .....94 D6
Caxton Pl 5 NP20 .....119 B5
Caxton View NP25 .....96 B5
Caynham CE Prim Sch
SY8 .....5 D4
Caynham Ct SY8 .....5 D4
Caynham Rd SY8 .....5 F4
Caynham Woods SY8 .....5 D3
Cecil Sharp Rd NP19 .....120 F5
Cedar Ave
Madresfield WR13 .....85 F4
Malvern WR14 .....85 B3
Cedar Cl Chepstow NP16 ..116 E5
Moreton-On-L HR4 .....37 F8
Presteigne LD8 .....6 E3
Cedar Ct HR8 .....89 E4
Cedar Gr HR9 .....66 C8
Cedar La HR4 .....90 A7
Cedar Rd NP19 .....119 D5
Cedar Wlk NP44 .....106 B5
Cedardean 13 GL14 .....67 C1
Cedars The
Llanmartin NP18 .....121 F7
Malvern WR14 .....84 F3
Cefn Cl
Croesyceiliog NP44 .....107 B6
Rogerstone NP10 .....118 B5
Cefn Ct Newport NP20 ...119 A3
Rogerstone NP10 .....118 B5
Cefn Dr NP10 .....118 B5
Cefn Mawr La NP15 .....73 B6
Cefn Milwr NP44 .....112 D8
Cefn Rd
Michaelchurch-on-A HR3 ..23 D4
Rogerstone NP10 .....118 A6
Cefn Rise NP10 .....118 A6
Cefn Wlk NP10 .....118 B5
Cefn Wood Jun & Inf Sch
NP10 .....118 A5
Celandine Ct NP16 .....116 F5
Celtic Cl NP26 .....123 C3
Celtic Way NP10 .....128 C5
Cenfedd St NP19 .....119 D7
Central Ave Hereford HR1 ..93 B8
Mitcheldean GL17 .....67 D5
Newport NP19 .....120 D2
Pontypool NP4 .....103 B1
Severn Beach BS10 .....135 A3
Central Dr NP4 .....102 B1
Central Way NP44 .....106 C5
Centurion Ct NP26 .....78 C1
Centurion Gate NP18 .....114 C2
Centurion Way
Credenhill HR4 .....37 A6
Hereford HR1 .....91 B4
Ceredig Ct 6 NP44 .....107 B2
Chadwick Cl NP20 .....113 A2
Chaffinch Way NP10 .....128 F7
Chain Bridge Rd NP7 .....73 B8
Chain Cl NP7 .....95 C7
Chain Rd NP7 .....95 C7
Challenger Cl
Ledbury HR8 .....89 D6
Malvern WR14 .....85 B1
Chance La WR14 .....87 E8
Chancel View HR2 .....92 C6
Chancery Ct HR3 .....88 E3
Chancery La HR3 .....88 D3
Chandlers Cl
Kingstone HR2 .....46 A7
Ludlow SY8 .....79 C4
Chandos St HR4 .....136 A3
Channel View
Chepstow NP16 .....116 E5
Cwmbran NP44 .....106 C5
Pontypool NP4 .....104 D7
Chantry Cl WR15 .....80 C5
Chantry Ct HR2 .....92 C6
Chantry High Sch The
WR6 .....22 D7
Chantry The NP25 .....137 B3
Chapel Cl
Chepstow NP16 .....116 B5
Leigh Sinton WR13 .....32 D5
Monmouth NP25 .....96 F3
23 Newport NP20 .....119 C3
Chapel Gr NP7 .....61 F7
Chapel Hill GL16 .....66 A1
Chapel La
Abergavenny NP7 .....95 C7

Chapel La continued
Bodenham Moor HR1 .....28 E5
Bransford WR6 .....32 E6
Chepstow NP16 .....116 B5
Cradley WR13 .....31 D2
Croesyceiliog NP44 .....107 A7
Dorstone HR3 .....34 E4
Gorsley HR9 .....59 B4
Llandevaud NP18 .....77 B1
Menithwood WR6 .....13 B8
Peterchurch HR2 .....35 B1
Chapel Mead NP4 .....103 E7
Chapel Mews SY8 .....79 C5
Chapel Orch
Abergavenny NP7 .....95 C7
Weobley HR4 .....26 B6
Chapel Pitch
Clifford's Mesne GL18 .....59 D2
King's Thorn HR2 .....47 C3
Chapel R
Abergavenny NP7 .....95 C6
Goldcliff NP18 .....131 A5
Hereford HR2 .....93 F5
Llangwm NP15 .....74 D2
Ross-on-W HR9 .....94 D3
Whitney-on-W HR3 .....23 F3
Chapel Row SY8 .....79 C5
Chapel St NP4 .....106 C5
Chapel Terr NP26 .....123 B2
Chapel Wlk 5 HR6 .....82 D5
Chapelfields HR9 .....65 B6
Chapman Cl NP20 .....113 A3
Chapman Ct 10 NP20 .....118 F4
Charles Cl
Abergavenny NP7 .....95 E8
Newport NP20 .....96 D7
Charles Cres NP7 .....95 E8
Charles Edwards Cl NP7 .....95 C3
Charles R NP25 .....71 A5
Charles St
Blaenavon NP4 .....101 D6
Cwmbran NP44 .....106 E6
Newport NP20 .....119 C4
Pontypool NP4 .....104 E3
Charles Way HR4 .....23 B8
Charles Witts Ave HR2 .....136 A1
Charlesville HR2 .....102 A1
Charlock Rd WR14 .....87 D7
Charlotte Dr NP20 .....119 C3
Charlotte St 16 NP20 .....119 C3
Charlotte Wlk 12 NP20 .....119 C3
Charlton Ave HR7 .....92 E5
Charlton Rise SY8 .....79 E4
Charnwood Rd NP19 .....119 D8
Charston NP44 .....106 C3
Chartist Dr NP10 .....118 A5
Chartist La GL19 .....51 F2
Chartists Way NP16 .....116 E5
Chartwell Rd HR1 .....91 C1
Charwood Ho 8 NP44 .....106 C2
Chase Ind Est HR9 .....94 F4
Chase Mews NP4 .....94 E5
Chase Rd Colwall WR13 .....36 B2
Malvern WR14 .....42 C4
Ross-on-W WR6 .....94 E4
Chase Sch The WR14 .....87 B6
Chase Side HR9 .....94 E4
Chase The NP15 .....109 B5
Chase View Rd WR6 .....94 C3
Chatsworth Cl HR9 .....94 F6
Chatsworth Rd HR4 .....90 C4
Chaucer Cl NP26 .....124 E4
Chaucer Cl 4 NP19 .....119 F5
Chaucer Rd NP19 .....119 F5
Chaucer Way NP25 .....137 B4
Chave Court Cl HR4 .....136 B4
Chave Ct HR4 .....136 B4
Cheaton Cl HR6 .....82 D6
Checkley Cl HR4 .....90 C4
Cheeseman's Trad Est NP26 .....124 C5
Chelmer Cl NP20 .....112 C1
Chelmer Wlk NP20 .....112 C1
Chelston Pl NP20 .....119 B7
Cheltenham Ave HR4 .....90 D5
Chepstow Camp (Fort)* NP16 .....116 F6
Chepstow Castle* NP16 .....110 E1
Chepstow Com Hospl NP16 .....116 D8
Chepstow Comp Sch NP16 .....110 D2
Chepstow Mus* NP16 .....110 F1
Chepstow Rd
Gwernesney NP15 .....74 C4
Langstone NP18 .....121 B8
Newport NP10 .....120 C5
Raglan NP15 .....70 C2
Trellech NP25,NP16 .....75 E7
Usk NP15 .....97 C4
Chepstow Rise NP44 .....107 A6
Chepstow Sta NP16 .....116 B8
Chepstow Wlk HR4 .....90 C5
Chequers Cl Hereford HR4 .....90 A1
Malvern WR14 .....85 C4
Cheriton Path NP44 .....106 B6
Cherry Orchard Cotts HR4 .....37 B8
Cherry Orchard La HR8 .....49 D3
Cherry Tree Cl
Bromyard NP7 .....83 B6
Caerleon NP18 .....114 B3
Croesyceiliog NP44 .....107 B5
Ewyas Harold HR2 .....54 C6
Langstone NP18 .....121 B8
Newport NP18 .....113 B3

Cherry Tree Dr WR14 .....86 F4
Cherry Tree La NP15 .....74 F1
Cherry Wlk NP25 .....96 B4
Cherrybrook Cl HR26 .....27 F7
Cherwell Wlk NP20 .....112 C2
Chesnut Gr NP18 .....113 E2
Chessell Ave BS35 .....135 C7
Chessgrove La GL17 .....67 F6
Chester Cl Hereford HR4 .....136 B4
Chester Pl WR14 .....84 E4
Chesterholme NP20 .....119 A3
Chestnut Ave HR6 .....18 D8
Chestnut Cl Ledbury HR8 .....89 D3
Magor NP26 .....123 B3
Pontypool NP4 .....105 B5
Welland WR13 .....42 E3
Chestnut Dr Hereford HR2 .....93 A6
Malvern WR14 .....86 F4
Rogiet NP26 .....124 C4
Chestnut Drive/Rhodfa'r Gastanwydden NP7 .....95 F6
Chestnut Gn NP44 .....106 B6
Chestnut Gr SY8 .....79 E4
Chestnut La HR4 .....90 A7
Chestnut Mdw SY7 .....2 C5
Chestnut Terr NP25 .....96 F3
Chestnut Way HR7 .....83 B5
Chevenham Cl WR13 .....86 A1
Cheviot Cl HR4 .....90 A3
Chichester Cl
Hereford HR2 .....92 C5
Newport NP20 .....113 F1
Chick La NP20 .....118 F4
Chickadee GL15 .....76 E7
Chickward La HR5 .....24 B8
Childer Rd HR8 .....89 B3
Chiltern Cl NP19 .....120 C6
Chilton Sq HR1 .....91 D2
Chimneys Mdw HR2 .....46 D4
Chippenham Cl NP25 .....137 B2
Chippenhamgate St NP25 .....137 B2
Chirk Cl NP10 .....128 D5
Chisel Cl HR4 .....90 D2
Chockbury La WR13 .....31 D2
Cholstrey Rd HR6 .....82 D5
Christ Church Rd WR14 .....87 A8
Christchurch Hill NP18 .....120 D7
Christchurch Rd NP19 .....119 E6
Christina Cres NP10 .....118 C4
Church Ave NP4 .....102 C1
Church Bank HR6 .....18 E8
Church Barn HR2 .....
Church Cl Caldicot NP26 .....125 A6
Croesyceiliog NP44 .....107 A5
Pontypool NP4 .....105 A2
Rogerstone NP10 .....118 C4
Ross-on-W HR9 .....94 D5
Upper Sapey WR6 .....12 F2
Church Cres
Bassaleg NP10 .....118 A3
Coedkernew NP10 .....128 A5
Pembroke HR6 .....16 D5
Church Croft
Fownhope HR1 .....48 E5
Madley HR2 .....36 C1
Church Ct Newport NP19 .....120 A8
Newport, Barnardtown NP19 .....119 E5
Church Farm NP25 .....96 F3
Church Farm Barns WR13 .....41 E8
Church Farm Cl
Bettws NP20 .....112 E1
Monmouth NP25 .....96 F3
Church Hill GL17 .....66 D2
Church Hill Cl GL16 .....66 B2
Church House Farm Barns WR6 .....13 D1
Church La Ashperton HR8 .....40 B4
Bettws Newydd NP15 .....73 B7
Bredwardine HR3 .....35 A7
Broadwas WR6 .....22 D2
Bromyard HR7 .....83 C6
Cilcenni CH4 .....128 A4
Cusop HR3 .....88 F2
Glascoed NP4 .....73 A4
Gorsley NP7 .....95 B8
Hampton Bishop HR1 .....48 B8
Ledbury HR8 .....89 E4
Ledbury, Wellington Heath HR8 .....41 C3
Letton HR3 .....25 A1
Llanddewi Rhydderch NP7 .....69 C7
Llanfoist NP7 .....95 B3
Llansoy NP15 .....74 F5
Madley HR2 .....36 A5
Much Marcle HR8 .....49 F3
Orleton SY8 .....9 E6
Pontypool NP4 .....104 B8
Pontypool, Panteg NP4 .....105 B2
St Arvans NP16 .....110 B6
Suckley WR6 .....30 B4
Undy NP26 .....123 E2
Upper Sapey WR6 .....12 F2
Whitney-on-W HR3 .....23 F2
Church Meadow Ct WR14 .....84 F2
Church Mews NP4 .....104 C6
Church Rd
Abbey Dore HR2 .....45 B3
Blaenavon NP4 .....101 C6
Bredwardine HR3 .....35 B7
Brockhampton HR1 .....89 B3

Church Rd continued
Burghill HR1 .....37 F7
Caldicot NP26 .....124 F7
Chepstow NP16 .....110 F1
Clehonger HR2 .....63 E6
Clifford HR3 .....33 E8
Clodock HR2 .....53 E6
Cusop HR3 .....88 F2
Cwmbran NP44 .....106 D5
Dorstone HR3 .....34 E4
Eardisley HR3 .....24 E4
Eardisley, Winforton HR3 .....24 B4
Gilwern NP7 .....60 C1
Govilon NP7 .....99 F8
Hereford HR1 .....91 D1
Hewelsfield GL15 .....76 F5
Holme Lacy HR2 .....48 C5
Hoptonheath SY7 .....2 F8
Kingstone HR2 .....46 E7
Kington HR5 .....64 E7
Ledbury HR8 .....89 E4
Llanfrechfa NP44 .....113 D8
Llanishen NP16 .....75 C6
Longhope GL17 .....67 F6
Maesygwartha NP7 .....98 D8
Malvern WR14 .....85 A4
Newport NP19 .....119 D6
Peterchurch HR2 .....35 B1
Pilning BS35 .....135 B7
Severn Beach BS35 .....135 A6
St Brides Wentlooge NP10 .....128 E1
Staunton-On-W HR4 .....35 E7
Undy NP26 .....123 D2
Upper Lydbrook GL17 .....66 D2
Weobley HR4 .....26 B6
Church Rise NP26 .....123 E3
Church Row
Chepstow NP16 .....110 F1
Redwick NP26 .....132 E5
Sudbrook NP26 .....125 F4
Church St Bromyard HR7 .....83 D6
Caerleon NP18 .....114 B2
Crickhowell NP8 .....60 A5
Hay-on-W HR3 .....88 D3
Hereford HR1 .....136 B2
Kington HR5 .....81 D6
Ledbury HR8 .....89 E4
Leintwardine SY7 .....3 B5
Leominster HR6 .....82 D5
Ludlow SY8 .....79 C4
Malvern WR14 .....86 F8
Monmouth NP25 .....96 E6
Newport NP20 .....119 D2
Presteigne LD8 .....6 E3
Ross-on-W HR9 .....94 D5
St Briavels GL15 .....76 E7
Tenbury Wells WR15 .....80 C5
Trellech NP25 .....75 F8
Usk NP15 .....97 B4
Wigmore HR6 .....18 C4
Church Terr
Hay-on-W HR3 .....88 D3
7 Pontypool NP4 .....102 A1
Church View
8 Blaenavon NP4 .....101 C6
Monmouth NP25 .....96 F3
Much Dewchurch HR2 .....47 A2
Raglan NP15 .....70 C6
Church Villas 3 HR7 .....83 C6
Church Way HR1 .....90 F5
Church Wlk
Bodenham Moor HR1 .....28 B5
Little Hereford HR6 .....10 E7
Malvern WR14 .....85 B4
Church Wood Rd NP44 .....106 D5
Churchdown Rd WR14 .....87 C5
Churchfield Ave HR6 .....124 F6
Churchfield Terr WR6 .....13 F6
Churchfields NP16 .....75 D2
Churchill HR6 .....18 E8
Churchill Ave HR6 .....82 C3
Churchill Cl Hereford HR1 .....91 B2
Ludlow SY8 .....79 D3
Churchill House Mus* HR1 .....91 C2
Churchill Mdw HR8 .....89 C3
Churchill Pl HR9 .....94 D2
Churchill Rd HR5 .....81 C6
Churchill Way GL17 .....67 D5
Churchmead
Bassaleg NP10 .....118 B2
Rogiet NP26 .....124 B4
Churchward Dr NP19 .....120 B4
Churchward Trad Est HR1 .....136 C4
Churchway Bromyard WR6 .....30 F7
Sutton St Nicholas HR1 .....38 C8
Churchway Cotts HR4 .....90 F5
Churchwood Cl NP4 .....104 C7
Cibi Wlk NP7 .....95 D5
Cider Mus* HR4 .....136 A2
Cidermill Cl NP16 .....116 F4
Cilcennin Cl NP16 .....91 D2
Cilgerram Cl NP44 .....107 B3
Cinder Hill GL15 .....76 E7
Cinderhill St NP25 .....137 B1
Cinderhill Way GL17 .....62 D7
Cinders La WR15 .....11 B3
Cinders Rd WR15 .....80 B1
Circle The NP44 .....106 D1
Civil War Fort NP18 .....114 C5
Clairwain NP44 .....105 A3
Clapham Terr NP10 .....101 B5
Clare Dr NP16 .....116 F4
Clare Drew Way NP44 .....107 A5
Clare Rd NP16 .....85 B1
Claremont NP20 .....113 B4

Claremont Ct WR14 .....86 E1
Claremont Orch SY8 .....9 E6
Clarence Cl WR14 .....87 A2
Clarence Cnr NP4 .....104 C6
Clarence Pl
Newport NP19 .....119 C5
Pontypool NP4 .....104 D6
Clarence Rd
Malvern WR14 .....87 A8
Pontypool NP4 .....104 D6
Clarence St
Newport NP20 .....119 D2
Pontypool NP4 .....104 C6
Clarendon Cl NP16 .....117 A4
Clarendon Ct WR14 .....86 F8
Clark Ave NP44 .....106 E6
Clarksons La HR1 .....91 C1
Clatterbrune LD8 .....6 F3
Clawdd Du NP25 .....137 A1
Clay Hill Pitch HR1 .....39 A2
Clayfield Dr WR14 .....86 A2
Claygreen WR6 .....31 F8
Claypatch Rd NP25 .....137 C1
Clayton St NP19 .....119 D6
Claytons HR9 .....94 A6
Clearview NP25 .....72 B1
Clearview Ct NP16 .....78 D4
Clearwater Rd NP19 .....130 D8
Clee Gdns SY8 .....79 D5
Clee Hill Rd WR15 .....80 C7
Clee Stanton Rd SY8 .....5 F8
Clee View SY8 .....79 E5
Clee View Cl SY8 .....79 E5
Cleeve La HR9 .....94 C3
Cleeve Orch HR1 .....
Clehonger CE Prim Sch HR2 .....46 D8
Clement Atlee Dr NP19 .....120 D7
Clencher's Mill La HR8 .....51 B7
Cleppa Park Ind Est NP10 .....128 C7
Clerkenwell Cres WR14 .....85 A2
Clevedon Cl 7 NP19 .....119 F6
Clevedon Rd NP18 .....120 F8
Clewer Court Mews 9 NP20 .....118 F4
Clewer Croft WR13 .....32 C5
Clewer Ct 6 NP20 .....119 A4
Cliff View NP16 .....117 B7
Cliff Villas SY8 .....79 C3
Clifford Castle HR3 .....23 D1
Clifford Castle HR3 .....33 F7
Clifford Prim Sch HR3 .....33 E8
Clifford Rd HR4 .....82 A4
Clifford St HR4 .....90 D1
Clifton Pl NP20 .....119 B4
Clifton Rd
Abergavenny NP7 .....95 F6
Hereford HR1 .....91 C1
Newport NP19 .....119 B4
Clifton Sq NP4 .....104 E3
Clifton Terr NP4 .....101 C7
Clifton upon Teme Prim Sch WR6 .....21 F8
Clingo Rd HR1 .....82 A4
Clinton Rd HR6 .....82 E4
Clipper Cl NP19 .....121 F1
Clist Rd NP20 .....112 C2
Clive Cotts SY8 .....79 B4
Clive St HR1 .....93 B8
Cliveden Gr HR4 .....90 C2
Clock Ho The 6 HR6 .....82 D4
Cloisters The NP16 .....110 D2
Clomendy Rd NP44 .....106 E2
Clos Afon Llwyd NP4 .....104 C7
Clos Alun NP26 .....125 A6
Clos Alwen NP26 .....125 A7
Clos Bury Capel NP7 .....95 F6
Clos Croeso NP15 .....97 B3
Clos Durand NP7 .....95 F6
Clos Rheidol NP26 .....125 A6
Close The Caldicot NP26 .....124 E5
Kington HR5 .....112 F8
Kington HR5 .....15 D2
Portskewett NP6 .....125 D5
4 Ross-on-W HR9 .....94 F5
Closure Pl HR2 .....35 B1
Clover Cl 6 HR7 .....83 C6
Clover Rd HR7 .....83 C6
Clover Terr HR7 .....83 C6
Clover Way WR14 .....86 A2
Cloverdale Dr HR2 .....35 F4
Clows Top Rd WR6 .....13 F6
Club Rd NP4 .....104 B8
Club Row NP7 .....98 D6
Clwyd-Y-Ciap La NP4 .....103 C4
Clydach Cl NP20 .....112 E1
Clydach Sch NP7 .....98 D6
Clyffard Cres NP20 .....119 B4
Clyffes NP44 .....106 B3
Clyro CW Sch HR3 .....88 A5
Clyro Pitch HR3 .....88 B7
Clyst La HR1 .....93 D7
Clytha Cres 3 NP20 .....119 C3
Clytha Inf & Jun Sch NP20 .....119 C3
Clytha Park Rd NP20 .....119 A5
Clytha Sq NP20 .....119 B3
Coach House Field SY8 .....79 D4
Coach La HR9 .....94 D4
Coach Rd HR9 .....94 D4
Coal Rd NP16 .....75 D1
Cobb Cres NP25 .....72 B1
Cobhall Cl HR2 .....92 F5
Coham Cl WR13 .....42 E3
Cobnash Ind Est HR6 .....17 C7

Cobner Cl NP4 .....102 C1
Cock St NP26 .....132 B6
Cockatoos La HR9 .....59 B5
Cocker Ave NP44 .....106 D1
Cockshot Rd WR14 .....84 F2
Coddington Vineyard*
HR8 .....41 C5
Coder Rd SY8 .....79 F4
Coed Cae NP44 .....106 C5
Coed Camlas NP4 .....104 F5
Coed Eithen St NP4 .....101 D6
Coed Eva Jun & Inf Schs NP44 .....106 B1
Coed Garw NP44 .....107 A6
Coed Glas NP44 .....106 D1
Coed Glas La NP7 .....95 E5
Coed Lee NP44 .....106 C1
Coed Lee Ct NP44 .....106 C1
Coed Llydd NP4 .....101 D6
Coed Rd NP4 .....101 D6
Coed Terr NP4 .....101 D6
Coed y Cerrig Nature Reserve* NP7 .....61 C8
Coed-Y-Cando Rd NP4 .....104 F5
Coedcae Pl NP4 .....104 B6
Coedcae Rd NP4 .....101 D7
Coedcae Terr NP4 .....104 B6
Coedeva Mill NP44 .....112 C8
Coedygric Rd NP4 .....104 E3
Coity Terr NP4 .....101 A5
Colchester Cl GL17 .....67 D5
Cold Bath Rd HR2 .....
Cold Store The NP44 .....107 A1
Cold Western Dr SY8 .....79 E5
Coldharbour La GL18 .....59 F6
Coldharbour Rd GL15 .....76 E6
Coldnose Rd HR2 .....93 E4
Coldra Est NP18 .....120 F7
Coldra Rd NP20 .....119 A3
Coldra The NP18 .....120 F7
Coldra Wood Dr NP18 .....120 E8
Coldstream Ct NP44 .....107 A5
Coldwells Rd HR1 .....90 F6
Coleford Rd NP16 .....110 F2
Coleg Gwent NP15 .....73 D5
Coleridge Cres HR14 .....90 B2
Coleridge Gn NP44 .....106 C2
Coleridge Rd NP19 .....120 A5
College Cres HR14 .....114 B3
College Ct Ludlow SY8 .....79 C4
Tenbury Wells WR15 .....80 C4
College Glade NP18 .....114 A4
College Gn HR1 .....91 A3
College Gr WR14 .....86 F6
College Mews WR14 .....85 A4
College Rd
Caerleon NP18 .....114 B3
18 Cinderford GL14 .....67 C1
Hereford HR1 .....91 B3
Malvern WR14 .....86 F7
Pontypool NP4 .....104 D7
College Terr
7 Pontypool NP4 .....102 A1
Tenbury Wells WR15 .....80 C5
College Wlk WR15 .....11 B4
Collier St NP19 .....119 D6
Colliers Field 15 GL14 .....67 C1
Collingwood Ave 1 NP19 .....120 B2
Chepstow NP16 .....117 A4
4 Newport NP19 .....120 A4
Collingwood Cres 3 NP19 .....120 A4
Collingwood Ct NP19 .....91 D2
Collingwood Rd 6 NP19 .....120 A3
Collins Cl NP20 .....118 E2
Collins Dr BS35 .....135 C3
Colne St NP19 .....119 D5
Colston Ave NP19 .....120 A3
Colston Cl NP19 .....120 A3
Colston Pl NP19 .....120 A3
Colts Foot Cl NP10 .....129 A6
Colwall Prim Sch WR13 .....42 A4
Colwall Sta WR13 .....36 B1
Comfrey Cl NP20 .....119 A6
Commercial Pl 8 NP44 .....106 E5
Commercial Rd
Hereford HR1 .....136 C3
Newport NP19 .....119 C3
Commercial Sq HR1 .....136 C3
Commercial St
Abergavenny NP7 .....95 C5
8 Blaenavon NP4 .....101 C6
Cwmbran NP44 .....106 E2
Newport NP20 .....119 C4
Pontypool NP4 .....104 C6
Pontypool,Griffithstown NP4 .....104 E3
Common Cl NP16 .....81 D6
Common Hill La HR1 .....48 E5
Common Rd NP7 .....60 D2
NP25 .....71 E5
Common Rd Heol y Comin NP7 .....44 E1
Common Road (Heol Y Comin) NP7 .....60 D1

Common The
Abberley WR6 . . . . .13 F6
Ledbury HR8 . . . . .41 C3
Como Rd WR14 . . . . .84 F1
Compton Cl NP10 . . . . .118 B6
Conde Cl HR9 . . . . .94 C3
Conifer Cl NP18 . . . . .113 E2
Conifer Hts WR6 . . . . .22 B3
Conifer Wlk HR4 . . . . .37 C4
Conigar Cres NP15 . . . . .97 A4
Coningsby Ct HR1 . . . . .136 C3
Coningsby Hospl Cotts
HR1 . . . . .136 C3
Coningsby Rd HR6 . . . . .82 D4
Coningsby St HR1 . . . . .136 C3
Coniston Cl Malvern WR14 . . .87 C6
Newport NP19 . . . . .119 F8
Coniston Ho HR44 . . . . .106 B3
Coniston Wlk HR4 . . . . .90 D3
Connaught Pl HR4 . . . . .90 C4
Constable Dr NP10 . . . . .120 A8
Constables Cl NP20 . . . . .119 D2
Constance St NP19 . . . . .119 D7
Conway Cl NP44 . . . . .106 E4
Conway Croft NP19 . . . . .120 A4
Conway Rd
Newport NP19 . . . . .119 F5
Pontypool NP7 . . . . .104 B7
Conway Sac 2 NP19 . . . . . . .120 A4
Conway Terr NP44 . . . . .106 F5
Cook's La GL19 . . . . .51 F4
Cooks La HR2 . . . . .46 A6
Coolgreany HR2 NP20 . . . . . . .11 F4
Coolgreany Cres NP20 . . . . . .113 A1
Coomassie St NP20 . . . . .119 C1
Coombe La WR13 . . . . .31 D2
Coombe Lea Ho HR2 . . . . .76 A5
Cooper Cl NP18 . . . . .115 E1
Copper Beech Cl NP18 . . . . .113 E2
Copper Beeches Cl HR2 . . . .47 A2
Coppice Cl WR6 . . . . .13 B8
Coppice Cl Malvern WR14 . . .84 E6
Withington HR1 . . . . .38 F6
Coppice Rd GL17 . . . . .66 D3
Coppin Rise NP2 . . . . .92 D5
Coppins The NP20 . . . . .113 B3
Copse Cross St NP44 . . . . . . .94 D4
Copsewood Dr HR1 . . . . .93 F8
Copy Well HR2 . . . . .44 D3
Corbetts The WR13 . . . . .32 D5
Corelli St NP19 . . . . .119 D6
Coriander Cl NP20 . . . . .119 A6
Corinium Bsns Pk GL14 . . . .62 F1
Corinium Rd NP4 . . . . .94 C2
Cormorant Way NP10 . . . . . .128 F7
Corn Sq 9 HR6 . . . . .82 D5
Corn St Leominster HR6 . . . . .82 D5
Newport NP19 . . . . .119 C5
Cornbrook Rd NP20 . . . . .112 E2
Cornewall Cl HR2 . . . . .35 C5
Cornewall St HR4 . . . . .90 D1
Cornford Cl NP25 . . . . .137 B4
Cornhill Rd HR6 . . . . .17 F5
Cornwall Gdns WR15 . . . . . . .80 C5
Cornwall Rd NP19 . . . . .119 E7
Cornwallis Way / Ffordd
Cornwallis NP25 . . . . .96 B4
Coronation Ave
Bromyard HR7 . . . . .83 B6
Ludlow SY8 . . . . .79 B5
Coronation Rd
Kington HR5 . . . . .81 E6
Malvern WR14 . . . . .85 C5
Corporation Rd
Newport NP19 . . . . .119 C4
Newport NP19 . . . . .130 A8
Corpus Christi La 3 NP4 . . .94 E5
Corris HR4 . . . . .106 F6
Corve St SY8 . . . . .79 C5
Corve View SY8 . . . . .79 B6
Cory Pk NP44 . . . . .114 B3
Cot Farm Circ NP19 . . . . .120 F6
Cot Farm Cl NP19 . . . . .120 F6
Cot Farm Wlk NP19 . . . . .120 F6
Cot Hill NP18 . . . . .121 A6
Cotfarm Gdns NP19 . . . . .120 F6
Cothar's Pitch HR9 . . . . .59 A5
Cothill Farm HR2 . . . . .44 E6
Cotman Cl NP12 . . . . .120 A7
Cotswold Cl NP11 . . . . .90 D1
Cotswold Dr HR4 . . . . .90 B3
Cotswold Rd WR14 . . . . .85 B1
Cotswold Way NP11 . . . . .90 D1
Cotterell St HR4 . . . . .90 D1
Cotterells Hos NP4 . . . . .101 D6
Cotters Mdw HR2 . . . . .46 A7
Cottonwoods HR2 . . . . .92 C5
Cotts La HR5 . . . . .38 D4
Coughton Pl HR9 . . . . .66 C8
Coulson Cl NP20 . . . . .119 C3
Council Bglws WR6 . . . . .13 D4
Council Hos Birchall HR8 . . . .40 C1
Broadheath WR15 . . . . .12 B4
Bromyard WR6 . . . . .30 E8
Clyro HR3 . . . . .88 A5
Cwmbran NP44 . . . . .106 C4
Eastnor HR8 . . . . .51 C7
Ledbury HR8 . . . . .41 F4
Much Cowarne HR7 . . . . .29 F1
Stockton on T WR6 . . . . .13 D5
Council Hos The WR13 . . . . . .32 C5
Council Villas
Clearwell GL16 . . . . .72 F3
English Bicknor GL16 . . . . .66 B1

County Hospl
Hereford HR1 . . . . .91 B1
Pontypool NP4 . . . . .104 E4
Court Cl
Little Dewchurch HR2 . . . . .47 F2
Lugwardine HR1 . . . . .38 D4
Court Cres
Bassaleg NP10 . . . . .118 B2
Hereford HR2 . . . . .93 A6
Court Farm Bsns Pk
HR6 . . . . .30 D3
Court Farm Cl NP44 . . . . .113 A8
Court Farm Dr HR4 . . . . .37 B8
Court Farm La GL17 . . . . .67 D5
Court Farm Rd NP44 . . . . .113 A8
Court Fold LD8 . . . . .14 B5
Court Gdns Malvern WR14 . . .87 B8
St Arvans NP16 . . . . .110 B6
Court Mdw
Langstone NP18 . . . . .121 C8
Pembridge HR6 . . . . .16 C4
Court Orch HR1 . . . . .48 D5
Court Perrott Cotts
NP18 . . . . .108 B4
Court Rd Clodock HR2 . . . . . . .53 F5
Cwmbran NP44 . . . . .107 A1
Malvern WR14 . . . . .87 A7
Ross-on-W HR9 . . . . .94 F7
Walterstone HR2 . . . . .53 E3
Court Rise
Blaenavon NP4 . . . . .101 D7
Llanddewi Rhydderch NP7 . . . .69 C7
Court Robin La NP15 . . . . .74 D3
Court View NP18 . . . . .121 C8
Courtfield Cl NP25 . . . . .137 A1
Courthouse Rd NP16 . . . . .77 F3
Courtlands The
7 Cwmbran NP44 . . . . .106 B3
Winforton HR3 . . . . .24 C2
Courtnay Rise HR1 . . . . .91 B2
Courtney St NP19 . . . . .119 D6
Courtyard The
Abergavenny NP7 . . . . .95 F3
Hereford HR2 . . . . .93 B4
Newport NP18 . . . . .128 D6
Courtybella Gdns NP19 . . . . .119 D2
Courtybella Terr
Newport NP20 . . . . .119 B2
Newport NP20 . . . . .119 D2
Coverack Rd NP19 . . . . .119 F4
Covert Wlk NP44 . . . . .106 B1
Cowl Barn La WR13 . . . . .86 B2
Cowleaze NP26 . . . . .123 B3
Cowleigh Bank WR14 . . . . . . .84 D4
Cowleigh Ct WR14 . . . . .84 D3
Cowleigh Rd WR13,WR14 . . . .84 C4
Cowley La HR9 . . . . .59 C2
Cowper Cl NP20 . . . . .118 C2
Cowshed La NP10 . . . . .118 A2
Coxbury & Wyegate La
GL15 . . . . .72 D2
Coxwell Dr WR14 . . . . .85 B3
Crabtree Rd
Cinderford GL14 . . . . .67 B1
Kington HR5 . . . . .81 D6
Craddock Rd GL18 . . . . .59 F4
Cradley CE Prim Sch
WR13 . . . . .31 E2
Cradley Cl HR2 . . . . .92 C4
Craft The HR1 . . . . .38 C8
Craig Ho HR1 . . . . .93 F7
Craig Rd NP44 . . . . .106 A3
Craig View NP7 . . . . .63 B7
Craig Yr Afon NP16 . . . . .116 F7
Craig-Y-Dorth View
NP25 . . . . .96 B4
Cralves Mead WR15 . . . . .80 C5
Cranborne Cl HR2 . . . . .92 B5
Crane St NP44 . . . . .104 C6
Cranes La HR6 . . . . .82 C5
Cranham Ho NP44 . . . . .106 C2
Cranmoor Gn BS35 . . . . .135 D6
Cranstone HR4 . . . . .37 B3
Cranwell Dr HR4 . . . . .36 F6
Crawford St NP19 . . . . .119 D6
Crawford Trad Est
NP19 . . . . .119 D7
Credenleigh WR13 . . . . .31 D1
Crescent Ct 4 NP19 . . . . . . .119 F6
Crescent Pl WR15 . . . . .80 D3
Crescent Rd Colwall WR13 . .86 A1
Newport NP19 . . . . .119 F6
Crescent The
Colwall WR13 . . . . .86 A2
Cwmbran NP44 . . . . .106 D1
Hereford HR2 . . . . .90 E5
Kington HR5 . . . . .81 C6
Crest Ct WR14 . . . . .90 C4
Crest The HR7 . . . . .20 E5
Cresta Rd NP7 . . . . .95 B6
Crew's Pitch HR1,HR8 . . . . . .39 D7
Criccieth Cl NP18 . . . . .128 E5
Cricket Rd Caerwent NP16 . . .78 D1
Portskewett NP26 . . . . .125 D6
Shirenewton NP16 . . . . .78 D4
Crickhowell High Sch
NP8 . . . . .60 A5
Crickhowell Prim Sch
NP8 . . . . .60 A6
Criftins The SY7 . . . . .3 B8
Crindau Ave & Ind Sch
NP20 . . . . .119 C7
Crindau Rd NP20 . . . . .119 B8
Croes Y Gareg NP15 . . . . .70 B7

Croes-Y-Pant La NP4 . . . . . .103 C5
Croesonen Inf Sch NP7 . . . . .95 F6
Croesonen Parc NP7 . . . . .95 F6
Croesonen Rd NP7 . . . . .95 F7
Croeswen NP44 . . . . .112 F8
Croesyceiliog By-Pass
NP44 . . . . .107 B5
Croesyceiliog Comp Sch
NP44 . . . . .107 A4
Croesyceiliog Jun Sch
NP44 . . . . .107 A5
Croesyceiliog North Road Inf
Sch NP44 . . . . .107 A5
Croft Bank WR14 . . . . .84 C1
Croft Bsns Pk HR6 . . . . .82 E3
Croft Cl Bartestree HR1 . . . . . .38 E4
Hereford HR2 . . . . .92 D5
Croft Cres HR6 . . . . .84 C5
Croft Ct 1 HR9 . . . . .94 E5
Croft Farm Dr WR14 . . . . .84 C1
Croft La Leominster HR6 . . . . .18 A8
Yarpole HR6 . . . . .9 C2
Croft Rd HR2 . . . . .46 C8
Croft St HR4 . . . . .82 C4
Croft The NP15 . . . . .109 C6
Croften Mede HR44 . . . . .104 D4
Crofts Cnr 8 NP44 . . . . .106 B3
Crofts La HR9 . . . . .94 E5
Crompton Cl NP25 . . . . .137 A2
Cromwell Ct
Malvern WR14 . . . . .85 A4
6 Newport NP19 . . . . .120 A4
Cromwell Pl 9 NP44 . . . . . . .106 E5
Cromwell Rd
Chepstow NP16 . . . . .116 E5
Malvern WR14 . . . . .85 A4
Newport NP19 . . . . .120 A4
Crooked End Pl GL17 . . . . . . .66 F4
Crooked Well HR5 . . . . .81 C6
Croome Cl HR1 . . . . .91 E1
Cropper Row HR9 . . . . .94 F4
Cross Ash Jun & Inf Sch
NP7 . . . . .63 B6
Cross Collar HR2 . . . . .56 D8
Cross Elm NP15 . . . . .70 C8
Cross Gn NP26 . . . . .77 D4
Cross Hands Rd BS35 . . . . . .135 D7
Cross La
16 Newport NP19 . . . . .119 C4
Trellech NP25 . . . . .75 E7
Cross of the Tree SY7 . . . . .76 F7
Cross Roads NP7 . . . . .60 E1
Cross St Abergavenny NP7 . . .95 E5
Blaenavon NP4 . . . . .101 C6
Caerleon NP18 . . . . .114 C2
Hereford HR4 . . . . .136 B3
Hereford, Blackmarstone
HR2 . . . . .136 B1
Tenbury Wells WR15 . . . . .80 C4
Cross The NP26 . . . . .125 A5
Cross Vane NP25 . . . . .72 B3
Cross Way HR5 . . . . .24 C8
Crossfields HR4 . . . . .90 D1
Crosshands The
Llanishen NP16 . . . . .75 C4
Usk NP15 . . . . .74 E6
Crossroads The NP4 . . . . .73 A4
Crossway NP26 . . . . .124 C4
Crossway Rattle Hill NP2 . . .49 B2
Crossways Coleford GL16 . . .72 F6
Hereford HR4 . . . . .90 A2
How Caple HR1 . . . . .49 B2
Peterchurch HR2 . . . . .35 B1
Crossways Ct NP20 . . . . .123 D2
Crouch Cl NP20 . . . . .112 D1
Crowfield La GL18 . . . . .50 E2
Crowmoor La HR4 . . . . .90 E5
Crown Cl Caerleon NP18 . . . .114 C2
Cwmbran NP44 . . . . .106 D6
Crown Lea Ave WR14 . . . . .87 C8
Crown Lea Ave WR14 . . . . . . .87 C8
Crown Rd NP44 . . . . .107 B1
Crown Rise NP44 . . . . .107 B1
Crown Sq 2 NP15 . . . . .70 C2
Crown St NP19 . . . . .119 E6
Crownbridge Specl Day Sch
NP4 . . . . .106 D4
Crownlea Cl HR4 . . . . .91 C1
Crows Nest La HR2 . . . . .47 D2
Crowthers Pool HR3 . . . . .23 B3
Croydon Cl NP19 . . . . .119 E8
Croydon Ct 8 NP19 . . . . .119 E8
Crozen La HR1 . . . . .93 C7
Crumlin St NP4 . . . . .104 B6
Crumpton Hill Rd WR13,
WR14 . . . . .84 D3
Crundel End La HR4 . . . . .13 D5
Cruxwell St HR7 . . . . .83 C6
Crypt The GL18 . . . . .50 D2
Cublington Court Rd
HR2 . . . . .36 A1
Culver St GL18 . . . . .59 F3
Cumberland Pl HR4 . . . . .90 C4
Cumberland Rd 7
NP19 . . . . .119 E8
Cumbrae Ave HR2 . . . . .93 A6
Cunningham Rd NP19 . . . . . .120 F7
Curie Cl NP20 . . . . .113 A3
Curl View HR6 . . . . .16 C5
Curl View Cres HR6 . . . . .16 C5
Curlew Ave NP26 . . . . .123 B2
Curlew Cl Hereford HR2 . . . . . .92 C5
Newport NP19 . . . . .120 E1
Cursneh Ho HR6 . . . . .82 C5
Cursneh Rd HR6 . . . . .82 C5
Curwood NP4 . . . . .101 C6

Cusop Cl HR2 . . . . .92 D4
Cusop Dingle HR3 . . . . .88 F2
Cut Throat La
Gorsley HR9 . . . . .59 A2
Ledbury HR8 . . . . .89 F6
Cutmill Bridge WR15 . . . . .13 A7
Cutmill Bridge Est WR15 . . .13 A7
Cutmill Gdns WR15 . . . . .13 A7
Cutter Cl NP19 . . . . .113 F1
Cutterbach La HR5 . . . . .81 B5
Cutting The NP7 . . . . .95 B3
Cwarelau Rd HR2 . . . . .44 E2
Cwm Farm La NP44 . . . . .104 D5
Cwm La NP10 . . . . .118 B6
Cwm Rd Abbey Dore HR2 . . . .45 C1
Glascoed NP7 . . . . .73 A4
Govilon NP7 . . . . .99 F8
Cwm Sor Cl NP44 . . . . .105 B4
Cwm Stocking HR2 . . . . .53 D5
Cwm-y-Nant Fields
NP44 . . . . .106 D2
Cwmavon Rd
Abersychan NP4 . . . . .102 A6
Blaenavon NP4 . . . . .101 F4
Cwmbeth Cl NP8 . . . . .60 A6
Cwmbran Dr NP44 . . . . .106 F4
Cwmbran Sta NP44 . . . . .106 F4
Cwmcoched HR2 . . . . .53 C5
Cwmhir Rd NP44 . . . . .105 D7
Cwmma Rd HR3 . . . . .24 A6
Cwmynyscoy Rd NP4 . . . . . .104 C4
Cwrdy Cl NP44 . . . . .104 D2
Cwrdy La NP44 . . . . .104 D2
Cwrdy Rd NP44 . . . . .104 D2
Cwrdy Wlk NP44 . . . . .104 D2
Cwrt Bleddyn NP44 . . . . .106 D1
Cwrt Bryn Derwen NP15 . . . .97 C5
Cwrt Dowlas NP44 . . . . .112 E8
Cwrt Morgan NP26 . . . . .78 C1
Cwrt Newydd NP8 . . . . .60 A5
Cwrt Severn NP26 . . . . .124 E4
Cwrtglas NP44 . . . . .107 A4
Cypress Cl NP18 . . . . .113 E2
Cyril St NP19 . . . . .119 D4

D

D Row NP4 . . . . .101 A6
Dabinett Ave HR4 . . . . .90 D2
Daffaluke La NP4 . . . . .57 B2
Dahn Dr SY8 . . . . .79 E5
Dairy Cotts WR14 . . . . .58 D3
Daisy View NP4 . . . . .104 D5
Dalbury Cl WR14 . . . . .84 F4
Dale Dr HR4 . . . . .90 E5
Dale Path NP44 . . . . .106 B2
Dale Rd NP20 . . . . .120 D6
Dalebrook HR9 . . . . .59 B4
Dales The HR2 . . . . .93 B5
Dame Anna Child's Sch
LD7 . . . . .6 A6
Damson Cl SY8 . . . . .9 C6
Damson Tree La HR7 . . . . .83 B6
Damson Way WR6 . . . . .31 D6
Dan-y-Deri HR7 . . . . .95 E8
Dan-y-Graig NP26 . . . . .123 B4
Dancing Cl NP26 . . . . .123 B4
Dancing Hill NP26 . . . . .123 B3
Danbury Pk WR14 . . . . .84 E3
Danemoor Cross WR13 . . . . .42 E3
Danes Cl Chepstow NP16 . . .116 D8
Malvern WR14 . . . . .85 B1
Danesfold Dr HR6 . . . . .82 B4
Dangarga Dr NP26 . . . . .124 F5
Daniel Pl 11 NP20 . . . . .119 C3
Danton Ho NP44 . . . . .107 B4
Danum Rd HR9 . . . . .94 C2
Danybryn NP7 . . . . .68 D6
Danycoed NP7 . . . . .68 D6
Danygraig NP44 . . . . .107 A7
Darenfelin Prim Sch NP7 . . .98 B5
Darent Cl NP20 . . . . .112 C1
Darent Rd NP20 . . . . .112 C1
Darent Wlk NP20 . . . . .112 D1
Dark La Ewyas Harold HR2 . . .54 C7
Leintwardine SY7 . . . . .3 B5
Ludlow SY8 . . . . .79 E4
Dark Orch WR15 . . . . .80 D3
Darks Rd GL18 . . . . .59 C3
Darlington Ct NP19 . . . . .119 D8
Darnell's La HR9 . . . . .59 B4
Darren View NP7 . . . . .60 A6
Dart Rd NP20 . . . . .112 E1
Dartmouth Ct HR1 . . . . .91 D2
Darwin Dr NP20 . . . . .113 A3
Davenham Ct WR14 . . . . .85 A2
David Cl NP20 . . . . .119 C1
Davis Cl NP4 . . . . .104 C7
Davis Sq 14 NP20 . . . . .119 C3
Davy Cl NP20 . . . . .113 A3
Daw's Rd HR1 . . . . .136 C2
Dawes Ct HR8 . . . . .89 D5
Daymerslea Cl NP19 . . . . .94 D4
De Ballon Cl NP7 . . . . .95 E3
De Braose Cl NP7 . . . . .95 E3
De Cantelupe Cl NP7 . . . . . . .95 E3
De Clere Way NP25 . . . . .75 F8
De Grosmont Cl NP7 . . . . .95 E3
De Lacy Ct 6 HR1 . . . . .93 B8
De Montfort Cl NP7 . . . . .95 E3
De Wallingford Cl NP7 . . . . . .95 E3
Deaconsfield HR1 . . . . .93 E8
Dean Cl WR15 . . . . .80 D6
Dean Mdws GL17 . . . . .67 D5
Dean St NP19 . . . . .119 E6

Dean Swift Cl HR9 . . . . .65 F6
Dean's Wlk GL17 . . . . .67 B4
Deanery Gdns NP20 . . . . .119 B4
Deans Gdns NP16 . . . . .110 D1
Deans Hill NP16 . . . . .116 D8
Deans The HR2 . . . . .46 A6
Declere Way NP25 . . . . .75 F8
Deen's Ct HR4 . . . . .136 B2
Deepweir NP26 . . . . .125 B4
Deepweir Gdns NP26 . . . . . . .125 B4
Deepweir Gdns NP26 . . . . . . .125 B4
Deer Park Cl HR2 . . . . .35 C5
Deerbrook NP44 . . . . .106 B2
Deerfold HR2 . . . . .92 F6
Deerhurst Dr HR2 . . . . .92 C6
Delafield Rd NP7 . . . . .95 B6
Delamere Rd
Malvern WR14 . . . . .85 B1
Tedstone Delamere HR7 . . . . . .21 B5
Delius Cl Newport NP19 . . . .120 C5
Rogerstone NP10 . . . . .118 A6
Dell Prim Sch The NP16 . . . .110 E1
Dell The HR3 . . . . .35 A7
Dell View NP16 . . . . .116 E8
Dempsey Cl HR2 . . . . .93 A5
Denbigh Dr NP16 . . . . .117 A5
Denbigh Rd NP19 . . . . .119 F8
Denbury Mews NP15 . . . . . . .97 B4
Dene Ind Est HR2 . . . . .46 C8
Dene Magna Sch GL17 . . . . . .67 D4
Denehurst GL17 . . . . .66 F3
Denison Cl WR14 . . . . .85 B2
Denmark Dr HR6 . . . . .82 B7
Denny Isle Dr BS35 . . . . .135 A6
Denny View NP26 . . . . .125 B4
Dents Cl NP19 . . . . .120 D5
Dents Hill NP19 . . . . .120 D5
Derby Gr NP19 . . . . .120 E6
Dereham Ct WR14 . . . . .84 F3
Deri Rd Abergavenny NP7 . . . .95 E6
Abergavenny, Pen-y-Pound
NP7 . . . . .95 D6
Dernside Cl HR4 . . . . .27 E3
Derry The HR4 . . . . .24 C4
Derwen Deg NP7 . . . . .99 F8
Derwen Deg Cl NP7 . . . . .99 F8
Derwen Fawr NP7 . . . . .60 B5
Derwen Way NP7 . . . . .95 B6
Derwent Cl NP20 . . . . .112 C1
Derwent Dr HR4 . . . . .90 D3
Derwent Ho 3 NP44 . . . . .106 C2
Devauden Rd NP16 . . . . .110 B7
Devereux Cl HR1 . . . . .91 E1
Devon Ct NP18 . . . . .114 A3
Devon Pl NP20 . . . . .119 B5
Dewpond Cl HR4 . . . . .90 E5
Dewsland Park Rd
NP20 . . . . .119 B3
Dewston Gdns NP26 . . . . . . .124 E5
Dewstow Cl NP26 . . . . .124 E5
Dewstow Rd NP26 . . . . .124 E5
Dewstow St NP19 . . . . .119 F4
Dibdin Cl NP19 . . . . .120 C5
Dickens Dr NP20 . . . . .118 E2
Dicks Pitch HR7 . . . . .54 C8
Digeddi Villas HR3 . . . . .33 A3
Dilwyn Sch HR4 . . . . .16 F1
Dinas Path NP44 . . . . .106 B2
Dinch Hill NP26 . . . . .123 B3
Dinch Hill La NP26 . . . . .123 B3
Dinedor Ave HR2 . . . . .92 F5
Dingle La 2 NP44 . . . . .106 C1
Dingle Rd
Abergavenny NP7 . . . . .95 B6
Leigh WR6 . . . . .32 C8
Pontypool NP4 . . . . .104 D5
Dingle The HR4 . . . . .90 B3
Dinham SY8 . . . . .79 B3
Dinham House Mus*
SY8 . . . . .79 B3
Dinmore Rd NP26 . . . . .78 C1
Dishley St HR6 . . . . .82 C4
Disraeli Ct HR4 . . . . .136 B3
Ditch Hill La NP26 . . . . .123 B2
Dixey Ct WR14 . . . . .84 E2
Dixton Cl NP25 . . . . .137 C3
Dixton Rd NP25 . . . . .137 C3
Dockins Hill Way GL17 . . . . . .67 F4
Docks Way NP20 . . . . .129 A8
Dockwell Terr NP18 . . . . .121 B4
Dodmore La SY8 . . . . .79 D5
Dog Kennel La SY7 . . . . .2 C5
Dogwood Cl WR14 . . . . .85 D3
Dolphin St NP20 . . . . .119 B3
Don Cl NP20 . . . . .112 C1
Doncaster Ave HR4 . . . . .90 C4
Donkey Lane (Avenue Road)
SY8 . . . . .5 B1
Dorchester Way HR2 . . . . .92 B6
Dore Abbey (rems of)*
HR2 . . . . .45 C1
Dore Hamlet HR2 . . . . .45 C1
Dorleigh Ct NP44 . . . . .106 B1
Dormington Dr HR1 . . . . .91 D1
Dorset Cl NP19 . . . . .119 B5
Dorset Cres NP19 . . . . .120 B2
Dorstone Hill HR3 . . . . .34 F5
Dorstone Wlk NP44 . . . . .107 B4
Dos Cotts HR2 . . . . .119 B6
Dos Rd NP20 . . . . .119 B6
Dove Cots HR4 . . . . .36 D8
Dovecote HR4 . . . . .37 A6
Dovecote La HR4 . . . . .37 A6
Doward Cl HR1 . . . . .91 B4
Downhams The NP25 . . . . . . .96 F4
Downing St NP19 . . . . .120 A3

Downs Sch The WR13 . . . . . . .86 B3
Downton View SY8 . . . . .79 E5
Drag Rd HR9 . . . . .65 E3
Dragon La NP7 . . . . .60 F1
Dragons Cross WR13 . . . . .32 C5
Dragons La WR13,WR14 . . . . .32 C5
Drain The HR3 . . . . .34 B3
Drake Cl NP19 . . . . .120 E6
Drake Ct HR4 . . . . .90 C3
Drake St WR13 . . . . .42 F2
Drapers La **8** HR6 . . . . .82 D5
Drayton Cl NP4 . . . . .106 C3
Drinkwater Cl HR8 . . . . .89 C5
Drinkwater La NP18 . . . . .118 F2
Drovers Mews **8** NP20 . . . . .119 C3
Drugger's End La WR13 . . .42 E1
Drury La GL19 . . . . .51 D2
Dry Thistle Cl HR7 . . . . .83 B6
Drybridge Ho HR2 . . . . .136 B1
Drybridge Pk NP25 . . . . .137 A2
Drybridge St NP25 . . . . .137 A2
Drybridge Terr NP25 . . . . . . .137 A2
Drybrook Cl NP44 . . . . .106 F3
Drybrook Rd GL17 . . . . .67 B4
Dryden Cl WR14 . . . . .85 A2
Duchess Cl NP25 . . . . .96 D7
Duchess Rd NP25 . . . . .96 D7
Duck St HR4 . . . . .35 E8
Duckpool La NP26 . . . . .77 B3
Duckpool Rd NP19 . . . . .119 E6
Dudley St NP19 . . . . .119 E4
Duffield's La NP25 . . . . .72 C5
Duffryn Cl NP10 . . . . .118 A3
Duffryn Dr NP10 . . . . .118 A3
Duffryn High Sch NP10 . . . .128 F6
Duffryn Jun Sch NP10 . . . . .128 F7
Duffryn Way NP10 . . . . .128 E6
Duke of Edinburgh Way
WR14 . . . . .85 C6
Duke of York Rd GL16 . . . .72 C7
Duke St
4 Blaenavon NP4 . . . . . . .101 C6
Kington HR5 . . . . .81 D6
Newport NP20 . . . . .119 D3
Duke's Way WR14 . . . . .87 C6
Duke's Wlk HR6 . . . . .82 D4
Dulas Ave NP44 . . . . .92 E5
Dulas Terr HR3 . . . . .88 E4
Dumbrehole La
Ashford Carbonell SY8 . . . . . .5 B1
Brimfield SY8 . . . . .10 B8
Dumbleton La WR15 . . . . . .13 A7
Dumfries Cl NP7 . . . . .95 B3
Dumfries Pl **16** NP20 . . . . .119 D4
Dunfield La HR5,LD8 . . . . . .14 D5
Dunkerton's Cider Mill*
HR6 .16 D3
Dunn Sq **20** NP20 . . . . .119 C3
Dunnet Gdns NP4 . . . . .105 B3
Dunns Copse HR8 . . . . .89 E3
Dunoon Mead HR2 . . . . .92 E5
Dunraven Dr NP10 . . . . .128 D5
Dunraven Rd NP44 . . . . .107 B2
Dunstable Rd NP19 . . . . . . .120 E5
Dunster Cl HR2 . . . . .92 D6
Dunstone Pl GL17 . . . . .67 D5
Durand Jun & Inf Sch
NP26 . . . . .125 A4
Durand Rd NP26 . . . . .124 F4
Durbridge Rd GL19 . . . . .51 C1
Durham La NP19 . . . . .119 D7
Durham Rd NP19 . . . . .119 E7
Durham Road Jun & Inf Sch
NP19 . . . . .119 D7
Duttons La GL17 . . . . .66 C7
Duxmere Dr HR9 . . . . .94 D3
Dyffryn La
Coedkernew NP10 . . . . .128 C4
Newport NP20 . . . . .128 B6
Dyffryn The NP15 . . . . .74 E2
Dyke House La HR8 . . . . .51 B4
Dymond Cl HR1 . . . . .93 C7
Dynevor Cl NP44 . . . . .107 B3
Dyson Dr WR14 . . . . .85 D1
Dyson Perrins CE High Sch
WR14 . . . . .84 F5

E

E Row NP4 . . . . .101 A6
Eagle Cl NP26 . . . . .125 A4
Eardisley CE Prim Sch
HR3 .24 E4
Eardisley Cl HR2 . . . . .92 D4
Eardisley Rd HR5 . . . . .81 E5
Eardiston Ho WR15 . . . . . . .13 A7
Earlsmede **8** NP44 . . . . . . .106 B3
Earlswood Rd NP16 . . . . .78 C4
Easinghope La WR6 . . . . .22 C3
East Ave NP4 . . . . .104 E1
East Bank Rd NP19 . . . . .119 F8
East Dock Rd NP20 . . . . .119 C1
East Grove Rd NP19 . . . . . . .120 C5
East Jefferson St NP16 . . . .78 D2
East Link GL17 . . . . .67 D5
East Lynne Gdns NP18 . . . .114 C3
East Market St NP20 . . . . . .119 D3
East Penn St NP16 . . . . .78 D2
East Rd NP44 . . . . .112 F8
East Roedin NP44 . . . . .112 C8
East St Hereford HR1 . . . . . .136 C2
Newport NP20 . . . . .119 C3
Pembridge HR6 . . . . .28 B1
St Briavels GL15 . . . . .76 F7
East Usk Lighthouse*
NP18 . . . . .130 A2

East Usk Rd NP19 . . . . .119 C6
East View Pontypool NP4 . .104 E2
Pontypool, Sowhill NP4 . . . .104 B6
East Way Rd NP20 . . . . .119 D1
Eastabrook Cl WR14 . . . . . . .84 F5
Eastern Ave Hereford HR4 . .90 B2
Mitcheldean GL17 . . . . .67 D5
Eastfield Cl NP18 . . . . .114 A4
Eastfield Dr NP18 . . . . .114 A4
Eastfield Mews NP18 . . . . .114 A4
Eastfield Rd
Caerleon NP18 . . . . .114 A4
Ross-on-W HR9 . . . . .94 D3
Eastfield View NP18 . . . . . .114 A4
Eastfield Way NP18 . . . . . . .114 A4
Eastgate Cres NP26 . . . . .78 C1
Easthampton Barn HR6 . . .42 A2
Eastholme Cl NP18 . . . . .92 C5
Eastholme Ct HR2 . . . . .92 C5
Eastmoor Rd NP19 . . . . .120 C3
Eastnor Castle* HR8 . . . .51 B7
Eastnor CE Prim Sch
HR8 .51 B8
Eastnor Dr HR1 . . . . .91 D2
Eastnor Rd HR8 . . . . .51 B4
Eastway NP4 . . . . .103 B2
Eastwood Durlow Comm
HR1 .39 F1
Eastwood Rd GL17 . . . . .67 B3
Eaton Barns HR6 . . . . .82 F3
Eaton Cres NP26 . . . . .82 D4
Eaton Pl HR4 . . . . .136 B3
Eaton Rd WR14 . . . . .86 C3
Ebbw Rd NP26 . . . . .124 F6
Ebenezer Dr NP10 . . . . .118 B4
Ebenezer Terr **14** NP20 . . .119 C4
Ebley Gdns NP26 . . . . .125 B4
Ebnal Cl HR6 . . . . .82 A4
Ebrington Rd WR14 . . . . . . .84 C2
Ebury Ho NP44 . . . . .107 B4
Eccroyd Pk HR4 . . . . .89 B4
Edde Cross St HR9 . . . . .94 D5
Eddys La GL17 . . . . .66 C3
Eden La HR2 . . . . .47 C3
Edgar St HR4 . . . . .136 B4
Edgcort NP4 . . . . .106 B1
Edge Hills Cl **16** GL16 . . . .67 C1
Edge Hills Rd GL14 . . . . .67 C1
Edgecombe HR4 . . . . .89 A4
Edgehill HR4 . . . . .107 B1
Edinburgh Ct NP44 . . . . . . .106 A3
Edison Ridge NP20 . . . . .113 A3
Edith Berry Ct WR14 . . . . . .85 B1
Edith Wlk WR14 . . . . .84 F1
Edlogan Sq NP44 . . . . .107 A6
Edlogan Way NP44 . . . . . . .107 A5
Edlogan Way (Ffordd
Eologan) NP44 . . . . .106 F4
Edmond Rd NP20 . . . . .117 B8
Edmonton Ct NP44 . . . . . . .104 C7
Edney View NP10 . . . . .128 F7
Ednoll Cotts WR6 . . . . .32 D7
Edward German Cres
NP19 . . . . .120 E5
Edward St
Pontypool, Sowhill NP4 . . . .104 B7
Pontypool,Griffithstown
NP4 . . . . .104 A3
Edward Vii Ave NP20 . . . . .118 F4
Edward VII Cres NP20 . . . . .119 A5
Edward VII La NP20 . . . . . . .119 A5
Edwards Cl GL17 . . . . .66 D3
Edwin Ind Est NP19 . . . . . . .119 D7
Edwin St NP20 . . . . .119 C7
Eign Gate HR4 . . . . .136 B3
Eign Mill Rd HR1 . . . . .93 C7
Eign Rd HR1 . . . . .93 B7
Eign St HR4 . . . . .136 B3
Eisteddfod Gr NP19 . . . . . . .120 E6
Elaine Cres NP19 . . . . .119 F7
Elan Cl NP20 . . . . .112 E1
Elan Way NP20 . . . . .112 E1
Elan Wlk NP44 . . . . .106 C2
Elder Cl NP18 . . . . .113 F2
Eleanor Ave HR1 . . . . .93 F7
Elgam Ave NP4 . . . . .101 C2
Elgam Gn NP4 . . . . .101 C2
Elgar Ave Hereford HR1 . . . .93 D7
Malvern WR14 . . . . .85 A3
Elgar Circ NP19 . . . . .120 D5
Elgar Cl Ledbury HR8 . . . . . .89 C3
Newport NP19 . . . . .120 D5
Elizabeth Ct HR1 . . . . .91 C1
Elizabeth Dr HR5 . . . . .81 E6
Elizabeth Sparks Cl
NP26 . . . . .124 B4
Elled Rd HR4 . . . . .104 A8
Ellick St NP4 . . . . .101 C7
Elliot Cl NP4 . . . . .85 A2
Ellipse The NP4 . . . . .104 D1
Ellwood Path NP44 . . . . . . .106 B2
Elm Ave NP26 . . . . .123 C2
Elm Cl Leominster HR6 . . . . .82 D3
Llantarnam NP18 . . . . .114 E6
Pontypool NP4 . . . . .102 B2
Tutshill NP16 . . . . .111 A2
Elm Dr Llanellen NP7 . . . . . .68 D5
Monmouth NP25 . . . . .96 B4
Elm Drive (Rhodfa Llwyfen)
NP4 .68 D5
Elm Gr Clehonger HR2 . . . . .46 D8
Pontypool NP4 . . . . .60 D8
Newport NP20 . . . . .113 B2
Pontypool NP4 . . . . .60 D8
Elm Rd Caldicot NP26 . . . . .124 E6
Credenhill HR4 . . . . .37 A6
Hereford HR1 . . . . .91 B1

Elm Rd continued
Tutshill NP16 . . . . .111 A2
Elm Wlk SY8 . . . . .79 C6
Elmdale Chepstow NP16 . .110 E1
Ewyas Harold HR2 . . . . .54 D7
Elmdean **5** GL14 . . . . .67 C1
Elmhurst Cl NP4 . . . . .102 B1
Elmley Cl WR14 . . . . .85 B1
Elms Dr WR13 . . . . .42 F2
Elms Hill NP26 . . . . .123 D3
Elms La Abergavenny NP7 . .61 F1
Llanvapley NP7 . . . . .62 A2
Elms Rd NP7 . . . . .99 F8
Elms Sch The WR13 . . . . . . .42 A4
Elms The NP26 . . . . .123 D4
Elmsdale Rd HR8 . . . . .89 D3
Elmtree Cotts HR8 . . . . .89 D8
Elstob Way NP44 . . . . .137 A1
Elvicta Est HR8 . . . . .60 B4
Elysia St NP19 . . . . .119 D7
Emlyn Ave HR4 . . . . .90 C1
Emlyn Sq **20** NP20 . . . . . . .119 C4
Emlyn St **20** NP20 . . . . . . .119 C4
Endyngs NP44 . . . . .106 B1
Engadine Cl WR14 . . . . .84 A2
Engine Row NP4 . . . . .101 B7
English Bicknor CE Prim Sch
GL16 . . . . .66 B2
Ennerdale Cl NP19 . . . . .119 F8
Enterprise Park Ind Est
NP20 . . . . .119 D3
Enterprise Way NP20 . . . . .119 D3
Enville Cl NP19 . . . . .118 E4
Enville Rd NP19 . . . . .118 E4
Epsom Wlk NP4 . . . . .90 D4
Eric Brown Cl HR2 . . . . .92 C4
Eric Coates Cl NP19 . . . . . .120 E4
Eric Coates Wlk NP19 . . . .120 E4
Eschol Cl NP20 . . . . .120 B3
Eschol Ct NP19 . . . . .120 A3
Escley Dr HR2 . . . . .92 E6
Esmond Rd HR1 . . . . .136 C4
Esperanto Way NP19 . . . . .119 E1
Essex Ct NP18 . . . . .114 A3
Essex St NP19 . . . . .119 D6
Estate Rd Blaenavon NP4 . .101 B7
Cinderford GL14 . . . . .67 B1
Pontypool NP4 . . . . .104 B8
Estavarney La NP15 . . . . . . .73 C6
Eston Ave WR14 . . . . .87 C8
Estuary Rd NP19 . . . . .120 D1
Estuary View NP19 . . . . . . .125 B4
Ethelstan Cres HR2 . . . . .92 D5
Ethley Dr HR5 . . . . .70 C2
Etnam St HR6 . . . . .82 D4
Etna Rd NP19 . . . . .119 D5
Etonhurst Wlk HR4 . . . . . . .87 B8
Evans St NP20 . . . . .119 C5
Eve's Well Ct NP19 . . . . . . .119 E5
Evendine Cnr WR13 . . . . . . .42 A4
Evendine La WR13 . . . . .42 A4
Everest Cres NP44 . . . . .90 B3
Everest Dr NP8 . . . . .60 A5
Evergreen NP20 . . . . .106 B2
Eversley Cl WR14 . . . . .85 B2
Eversley Gr WR14 . . . . .85 B2
Everstone Rise HR9 . . . . .57 A4
Evesham Ct NP20 . . . . .120 B3
Eveswell Jun & Inf Sch
NP19 . . . . .119 F5
Eveswell La **1** NP19 . . . . .119 F5
Eveswell Park Rd NP19 . . .119 F5
Eveswell St NP19 . . . . .119 F5
Evtol Ind Est NP20 . . . . .119 D2
Ewyas Harold Comm
HR2 .45 B1
Ewyas Harold Prim Sch
HR2 .54 C7
Exe Rd NP20 . . . . .112 E1
Exeter Cl NP44 . . . . .106 A3
Exeter Rd **8** NP19 . . . . . . .119 E6
Exeter St NP19 . . . . .119 E5
Exford Gr NP7 . . . . .60 D1
Eye La HR6 . . . . .9 E2
Eywood La HR5 . . . . .15 C6

F

Factory Rd NP20 . . . . .119 B6
Fair View NP16 . . . . .116 D6
Fairfax Rd NP19 . . . . .120 A4
Fairfax View **3** NP15 . . . . .70 C7
Fairfield Penperlleni NP4 . .103 E6
Pontypool NP4 . . . . .104 A7
Fairfield Cl
Caerleon NP18 . . . . .113 F3
Caldicot NP26 . . . . .124 E5
Fairfield Gn HR1 . . . . .48 D5
Fairfield High Sch HR4 . . . .35 B1
Fairfield Rd
Caerleon NP18 . . . . .113 F3
Chepstow NP16 . . . . .116 E6
Fairfields Rd HR8 . . . . .89 D3
Fairhill NP44 . . . . .106 B2
Fairhill Wlk NP44 . . . . .106 B2
Fairholme Rd NP7 . . . . .60 D2
Fairoak NP16 . . . . .75 F1
Fairoak Ave NP19 . . . . .119 E6
Fairoak Ct **4** NP19 . . . . . .119 E6
Fairoak Gdns **8** NP19 . . .119 E6
Fairoak La NP44 . . . . .107 A4
Fairoak Terr NP19 . . . . .119 E5
Fairplay Cotts GL17 . . . . . . .55 C1
Fairview HR2 . . . . .85 E5
Fairview Cl NP25 . . . . .96 F4
Fairview Ct NP44 . . . . .104 A8

Fairwater Cl NP44 . . . . .106 B2
Fairwater High Sch
NP44 . . . . .106 A2
Fairwater Jun & Inf Schs
NP44 . . . . .106 C2
Fairwater Square Shops
NP44 . . . . .106 B1
Fairwater Way Ffordd
Fairwater NP44 . . . . .106 B1
Fairway Cl NP10 . . . . .118 A7
Fairway The NP44 . . . . .105 B4
Fakenham Dr HR4 . . . . .90 D5
Falaise Cl HR9 . . . . .94 D3
Falcon Cl NP26 . . . . .125 A4
Falcon Cotts HR1 . . . . .49 A3
Falcon La HR8 . . . . .40 E1
Falconer Pl HR4 . . . . .90 D4
Fallowfield **8** NP44 . . . . . .106 B1
Fallowfield Cl HR2 . . . . .92 E6
Fallowfield Dr NP19 . . . . . .120 C3
Falstaff Rd HR2 . . . . .92 E4
Far Meadow Rd HR6 . . . . . . .17 F5
Faraday Cl NP20 . . . . .112 F2
Faraday Rd HR4 . . . . .90 E3
Farjeon Cl HR8 . . . . .89 C4
Farlays NP44 . . . . .106 A1
Farley Rd WR14 . . . . .85 B4
Farleys The WR13 . . . . .31 D2
Farlow Wlk NP44 . . . . .106 D2
Farm Ct
Bishops Frome WR6 . . . . . . .30 D3
Lucton HR6 . . . . .29 A6
Farm House Cl HR1 . . . . .91 B4
Farm La Cwmbran NP44 . . .106 F4
Easter Compton BS35 . . . . .135 E2
Llangrove HR9 . . . . .65 B5
Newport NP19 . . . . .119 F7
Farm Rd Pontypool NP4 . . .104 C5
Ruardean Woodside GL17 . .66 F3
Farmfield La NP18 . . . . .130 D3
Farmhouse Mews NP25 . . .96 D7
Farmwood Cl NP19 . . . . . . .120 B5
Farnaby Cl NP19 . . . . .120 E5
Farr Cl HR1 . . . . .91 D1
Farriers Orch WR6 . . . . .30 F1
Farriers Way HR14 . . . . .136 C4
Farringdon Ave HR2 . . . . . . .92 C5
Faulkner Rd NP20 . . . . .119 B5
Fawley Cl HR1 . . . . .91 B4
Fawley Cross HR1 . . . . .48 E1
Fayre Oakes Dr HR4 . . . . . . .90 B2
Fayre Oakes Gn HR4 . . . . . . .90 C2
Fayre Oakes Rd HR4 . . . . . . .90 C2
Fayre Oaks Home Pk
HR4 .90 A2
FC Morgan Cl HR2 . . . . .93 B5
Fedw Wood HR4 . . . . .116 C8
Feering St NP19 . . . . .119 E4
Felnex Ind Est NP19 . . . . . .119 E1
Fenner Brockway Cl **1**
NP19 . . . . .120 D7
Fern Bank HR2 . . . . .54 C8
Fern Ct NP16 . . . . .116 F5
Fern Rise NP20 . . . . .113 B3
Fernbank Rd NP44 . . . . .106 B2
Fernbank Rd HR9 . . . . .94 D3
Ferncroft Way NP4 . . . . . . .102 B2
Ferndale Cl **28** GL14 . . . . .67 C1
Ferndale Rd HR4 . . . . .90 B4
Ferndown Rd HR8 . . . . .89 D2
Ferneycross NP26 . . . . .124 E5
Fernhill Gr WR14 . . . . .85 A1
Fernleigh Rd NP20 . . . . .113 B3
Fernside NP10 . . . . .118 A7
Ferrers St HR1 . . . . .136 C2
Ferrie La HR1 . . . . .65 E3
Ferry La HR1 . . . . .48 D5
Ferry Way NP16 . . . . .117 B4
Festival Cres NP44 . . . . .105 B4
Fetty Pl HR4 . . . . .106 B1
Fforest Glade NP19 . . . . . . .119 F6
Ffrwd Rd NP4 . . . . .102 A4
Ffynnonau HR9 . . . . .60 A6
Fidler's Cross HR9 . . . . .58 E3
Field Farm Mews HR2 . . . . .92 D5
Field Grove View HR1 . . . . .91 B4
Field La Eardisley WR14 . . . .24 C5
Little Hereford SY8,WR15 . .10 E6
Field View NP44 . . . . .107 A5
Field Way HR1 . . . . .91 B4
Fieldfare HR2 . . . . .47 F2
Fieldfare Cl WR14 . . . . .84 D6
Fielding Ho HR1 . . . . .93 F7
Fieldings **7** NP44 . . . . . . .106 B1
Fields Ave NP44 . . . . .106 D6
Fields Park Cres NP20 . . . .119 A5
Fields Park Cres NP20 . . . .119 A5
Fields Park Gdns NP20 . . .119 A5
Fields Park Rd NP20 . . . . . .118 F5
Fields Rd Cwmbran NP44 . .112 F8
Newport NP19 . . . . .119 A5
Fieldway HR1 . . . . .91 B4
Fifth St NP19 . . . . .94 D7
Fifth St NP19 . . . . .119 F7
Filey Rd NP19 . . . . .119 D7
Fincher's Cnr WR13 . . . . . . .31 D1
Fine St NP20 . . . . .35 A2
Fir Tree La HR2 . . . . .93 C6
Firbank Ave NP19 . . . . .120 A7
Firbank Cl NP19 . . . . .120 A7
Firemens Qtrs HR1 . . . . .93 D5
Firs Cl WR14 . . . . .86 F6
Firs La Bromyard HR7 . . . . . .83 B6
Bromyard HR7 . . . . .83 C6
Firs Mead HR9 . . . . .94 C3
Firs Orch HR7 . . . . .83 B6

Fairwater Cl NP44 . . . . .106 B2
Firs Rd Abergavenny NP7 . . .95 F5
Abergavenny, Mardy NP7 . . .95 F8
Caldicot NP26 . . . . .124 F6
Llanvapley NP7 . . . . .62 D1
Ross-on-W HR9 . . . . .94 C3
Firs The Blaenavon NP4 . . .101 E6
Newport NP20 . . . . .113 C2
The Bage HR3 . . . . .34 B6
Firs Wlk **11** HR7 . . . . .83 C6
First Ave HR4 . . . . .94 D7
First St NP19 . . . . .130 B8
Firtree Cl NP18 . . . . .113 E2
Fish House La NP18 . . . . . . .130 B3
Fish St SY8 . . . . .79 C4
Fisher Cl NP19 . . . . .120 F7
Fisherman's Reach HR9 . . .94 B5
Fisherman's Wlk NP16 . . . .116 F5
Fishmore Cl SY8 . . . . .79 C6
Fishmore Rd SY8 . . . . .79 C6
Fishmore View SY8 . . . . .79 C6
Fitzosborn Cl NP16 . . . . . . .116 E7
Fitzosborn Cl NP16 . . . . . . .116 E7
Fitzjames Cl NP25 . . . . .137 A1
Fitzwalter Rd NP26 . . . . . . .124 F4
Five Locks Cl NP44 . . . . . . .106 D7
Five Locks Rd NP44 . . . . . . .106 D6
Five Oaks Cl WR14 . . . . .87 D8
Five Oaks La NP44 . . . . . . .107 A5
Flaggoner's Cl HR7 . . . . .83 A6
Flannel St HR7 . . . . .95 D5
Flaxley Dr HR2 . . . . .92 D6
Fleetwood Cl NP19 . . . . . . .119 F4
Fleming Cl NP19 . . . . .113 A2
Flint Cl NP19 . . . . .120 A7
Flint Ct NP19 . . . . .120 A7
Floodgates HR5 . . . . .81 B6
Florence Pl NP4 . . . . .104 E2
Floyds La HR8 . . . . .41 C3
Foldgate La SY8 . . . . .79 F3
Foldgate View SY8 . . . . .79 F3
Foley Ho NP44 . . . . .107 B4
Foley St HR1 . . . . .93 B8
Foley Terr WR14 . . . . .86 E7
Foley Trad Est HR1 . . . . .93 C8
Folly Cl WR6 . . . . .31 F8
Folly La
English Bicknor GL16 . . . . . .66 A1
Hereford HR1 . . . . .93 C1
Penperlleni NP4 . . . . .103 A3
Pontypool NP4 . . . . .102 D1
Folly Rd Alfrick WR6 . . . . . . .32 A8
Pontypool NP4 . . . . .102 C1
Fonteine Ct HR9 . . . . .94 D5
Footway Croft HR6 . . . . .17 F5
Ford Cl WR14 . . . . .87 C8
Ford Farm La HR8 . . . . .51 B4
Ford La GL18 . . . . .59 D4
Ford St Newport NP20 . . . .119 B5
Presteigne LD8 . . . . .6 E3
Wigmore HR6 . . . . .18 E3
Fording La HR9 . . . . .58 F4
Fordshill Rd HR2 . . . . .92 C6
Fordwich Cl NP16 . . . . .110 B5
Forest Cl Cwmbran NP44 . .112 B8
Newport NP19 . . . . .119 F6
Staunton GL16 . . . . .72 E7
Forest Dr NP7 . . . . .60 D1
Forest of Dean Mechanical
Organ Mus* GL17 . . . .67 B5
Forest Pl HR1 . . . . .93 F7
Forest Rd Hay-on-W HR3 . .88 D2
Ruardean Woodside GL17 . .66 F3
Forest Rise
8 Cinderford GL14 . . . . . .67 D1
Upper Lydbrook GL17 . . . . .66 E4
Forest Vale Ind Est GL14 . .67 B1
Forest Vale Rd GL14 . . . . . .67 B1
Forest View NP25 . . . . .72 B1
Forest View Prim Sch
GL14 . . . . .67 D1
Foresters' Almshouses
HR4 .90 D1
Forge Cl NP18 . . . . .114 B4
Forge Cotts
Fownhope HR1 . . . . .48 D5
Monmouth NP25 . . . . .137 A4
Forge Ctyd HR8 . . . . .40 B6
Forge Gdns NP16 . . . . .110 B6
Forge Hammer Ind Est
NP44 . . . . .106 D4
Forge Hill GL17 . . . . .67 C4
Forge La Bassaleg NP10 . . .118 B2
King's Thorn HR2 . . . . .47 B2
Leintwardine SY8 . . . . .7 F5
Forge Mdws HR1 . . . . .21 F8
Forge Mews NP10 . . . . .118 B2
Forge Rd Bassaleg NP10 . .118 C1
Blaenavon NP4 . . . . .101 B6
Monmouth NP25 . . . . .137 A4
Forge Row Cwmavon NP4 . .68 A1
Maesygwartha NP7 . . . . .98 E8
Forge Side Rd NP4 . . . . . . .101 B5
Forge The Kington HR5 . . . .15 D6
Lower Lydbrook GL17 . . . . .66 C3
Forgebank HR8 . . . . .41 A6
Forgeside NP4 . . . . .106 E4
Forresters Rd WR15 . . . . . .136 F5
Fort View NP10 . . . . .118 A4
Fortlee NP20 . . . . .118 E3
Forty's Pitch HR9 . . . . .94 D3
Fosse Cl NP4 . . . . .120 C2
Fosse Rd NP19 . . . . .120 C2
Fosterville Cres NP7 . . . . . . .95 E4

Foundry Rd **17** GL14 . . . . .67 C1
Fountain Rd NP4 . . . . .104 E5
Fountain Way NP16 . . . . .116 F4
Fountains Cl HR2 . . . . . . .92 C6
Four Acres HR4 . . . . .37 B4
Four Ash Ct NP15 . . . . . . .97 B4
Four Ash St NP15 . . . . . . .97 B4
Fourteen Locks Canal Ctr*
  NP10 . . . . .118 B6
Fourth Ave HR9 . . . . .94 D7
Fourth St NP19 . . . . .130 B8
Fowbridge Gdns HR9 . . . . .66 C8
Fowler St NP4 . . . . .104 A8
Fownhope Cl HR1 . . . . . . .48 D5
Fox La WR6 . . . . .13 B8
Foxes Bridge Rd GL14 . . . .67 B1
Foxglove Cl
  Malvern WR14 . . . . .87 D7
  Ross-on-W HR9 . . . . .94 D6
Foxhalls Rattle Hill HR1 . .49 C3
Foxwhelp Cl HR4 . . . . .36 A2
Foxwood Cl HR2 . . . . .92 E6
Francis Cl NP20 . . . . .119 C3
Francis Dr NP20 . . . . .119 C3
Francis Morris Est NP4 . .101 D6
Francis St **21** NP20 . . . . .119 C3
Frank Owen Ct HR1 . . . . . .91 B2
Frank St NP19 . . . . .119 C6
Franklin Wlk HR4 . . . . .90 B1
Franks Ave HR2 . . . . .93 B5
Fraser Cl WR14 . . . . .87 A6
Fraser Ct HR4 . . . . .136 B3
Fred Edwards Cl NP19 . . .120 F5
Freda Pearce Cl HR2 . . . .92 E6
Frederick Ave HR1 . . . . . . .91 A3
Frederick Mews NP20 . . . .119 D3
Frederick Rd WR14 . . . . . .84 F4
Frederick St NP20 . . . . . .119 D3
Freehold Land Rd NP4 . . .102 A1
Freeminers Way **2** GL14 .67 D1
French La NP25 . . . . .72 C4
Freshwater Rd NP19 . . . .120 D1
Friars Ct NP20 . . . . .119 B4
Friars Field Ludlow SY8 . . .79 D3
  Newport NP20 . . . . .119 B3
Friars Gdn
  Llanyravon NP44 . . . . . . .107 B1
  Ludlow SY8 . . . . .79 C4
Friars Rd NP20 . . . . .119 B3
Friars St Hereford HR4 . . .136 B2
  1 Newport NP20 . . . . .119 B3
Friars The NP20 . . . . .119 B3
Friars Wlk SY8 . . . . .79 C4
Frobisher Ct HR4 . . . . . . .101 B7
Frobisher Rd NP19 . . . . . .120 B3
Frog La HR7 . . . . .83 D6
Frogmore St NP7 . . . . .95 D5
Frome Ave HR2 . . . . .92 E5
Frome Brook Rd HR8 . . . . .95 F2
Frome Cl HR7 . . . . .83 C6
Frome Pk HR1 . . . . .38 F3
Frome Wlk NP20 . . . . . . .112 C2
Fromington Cotts HR1 . . . .28 C2
Frondeg NP4 . . . . .103 E6
Frost Rd HR8 . . . . .89 C5
Frowens La HR9 . . . . .59 B4
Fruitlands WR14 . . . . .86 F4
Frythe Wood NP16 . . . . . .116 C8
Furlong Cl HR8 . . . . .89 D2
Furlong La HR5 . . . . .81 D6
Furnace La GL18 . . . . .59 F5

G

Gadbridge Rd HR4 . . . . . . .26 C7
Gaer Inf Sch NP20 . . . . . .118 F3
Gaer Jun Sch NP20 . . . . .118 E2
Gaer La NP20 . . . . .119 A3
Gaer Park Ave NP20 . . . .118 E3
Gaer Park Dr NP20 . . . . .118 E3
Gaer Park Hill NP20 . . . .118 E3
Gaer Park La NP20 . . . . .118 E3
Gaer Park Par NP20 . . . .118 E2
Gaer Park Rd NP20 . . . . .118 D3
Gaer Rd NP20 . . . . .118 F2
Gaer St NP20 . . . . .119 A2
Gaer Vale NP20 . . . . .118 F1
Gainsborough Cl
  Cwmbran NP44 . . . . .113 A8
  Welland WR13 . . . . .4 D2
Gainsborough Dr NP19 . .128 A8
Gaisford Cl HR1 . . . . .93 F7
Gaol St HR1 . . . . .136 C2
Garbrook HR1 . . . . .39 F3
Garden City Way NP16 . .116 E8
Gardeners Way GL18 . . . . .59 F4
Gardens The Gilwern NP7 .60 D2
  Hay-on-W HR3 . . . . .88 E4
  Magor NP26 . . . . .123 A3
  Monmouth NP25 . . . . . . .137 C3
Garibaldi Terr HR3 . . . . . . .88 E3
Garn Dyrus Mount NP4 . .101 D7
Garn Rd NP4 . . . . .101 A8
Garn-Galed HR2 . . . . .53 C6
Garn-yr-erw NP4 . . . . . . .100 F8
Garnstone Rise HR1 . . . . . .91 D2
Garren View HR9 . . . . .65 C7
Garrick Ave HR9 . . . . .92 F5
Garth Cl Bassaleg NP10 . .118 A8
  Pontypool NP4 . . . . .102 B2
Garth Rd NP44 . . . . .104 C6
Garth The HR8 . . . . .89 D6
Garthalan Dr NP26 . . . . . .124 E4
Garthi Cl NP25 . . . . .71 E4

Garvey Cl NP16 . . . . .116 F4
Garw Row NP44 . . . . .107 B5
Garw St NP44 . . . . .107 B5
Garw Wood Dr NP44 . . . .107 A6
Garway Prim Sch HR2 . . . .55 E1
Gaskell St NP19 . . . . .119 F3
Gatehouse Rd HR2 . . . . . .93 E4
Gateway La HR6 . . . . .82 C3
Gattimer La HR3 . . . . .34 F3
Gaudi Wln NP20 . . . . .118 A6
Gavenny Way NP7 . . . . .95 E5
Gaynors NP44 . . . . .106 B1
Geldof Gr HR1 . . . . .136 C4
Gellyfelen NP7 . . . . .98 B5
General Hospl HR1 . . . . . .136 C1
General Rees Sq **5**
  NP44 . . . . .106 E4
Geneva Ave WR14 . . . . . . .87 A5
Geoffrey Ave HR1 . . . . .91 B2
Geoffrey Dr NP25 . . . . . . .137 A1
George Bew Cl HR2 . . . . . .92 C4
George La GL14 . . . . .67 E1
George Lansbury Dr **2**
  NP20 . . . . .119 B3
George Pl NP9 . . . . .94 E5
George St
  7 Blaenavon NP4 . . . .101 C6
  Cwmbran NP44 . . . . .106 E4
  Leominster HR6 . . . . .82 C3
  Newport NP19,NP20 . . . .119 D4
  Pontypool NP4 . . . . .104 B7
  Pontypool, Mount Pleasant
   NP4 . . . . .104 A8
George Street Prim Sch
Georges Delight NP15 . . . .74 F2
Geraldine Cl WR14 . . . . . .87 B7
Geraldine Ct WR14 . . . . . .87 B7
Geraldine Rd WR14 . . . . . .87 B7
Gethin Pl HR7 . . . . .69 B2
Gething Terr NP4 . . . . . . .101 A6
Gibbons Cl NP19 . . . . .120 C4
Gibbs Rd NP19 . . . . .120 B5
Gibraltar Dr NP25 . . . . . . .96 B4
Gibraltar La HR2 . . . . .56 C7
Gibraltar Way NP16 . . . . .117 B4
Gibson Gr WR14 . . . . .84 E3
Gibson Rd HR8 . . . . .89 C5
Giffard Dr WR13 . . . . .42 E3
Gifford Cl NP44 . . . . .106 D1
Gilbert Cl NP19 . . . . .120 D4
Gilbert Rd NP19 . . . . .87 B8
Gilberts Wood HR2 . . . . . .54 D7
Gilchrist Thomas Ct
Gilchrist Wlk NP4 . . . . . . .101 C6
Gilchrist-Thomas Ind Est
Giles Rd NP4 . . . . .101 E6
Gileston Wlk **6** NP44 . .106 C2
Gilfach HR2 . . . . .44 E5
Gilwern Farm Cl NP18 . . .113 F7
Gilwern Park Ind Est
  NP7 . . . . .60 E1
Gilwern Pl NP44 . . . . .106 D2
Gilwern Prim Sch NP7 . . . .60 D2
Ginhall La HR6 . . . . .82 A5
Gipsy La NP7 . . . . .95 B3
Glade Cl NP44 . . . . .112 A8
Glade The WR14 . . . . .85 F6
Glade Willow HR3 . . . . .33 A3
Gladstone Dr HR4 . . . . . .136 B3
Gladstone Pl NP44 . . . . . .104 E1
Gladstone Terr NP4 . . . . .101 D6
Glady's Terr NP7 . . . . .95 B3
Glan Gavenny NP7 . . . . . . .95 F6
Glan Rhyd NP44 . . . . .112 A8
Glan-Y-Nant Cl NP44 . . . .106 D1
Glangrwyney Rd NP7 . . . . .60 D2
Glanhonddu Cl NP17 . . . . .53 D1
Glanmoor NP7 . . . . .60 D1
Glanmor Cres NP19 . . . . .120 B5
Glanmor Park Ave NP19 .120 B5
Glantorvaen Rd NP4 . . . .104 C6
Glantorvaen Terr Upper
  NP4 . . . . .99 FB
Glanwern Ave NP19 . . . . .120 C6
Glanwern Cl NP19 . . . . . .120 C6
Glanwern Dr NP18 . . . . . .120 C5
Glanwern Ho NP44 . . . . . .106 B6
Glanwern Rise NP19 . . . .120 C6
Glanynant NP15 . . . . .109 C6
Glascoed La Glascoed NP4 .73 A4
  Pontypool NP4 . . . . .105 E6
Glascoed Rd NP4 . . . . . . .105 B4
Glasllwch Cres NP10,
  NP20 . . . . .118 D4
Glasllwch Jun & Inf Sch
  NP20 . . . . .118 D3
Glasllwch La NP20 . . . . . .118 D3
Glasllwch View NP20 . . . .118 C3
Glaslyn Ct NP44 . . . . .107 A6
Glass Works Cotts
  NP20 . . . . .119 C8
Glastonbury Cl
  Hereford HR2 . . . . .92 D6
  4 Newport NP20 . . . .119 C6
Glebe Cl Credenhill HR4 . .36 F4
  Mitcheldean GL17 . . . . . .67 D6
Glebe Ct HR8 . . . . .95 F7
Glebe Ct The GL18 . . . . . . .54 C7
Glebe Ct GL18 . . . . .59 F5
Glebe Inf Sch GL18 . . . . . .59 F5
Glebe Orch HR8 . . . . .50 A3
Glebe Rd GL18 . . . . .59 F5
Glebe Rd The HR8 . . . . . . .49 F8

Glebe St NP19 . . . . .119 E5
Glebe The Pilning BS35 . .135 C7
  Ross-on-W HR9 . . . . .58 B3
Glebe Way GL18 . . . . .59 F5
Glebelands Cl SY8 . . . . .5 FB
Glebelands The HR4 . . . . . .16 F1
Glen The NP18 . . . . .115 D1
Glen View
  Cwmbran NP44 . . . . .106 D4
  Wigmore HR6 . . . . .8 C7
Glen View Rd NP4 . . . . . .102 B2
Glen-Usk View NP18 . . . .114 A4
Glencoe La GL17 . . . . .67 D4
Glencoe Terr SY8 . . . . .79 C4
Glencourt NP4 . . . . .104 E1
Glendale Cl HR4 . . . . .90 D4
Glendower Cl HR2 . . . . . . .92 E4
Glendower Rd HR6 . . . . . . .82 D3
Glendower St NP25 . . . . . .137 B2
Granada Park Ind Est
  NP8 . . . . .60 A4
Gleneagles Rd HR1 . . . . . . .91 A5
Glengarriff Cl NP4 . . . . . .104 E2
Glenrhyd NP7 . . . . .60 D1
Glenroyd Terr NP25 . . . . .137 A1
Glenside NP4 . . . . .106 D6
Glenthorne Rd HR4 . . . . . .90 E5
Glenwern Terr NP4 . . . . . .104 B5
Glevum Cl HR9 . . . . .94 D3
Gloster Pl **1** NP19 . . . .119 D6
Gloster St **3** NP19 . . . .119 D6
Gloster's Par NP4 . . . . . . .105 B3
Gloucester Cl
  Llanyravon NP44 . . . . . . .107 B3
  Malvern WR14 . . . . .85 C5
Gloucester Ct NP18 . . . . .114 A3
Gloucester Rd
  Mitcheldean GL17 . . . . . .67 D5
  Ross-on-W HR9 . . . . .94 E5
  Tutshill NP16 . . . . .111 A2
Glover Rd HR6 . . . . .82 A5
Glowson Wood Rd HR1 . . .49 C5
Glyndwr Gdns NP7 . . . . . . .95 E3
Glyndwr Ho NP4 . . . . .106 F3
Glyndwr Rd NP4 . . . . .106 F3
Glyntirion NP44 . . . . .106 D1
Gobannium Way NP7 . . . . .95 E3
Godfrey Rd
  Cwmbran NP44 . . . . .106 D5
  Newport NP20 . . . . .119 B5
Godiva Rd HR6 . . . . .82 A4
Godson's Cl WR15 . . . . . . .80 C5
Gold Tops NP20 . . . . .119 B5
Goldcliff Cl NP44 . . . . . . .106 F3
Goldcliff Ho NP44 . . . . . .106 F3
Goldcliff Rd NP18
  Goldcliff NP18 . . . . .131 B3
  Nash NP18 . . . . .130 E3
Goldcroft Ct NP18 . . . . . .114 B2
Golden Cross HR4 . . . . .17 B3
Golden Lion Cl HR4 . . . . . .90 E3
Golden Post HR2 . . . . .92 D6
Goldfinch Cl NP26 . . . . . .124 F4
Golding Way HR4 . . . . .89 D6
Goldsmith Cl
  Hereford HR1 . . . . .93 E8
  Newport NP20 . . . . .118 E2
Goldwire La NP25 . . . . . . .137 A1
Golf Rd NP4 . . . . .105 B4
Gomond St HR1 . . . . .136 C3
Good Neighbours La
  NP25 . . . . .72 B7
Goodrich Castle * HR9 . .66 A6
Goodrich CE Prim Sch
  HR9 . . . . .66 A6
Goodrich Cl HR9 . . . . .94 D3
Goodrich La NP20 . . . . . .119 B7
Goodson Rd WR14 . . . . . . .85 C5
Goodwin Way HR2 . . . . . . .93 C5
Goodwood Rd WR14 . . . . .85 A5
Goodwood Wlk HR4 . . . . . .90 C4
Gooses Foot Ind Est HR2 .45 F6
Goossens Cl NP19 . . . . . .120 C6
Gordings NP44 . . . . .106 B3
Gordon St NP19 . . . . .119 E5
Gordon Terr WR14 . . . . . . .86 E4
Gore St NP19 . . . . .119 D7
Gorse Cover Rd BS35 . . . .135 A7
Gorsley Gdns HR9 . . . . . . .59 B4
Gorsley Goffs Prim Sch
  HR9 . . . . .59 B5
Gorsty La Hereford HR1 . . .93 E8
  Kington HR5 . . . . .15 B6
Gosmore Rd HR2 . . . . .46 D8
Govier Way BS35 . . . . . . .135 C4
Govilon Pl NP44 . . . . .106 C5
Govilon Jun & Inf Sch
  NP7 . . . . .99 FB
Gower Cotts NP16 . . . . . .110 F2
Gower Gdn NP44 . . . . . . .107 A6
Goya Cl NP19 . . . . .120 A7
Goytre Fawr Prim Sch
  NP4 . . . . .103 E5
Goytre Wharf * NP7 . . . . .68 E3
Goytre Wharf Walks*
  NP7 . . . . .68 E1
Grafton Cl WR14 . . . . .84 F3
Grafton Court Cl HR2 . . . .92 D3
Grafton La Hereford HR2 . .92 D3
Grafton Rd NP19 . . . . . . .119 D5
Grafton Wlk HR2 . . . . .92 E5
Graftonbury Rise HR2 . . . .92 D3

Graham Bell Cl NP20 . . . .112 F4
Graham Ct WR14 . . . . .84 F1
Graham Rd WR14 . . . . .84 F2
Graham St NP20 . . . . .119 B4
Grahamstown Gr NP16 . .117 B8
Grahamstown Rd NP16 . .117 B8
Graig Cl NP10 . . . . .118 A3
Graig Park Ave NP20 . . . .113 B1
Graig Park Circ NP20 . . . .113 B1
Graig Park Hill NP20 . . . .113 B1
Graig Park La NP20 . . . . .113 B1
Graig Park Par NP20 . . . .113 B1
Graig Park Rd NP20 . . . . .113 B1
Graig Park Villas NP20 . .113 A1
Graig Rd NP20 . . . . .106 A5
Graig Wood Cl NP20 . . . .113 B1
Gramar School Cl HR9 . . .94 E5
Grampian Cl NP20 . . . . . .113 B1
Granada Park Ind Est
  NP8 . . . . .60 A4
Grandison Dr HR1 . . . . . . .91 D2
Grandison Rise HR1 . . . . . .91 E2
Grandstand Rd HR4 . . . . . .90 D3
Grange Ct NP20 . . . . .119 A4
Grange Gdns HR1 . . . . .93 D7
Grange Ind Site NP44 . . .106 F2
Grange La **2** NP44 . . . .106 F2
Grange Pk
  St Arvans NP16 . . . . .110 A6
  Whitchurch HR9 . . . . .65 D4
Grange Rd
  Cwmbran NP44 . . . . .106 F3
  Malvern WR14 . . . . .86 FB
  St Arvans NP16 . . . . .110 A6
  Undy NP26 . . . . .123 B4
Grange Wlk HR6 . . . . .82 D5
Granston Ho NP44 . . . . . .106 B2
Granston Sq NP44 . . . . . .106 B2
Grantham Cl HR2 . . . . .92 C6
Granville Cl NP10 . . . . . . .118 C4
Granville Ho NP44 . . . . . .106 F3
Granville St
  Monmouth NP25 . . . . . . .137 C2
  Newport NP20 . . . . .119 E5
Granville Terr NP16 . . . . .111 A1
Grasmere Cl HR4 . . . . .90 D3
Grasmere Way NP16 . . . .117 A4
Grassy Bank WR15 . . . . . . .80 D3
Gravel Hill SY8 . . . . .79 D5
Gravel Hill Dr HR5 . . . . . . .15 B8
Gravels Cl NP44 . . . . .106 B1
Great Malvern Prim Sch
  WR14 . . . . .87 C8
Great Malvern Sta WR14 .87 A8
Great Oak HR8 . . . . .24 C4
Great Oak Rd NP8 . . . . . . .60 B5
Great Western Ct
  Hereford HR4 . . . . .136 B3
  Ross-on-W HR9 . . . . .94 F5
Green Acre NP44 . . . . . . .106 D1
Green Acres SY8 . . . . .79 E3
Green Ash Cl HR2 . . . . .92 C5
Green Ave NP26 . . . . .124 F5
Green Cl
  Brampton Abbotts HR9 . . .58 A5
  Colwall Stone WR13 . . . . .41 F4
Green Cl HR2 . . . . .124 C4
Green Colley Cl HR9 . . . . . .66 B6
Green Croft HR2 . . . . .92 E5
Green Ct Caldicot NP26 . .124 E5
  Eaton Bishop HR2 . . . . . .36 F2
  Wilton HR9 . . . . .94 B5
Green Elms HR6 . . . . .16 F5
Green End LD8 . . . . .6 C5
Green La
  Bishops Frome WR6 . . . . .30 F3
  Bromyard HR7 . . . . .20 C1
  Caldicot NP26 . . . . .124 F5
  Eardisley HR3 . . . . .24 E2
  Easter Compton BS35 . . .135 C1
  King's Thorn HR2 . . . . . . .47 D3
  Kingstone HR2 . . . . .46 B8
  Kington HR5 . . . . .15 B8
  Kington, Titley HR5 . . . . .15 C6
  Lea HR9 . . . . .58 F1
  Ledbury HR8 . . . . .89 E4
  Leominster HR6 . . . . .82 C5
  Little Dewchurch HR2 . . .47 F3
  Madley HR2 . . . . .36 A5
  Malvern WR14 . . . . .86 B7
  Orleton SY8 . . . . .9 D6
  Severn Beach BS35 . . . . .135 B8
  Snodhill HR3 . . . . .33 A4
  St Brides Wentlooge NP10 .128 E3
  Swainshill HR4 . . . . .37 B3
  Yarpole HR6 . . . . .9 B4
Green Lane Cres HR6 . . . . .9 B4
Green Lane Park Homes
  HR4 . . . . .37 B3
Green Mews HR9 . . . . .94 A1
Green Moor La NP26 . . . .122 F3
Green Pastures NP25 . . . .72 A3
Green St Chepstow NP16 .116 E8
  Hereford HR1 . . . . .136 C2
  Redwick NP26 . . . . .133 A6
  Sennybridge NP26 . . . . .133 A6
Green The NP16 . . . . .116 B5
Green Willows NP44 . . . . .112 F8
Greenaways GL18 . . . . .59 F5
Greenbank Cl GL17 . . . . . .67 B3
Greenbanks NP25 . . . . . . .76 B7
Greencourt NP44 . . . . . . .107 A4
Greenfield Cl NP17 . . . . . .120 F5
Greenfield
  Caerleon NP18 . . . . .113 F3
  Kington HR5 . . . . .15 D6
Greenfield Cl
  Cwmbran NP44 . . . . .106 D6

Greenfield Cl continued
  Joy's Green GL17 . . . . . . .66 D3
Greenfield Dr HR5 . . . . . . .81 D6
Greenfield Pl NP4 . . . . . . .101 D6
Greenfield Rd
  Joy's Green GL17 . . . . . . .66 D3
  Presteigne LD8 . . . . .6 E3
  Rogerstone NP10 . . . . . .118 B4
Greenfield Stores NP10 . .118 C4
Greenfields HR1 . . . . .38 F5
Greenfields Rd WR14 . . . . .85 A5
Greenfields View NP19 . . .77 A1
Greenforge Way NP44 . . .106 C4
Greenhill Cl
  Cwmbran NP44 . . . . .106 D4
  Pontypool NP4 . . . . .104 E2
Greenhill Way NP8 . . . . . . .60 A5
Greenland Rd
  Hereford HR4 . . . . .136 A3
  Pontypool NP4 . . . . .104 E2
Greenlands Cl NP25 . . . . . .96 F4
Greenlawn Jun Sch
  NP4 . . . . .105 B4
Greenmeadow Ave
  NP19 . . . . .120 C3
Greenmeadow Cl
  Cwmbran NP44 . . . . .106 D2
  Llandevaud NP26 . . . . . . .77 B2
Greenmeadow Community
  Farm * NP44 . . . . .106 B4
Greenmeadow Cres
  NP44 . . . . .103 E3
Greenmeadow Dr NP26 . . .77 B2
Greenmeadow Ho NP44 . .106 D2
Greenmeadow Prim Sch
  (Ysgol Gynradd Maes-glas)
  NP44 . . . . .106 A3
Greenmeadow Rd NP19 . .120 C3
Greenmeadow Way
  NP44 . . . . .106 D2
Greenprice Cl LD8 . . . . .6 C5
Greenway Cl NP44 . . . . . .104 C2
Greenway Dr NP4 . . . . . . .104 C2
Greenway La
  Llandogo NP25 . . . . .76 A8
  Trelech NP25 . . . . .75 F8
Greenway Wlk NP44 . . . . .104 C3
Greenways The NP26 . . . . .123 A3
Greenwich Rd NP20 . . . . .119 B1
Greenwillows NP44 . . . . . .112 F8
Greenwood NP18 . . . . . . .120 A8
Greenwood Ave NP44 . . .106 C5
Greenwood Pl NP7 . . . . . .104 C6
Grenadier Dr NP18 . . . . . .121 C8
Grendon Firs HR7 . . . . .20 A3
Grenfell Rd HR1 . . . . .93 B8
Grenville Terr NP26 . . . . .124 C2
Gresleys The HR9 . . . . .94 E4
Greswolde WR6 . . . . .22 B1
Grey Waters HR4 . . . . . . .136 A3
Greyfriars Ave HR4 . . . . . .136 B2
Greys Rd HR1 . . . . .91 C4
Greystones Cl NP7 . . . . . . .61 D3
Greystones Ct NP7 . . . . . . .61 D3
Greystones Cres NP7 . . . . .61 D3
Greytree Rd HR9 . . . . .94 C4
Griffin Ave NP4 . . . . .101 D6
Griffin Cl NP4 . . . . .104 B7
Griffin St **9** NP20 . . . .119 C5
Griffin The NP10 . . . . .118 A2
Griffiths Cl NP4 . . . . .101 A6
Griffithstown Inf Sch
  NP4 . . . . .104 E2
Griffithstown Jun Sch
  NP4 . . . . .104 E2
Grimmer Rd HR4 . . . . . . .136 A3
Grindle Wlk HR10 . . . . . . .118 A6
Grit La WR14 . . . . .84 F6
Groes Cl NP10 . . . . .118 A7
Groes Rd NP10 . . . . .118 A7
Grosmont Castle * NP7 . .54 E3
Grosmont Cl NP25 . . . . . .137 A1
Grosmont Gr NP4 . . . . .92 D4
Grosmont Pl NP44 . . . . . .107 A4
Grosmont Rd NP4 . . . . . . .92 D4
Grosmont Way NP20 . . . .128 D5
Grosvenor Pl
  Hereford HR4 . . . . .90 C4
  Pontypool NP4 . . . . .104 A8
Grosvenor Rd NP7 . . . . . . .95 F6
Grove Ave NP7 . . . . .95 B2
Grove Cres NP4 . . . . .102 A1
Grove Est NP4 . . . . .102 A1
Grove Farm Rd HR5 . . . . . .23 C2
Grove Inf Sch The WR14 . .85 A2
Grove Jun Sch The
  WR14 . . . . .85 A2
Grove La **1** NP20 . . . . .119 C4
Grove Mans NP7 . . . . .95 B2
Grove Park Dr NP20 . . . . .113 A1
Grove Pk Cwmbran NP44 .106 F6
  Wormbridge HR2 . . . . . . .45 F4
Grove Pl NP4 . . . . .104 C2
Grove Rd Hereford HR1 . . .93 B8
  Pontypool NP4 . . . . .104 A8
Grove The
  Brampton Abbotts HR9 . . .58 A5
  Caldicot NP26 . . . . .125 A5
  Shobdon HR6 . . . . .16 C4
Groves Rd NP20 . . . . .118 C4
Groveside Villas **8** NP4 .102 A1

Grovewood Rd WR14 ....85 C4
Grundy's La WR14 ....86 E1
Gruneisen St HR4 ....90 D2
Guardian Ct HR1 ....136 C2
Guarlford Rd WR14 ....87 E7
Guildford Rd HR4 ....37 A6
Guildford St HR4 ....136 A3
Guildway Bglws 4 HR7 .83 C6
Gurney Ave HR1 ....9 E3
Guy Thornycroft Ct SY8 ..79 F3
Greaunfelin Wlk NP4 ....101 D7
Gwenherrion Cross NP25 .64 F5
Gwent Cragg Grass Ski Ctr*
NP15 ....74 B1
Gwent Pl NP7 ....95 F8
Gwent Rd NP7 ....95 F8
Gwent Rural Life Mus*
NP15 ....97 B4
Gwent Sq NP44 ....106 E3
Gwent St NP4 ....104 B6
Gwentlands Cl NP16 .....116 E7
Gwern Ddu Rd
Coed-Cwnwr NP15 ......74 B1
Llantrisant NP15 ....77 A8
Gwladys Pl NP18 ....116 A3
Gwy Ct NP16 ....110 F1
Gwyndy Rd NP26 ....123 C3
Gwynllyw 3 NP44 ....106 C6
Gwynn's Almshouses
HR3 ....88 D3
Gwynne St HR4 ....136 B2
Gwynns Hill HR4 ....49 E2
Gypsy Castle La HR3 .....88 C3
Gypsy Cres NP7 ....95 B3
Gypsy La Bredwardine HR3 .35 B7
Gorsley GL18 ....59 C3

H

Haberdasher's Monmouth
Sch for Girls NP25 ....137 C4
Hacton La HR2 ....35 F4
Haden St NP4 ....104 B6
Hadnock Rd NP25 ....96 F5
Hadnock Road Ind Est
NP25 ....96 F5
Hadrian Cl NP18 ....114 A3
Hafod Cl NP18 ....113 F6
Hafod Court Rd NP44 ...106 A5
Hafod Gdns NP18 ....113 F6
Hafod Rd Hereford HR1 ..93 C8
Ponthir NP18 ....113 F6
Hafon Mews NP18 ....113 F6
Hafren Rd (Heol Hafren)
NP44 ....106 A4
Hagley Dr HR1 ....38 E4
Hagley Pk HR1 ....38 F4
Haigh Ind Est HR9 ....94 F4
Haisbro' Ave NP19 ......119 D4
Haldane Pl NP20 ....113 A4
Haldens The NP44 ......106 B1
Haldon Way HR4 ....90 D5
Hales Ho WR14 ....86 E2
Half Acre Cnr NP26 .....131 E6
Half Acre La NP18 ......131 D4
Halfkey Rd WR13,WR14 ..84 D7
Halfpennys The NP7 .....60 D2
Hall East NP7 ....99 E7
Hall Gn WR14 ....87 E8
Hall Green Cl WR14 .....87 E8
Halle Cl NP19 ....121 A5
Hallets Well SY8 ....9 E6
Hallwood Dr HR8 ....89 B3
Halstead St NP19 ....119 E4
Halton La SY8 ....79 A4
Halton Way HR4 ....38 F4
Hamilton St NP19 ....119 F3
Hamilton Way NP25 ......96 F5
Hamlet Cl SY8 ....79 D6
Hamlet Rd SY8 ....79 D6
Hammett Ct NP25 ....72 B7
Hammond Dr NP19 ......119 F4
Hampden Ct NP19 ....120 A3
Hampden Mews WR14 ....85 A4
Hampden Rd
Malvern WR14 ....85 A4
Newport NP19 ....120 A3
Hampshire Ave NP19 ...120 B2
Hampshire Cl NP19 .....120 B2
Hampshire Cres NP19 ..120 B2
Hampton Court Gdn*
HR6 ....28 B7
Hampton Dene Prim Sch
HR1 ....93 E8
Hampton Dene Rd HR1 ..93 E8
Hampton Gdns 2 HR6 ...82 D5
Hampton Manor Cl HR1 ..93 E8
Hampton Park Rd HR1 ...93 E7
Hampton St HR1 ....93 B7
Hanbury Cl
Caerleon NP18 ....114 C1
Cwmbran NP44 ....106 E4
Hanbury Gdns NP4 .....104 A8
Hanbury Gn HR6 ....16 E8
Hanbury Ho NP19 ......119 E4
Hanbury Rd
Pontypool NP4 ....104 C6
Pontypool, Mount Pleasant
NP4 ....104 A8
Hancocks La NP4 13,WR14 .42 C2
Hand Farm Rd NP4 .....104 F5
Handbury Rd WR14 ......85 A5
Handel Cl NP19 ....121 A5
Handsworth St NP19 ....119 F4
Hanfield Pk NP44 ......107 A4

Hangerberry New Rd
GL17 ....66 D1
Hanley La NP16 ....111 E6
Hanley Path 3 NP44 ...106 C2
Hanley Rd WR14 ....86 F1
Hanley Terr WR14 ....86 E3
Hanley Workshops WR8 .87 D1
Hanover Cl NP16 ....110 D1
Hanover Ho NP16 ....117 A8
Hanter La LD8 ....14 B5
Happy Valley WR14 ......84 E1
Harbinger Ave WR14 ....85 B1
Harbour Dr WR13 ....86 B2
Harcourt Rd WR14 ....86 C6
Harding Ave NP20 ......113 A3
Hardinge Cl HR2 ....48 B6
Hardwick Ave HR1 ......116 C6
Hardwick Cl HR7 ....83 A6
Hardwick Hill NP16 ....116 E8
Hardwick Hill La NP16 ..116 E8
Hardwicke Ho WR14 .....86 F7
Hardwicke Rd HR3 ....88 F3
Hardy Cl NP20 ....118 E1
Hardy Ct 17 NP4 ....102 A1
Harefields 2 NP4 ....94 F5
Hareley Open Farm*
WR6 ....31 A8
Hargreaves Dr NP20 ...113 A4
Harlech Cl NP44 ....107 A6
Harlech Ret Pk NP20 ..119 A1
Harlequin Cl NP44 ......119 C6
Harlequin Dr NP20 .....119 C6
Harlequin Rdbt 3 NP20 .119 C6
Harley Cl HR1 ....136 C2
Harley's Almshouses
HR3 ....88 D2
Harling Ct HR8 ....89 D4
Harold Rd NP7 ....95 C6
Harold Road Jun Sch
NP7 ....95 C6
Harp La SY8 ....79 C4
Harper's La LD8 ....6 E3
Harptres Way GL17 .....67 D6
Harrington Gdns SY8 ...79 C4
Harrison St HR1 ....136 C2
Harrogate Rd 2 NP19 ..119 E8
Harrow Rd Hereford HR4 .136 A3
Newport NP19 ....119 D5
Hart Gdns 16 NP20 ....119 C3
Hart La GL17 ....66 F4
Hartland Cl HR2 ....92 F8
Hartridge Comp Sch
NP18 ....120 C4
Hartridge Farm Rd
NP18,NP19 ....120 E4
Harts Barn Flower & Craft
Ctr* GL17 ....67 E5
Harvey Cl NP20 ....113 A2
Harvey Rd HR1 ....93 E8
Harvey Wlk NP20 ......112 C1
Hassocks Lea 5 NP44 ..106 B1
Hastings Cl
Abergavenny NP7 ....95 E3
Martley WR6 ....22 D6
Hastings Rd WR14 ....87 B3
Haston Cl HR4 ....90 B3
Hathaway St NP19 .....119 F4
Hatherleigh Pl NP19 ...120 B6
Hatherleigh Pl NP7 .....95 C5
Hatherleigh Rd NP7 ....95 C6
Hatton Cl GL17 ....66 D1
Hatton Gardens Ind Est
HR5 ....81 F7
Hatton Pk HR7 ....83 B5
Haugh Wood Forest Trails*
HR1 ....48 F7
Haulfryn NP7 ....94 A4
Havelock Rd HR6 ....82 B4
Havelock St 6 NP20 ...119 B4
Haven Dr HR6 ....27 F5
Haven The NP4 ....103 E6
Haven Way NP7 ....95 B7
Hawarden Gn NP44 ....107 B2
Hawarden Rd NP19 ....120 A5
Hawke Cl NP10 ....120 C7
Hawker Hill GL17 ....67 D5
Hawkers La HR1 ....136 A3
Hawkins Cres NP19 ....120 E6
Hawkins Ct HR4 ....90 B5
Hawks Moor Cl NP10 ..118 B6
Hawksworth Gr NP19 ..120 D4
Hawkswell Cotts GL17 ..67 B3
Hawkwood Cl WR14 .....84 E3
Hawse La NP10 ....120 E3
Hawthorn Ave NP19 ...120 B4
Hawthorn Cl
Chepstow NP16 ....116 E4
Llanmartin NP18 ....121 E6
Undy NP26 ....123 B4
Hawthorn Ct NP44 .....107 A5
Hawthorn Dr HR2 ....93 A6
Hawthorn La
Madresfield WR13 ......85 F8
Malvern WR14 ....87 B5
Hawthorn Pl HR2 ....93 A6
Hawthorn Rd NP4 .....104 D1
Hawthorn Rise HR2 .....65 F1
Hawthorne Fosse NP19 .120 B4
Hawthorne Hill GL18 ...59 D5
Hawthorne La HR9 ......114 B6
Hawthorne Pl HR6 ......82 D4
Hawthorn Sq 7 NP19 ..120 A4
Hawthorns GL17 ....67 B5

Hawthorns The
Caerleon NP18 ....114 B3
Cwmbran NP44 ....106 B6
12 Raglan NP15 ....70 C2
Hay Croft HR1 ....93 F8
Hay-on-Wye Cty Prim Sch
HR3 ....88 D3
Haydock Ave HR4 ....90 C4
Hayes Almshouses HR1 .136 C1
Hayes Bank Rd WR14 ...87 B5
Hayes La WR15 ....10 F5
Hayes The NP16 ....117 B8
Haylease Cres HR2 .....92 D6
Hayles The SY8 ....5 B1
Hayling Cl NP19 ......119 F7
Haymeadow La HR4 .....37 B7
Haynes Cl Malvern WR14 .85 B5
Newport NP20 ....119 D2
Haysfield The WR14 ....85 C4
Hayslan Ave WR14 ......85 B2
Hayslan Gn WR14 ....85 B2
Hayslan Rd WR14 ....85 B2
Hayswayn 2 NP44 .....106 B1
Hayton Way SY8 ....79 D6
Haywood High Sch HR2 ..92 E5
Haywood Ind Est HR4 ...27 F3
Haywood Pitch HR9 .....59 C5
Hazel Ave NP26 ....124 E6
Hazel Cl NP4 ....105 B5
Hazel Field GL17 ....67 B5
Hazel Gr HR2 ....92 E6
Hazel Rd Drybrook GL17 .67 B4
Malvern WR14 ....85 D5
Hazel Wlk Caerleon NP18 .113 F2
Croesyceiliog NP44 .....107 A6
Hazeldean 8 GL14 ......67 C1
Hazelhurst Bglws HR9 ...66 B5
Hazle Cl HR8 ....89 D2
Headbrook HR5 ....81 E5
Headland The HR6 .....117 A4
Heads Of The Valleys Rd
Clydach NP7 ....98 D6
Gilwern NP7 ....60 E1
Llanfoist NP7 ....95 C4
Heath Cl NP19 ....120 C2
Heath St NP25 ....96 F3
Heather Cl NP16 ....116 F5
Heather Rd NP19 ......119 F7
Heathlands Cl WR14 ...92 C4
Helensdale Cl HR1 ......91 B3
Helford Sq NP20 ......112 D2
Heliston Pl HR2 ....54 D6
Heliston Terr HR2 ....54 D6
Hellens* HR8 ....50 A4
Helpstone Terr NP4 ...104 A7
Hendon Dr HR4 ....90 C5
Hendre Close / Clos Hendre
NP25 ....96 B4
Hendre Ct NP44 ....112 A8
Hendre Farm Ct NP19 ..120 F6
Hendre Farm Dr NP19 ..120 D6
Hendre Farm Gdns
NP19 ....120 E5
Hendrick Dr NP16 .....117 A8
Hengrave Gn HR4 ....17 F3
Henley La SY8 ....5 C7
Henley Orchards SY8 ...79 D6
Henley Pl WR14 ....84 F3
Henley Rd SY8 ....79 D6
Henllan La NP25 ....96 D4
Henllys Way
Cwmbran, Fairwater NP44 .106 A1
Cwmbran, St Dials NP44 ..105 F2
Henry Burton Cl NP25 .137 B2
Henry Morgan Cl NP10 .128 F6
Henry St HR9 ....94 E5
Henry Wood Cl NP19 ..120 C4
Henry Wood Wlk NP19 ..120 C4
Hensol Cl
Llanyravon NP44 ......107 A3
Rogerstone NP10 ......118 B6
Henson St NP19 ....119 F4
Henton Rd NP18 ....130 E4
Henwood Cl HR4 ....116 A3
Herbert Rd Caldicot NP26 .124 F6
Leominster HR6 ....82 A4
Newport NP19 ....119 D6
Herbert St 2 NP20 ....119 C3
Herbert Wlk NP20 .....119 C3
Herbert's Hill HR9 ......65 B8
Herbie Samuels Way
NP4 ....90 F4
Herbert La
Hereford Cathedral Jun Sch
HR1 ....136 B2
Hereford Cathedral Sch
HR1 ....136 C2
Hereford City Mus, Libg & Art
Gal* HR1 ....136 B2
Hereford Ct
Abergavenny NP7 ......95 E5

Hereford Ct continued
Caerleon NP18 ....114 A3
Hereford Football Ground*
HR4 ....136 B3
Hereford La
Kingsland HR6 ....17 A8
Mortimer's Cross HR6 ...8 D2
Hereford Rd
Abergavenny NP7 ......95 F7
Bromyard HR7 ....83 B4
Hope u D HR6 ....28 A8
Ledbury HR8 ....40 E2
Ledbury, New Mills HR8 ..89 D6
Leominster HR6 ....82 D2
Monmouth NP25 ....96 D7
Weobley HR4 ....90 D4
Hereford Sixth Form Coll
HR1 ....91 C2
Hereford St
Newport NP19 ....119 D6
Presteigne LD8 ....6 E3
Hereford Sta HR1 ......91 B2
Hereford Tech Coll (Annexe)
HR1 ....136 C2
Hereford Terr HR6 ......82 D3
Hereford Waldorf Sch
HR2 ....47 A2
Herefordshire Coll of Art
HR1 ....91 C2
Herefordshire Coll of
Technology HR1 ......91 C2
Hergest Croft Gdns*
HR5 ....81 A5
Hergest Rd HR5 ....81 B5
Heritage Ct
Blaenavon NP4 ....101 B7
Cwmbran NP44 ....113 B7
Heritage Dr HR4 ....37 A6
Heron Cl HR2 ....92 C5
Heron Rd NP4 ....125 A4
Heron Way NP10 ......128 F7
Heronston Cl NP25 ....123 D3
Hertford Pl NP19 ......119 F6
Heston Cl NP26 ....125 F5
Hever Rd HR2 ....93 B4
Hewelsfield La GL15 ....76 F7
Hewitt Ave HR4 ....90 B2
Hewlins La HR9 ....65 D3
Heywood Ave HR1 ....92 C4
Heywood Com Sch GL14 .67 D1
Heywood Cres NP44 ..107 A6
Heywood Rd GL14 ......67 C1
High Banks NP19 .....119 E8
High Beech La NP16 ..116 D6
High Gn NP4 ....107 B1
High Cross Cl NP10 ...118 C4
High Cross Jun & Inf Sch
NP10 ....118 C5
High Gdns HR3 ....24 D4
High La WR6 ....21 B7
High Orch NP7 ....29 C7
High Rd GL17 ....67 D5
High Row GL17 ....66 F3
High St Abergavenny NP7 .95 D5
Blaenavon NP4 ....101 C6
Brierley GL17 ....66 F2
Bromyard HR7 ....83 C6
Caerleon NP18 ....114 B2
Chepstow NP16 ....116 E8
Cinderford GL14 ....60 A5
Drybrook GL17 ....67 B4
Hereford HR4 ....136 B3
Kington HR5 ....81 D6
Ledbury HR8 ....89 E4
Leintwardine SY7 ....3 B5
Leominster HR6 ....82 D4
Ludlow SY8 ....79 C4
Mitcheldean GL17 ......67 D5
Newport NP20 ....119 C5
Pembridge HR6 ....16 D5
Pontypool NP4 ....104 B6
Pontypool NP4 ....104 C6
Presteigne LD8 ....6 D3
Raglan NP15 ....70 C2
Ross-on-W HR9 ....94 D5
Ruardean GL17 ....66 F4
St Briavels GL15 ....76 E7
Upper Lydbrook GL17 ...66 E3
Weobley HR4 ....90 D4
High Town Hay-on-W HR3 ..88 D3
High Trees Rd NP7 ......60 D1
High Towy NP26 ....125 A4
High Vinnalls Forest Wlks*
SY8 ....54 D1
High Way The NP4 .....105 A4
Highbeech Rd GL17 .....66 E3
Highbury Rd NP25 ......72 C4
Highbury Terr NP25 ....72 C4
Highcroft Rd NP20 ....119 A6
Highcross Rd NP10 ....118 A4
Highfield
Caerwent NP26 ....78 C1
Penperlleni NP4 ....103 E7
Highfield Cl
Caerleon NP18 ....113 F4
Hereford HR4 ....17 B8
Malvern WR14 ....85 A4
Monmouth NP25 ....96 D7
Highfield Cl (Clos Uchel)
NP44 ....113 B8
Highfield Cres NP7 .....95 E7
Highfield Gdns NP10 ..118 A3

Highfield Rd
Bassaleg NP10 ....118 A3
Caerleon NP18 ....113 F4
Malvern WR14 ....84 F4
Monmouth NP25 ....96 D7
Newport NP20 ....118 E3
Ruardean GL17 ....66 F4
Highfield Way NP18 ...113 F4
Highgate Ct HR4 ....82 D3
Highgrove Bank HR1 ...93 C8
Highland Gr NP44 .....106 E6
Highmeadow NP25 .....96 F3
Highmore Cl HR4 ....90 D4
Highmore St HR4 ....90 D4
Highview Rd GL17 ......67 A3
Highway The
Croesyceiliog NP44 ...107 B5
Cwmbran NP44 ....112 F8
Highwell Ave HR7 ......83 C5
Highwell La HR7 ....83 C5
Highlands The HR6 .....82 F6
Hildersley Ave 5 HR9 ..94 F5
Hildersley Rise 3 HR9 ..94 F5
Hiley Ave NP7 ....60 D1
Hileys Row NP7 ....98 E7
Hill (Coll) The NP7 .....95 D7
Hill Barn View NP26 ..125 E6
Hill Crest NP7 ....63 B7
Hill Flats NP4 ....104 B6
Hill Gate HR5 ....14 F5
Hill Rd Abergavenny NP7 .95 D7
Craswall HR2 ....43 E5
Ravenhills Green WR6 ..22 C2
Hill Rd The NP7 ....54 B6
Hill Side Rd NP4 ......104 D3
Hill St Blaenavon NP4 ..101 C7
Cwmbran NP44 ....106 E1
Llanwihangel Crucorney NP7 .62 A6
Newport NP20 ....119 C4
Pontypool, Griffithstown
NP4 ....104 E3
Pontypool, Mount Pleasant
NP4 ....104 A8
Ross-on-W HR9 ....94 E5
Hill Top NP16 ....116 D7
Hill Top Rd NP44 ......106 D2
Hill View Gilwern NP7 ..60 D2
Hope u D HR6 ....27 F7
Leominster HR6 ....17 F5
Hill View Cl Colwall WR13 .86 B2
Malvern WR14 ....85 B5
Hill View Rd HR9 ......94 F6
Hillary Dr HR4 ....90 B3
Hillbrook Ct NP8 ....60 A6
Hillcrest Caerleon NP18 .113 F4
Much Dewchurch HR2 ...47 A5
Pontypool NP4 ....105 B4
Hillcrest Cl NP25 ....96 F4
Hillcrest Pentwyn Sch
HR1 ....88 A6
Hillcrest Ave
Abergavenny NP7 ......95 E7
Ross-on-W HR9 ....
Monmouth NP25 ....72 E5
Pontypool NP4 ....104 F5
Hillfield Dr HR8 ....89 B4
Hillgrove Ave NP7 .....61 D3
Hillside Abergavenny NP7 .95 F7
Ludlow SY8 ....79 C5
Hillside Ave
Blaenavon NP4 ....101 D7
Hereford HR2 ....92 F5
Hillside Cl HR2 ....92 F5
Hillside Cres NP10 ....118 B4
Hillside Ct NP44 ......106 D5
Hillside Dr Norton LD8 ...6 C5
NP44 ....106 E5
Hillside Prim Sch NP4 .101 D7
Hillside Rd Drybrook GL17 .67 B5
Llangattock NP8 ....60 A4
Mitcheldean GL17 ......67 D5
Hillside Terr GL17 ......66 D3
Hillside View HR4 ....37 A6
Hillstone Ct WR14 ......84 F1
Hillstone Malvern Coll
WR14 ....86 F7
Hiltop Gn NP44 ....106 C5
Hillview NP20 ....118 F3
Hillview Cres NP19 ....120 B3
Hillview Dr WR14 ....84 E4
Hilton Rd WR14 ....87 C7
Hilton Terr HR9 ....94 F5
Hinter Path NP44 .....106 B1
Hinton Ave HR2 ....92 F6
Hinton Cres HR2 ....92 F6
Hinton Ct HR2 ....35 B1
Hinton La HR4 ....25 F1
Hinton Nags Head HR2 ..35 B1
Hinton Rd HR2 ....136 B1
Hitchen Hollow HR1 ...117 B4
Hither Bush HR4 ....37 F7
Hoarwithy Rd HR2 ......93 A5
Hobart Cl NP20 ....118 E4
Hocker Hill St NP16 ..116 E8
Hodges Cl NP20 ....119 A6
Hodges Terr NP44 .....106 D3
Hogarth Cl
Cwmbran NP44 ....113 A8
Newport NP19 ....119 F7
Holbein Rd NP19 ....120 A7
Holborn La HR3 ....23 F5
Holbrook Cl GL17 ......66 D2
Holbrook Cl HR1 ....93 D7
Holders La GL18 ....59 E6
Holland Cl NP4 ....118 A7

Holland Rd HR6 ....82 C4
Hollies Mews The WR14 ..85 B5
Hollies The HR2 ....46 C8
Hollins CI NP16 ....110 F1
Hollins La WR6 ....22 D5
Hollow Halt HR6 ....41 B4
Hollow The GL17 ....67 A4
Holloway Rd BS35 ....135 C4
Holly Bush La
  Clifton u T WR6 ....21 D8
  Llanwarne HR2 ....56 D8
  Much Birch HR2 ....47 D1
Holly CI NP16 ....116 E5
Holly La NP18 ....119 C6
Holly Lodge Gdns NP44 ..107 B6
Holly Lodge Gn NP44 ....107 A6
Holly Lodge Rd NP44 ....107 A6
Holly Rd WR15 ....80 D6
Hollybush NP44 ....106 D1
Hollybush Ave NP20 .....113 A2
Hollybush CI NP20 ......113 A2
Hollybush Prim Sch
  NP44 ....106 C1
Hollybush Terr NP4 .....104 A8
Hollybush View NP44 ....112 D8
Hollybush Way NP44 ....112 D8
Hollybush Wlk HR2 ......92 F6
Hollydean 4 GL14 ....67 C1
Hollyhill Pk GL14 ....67 B1
Hollyhill Rd GL14 ....67 B1
Hollylea CI HR1 ....38 F4
Hollylodge CI NP44 .....107 B6
Hollywell Cres NP7 ......95 E4
Hollywell Rd GL17 ....67 D6
Holm Oak Rd HR2 ....92 C5
Holmdale 3 NP44 ....106 B3
Holme Lacy Coll HR2 ....48 B6
Holme Lacy Prim Sch
  HR2 ....48 B6
Holme Lacy Rd HR2 ......93 B5
Holme Oaks HR1 ....29 B1
Holmer CE Prim Sch HR4 .90 F3
Holmer Hall HR4 ....90 E5
Holmer Manor CI HR4 ....90 E5
Holmer Rd HR4 ....90 F4
Holmer St HR4 ....90 D1
Holmer Trad Est HR1 .....91 B4
Holmes Marsh HR5 ....15 D1
Holmfield Dr NP25 ....76 B7
Holmfirth CI HR2 ....92 C5
Holst CI NP19 ....121 A6
Holts Rd GL18 ....59 F4
Holy Thorne La HR2 ......47 C3
Holy Well Rd WR14 ....86 E1
Holyoake Terr NP4 ......104 A8
Holywell CI
  Abergavenny NP7 ......95 E5
  Monmouth NP25 ....137 A1
Holywell Gutter La
  Hereford HR1 ....93 E8
  Hereford, Hampton Park
  HR1 ....
Holywell Rd NP7 ....95 E4
Holywell Rd E NP7 ....95 E4
Home Farm CI NP18 .....113 F2
Home Farm Cres NP18 ...113 F2
Home La HR2 ....92 E6
Homend Cres HR8 ....89 E5
Homend The HR8 ....89 D6
Homend Trad Est HR8 ....89 D6
Homestead HR2 ....93 A5
Homestead CI WR14 .....42 C4
Homeway HR4 ....20 C1
Honddu CI Caldicot NP26 .124 F6
  Hereford HR2 ....92 E5
Honey Mdw SY8 ....79 F4
Honeysuckel CI NP10 ...118 B3
Honeysuckle CI
  Hereford HR1 ....93 E8
  Ross-on-W HR9 ....94 D6
Hood Rd NP19 ....120 F7
Hook CI NP15 ....109 C6
Hook La WR6 ....31 A3
Hoopers CI WR13 ....32 C5
Hoovers La HR9 ....67 B8
Hop Gdn The NP16 ......116 F4
Hop Kilns The WR6 ......30 D3
Hop Pole Gn WR13 ......32 C5
Hope Brook CE Prim Sch
  GL17 ....67 F6
Hope Cotts HR6 ....82 C4
Hope La WR6 ....21 E7
Hopefield NP20 ....119 B7
Hopehouse La WR6 ......22 E6
Hopewell 8 GL14 ....67 D1
Hopewell CI NP16 ......117 A4
Hopkins WR15 ....13 A7
Hopkins The WR15 ......30 E4
Hopkins Wlk NP19 ......120 F5
Hopleys Green Rd HR5 ...25 A7
Hopton CI Bartestree HR1 .38 F4
  Ledbury HR8 ....89 C5
  Ludlow SY8 ....59 C5
Hopton La HR6,WR13 ....32 A7
Hopton Rd HR1 ....91 B2
Hopton Yd HR8 ....40 B6
Hoptonheath Sta SY7 ....2 F8
Hopyard CI HR6 ....17 F5
Hopyard Gdns HR6 ......82 C4
Horn La WR6 ....22 E8
Hornbeam CI NP18 ......113 E2

Hornyold Ave WR14 .....84 E3
Hornyold Ct WR14 ....86 E2
Hornyold Rd WR14 ......84 E3
Horrocks CI NP20 ....113 A4
Horse Lane Orch HR8 ....89 E4
Horse Pool La HR9 ....65 E2
Horse Rd HR8 ....89 D8
Horsecroft HR2 ....54 C7
Horsefair La GL18 ....59 F5
Horsepool La GL15 ......76 E6
Horseway Herb Gdn*
  HR6 ....15 E7
Horslea GL17 ....66 D3
Hoskins St NP20 ....119 C6
Hospital Bank WR14 ....84 F3
Hospital Rd
  Malvern WR14 ....84 D6
  Pontypool NP4 ....104 B8
Housman CI SY8 ....79 E4
Housman Cres SY8 ......79 D4
Hove Ave NP19 ....120 A6
How Caple Court Gdns*
  HR1 ....49 B1
Howard Bowen CI NP25 ..96 C7
Howard Ct WR14 ....96 C7
Howard Ct HR4 ....90 C2
Howe Circ NP19 ....120 F7
Howe Terr HR5 ....15 D2
Howells PI NP25 ....137 B2
Howsell Rd WR14 ....85 A4
Howsells The WR14 .....85 B6
Hubert Rd NP19 ....119 E7
Hubert Rise NP10 ....118 B5
Hucklemarsh Rd SY8 ....79 D6
Hudnalls View NP25 .....76 F4
Hugh Thomas Ave HR4 ..90 E5
Hughes Cres NP16 .....116 E7
Humber CI Bettws NP20 ..112 E1
  Stoke Prior HR6 ....48 F8
Humber Marsh Visitor Ctr*
  HR6 ....18 F4
Humber Marsh Wetlands
  Reserve* HR6 ....18 F3
Humber Rd NP20 ....112 E1
Humble Bee Pk HR1 .....48 B8
Hunderton Ave NP20 ....92 E6
Hunderton Inf Sch HR2 ..136 A1
Hunderton Jun Sch
  HR2 ....136 A1
Hunderton Rd HR2 ......92 D6
Hundred La HR6 ....10 B2
Hunter CI NP10 ....118 A6
Huntfield Rd NP16 .....116 D8
Hunthouse La HR4 ......53 C6
Huntington WR13 ....31 D2
Huntington Ave NP44 ...106 A3
Huntington Gn SY8 ......35 B2
Huntington La SY8 ......5 C1
Huntington La HR4 ......90 A1
Huntsmans Dr HR4 ......90 B2
Hurdman Wlk HR4 ....90 C3
Hurstbourne Dr HR1 ....136 C4
Huxley Gn NP20 ....113 A2
Hyde Park Cnr GL19 ....51 D2
Hyde The HR1 ....49 B5
Hyde View GL16 ....72 F3
Hydrangea CI NP10 .....118 B3
Hyes CI NP25 ....137 B2

I

Ifton Ave NP26 ....124 C4
Ifton Ind Pk NP26 ......124 C5
Ifton La NP26 ....124 C5
Ifton Quarry Ind Est
  NP26 ....124 C5
Ifton Rd NP6 ....124 C4
Ifton St NP19 ....120 A3
Ifton Terr NP6 ....124 C4
Imperial Rd NP4 ....87 A8
Imperial Way NP10 .....128 D6
In the Nick of Time*
  NP20 ....119 C4
Ind Est E NP25 ....96 B3
Ind Est W NP25 ....96 B3
Ingestre St NP20 ....119 D3
Ingham Pedl CI WR13 ...26 A1
Ingles 15 NP44 ....106 B1
Ingram Ave HR4 ....90 E5
Inner Loop Rd NP16 ....117 B6
Innesfield HR2 ....46 D8
Iron Cross HR6 ....82 D4
Irvine CI HR4 ....90 B3
Isca CI Cwmbran NP44 ..106 F4
  Newport NP20 ....119 B3
Isca Ct NP18 ....114 B3
Isca Mews NP18 ....114 C2
Isca Rd NP18 ....114 C1
Isobel Harrison Gdns
  WR14 ....85 C5
Itchen CI NP20 ....113 D3
Itchen Rd NP20 ....112 D3
Itton Rd NP16 ....110 B2
Iverley Ct WR15 ....30 E4
Ivington CE Prim Sch
  HR6 ....17 F3
Ivington Rd
  Leominster HR6 ....82 A3
  Newtown HR6 ....17 F4
Ivor John Wlk NP18 .....114 A4
Ivor St Blaenavon NP4 ...105 C6
  Newport NP20 ....119 C4
Ivy Dene CI NP4 ....102 B1
Ivy House Est NP19 .....59 B5
Ivy House La HR9 ....59 B5
Ivy Rd NP20 ....119 A4

J

Jack's Ditch La HR5 .....15 B2
Jacks Pill Ind Est NP20 .119 D3
Jackson CI BS35 ....135 D7
Jackson CI 2 NP19 .....119 E6
Jackson PI 3 NP19 .....119 E6
Jamaica Cres WR14 ......85 A4
Jamaica Rd WR14 ....85 A5
James CI SY8 ....79 E4
James St Blaenavon NP4 .101 C6
  Newport NP20 ....119 D2
  Pontypool NP4 ....104 D7
James Terr NP7 ....98 C6
Jameson Ct HR4 ....136 A3
Jane Austen CI NP20 ...118 E1
Jane CI NP10 ....128 F5
Japonica CI NP20 ......113 B3
Jarvis CI HR4 ....35 D7
Jasmine La HR4 ....90 B7
Jasmine Rd WR14 ....86 F4
Jay La SY7 ....24 A5
Jay's Gn HR9 ....59 A5
Jeans CI NP20 ....113 A3
Jeddo CI NP20 ....119 C2
Jeddo St NP20 ....119 C2
Jeffrey St NP19 ....119 E5
Jellicoe CI NP19 ....120 F7
Jenkins St NP19 ....119 F3
Jenks Orch HR7 ....92 B5
Jennett Tree La WR13 ...85 F5
Jerusalem Rd NP44 .....105 B3
Jerusalem La NP4 ......105 B4
Jervis Wlk NP20 ....120 E6
Jessop CI NP10 ....118 B6
Jessop Rd NP10 ....118 B6
Jew's La HR2 ....53 B8
Jewell La NP20 ....119 B8
Jockey Field SY8 ....79 F2
Joe Deakins Rd (Heol Joe
  Deakins) LD8 ....6 E2
John Abel CI HR6 ....82 D4
John Baker CI NP44 ....112 F8
John Beddoes Sch LD8 ...6 E3
John CI NP19 ....120 E6
John Field Wlk NP19 ...120 E4
John Frost Sq NP20 ....119 C4
John Haider Bldg HR6 ..136 C2
John Ireland CI NP19 ...120 D5
John Kyrle High Sch HR9 .94 E7
John Lee Rd HR8 ....89 C5
John Masefield High Sch The
  HR8 ....89 E3
John St Newport NP20 ..119 D7
  Pontypool NP4 ....104 C6
John Tarrant CI HR2 ....92 D4
Johns Croft HR1 ....93 D7
Johnston CI NP10 .....118 A7
Johnstone Rd GL18 .....59 F4
Jolyons CI NP26 ....125 A5
Jones Ho NP20 ....137 C3
Jones St NP20 ....119 B4
Joy's Green Prim Sch
  GL17 ....66 D3
Joyce CI NP20 ....118 E2
Joys Green Rd GL17 ....66 D2
Jubilee CI HR8 ....89 E2
Jubilee Ct NP7 ....95 F8
Jubilee Pk* HR9 ....65 E4
Jubilee Terr NP4 ......104 A8
Jubilee Way NP26 ......124 F5
Judge's CI HR1 ....91 C1
Judge's La GL18 ....59 F1
Judge's Lodging Mus The*
  LD8 ....6 E3
Jule Rd NP44 ....106 B1
Julian Rd SY8 ....79 D5
Julius CI NP18 ....113 F3
Junction Rd NP19 .....119 D6
Juniper Cres NP44 .....112 A7
Juniper PI HR9 ....94 C3
Juniper Way WR14 .....86 F4
Jury Gdns HR1 ....91 C1
Jury La NP6 ....22 D6
Justin's Hill NP25 ......96 F4

K

Karen Ct HR4 ....16 F1
Katharine's Wlk HR4 ....89 D2
Kays & Kears Ind Est
  NP4 ....101 A7
Kear Ct NP20 ....120 A7
Kear's Row NP4 ....101 F1
Keats CI Cwmbran NP44 .106 D2
  Newport NP20 ....118 D5
Keats Rd HR6 ....124 E5
Keelings The 17 GL14 ...67 C1
Keen's Gr BS35 ....135 C2
Keene Ave NP10 ....118 C3
Keene St NP19 ....119 F4
Keepside CI NP44 ......79 A6
Keir Hardie CI HR4 .....136 B4
Keir Hardie Cres NP19 ..120 C7
Kellys La NP16 ....76 F1
Kelvedon St NP19 .....119 E4
Kelvin CI NP20 ....113 A2
Kemble CI HR2 ....92 F5
Kemeys Fawr NP4 .....104 D1
Kempley Brook Dr HR8 ..89 D4
Kempton Ave HR4 ......90 C5

Kemys Fawr Inf Sch
  NP4 ....104 D1
Kemys St NP4 ....104 E2
Kemys Wlk NP44 ......106 D1
Kenchester Water Gdns*
  HR4 ....37 F7
Kendall Sq NP16 ......110 F1
Kenchen CI WR6 ....22 E4
Kenelm CI HR6 ....82 C5
Kenelm Rd WR6 ....21 F8
Kenfig PI NP44 ....107 A3
Kenilworth CI HR2 .....92 B5
Kenilworth PI NP44 ....106 C1
Kenilworth Rd 3 NP19 .120 A5
Kennard Cres NP44 ....101 B6
Kennard Ct NP44 ......101 B6
Kennard PI NP44 ......101 B7
Kennedy PI HR9 ....94 E6
Kennet Bank SY8 ......79 B6
Kennett Grange NP15 ..109 C6
Kensington Gdns 6
  NP19 ....119 F6
Kensington Gr NP19 ...119 F5
Kensington Pk NP26 ...122 E3
Kensington PI NP19 ...119 F5
Kent Ave HR9 ....94 D4
Kent CI Malvern WR14 ..85 C6
  Rogerstone NP10 .....118 A2
Kent CI NP18 ....114 A3
Kentchurch CI HR1 .....91 D1
Kenwater CI HR6 ....82 C5
Kernal Rd HR4 ....35 D3
Kershaw CI SY8 ....79 E6
Kestrel CI NP26 ....125 A4
Kestrel Rd HR2 ....92 C4
Kestrel Way NP10 .....128 E7
Keswick CI HR4 ....90 A6
Kews La GL18 ....59 D4
Keynsham Ave NP20 ...119 C3
Keyse CI SY8 ....79 E4
Keystone Gdns SY8 ....79 D4
Kidwelly CI HR4 ....107 A2
Kidwelly Rd NP44 .....107 B2
Kier Hardie Dr NP19 ...120 D7
Kier Hardie Dr NP19 ...120 D7
Killhorse La SY8 ....4 B1
Kiln La WR13 ....32 D5
Kiln Rd NP7 ....95 B3
Kiln Way NP26 ....123 C3
Kilpeck Ave HR2 ......92 D4
Kilvert Rd HR2 ....92 C5
Kilvert View HR3 ......88 A6
Kimbolton St James CE Prim
  Sch HR6 ....18 E8
Kinford Cross HR4 .....27 B4
King Alfreds Rd NP16 ..117 A8
King Edward's Rd WR14 .86 E4
King Georges Terr HR2 ..136 B1
King Henry V Dr NP25 ..137 A1
King Henry VIII Comp Sch
  NP7 ....95 D7
King La 12 NP20 ......119 C4
King St Abergavenny NP7 .95 D5
  Hereford HR4 ....136 B2
  Ludlow SY8 ....79 C4
  Newport NP20 ....104 B7
King's Acre Rd HR4 ....90 B2
King's Caple Prim Sch
  HR1 ....57 C7
King's Fee NP20 ......137 A1
King's Fee 7 NP20 ....119 D2
Kingfisher CI NP26 ....125 A4
Kingfisher PI NP10 ....128 E7
Kingfisher Rd HR2 .....92 C5
Kingfisher Rise HR4 ....27 E3
Kings Acre NP20 ......118 F5
Kings Acre Halt NP4 ...37 B4
Kings Cres HR1 ....91 A3
Kings Ct (Llys Y Brenin)
  LD8 ....6 E2
Kings Fee NP25 ....96 B3
Kings Orch WR13 ......31 E1
Kings Rd Malvern WR14 .42 C4
  Orleton SY8 ....9 E6
Kingsdale CI NP20 ....119 A3
Kingshill CI WR14 .....85 A1
Kingshill Ct NP20 .....119 C4
Kingsland CE Prim Sch
  HR6 ....17 C8
Kingsland Wlk NP44 ...106 B2
Kingslea 16 NP44 .....106 B1
Kingsleane HR6 ....17 C8
Kingsmark La NP16 ...110 D1
Kingsmead NP25 ......137 A2
Kingsmeadow HR6 .....8 C7
Kingsmill Terr 3 NP20 .119 B4
Kingston CI 2 NP20 ...82 D4
Kingston Rd NP19 ....119 F5
Kingstone & Thruxton Prim
  Sch HR2 ....45 F7
Kingstone CI WR14 ....84 D2
Kingstone Wlk HR4 ...136 A2
Kingsvale 18 NP20 ....119 C4
Kingsway Hereford HR1 .91 A3
  Newport NP20 ....119 D4
Kingsway Ctr 8 NP20 ..119 C4
Kingsway La GL17 .....66 F4
Kingswood Comm HR5 .81 B1
Kingswood Rd
  Kington HR5 ....81 D3
  Monmouth NP25 ......96 B5
Kington Cott Hosp† HR5 .81 E6
Kington Mus* HR5 ....81 D6
Kington cum Sch HR5 ..81 D6
Kington Rd HR4 ....26 A6

Kington Road Ind Est
  HR4 ....26 A7
Kinley La HR4 ....24 F2
Kinnersley CI HR2 .....92 D4
Kinnersley Rd WR14 ...84 E6
Kinnock Ct NP44 ......107 A6
Kinthall La WR15 ......12 D3
Kipling CI WR14 ....85 A2
Kipling Hill NP20 .....118 E2
Kipling Rd NP26 ......124 E5
Kirby Daniel Ct 28 NP20 .119 C3
Kirby La NP20 ....119 C3
Kirkham Gdn HR7 ......83 C6
Kirkham Villas 1 HR7 ..83 C6
Kirkland CI HR1 ....93 F7
Kirrlach CI NP20 ......125 E5
Kitchen Hill Rd SY8 ....9 F5
Kitty Hawk Dr SY8 ....120 B3
Kitty's La HR4 ....25 E3
Knapp & Papermill Nature
  Reserve* HR6 ....31 F6
Knapp CI Goodrich HR9 .66 A6
  Ledbury HR8 ....89 D5
Knapp Cotts GL18 .....51 B3
Knapp La HR8 ....89 E5
Knapp Ridge HR8 ......89 E5
Knapp Way WR14 .....89 E5
Knight CI 28 NP20 ....119 C3
Knighton CI NP18 .....114 B2
Knighton Rd LD8 ......6 A8
Knights Cres GL18 .....59 F4
Knights CI HR9 ....30 D3
Knights Way GL18 .....59 F4
Knightshill HR9 ....67 D8
Knightswood HR1 .....93 E8
Knoll La HR4 ....87 C6
Knoll Rd NP7 ....95 F6
Knoll The HR1 ....93 D8
Kymin Lea NP25 ......96 F4
Kymin Rd NP25 ....72 B7
Kynaston HR8 ....49 E6
Kyre Park Gdns* WR15 .11 F2
Kyreside HR15 ....80 D4
Kyrewood Ct WR15 ...80 D4
Kyrle PI HR9 ....94 D5
Kyrle Pope Ct HR1 ....93 E7
Kyrle St Hereford HR1 ..136 C3
  Ross-on-W HR9 ......94 D5

L

Laburnham Bush La
  NP19 ....120 C3
Laburnum Ave NP19 ...120 B4
Laburnum CI
  Ross-on-W HR9 ......94 C3
  Undy NP26 ....123 C4
Laburnum Dr
  Cwmbran NP44 ......112 A8
  Pontypool NP4 ....105 B5
Laburnum Gr NP18 ....77 B1
Laburnum Gr
  Hereford HR4 ....92 F6
  Portskewett NP26 ....125 F5
Laburnum Terr NP26 ..125 F5
Laburnum Way NP16 ..116 E5
Laburnum Wlk
  Abergavenny NP7 .....95 F5
  Malvern WR14 ....84 F3
Lacy Rd SY8 ....79 D6
Lacy Way HR4 ....17 F5
Lady Gdns HR3 ....24 E4
Lady Hawkins' High Sch
  HR5 ....81 C6
Lady Margaret Ct NP16 .116 F4
Lady Somerset Dr HR8 ..89 C5
Ladybench HR4 ....106 B1
Ladygrove Bsns Pk GL17 .67 E5
Ladyhill CI NP15 ....97 C5
Ladyhill Ct NP15 ......120 C4
Ladyhill Gn NP19 .....120 C4
Ladyhill Rd NP19 .....120 D5
Ladywell Bucknell SY7 ...2 C5
  Cwmbran HR42 ....106 E5
Ladywell La HR22 .....47 C2
Ladywood NP15 ....97 C5
Lake Ho NP19 ....120 C1
Lake Rd WR14 ....113 A6
Lakeside Dr Norton LD8 ..6 C5
  Ross-on-W HR9 ......94 E3
Lamb Bank HR4 ....84 D3
Lamb CI Abergavenny NP7 .95 C5
  Newport NP20 ....118 E1
Lamb La NP18 ....113 E7
Lamb St NP16 ....60 A5
Lambert CI NP20 ......119 B7
Lambert St NP20 .....119 B7
Lambourne Ave WR14 ..85 A1
Lambourne CI HR8 .....89 C3
Lambourne Cres NP20 ..112 D2
Lambourne Gdns HR4 ..37 C4
Lambourne Rd NP20 ..112 D2
Lambourne Wlk NP20 ..112 D1
Lambs Cross HR9 ......59 B4
Lammas CI HR6 ....82 C4
Lancaster Dr NP7 .....60 E1
Lancaster Ho NP25 ...137 B3
Lancaster Rd NP4 ....105 A2
Lancaster Way
  Chepstow NP16 ......116 D8
  Monmouth NP25 .....96 C7
Lancaut La NP16 ......110 F6
Lancers Way NP10 ....128 F7
Landau CI NP20 ....123 C3
Landimore CI NP19 ...120 A7
Landseer CI NP19 ....120 A7
Lane The BS35 ....135 F7
Langford La SY8 ......79 F4

Langham Ho NP16 ....116 F5
Langland Ave WR14 ....85 C1
Langland Cl WR14 ....85 C1
Langland Dr HR4 ....90 C2
Langland The HR8 ....89 D5
Langland Way NP19 ....120 A1
Langley Cl NP26 ....123 A4
Langstone Bsns Vill
  NP18 ....121 B8
Langstone Cotts NP18 ..121 A8
Langstone Court Rd
  NP18 ....121 C8
Langstone Ct
  Cwmbran NP44 ....106 C1
  * St Weonards HR9 ....56 F1
Langstone Jun & Inf Sch
  NP18 ....115 E2
Langstone La NP18 ....121 B6
Lansdown Dr NP7 ....95 E7
Lansdown Rd NP7 ....95 E7
Lansdowne NP4 ....104 E1
Lansdowne Cl WR14 ....85 B1
Lansdowne Cres WR14 ..85 A1
Lansdowne Ho WR14 .....85 A1
Lansdowne Rd
  Caerleon NP18 ....114 B2
  Malvern WR14 ....84 F4
  Newport NP20 ....118 F2
Lansdowne Row WR14 ...85 B1
Lansdowne Terr WR14 ...85 A1
Lanstone Rise NP18 .....115 F2
Lapwing Ave NP26 ....125 B4
Larch Cl NP4 ....105 A4
Larch Ct NP20 ....113 A3
Larch Gr Llanmartin NP18 .121 E6
  Newport NP20 ....113 B3
Larchfield Cl WR14 ......84 E4
Larkfield Ave NP16 .....116 E7
Larkfield Cl NP18 ....113 F4
Larkfield Pk NP16 ....116 E7
Larkfield Pk NP16 ....116 D7
Larkhill Cl NP16 ....116 E7
Larksfield Rd GL17 ......67 B4
Larport La HR1 ....39 A1
Lasgarn La NP4 ....102 A3
Lasgarn Pl NP4 ....102 A3
Laskett La HR2 ....56 D8
Lassen Dr HR2 ....93 A4
Latchen GL17 ....67 F5
Latchen Orch GL17 ......67 F5
Latimer Rd GL14 ....107 D1
Laundry La HR6 ....82 D3
Laundry Pl NP7 ....95 C5
Laural Rd GL16 ....72 E4
Laural Wlk NP44 ....106 B6
Laurel Cl NP26 ....123 C4
Laurel Cres
  Newport NP20 ....113 B2
  Undy NP26 ....123 D3
Laurel Dr Bassaleg NP10 .118 A4
  Penperlleni NP4 ....103 E7
Laurel Gn NP44 ....106 B6
Laurel Pk NP16 ....110 B6
Laurel Rd NP10 ....118 A3
Laurels Ct HR6 ....82 C4
Laurels The NP16 ....70 D5
Lavender Wlk WR14 .....87 C7
Lavery Cl NP19 ....120 A7
Lawns The NP26 ....123 A3
Lawnside WR14 ....87 A8
Lawnside Rd HR8 ....89 D4
Lawrence Cres NP6 ......78 C1
Lawrence Hill NP19 ....120 B5
Lawrence Hill Ave NP19 .120 B5
Lawton Cross HR6 ....17 B6
Laybourne Cl NP44 .....106 C5
Laycock Dr HR2 ....93 A4
Laymore Rd GL14 ....67 B1
Laysters Ave HR2 ....92 E4
Laystone Gn HR1 ....28 A2
Layton Ave WR14 ....85 B3
Lea CE Prim Sch The
  HR9 ....67 C8
Lea Cl Bettws NP20 ....112 D2
  Undy NP26 ....123 B4
Lea Hill HR1 ....93 A4
Lea Villa Cvn Pk HR9 ....67 D8
Leach Rd NP20 ....112 D3
Leadon Ct NP44 ....106 A4
Leadon Rd WR14 ....87 D7
Leadon Way HR8 ....89 C3
Leaping Stocks Rd HR9 .65 D3
Leas The NP44 ....106 C5
Leasdown HR4 ....37 C7
Lechmere Cres WR14 ...85 A5
Ledbrooke Cl HR4 ....44 C5
Ledbury Dr NP20 ....119 C6

Leicester Dr NP44 ....106 A3
Leicester Rd NP19 .....119 E6
Leigh & Bransford Prim Sch
  WR13 ....32 D5
Leigh Court Barn* WR6 32 D8
Leigh Hurst WR6 ....32 E7
Leigh Rd NP4 ....102 B1
Leigh Sinton Rd WR14 ..84 F6
Leigh St HR4 ....90 C4
Leighton Ct NP44 ....106 C2
Leintwardine Endowed Prim
  Sch SY7 ....3 B5
Lennard St NP19 ....119 E4
Leofric Ho HR6 ....82 D4
Leominster Com Hospl
  HR6 ....82 D4
Leominster Folk Mus*
  HR6 ....82 C3
Leominster Inf Sch HR6 .82 C3
Leominster Sta HR6 .....82 C3
Leslie Green Ct NP10 ..128 C8
Leslie Terr NP10 ....118 B4
Lettuce Sq NP20 ....119 C3
Levitsfield Close NP25 ..96 B5
Lewes Rd HR2 ....93 A5
Lewis Cl NP19 ....120 B4
Lewis Smith Ave HR2 ..136 A1
Lewis Terr NP44 ....104 B8
Lewis View NP10 ....118 B5
Lewis Way
  Chepstow NP16 ....116 F4
  Peterchurch HR2 ....35 B1
Lewis's La NP7 ....95 C5
Lewis's Wlk NP7 ....95 C5
Leys La HR6 ....9 C5
Leys The WR13 ....31 E2
Leysters Pole HR6 ......10 F2
Libeneth Rd NP19 ......120 B4
Library Mews 4 HR8 ....94 E5
Lichfield Ave HR1 ....93 C8
Lighthouse Rd NP10 ...129 A4
Lighton Cl HR1 ....93 D7
Lilac Gr Hereford HR2 ..92 F6
  Luston HR6 ....9 D1
Lilleshall St NP19 .....119 E4
Lilly Hall La HR8 ....58 C7
Limburne Dr NP19 .....119 F4
Lime Cl Ludlow SY8 .....79 D6
  Newport NP20 ....119 C2
Lime Cres NP19 ....120 B4
Lime Gr Hereford HR2 ..93 A6
  Llanmartin NP18 ....121 F7
  Welland WR13 ....42 E3
Lime Tree Ave WR14 ...86 E4
Lime Tree Cl NP7 ....95 E4
Limekiln Rd NP4 ....102 A3
Limes The NP26 ....123 B3
Limetree Ave NP25 .....96 F3
Limetree Mews NP7 .....95 E4
Lincoln Cl Hereford HR1 .93 E8
  Newport NP19 ....119 E6
  Ross-on-W HR9 ....94 C3
Lincoln Ct NP18 ....114 A3
Lincoln Hill HR9 ....94 B3
Lindbergh Cl NP20 .....120 A3
Linden Ave NP7 ....95 C7
Linden Cl NP16 ....106 A4
Linden Gr NP7 ....99 F8
Linden Rd NP19 ....120 A5
Linden Villas HR1 .....136 C2
Lindon Ct HR1 ....91 C1
Lindridge St Lawrence's CE
  Prim Sch WR15 ....12 E7
Line The HR9 ....59 A3
Lingen Ave HR1 ....91 B2
Lingen Gdns* SY7 ....2 D5
Lingen Rd SY8 ....79 F4
Lingfield Wlk HR4 ....90 C5
Link Ind Est WR14 ....85 A4
Link Rd Hereford HR1 ...91 B2
  Monmouth NP25 ....96 C2
  Pontypool NP4 ....105 A4
Linley Ct HR1 ....84 F2
Link Way Hereford HR4 ..90 A2
  Malvern WR14 ....85 A4
Links The NP4 ....102 C1
Linley Cl NP19 ....121 A6
Linnet Cl HR2 ....92 C5
Linnet Rd NP26 ....124 F4
Linney SY9 ....79 C4
Linton Cl NP4 ....102 A3
Linton La HR7 ....83 D5
Linton Park Cvn Pk HR7 .83 D5
  Gorsley HR9 ....59 B4
Linton St NP19 ....119 D2
Linton Trad Est HR7 ....83 E5
Linton Villas HR7 ....83 E5
Lion Cl 1 NP4 ....101 C6
Lion Ind Est HR6 ....9 D2
Lion St Abergavenny NP7 ..95 E5
  Blaenavon NP4 ....101 C6
  Hay-on-W HR3 ....88 E3
Lion Terr
  Evans Harold HR2 ....54 D6
  Gilwern NP7 ....60 D1
Liscombe St NP20 .....120 A4
Lister Gn NP20 ....113 A2
Liswerry Cl 2 NP44 ....107 B2
Liswerry Dr NP44 .....107 B2
Liswerry Jun Sch NP19 .120 B3

Liswerry Park Dr NP19 .120 C4
Liswerry Rd NP19 .....120 C4
Litley Cl HR1 ....93 E7
Litley Ct HR1 ....93 E7
Little Berrington St
  HR4 ....136 B2
Little Birch Rd HR2 .....47 C2
Little Dell Cl HR7 ....46 A6
Little Dewchurch CE Prim
  Sch HR2 ....47 F2
Little Gn GL19 ....51 D2
Little Green La BS35 ..135 A7
Little Hereford St 9
  HR7 ....83 C6
Little London HR1 ....35 D8
Little Marcle Rd HR8 ...89 C3
Little Oaks HR8 ....51 B4
Little Oaks View NP10 .118 A6
Little Paradise HR1 ....28 B2
Little Pencombe Mdw
  HR7 ....29 D7
Little Trewen La HR9 ...65 C5
Littlene NP44 ....106 B3
Livale Cl NP20 ....112 C2
Livale Ct NP20 ....112 C2
Livale Rd NP20 ....112 C2
Livale Wlk NP20 ....112 C2
Liverpool St 5 NP19 ...119 E6
Livesey Ave SY8 ....79 D5
Livesey Rd SY8 ....79 C6
Livingstone Pl NP19 ...119 E5
Llan Arrow HR5 ....23 E6
Llan La NP4,NP15 ....73 A7
Llan-Yr-Avon Sq NP44 .107 A2
Llan-Yr-Avon Way
  NP44 ....107 A3
Llanarth Court Hospl
  NP15 ....69 F5
Llanarth St 3 NP20 ....119 C4
Llanbedr Rd NP8 ....60 B5
Llandaff Gn 3 NP44 ...106 C4
Llandaff St NP20 ....119 A3
Llanddewi Ct NP7 ....95 C4
Llandegefedd Way NP4 .105 A3
Llandegfedd Cl NP10 ..118 D2
Llandegfedd Resr* NP4 73 A2
Llandegveth Cl NP44 ..107 B6
Llandenny Wlk NP44 ...106 C3
Llanderfel Ct NP44 ....106 C4
Llandogo Jun & Inf Sch
  NP25 ....76 B7
Llandogo Rd NP25 ......75 F8
Llandowlais St NP44 ..106 E1
Llandudno Cl NP11 ....130 A7
Llanellen Rd NP7 ....95 B3
Llanellen Rd NP7 ....95 B3
Llanerch Path NP44 ...106 B2
Llanfair Kilgeddin CW Jun &
  Inf Sch NP7 ....69 B2
Llanfoist Cres NP44 ...101 D7
Llanfoist Jun & Inf Sch
  NP7 ....95 B3
Llanfrechfa Grange Hospl
  NP44 ....107 C2
Llanfrechfa Way 4 NP44 ..95 E4
Llangarron Bsns Ctr HR9 .65 B7
Llangattock Cl NP44 ...107 B5
Llangattock Sch NP8 ...60 A4
Llangenny La NP8 ....60 B5
Llangorse Dr NP10 ....118 B7
Llangorse Path NP44 ..107 A2
Llangorse Rd NP44 ....107 A2
Llangrove CE Prim Sch
  HR9 ....65 B6
Llanigon Cty Prim Sch
  HR3 ....33 A2
Llanishen Cross NP16 ..75 C5
Llanllowell La NP15 ....73 A4
Llanmartin Jun & Inf Sch
  NP18 ....121 E6
Llanon The Glibes HR4 .44 B7
Llanover Cl
  Blaenavon NP4 ....101 C6
  Newport NP20 ....113 A1
Llanover Rd
  Blaenavon NP4 ....101 D6
  Cwmavon NP4 ....68 A1
Llanover Way NP7 ....95 E3
Llantarnam Gdns NP44 .113 B7
Llantarnam Hall Rougemont
  Sch NP44 ....112 F4
Llantarnam Ind Pk
  NP44 ....113 A7
Llantarnam Park Way
  NP44 ....113 A6
Llanthewy Cl NP44 ....107 B6
Llanthewy Rd NP20 ...119 A4
Llanthomas La HR3 .....33 B3
Llanthony Ct NP44 .....125 A6
Llanthony Priory* NP7 .52 E6
Llantilo Pertholey Jun & Inf
  Sch NP7 ....61 D3
Llanvair Mews NP19 ...119 C6
Llanvair Rd
  Caerwent NP26 ....78 B1
  Newport NP19 ....119 C6
Llanvihangel Crucorney Prim
  Sch NP7 ....62 A8
Llanwarne Ct HR2 ....47 A1
Llanwenarth View NP7 .99 F8
Llanwern Hill Circular Wlk*
  NP18 ....121 C4
Llanwern St NP19 .....120 C7
Llanwern St NP19 .....119 D5

Llanwonog La HR2 ....53 C8
Llanwrithy HR9 ....65 C5
Llanwye Cl HR1 ....93 C7
Llanynant Rd NP15 .....74 C2
Llanyrafon Farm Mus*
  NP44 ....107 A2
Llanyrafon Prim Sch
  NP44 ....107 A2
Llewellin Rd HR5 ....81 D6
Llewellin St 4 NP19 ...120 A5
Llewellyn Gr NP20 .....113 A3
Llewellyn Rd NP20 ....113 A3
Lliswerry High Sch
  NP19 ....120 C1
Lloyd St Hereford HR1 ..93 B8
  Newport NP20 ....120 A3
Llwyn Celyn NP44 .....106 D1
Llwyn Onn NP44 ....107 B4
Llwynau La NP15 ....77 A6
Llwynderi NP20 ....119 A4
Llwynlon NP18 ....114 A6
Llwynu Inf Sch NP7 ....95 E8
Llwynu La NP7 ....95 E8
Llwynu Rd NP7 ....95 E6
Llyn Berwyn Cl NP10 ..118 B6
Llyn Celyn Cl NP10 ...118 B7
Llys Gwyrdd NP44 .....112 A7
Llys Tedcu NP15 ....97 B4
Llys-Yr-Afon NP8 ....60 A5
Llywelyn Rd NP44 .....107 A1
Llywelyn Ho NP44 ......85 D3
Llywelyn Rd NP44 .....106 C3
Locke St NP20 ....119 B5
Lockhill WR6 ....12 F2
Locksters La Clifford HR3 .23 F1
  Whitney-on-W HR3 ....23 F1
Loddon Cl NP20 ....112 C2
Loden Brook Cl HR8 ....89 D5
Loder Dr HR1 ....91 B3
Lodge Ave NP18 ....114 A3
Lodge Dr WR14 ....84 F2
Lodge Gdns GL15 ....76 E7
Lodge Hill Caerleon NP18 .113 F3
  Llanwern NP18 ....121 B5
Lodge Rd NP18 ....114 A3
Lodge Way NP26 ....125 C5
Lodge Wood NP4 ....104 E5
Lodon Ave HR7 ....83 C6
Logaston Rd HR3 ....25 C6
Lon Helyg NP44 ....107 B4
Lon Nant NP44 ....106 F5
London St NP19 ....119 E6
Lone La NP25 ....72 C2
Long Acre NP44 ....106 B1
Long Acres HR8 ....89 D4
Long Hollow 1 NP44 ..106 E4
Long House Barn Est
  NP4 ....103 E7
Long La Peterchurch HR2 ..35 A1
  Snodhill HR2 ....34 F1
Long Meadow Cl NP7 ..120 C3
Long Meadow Ind Est
  HR2 ....54 D6
Longbridge NP18 ....113 F6
Longcroft Rd NP26 ....124 F5
Longditch Rd NP4 .....120 E1
Longfellow Cl NP26 ...124 E1
Longfellow Pl NP26 ...124 E1
Longfellow Rd NP26 ...124 E1
Longlands La NP26 ....17 C8
Longlands La NP26 ....132 E6
Longmeadow Dr WR15 .80 D7
Longridge Rd WR14 ....87 B5
Longstone La NP44 .....38 F4
Longtown Castle* NP7 .53 B8
Longtown Comm Prim Sch
  HR2 ....53 B8
Longtown Gr NP10 ....128 E5
Longworth La HR1 ....38 F3
Longworth Rd HR1 .....93 D8
Loop Rd NP16 ....117 B5
Lord Eldon Dr NP16 ...116 F4
Lord Scudamore Prim Sch
  HR4 ....136 B2
Lord St 4 NP19 ....119 D6
Love La HR5 ....81 D6
Lovers Wlk HR9 ....59 B4
Lowe Croft SY7 ....3 B4
Lowe Farm La HR6 ....16 A5
Lowe The HR6 ....9 C3
Lower Bridge St HR3 ...23 A3
Lower Bridge St NP4 ..104 C6
Lower Broad St SY8 ....79 C3
Lower Brockhampton*
  WR6 ....21 C2
Lower Buckfield Cotts
  HR6 ....82 B4
Lower Bullingham La
  HR2 ....93 B4
Lower Castle St NP7 ...95 D5
Lower Chase Rd WR14 ..87 C8
Lower Church St NP16 .110 F1
Lower Comm NP4 ....44 E1
Lower Cross HR5 ....81 D6
Lower Dock St NP19 ...120 A4
Lower Fee NP7 ....79 C3
Lower Galdeford SY8 ...79 D3
Lower Giantorvaen Terr
  NP4 ....101 B6
Lower Hardwick La HR7 .83 C7
Lower Hill St NP4 .....101 C6
Lower Hope Cotts HR1 .29 B5
Lower House Gdns HR1 .48 D5
Lower House La NP18 ..53 F6
Lower Howsell Rd WR14 .85 B6

Lower Leigh Rd NP4 ...102 A2
Lower Mead HR3 ....88 E3
Lower Mill St SY8 ....79 C3
Lower Monk Street/Stryd Y
  Mynach Isaf NP7 ....95 E5
Lower Montpelier Rd
  WR14 ....84 C1
Lower Newton HR2 .....44 E2
Lower Orchs HR4 ....37 D7
Lower Park Gdns NP4 ..104 C7
Lower Park Terr NP4 ..104 C8
Lower Prospect Rd NP25 .96 D7
Lower Quest Hills Rd
  WR14 ....84 F4
Lower Raven La SY8 ....79 C3
Lower Rd
  Coldharbour GL15 ....76 E7
  Ledbury HR8 ....89 C3
  Malvern WR14 ....85 B6
Lower Thorn HR7 ....83 B5
Lower Waltons HR8 .....49 E4
Lower Waun St NP4 ...101 C7
Lower Welson HR3 ....24 C4
Lower Westfields
  Bromyard HR7 ....83 C5
  Cradley WR13 ....31 D2
Lower Wilton Rd WR14 .87 B8
Lower Woodland St
  NP4 ....101 D7
Lower Wyche Rd WR14 .86 E6
Lower Wyndcliff Nature
  Trail* NP16 ....110 D7
Lowfield Mdw HR2 ......46 A3
Lowlands Cres NP44 ...106 E6
Lowlands Ct NP44 .....106 E6
Lowlands Rd NP44 .....106 E6
Luard Wlk HR2 ....136 A1
Lucas Rd NP20 ....119 B6
Lucerne Ave WR14 ......87 A5
Lucton La HR6 ....8 E3
Lucton Sch HR6 ....8 E3
Ludford Almshouses SY8 .79 C3
Ludlow Cl Hereford SY8 ..79 F3
Ludlow Bsns Pk SY8 ....79 F4
Ludlow Castle* SY8 ....79 B4
Ludlow CE Sch SY8 ....79 A6
Ludlow Cl
  Llanyravon NP44 ....107 B1
  Newport NP20 ....119 F4
Ludlow Coll Ludlow SY8 .79 C4
  Ludlow SY8 ....79 C3
Ludlow Hospl SY8 ......79 C5
Ludlow Jun Sch SY8 ...79 D5
Ludlow Mus* SY8 ....79 D4
Ludlow Pl NP44 ....92 D4
Ludlow Rd Leominster HR6 .82 F7
  Snitton SY8 ....79 C5
Lugg Fields HR8 ....89 C5
Lugg Gn HR6 ....17 C8
Lugg Green Rd
  Kingsland HR6 ....17 C8
  Lugg Green HR6 ....8 F1
Lugg View HR1 ....91 C3
Lugg View Ind Est HR4 .38 A8
Lugg Way HR6 ....82 D4
Lugwardine Court Orch
  HR1 ....38 D3
Lugwardine Prim Sch
  HR1 ....38 E4
Lulworth Rd NP18 .....114 C1
Lumber La HR1 ....38 E4
Lundy Dr NP19 ....119 F7
Luston Cl HR6 ....9 D2
Luston Prim Sch HR6 ...9 D2
Lyall Cl HR1 ....93 E7
Lydbrook Prim Sch GL17 .66 D2
Lyde St HR4 ....90 D4
Lydes Rd WR14 ....85 A2
Lydham Bank WR14 .....84 F2
Lyn Pac Trad Est NP44 .106 E5
Lynch La HR9 ....10 D6
Lyncroft NP44 ....106 B3
Lyndalls La HR1 ....49 C3
Lyndhurst Ave
  Hereford HR1 ....91 D1
  Newport NP20 ....119 A2
Lyndon Way NP10 .....118 B4
Lyne Down HR8 ....49 E2
Lyne Rd NP20 ....119 C2
Lynn Cl WR13 ....32 C5
Lystep Ho NP44 ....106 C2
Lyston La HR2 ....56 A7
Lytham Dr HR1 ....91 A5
Lyttleton Sq WR14 .....85 A4

M

Mabel's Furlong HR8 ...89 E3
Mablethorpe Pl 1 HR9 ..94 F5
Macaulay Ave HR4 .....90 C1
Macaulay Gdns NP20 ..113 E8
Macaulay Rise WR14 ...85 A2
Machine Mdw 3 NP4 ..102 A1
Macmillan Cl HR4 .....136 B4
Maddox Cl NP25 ....96 C6
Madley Prim Sch HR2 ..36 C1
Madocke Rd NP16 ....117 A7
Madresfield CE Prim Sch
  WR13 ....85 D3

Madresfield Rd
Malvern WR14 . . . . .85 B1
Malvern,Sherrards Green
WR13,WR14 . . . . .85 D1
Maendy Pl NP44 . . . . .106 C6
Maendy Rd Sch NP44 . .106 E4
Maendy Sq NP44 . . . . . .106 C5
Maendy Way NP44 . . . .106 C5
Maendy Wood Rise
NP44 . . . . .106 C5
Maerdy Cl NP20 . . . . . . .118 F1
Maes Ebbw Sch NP20 . .128 F8
Maes Fynnon NP6 . . . . . .60 C7
Maes-Y-Celyn NP4 . . . . .104 D4
Maes-Y-Ffynnon NP8 . . .60 B5
Maes-Y-Rhiw Ct NP4 . .106 A3
Maes-Yr-Afon LD7,LD8 . . .6 A6
Maesderwen Cres NP4 .104 D5
Maesderwen Rd NP4 . . .104 C5
Maesglas Ave NP20 . . . .118 F1
Maesglas Cres NP20 . . .129 A8
Maesglas Gr NP20 . . . . .128 F8
Maesglas Ind Est NP20 .119 B1
Maesglas Jun & Inf Sch
NP20 . . . . .129 A8
Maesglas Rd NP20 . . . . .118 F1
Maesglas St NP20 . . . . .129 A8
Maesgwyn NP4 . . . . .106 D6
Maeshyfryd NP7 . . . . .99 F8
**Maesygwartha Road (Heol
Maes-Y-Gwartha)** NP7 .60 D1
Maghausel Cl NP26 . . . .124 F5
Magna Porta Gdns
NP44 . . . . .113 B6
Magnis Cl HR4 . . . . .37 A6
Magnolia Cl
Chepstow NP16 . . . . .116 F5
Newport NP20 . . . . .113 B3
Magnolia Terr NP7 . . . . . .95 C5
Magor Firm NP26 . . . . .123 B3
Magor Rd
Langstone NP18 . . . . .121 F8
Llanmartin NP18,NP26 . .122 C5
Magor NP19 . . . . .119 F3
Mahollam Rd
Huntington HR5 . . . . .23 E8
Kington HR5 . . . . .14 C1
Maidstone Cl HR2 . . . . . . .92 D5
Main Rd Cheltenham NP7 . .98 C6
Gilwern NP7 . . . . .60 D1
Portskewett NP26 . . . . . . .125 E5
Tintern Parva NP16,NP25,
GL15 . . . . .76 B3
Undy NP26 . . . . .123 B3
Maindee Jun & Inf Sch
NP19 . . . . .119 D5
Maindee Par NP19 . . . . .119 E6
Maindee Terr NP19 . . . . .119 D5
Maindiff Court Hospl
NP7 . . . . .61 E2
Majors Cl NP7 . . . . .95 E8
Malcolm Sargent Cl
NP19 . . . . .120 D4
Malford Gr NP7 . . . . .60 D1
Mall The NP44 . . . . .106 E3
Mallard Way NP20 . . . . .128 F6
Mallory Cl HR4 . . . . .90 A2
Mallow Cl WR14 . . . . .47 D7
Malmesbury Cl NP20 . . .119 C6
Malmo Pl HR9 . . . . .57 B1
Malpas Court Jun & Inf Sch
NP20 . . . . .113 B2
Malpas CW Jun & Inf Schs
NP20 . . . . .119 B8
Malpas La NP20 . . . . .119 B8
Malpas Park Prim Sch
NP20 . . . . .113 A3
Malpas Rd NP20 . . . . . . .113 A3
Malpas St NP44 . . . . .106 E2
Malthouse La NP4 . . . . . .104 B7
Malthouse Rd
Caerleon NP18 . . . . .114 A5
Ponthir NP18,NP44 . . . . .113 D6
Maltings The
Dormington HR1 . . . . .39 B3
2 Ross-on-W HR9 . . . . . . .94 E5
Malton Cl WR14 . . . . .84 E6
Malus Cl WR14 . . . . .85 C3
Malvern Cl
Hereford HR4 . . . . .90 B3
Newport NP19 . . . . .120 A8
Malvern Coll WR14 . . . . . .86 F7
Malvern General Hospl
WR14 . . . . .85 A1
Malvern Girls' Coll
WR14 . . . . .87 A8
Malvern Link CE Prim Sch
WR14 . . . . .85 A4
Malvern Link St WR14 . . .85 A3
**Malvern Nus* WR14 . . . . .86 F8
Malvern Parish CE Prim Sch
WR14 . . . . .85 A4
Malvern Pl HR1 . . . . .38 F4
Malvern Rd
Bromyard WR6 . . . . .30 E8
Leigh Sinton WR13 . . . . . . .32 D5
Malvern WR2,WR13 . . . . . .47 B5
Newport NP19 . . . . .119 D5
Malvern Wells CE Prim Sch
WR14 . . . . .42 C4
Malvern Wyche CE Prim Sch
WR14 . . . . .86 E5
Mamhilad Park Est NP4 .103 B1
Manby Rd WR14 . . . . .87 A8

Manchester St NP19 . . . .119 D6
Manley Cres HR6 . . . . . . .16 C4
Manley La HR6 . . . . .16 C5
Manley Rd NP20 . . . . . . .119 A4
Mannings Rd GL17 . . . . . . .67 B4
Manor Chase NP26 . . . . .123 D3
Manor Cl Almeley HR3 . . . .25 A6
Norton LD8 . . . . .6 C5
Manor Ct Fownhope HR1 . . .48 E5
Usk NP15 . . . . .97 B3
Manor Fields HR4 . . . . . . .37 C7
Manor Pk NP10 . . . . .128 F6
Manor Rd Clifton u T WR6 . .21 F8
Hereford HR2 . . . . .93 A5
Manor View NP16 . . . . . .110 B5
Manor Way NP26 . . . . . .125 D5
Manor Wood NP16 . . . . .116 C8
Manor Wood Forest Trail*
NP25 . . . . .76 B6
Manorbier Dr NP44 . . . . .107 A3
Mansbridge Ave HR1 . . . .93 B8
Manse La The HR9 . . . . . . .59 B5
Manse Rd GL17 . . . . .67 B4
Mansel St NP19 . . . . .120 A5
Mansfield Rd WR14 . . . . . .85 D3
Manson La NP25 . . . . .64 F2
Manson's La NP25 . . . . . . .96 F7
Maple Ave NP16 . . . . .116 C5
Maple Cl Bromyard HR7 . . .83 B5
Caldicot NP26 . . . . .124 F6
Llanmartin NP18 . . . . .121 C6
Ludlow SY8 . . . . .79 D6
Maple Cres NP4 . . . . .104 D1
Maple Gr HR2 . . . . .92 F6
Maple Rd Malvern WR14 . . .85 C3
Maple Rd S NP4 . . . . .104 D1
Mapledean **10** GL14 . . . . .67 C1
Mappa Mundi Mus*
HR4 . . . . .136 B2
Mappenors La HR6 . . . . . . .82 C5
Mararyat Wlk NP20 . . . . .118 E1
Marcle Orch SY8 . . . . .10 B6
Marcle Ridge Wlk* HR8 49 D5
Marcle Wlk HR2 . . . . .92 D4
Marconi Cl NP20 . . . . . . .112 F2
Marden Prim Sch HR1 . . .28 B2
Marfells Way GL17 . . . . . .66 F3
Margaret Ave NP20 . . . . .119 D7
Margaret Rd HR8 . . . . .89 D4
Margery La GL15 . . . . .72 F2
Margretts Way NP26 . . . .124 F6
Marina Ct **6** NP19 . . . . .119 E8
Marine Terr NP26 . . . . . . .125 E4
Mariner Way NP19 . . . . . .129 E8
Mariners Way NP16 . . . . .117 A4
Marion Pl NP20 . . . . .119 C2
Marion St NP20 . . . . .119 C2
Mark Cl WR14 . . . . .84 E6
Market Arc **1** NP20 . . . .119 C5
Market Hall St HR5 . . . . . .81 D6
Market Pl HR9 . . . . .94 D5
Market Sq Bromyard HR7 . .83 D6
Pontypool NP4 . . . . .104 C6
Tenbury Wells WR15 . . . . . .80 C5
Market St
Abergavenny NP7 . . . . .95 D5
Blaenavon NP4 . . . . .101 C6
18 Cinderford GL14 . . . . . .67 C1
Hay-on-W HR3 . . . . .88 D3
Ledbury HR8 . . . . .89 D4
2 Newport NP20 . . . . . . .119 C5
Pontypool NP4 . . . . .104 C6
Tenbury Wells WR15 . . . . . .80 C5
Markwick Cl HR5 . . . . .81 D6
Markyes Cl NP19 . . . . .94 D5
Marl Cl NP44 . . . . .106 B5
Marlbank Rd WR13,WR14 . .42 D3
Marlborough Cl HR8 . . . . .82 C3
Marlborough Gdns WR14 .85 B6
Marlborough Rd NP19 . . .119 D5
**Marlborough (Heol
Marlborough)** NP44 . . .106 A3
Marlbrook Rd HR2 . . . . . . .92 E4
Marloss Path 1 NP44 . . .106 B3
Marlow Cl NP10 . . . . .118 B6
Marlow Ct NP44 . . . . .106 B3
Marlowe Dr NP44 . . . . . . .90 C1
Marlowe Gdns NP20 . . . .118 E1
Marsh Cl WR14 . . . . .85 B2
Marsh Common Rd
BS35 . . . . .135 D6
Marsh Ct NP7 . . . . .95 E4
Marsh La HR2 . . . . .56 D6
Marsh Rd NP16 . . . . .116 F5
Marshall Ct HR4 . . . . .90 C1
Marshall's La GL15 . . . . . .67 C1
Marshfield St NP19 . . . . . .120 A3
Marston Ct NP20 . . . . . . .119 B7
Marston La HR4 . . . . .16 A4
Marstons Mill SY8 . . . . . . .79 C4
Marstow Cl NP44 . . . . .79 C4
Martell Way NP8 . . . . .60 E8
Martel Rd NP16 . . . . .116 E6
Martin Cl Malvern WR14 . . .85 C1
Rogiet NP26 . . . . .124 B4
Martin Terr NP4 . . . . .101 A6
Martin's Orch WR13 . . . . .42 A4
Martindale Rd NP4 . . . . . .104 E2
Martins La NP26 . . . . .78 C1
Martin The HR6 . . . . .111 A1
Martley CE Prim Sch
WR6 . . . . .89 D2
Mary De Bohan Cl NP25 .137 A1
Mary Elizabeth Rd SY8 . . .79 E3

Mary Knoll Forest Wlks*
SY8 .4 E5
Mary St **15** NP4 . . . . .101 C6
Maryport St NP15 . . . . .97 B4
Maryvale WR15 . . . . .80 B4
Masefield Ave HR2 . . . . . . .92 D5
Masefield Cl HR8 . . . . .89 D4
Masefield Rd NP26 . . . . . .124 E4
Masefield Vale NP20 . . . .118 F2
Mason Cl WR14 . . . . .85 B3
Massey Rd HR8 . . . . .89 C5
Mathern Cres NP16 . . . . .116 B4
Mathern Rd NP16 . . . . . . .116 C5
Mathern Way NP16 . . . . .116 B4
Mathon Rd Colwall WR13 . .86 B4
Malvern WR14 . . . . .84 C1
Matilda Cl HR9 . . . . .57 A1
Matravers Rd WR14 . . . . . .85 B2
Matthias Cl WR14 . . . . .85 A5
Maugham Cl NP20 . . . . . .118 F1
Maxworthy Rd NP4 . . . . . .101 C7
May Bush La HR9 . . . . .65 E2
May Meadow La GL17 . . . .67 D5
May St NP19 . . . . .119 C4
Maybank WR14 . . . . .85 C3
Mayberry Ave HR2 . . . . . . .92 E5
Maybury Ho **9** NP44 . . . .106 B3
Mayern Cl HR6 . . . . .82 C4
Mayfield Rd WR13,WR14 . .85 C2
Mayfields SY8 . . . . .79 C6
Mayflower Cl WR14 . . . . . .87 B8
Mayhill Ind Est NP25 . . . .137 C2
Mayhill Rd HR9 . . . . .94 E7
Maylite Trad Est WR14 . . .22 C6
Maylord St HR1 . . . . .136 C3
Mayne Ave HR2 . . . . .93 B5
Maynes 4 NP44 . . . . .106 B1
McMahon Cl HR4 . . . . .90 D4
Mead La Cwmbran NP44 . .106 E4
Redwick NP26 . . . . .132 F2
Mead The HR9 . . . . .58 B2
Meadow Bank NP4 . . . . . .103 E6
Meadow Cl Hereford HR2 .136 B1
Norton LD8 . . . . .6 C5
Meadow Cres HR1 . . . . . . .28 F1
Meadow Ct HR7 . . . . .83 B6
Meadow Dr
Canon Pyon HR4 . . . . .27 B3
Credenhill HR4 . . . . .36 F6
Meadow Gn NP4 . . . . .104 D1
Meadow Gn WR6 . . . . .21 F3
Meadow Hts HR7 . . . . .56 F3
Meadow La
Abergavenny NP7 . . . . .95 A7
Croesyceiliog NP44 . . . . . .107 B5
Meadow Rd
Cinderford GL14 . . . . .67 D1
Malvern WR14 . . . . .85 A3
Meadow Rise
Tenbury Wells WR15 . . . . . .80 D5
Undy NP26 . . . . .123 B3
Meadow St HR4 . . . . .26 A6
Meadow The NP26 . . . . . .123 A3
Meadow Way NP44 . . . . .103 E7
Meadow Wlk
Chepstow NP16 . . . . .116 D8
Colwall WR13 . . . . .86 B2
Meadowbank Rd HR1 . . . .93 C8
Meadowbrook Ave
NP44 . . . . .106 D6
Meadowcroft NP26 . . . . .124 C4
Meadowlands Cl NP26 . . .77 B2
Meadows End GL17 . . . . . .67 F6
Meadows Rd NP20 . . . . . .130 D8
Meadows The
Hereford HR2 . . . . .92 B5
Leominster HR6 . . . . .82 C5
Usk NP15 . . . . .97 C4
Meadowsweet Ct WR14 . .87 C7
Meads Cl Kington HR5 . . . .81 A6
Newport NP20 . . . . .120 C2
Meads The NP16 . . . . .116 E6
Meadway
Abergavenny NP7 . . . . .95 E7
Malvern WR14 . . . . .84 F5
Rogiet NP26 . . . . .124 A4
Medlock Cl NP20 . . . . . . .112 E2
Medlock Cres NP20 . . . . .112 E3
Medlock Wlk NP20 . . . . . .112 E2
Medway Cl NP20 . . . . .112 D3
Medway Ct NP20 . . . . . . .112 D3
Medway Rd NP20 . . . . . . .112 C2
Meeks Hill NP25 . . . . .72 B1
Meeks Well La HR9 . . . . . . .65 C3
Meend La GL17 . . . . .67 C1
Meeting House La LD8 . . . .6 D7
Melbourne Cl WR14 . . . . .106 D2
Melbourne Way NP44 . . .106 D2
Melfort Gdns NP20 . . . . .118 F3
Melfort Rd NP20 . . . . .118 F3
Mellon St NP20 . . . . .119 C4
Melon St NP20 . . . . .119 C4
Melyn Bach Ave NP4 . . . .103 E3
Mendalgief Ret Pk
NP20 . . . . .119 C1
Mendalgief Rd NP20 . . . .119 C2
Mendip Cl Malvern WR14 . .85 B1
Newport NP20 . . . . .120 D6
Meon Cl NP20 . . . . .112 F2
Merbach's Hill NP4 . . . . . .104 B8
Merchant's Hill Cl NP4 . .104 A8
Mercian Way NP16 . . . . . .117 A7
Mere Path NP44 . . . . .106 B3
Merebrook WR14 . . . . .42 C4
Merebrook Ind Est WR13 .87 D1
Meredith Cl NP20 . . . . . . .118 F2

Merestone Rd HR2 . . . . . . .92 E4
Merick Rd WR14 . . . . .85 B5
Merlin Cl NP26 . . . . .124 B4
Merlin Cres NP19 . . . . . . .119 F7
Merrick Cl HR9 . . . . .94 E6
Merrick Pl HR9 . . . . .94 E6
Merricks La NP20 . . . . .76 D4
Merrievale Ct WR14 . . . . . .87 B8
Merritt St GL17 . . . . .67 C5
Merriots Pl NP19 . . . . . . .119 E6
Merrivale Cres HR9 . . . . . .94 E3
Merrivale La HR9 . . . . .94 E4
Merrivale Rd HR9 . . . . .94 E3
Merryfields WR13 . . . . .42 E2
Merryhill Cres HR2 . . . . . .92 E6
Merryhill Terr HR2 . . . . . . .92 E4
Merthyr Rd
Abergavenny NP7 . . . . .95 C4
Llanfoist NP7 . . . . .95 B3
Merthyr Terr GL17 . . . . . . .66 D2
Merton Gn NP26 . . . . .78 B1
Merton Rd WR14 . . . . .85 A4
Mervyn Terr NP4 . . . . .104 B7
Merwald Cl HR6 . . . . .82 C6
Mescoed Rd NP10 . . . . . .118 B8
Mesne La HR2 . . . . .47 C2
Metcalfe Cl HR9 . . . . .94 D5
Methuen Rd NP19 . . . . . .119 E5
Metro Mon Ind Est
NP44 . . . . .106 F7
Mews The
Abergavenny NP7 . . . . .95 D5
Credenhill HR4 . . . . .37 A6
Hereford HR4 . . . . .136 B2
Ledbury HR8 . . . . .89 D5
Newport NP20 . . . . .119 A5
Tenbury Wells WR15 . . . . . .80 C4
Tenbury Wells WR15 . . . . . .80 C6
Meyrick St WR14 . . . . .94 E6
Meyricks NP44 . . . . .112 B8
Michael Cres WR14 . . . . . .84 F6
Michael Way HR4 . . . . . . .104 B7
**Michaelchurch Escley Prim
Sch** HR2 . . . . .44 A2
Middle Coedcae NP4 . . . .101 D6
Middle Coedcae Rd
NP4 . . . . .101 D6
Middle Maes Coed
Cardiff NP44 . . . . .44 D4
Middle Maes-coed HR2 . . .44 E4
Middle St NP16 . . . . .116 E8
Middle Way
Chepstow NP16 . . . . .116 F5
Hereford HR4 . . . . .90 A5
Middle Wood Rd SY8 . . . . .79 A3
Middlemarsh HR6 . . . . .82 D6
Midfield Cl NP44 . . . . .106 C6
Midfield NP4 . . . . .103 E6
Midsummer Ct HR6 . . . . . .82 D4
Midway NP7 . . . . .103 B2
Midway Cl NP7 . . . . .95 F8
Midway La NP7 . . . . .95 F8
Milbank Est LD8 . . . . .6 D5
Milford Ho NP44 . . . . .106 D2
Mill Bank HR4 . . . . .26 B6
Mill Cl HR4 . . . . .26 B6
Mill Comm NP26 . . . . .123 B3
Mill Ct HR1 . . . . .93 B8
Mill End GL17 . . . . .67 D1
Mill Heath NP20 . . . . .112 E3
Mill Hill HR6 . . . . .76 D4
Mill La Abbey Dore HR2 . . . .45 A1
Caldicot NP26 . . . . .125 A4
Colwall Stone WR13 . . . . . .41 F5
Credenhill HR4 . . . . .36 F6
Dorstone HR3 . . . . .34 E4
Eardiston WR6,WR15 . . . . .13 A7
Gorsley GL18 . . . . .59 C3
Govilon NP7 . . . . .99 F8
Kington HR5 . . . . .14 C1
Leintwardine SY7 . . . . .3 B4
Llanyravon NP44 . . . . .107 B2
Lowbands GL19 . . . . .51 F2
Malvern WR14 . . . . .87 D7
Much Cowarne HR7 . . . . . .29 F1
Presteigne LD8 . . . . .6 E3
Redmarley D'Abitot GL19 . .51 F1
Tenbury Wells WR15 . . . . . .12 B8
Wellington HR4 . . . . .27 C3
Mill Lane Ind Est WR15 . .13 A7
Mill Mdw WR15 . . . . .80 D3
Mill Orch HR9 . . . . .94 D5
Mill Par NP20 . . . . .119 D1
Mill St Abergavenny NP7 . . .95 E4
Crickhowell NP8 . . . . .60 A5
Hereford HR1 . . . . .136 B3
Kington HR5 . . . . .81 D6
Leominster HR6 . . . . .82 A3
Ludlow SY8 . . . . .79 C3
Newport NP20 . . . . .119 C4
Usk NP15 . . . . .97 B3
Mill Stream Pl HR1 . . . . . .91 B4
Mill Street NP15 . . . . .97 B3
Mill Street Ind Est NP7 . . .95 E4
Millard Cl HR2 . . . . .92 D5
Millbrook Cl SY8 . . . . .9 E6
Millbrook Ct
Magor NP26 . . . . .123 B3
Penperlleni NP4 . . . . .103 E3
Millbrook Gdns NP20 . . .112 F2
Millbrook Jun & Inf Schs
NP20 . . . . .112 F2
Millbrook La NP26 . . . . . . .77 D3

Millbrook Pl NP20 . . . . . .103 E2
Millbrook St HR4 . . . . . . .136 B4
Millbrook Way SY8 . . . . .9 C6
Millcroft Rd HR1 . . . . .28 D6
Miller Cl NP18 . . . . .115 F1
Miller Craddock Way
HR8 . . . . .89 D2
Millers Cl HR6 . . . . .82 C6
Millers Gn Abberley WR6 . .13 F4
Drybrook GL17 . . . . .67 A4
Millers Ride NP44 . . . . . . .107 A3
Millfield Pk NP26 . . . . . . .123 B4
Millhill La GL16 . . . . .72 F3
Millpond St HR9 . . . . .94 D4
Millstream Gdns HR3 . . . .24 E4
Millway
Sutton St Nicholas HR1 . . .38 C8
Wellington HR4 . . . . .27 D3
Milman St NP20 . . . . .119 C1
Milne Ho HR2 . . . . .92 E5
Milner St NP19 . . . . .119 F3
Milton Cl NP44 . . . . .106 D2
Milton Cross HR6 . . . . .16 C7
Milton Ct Malvern WR14 . . .85 A2
Newport NP19 . . . . .120 F6
Milton Hill NP18 . . . . .121 B5
Milton Inf Sch NP19 . . . . .120 F6
Milton Jun Sch NP19 . . . .120 F6
Milton Rd Ludlow SY8 . . . . .79 E4
Newport NP19 . . . . .120 A5
Milvern Cl HR7 . . . . .83 C6
Mine Pitts La HR9 . . . . .65 E3
Minnett's La NP26 . . . . . . .124 A5
Minories **1** NP44 . . . . . . .106 B1
Minster Coll The HR6 . . . .82 D3
Minster Ct **7** HR6 . . . . . . .82 D4
Minster Gr HR2 . . . . .92 C6
Miskin Cl NP44 . . . . .123 D3
Miskin Gn NP44 . . . . .107 A3
Miskin Ho NP44 . . . . .107 A3
Miss Grace's La NP16 . . . .76 E2
Mitch Pl HR2 . . . . .44 A4
**Mitcheldean Endowed Prim
Sch** GL17 . . . . .67 D5
Mitchell Cl NP44 . . . . .107 B1
Mitchell Terr 4 NP4 . . . . .102 A1
Mithras Way NP18 . . . . . .114 A4
Mitnell La
Richard's Castle SY8 . . . . . . .9 E8
Richards Castle SY8 . . . . . . .85 D1
Moat Cres WR14 . . . . .85 D1
Moatway WR14 . . . . .85 D1
Moccas St* HR2 . . . . .35 C6
Mocktree Turnpike SY7 . . .3 D7
Mole Cl NP20 . . . . .112 C2
Molescombe 6 NP44 . . . .106 B1
Mona Cl NP44 . . . . .106 D2
Monet Cres NP44 . . . . . . .120 A7
Monk St Abergavenny NP7 . .95 E5
Monmouth NP25 . . . . .137 B3
Monkland Rd HR6 . . . . . . .17 C5
Monkmoor St HR1 . . . . . .136 C3
Monks Cl NP26 . . . . .125 A6
Monks Mdw HR8 . . . . .49 F3
Monks' Ditch NP18 . . . . . .113 B7
Monksbury Cotts HR8 . . . .39 E6
Monkscroft Dr HR2 . . . . . . .92 C6
Monksfield La WR13 . . . . . .32 F5
Monkswell Cl NP25 . . . . . .137 B3
Monkton **7** HR2 . . . . .89 E2
Monmouth Castle*
NP25 . . . . .137 B2
Monmouth Cl NP44 . . . . .105 A2
Monmouth Comp Sch
NP25 . . . . .137 C3
Monmouth Dr NP19 . . . . .120 A8
Monmouth Ho NP44 . . . . .106 D2
Monmouth Hospl NP25 . .137 B3
Monmouth Mkt NP25 . . . .137 B3
Monmouth Rd
Abergavenny NP7 . . . . .95 E5
Gwernesney NP15 . . . . .74 C4
Raglan NP15 . . . . .70 C2
Trellech NP25 . . . . .75 F8
Usk NP15 . . . . .97 C5
Monmouth Sch NP25 . . . .137 C3
Monmouth Wlk NP44 . . . .106 E3
Monnington La HR4 . . . . . .35 E6
Monnington Wlk HR2,
HR4 . . . . .35 C6
Monnow WR14 . . . . .87 D8
Monnow Cres HR2 . . . . . . .92 E6
Monnow Ct NP44 . . . . . . .106 D2
Monnow Fm Ty Cradoc
HR2 . . . . .44 B3
Monnow Jun Sch NP20 . .112 D2
Monnow St NP25 . . . . . . .137 B3
Monnow Way NP20 . . . . .112 E2
Monnow Wlk NP20 . . . . . .112 E2
Mons Cl NP20 . . . . .119 A6
Montfort Fields HR5 . . . . . .81 B6
Montfort Rd HR5 . . . . .81 B6
Montgomery St HR4 . . . . . .90 A4
Montgomery Rd NP19 . . .119 A4
Montgomery St HR4 . . . . . .90 D1
Montpelier Rd HR4 . . . . . .84 C1
Montreal Cl NP20 . . . . . . .118 D3
Montresor Cl NP44 . . . . . .113 B7
Mood Wood Cl NP25 . . . . .55 C1
Moor Court La HR5 . . . . . . .15 F2
Moor Farm La HR4 . . . . . . .90 C3
Moor Mdw HR6 . . . . .110 B6
Moor Park Rd HR4 . . . . . . .90 C2
Moor Park Sch SY8 . . . . . . .4 F2
Moor St Chepstow NP16 . .116 E8
Hereford HR4 . . . . .136 B4
Moor The HR1 . . . . .28 D5

Moor View NP18 ....121 F3
Moore Cres NP19 ....121 A6
Moorfield Cotts HR1 ......29 B1
Moorfield Ct HR4 ....136 B3
Moorfield St HR4 ....136 B3
Moorings The
  Newport NP19 ....119 F8
  Newport NP19 ....120 A8
Moorland Av NP19 ....120 C3
Moorland Cl 81 GL14 .....67 C1
Moorland Pk NP19 ....120 C3
Moorlands Ct WR14 ......84 F2
Moorlands Rd WR14 ......84 F2
Moorlands The WR14 .....86 F4
Moorlands View NP26 ...125 B4
Moorings The NP4 ......104 E5
Mopla Rd NP16 ....116 E5
Morden La NP19 ....119 F2
Morden Rd NP19 ....119 E6
Mordiford CE Prim Sch
  HR1 ....48 D8
Mordiford Loop Wlk*
  HR1 ....39 A1
Moreland Ave HR1 ....91 B2
Moreton Rd HR4 ....37 E8
Morgan Ct WR14 ....84 F3
Morgan Rise NP4 ....101 D7
Morgan St
  Blaenavon NP4 ....101 C6
  Newport NP19 ....119 D6
Morgan Way NP10 ......128 F6
Morgans La GL17 ....67 A3
Morgans Orch HR5 ......81 D6
Morgraig Ave NP10 ....128 E5
Mork La GL15 ....76 E7
Mork Rd GL15 ....76 E7
Morley Cl NP19 ....120 E5
Morley Sq HR9 ....94 D5
Morman Cl GL17 ....67 B4
Morningside WR15 ......80 C4
Morris Rise NP4 ....101 D7
Morris St NP19 ....119 E4
Morse La GL17 ....67 A4
Morse Rd GL17 ....67 B4
Mortimer Cl
  Leominster HR6 ....82 C4
  Orleton SY8 ....9 E6
Mortimer Dr SY8 ....9 F8
Mortimer Pl SY8 ....79 D4
Mortimer St HR4 ....90 F3
Mortimer St HR6 ....82 C4
Mortimer Trad Ctr HR4 ..90 F3
Mortimer's Cross Water
  Mill* HR6 ....8 D2
Mortlake Dr WR6 ....22 D6
Morton Cotts HR8 ......41 A6
Morton Way NP20 ......118 F1
Morville Cl HR7 ....92 B5
Moseley Terr NP44 ....106 E7
Moss Rd NP44 ....106 B3
Mostyn St HR4 ....136 A3
Mount Cl GL17 ....84 E3
Mount Craig Hall HR9 ..65 F8
Mount Cres HR1 ....91 D2
Mount Orch WR15 ......80 C4
Mount Pleasant
  Chepstow NP16 ......116 E8
  Llanelly Hill NP7 ......98 C5
  Newport NP20 ....113 A3
  Ross-on-W HR9 ....94 E6
  Tenbury Wells WR15 ..80 D7
Mount Pleasant Cl
  NP10 ....106 D5
Mount Pleasant Ct NP4 104 C6
Mount Pleasant Jun & Inf
  Sch NP10 ....118 A6
Mount Pleasant Rd
  Cwmbran NP44 ....106 D5
  Pontypool NP4 ....104 A8
Mount Rd NP4 ....102 D1
Mount St NP7 ....95 C6
Mount Way
  Chepstow NP16 ......110 D1
  Chepstow NP16 ......116 D8
  St Weonards HR2 .....56 B3
Mountain La NP4 ......104 D3
Mountain Rd
  Cwmbran NP44 ....104 B7
  Pontypool NP4 ....104 B1
  Rogerstone NP10 ....118 A8
Mountain View
  Almeley HR3 ....25 A6
  Llanfoist NP7 ....95 B3
  Ruardean GL17 ....66 F4
Mountbatten Cl NP19 ..120 F7
Mountbatten Ct HR2 ...93 A6
Mountbatten St HR4 ...88 C2
Mountford Cl NP10 ....118 A4
Mountjoy Pl 4 NP20 ..119 C3
Mountjoy St 5 NP20 ..119 C3
Mountjoy St 6 NP20 ..119 C3
Mountjoy's La 23 GL14 ..67 C1
Mountjoy's Lane End 26
  GL14 ....67 C1
Mounton Cl NP16 ......116 B7
Mounton Dr NP16 ......116 C6
Mounton House Specl Sch
  NP16 ....116 B7
Mounton Hts NP16 ....116 B8
Mounton Rd NP16 ....116 C8
Mowbage La HR2 ......35 B2
Mowberry La HR6 .....17 F5
Moxon Rd NP20 ....113 A1
Moyle Gr NP18 ....119 F8
Moyle Old School La
  NP16 ....111 A4
Moyle's Cross NP25 ...64 E4
Much Birch Sch HR2 ..47 C1

Much Marcle CE Prim Sch
  HR8 ....49 F4
Muir Cl HR2 ....92 D4
Muirfield Cl HR1 ......91 A5
Mulberry Cl HR1 ......91 A5
Mulberry Ct WR6 .....13 C6
Mulberry Dr WR14 ....86 F4
Mulcaster Ave NP19 ..120 C2
Munnings Dr NP19 ....120 A7
Murrells Rd GL18 .....60 A6
Murren Ave WR14 ....87 A5
Museum Ct NP4 ....104 E2
Museum St NP18 .....114 B1
Mynachdy Pitch NP7 ..62 B1
Mynd Rd LD8 ....6 D6
Mynydd Bach Rd NP16 ..77 F8
Mynydd Cl NP4 ....104 C4
Mynydd Maen Rd NP44 106 C6
Mynydd View NP44 ....104 C4
Myra Hess Cl NP19 ...120 F6
Myrtle Cl NP18 ....118 B3
Myrtle Cotts NP18 ...114 C2
Myrtle Dr NP10 ......118 B3
Myrtle Gr NP19 ......120 B5
Myrtle Pl NP16 ......110 F1
Myrtles The NP16 ....111 A2

N

Nailer's La NP25 .....137 B2
Nailers La GL18 .....59 D3
Nan Belville Day Hospl The
  HR4 ....92 D8
Nant Celyn Cl NP44 ..106 C6
Nant Coch Dr NP20 ..118 E4
Nant Coch House Rougemont
  Sch NP20 ....118 E4
Nant-Y-Banw La NP15 ..77 B8
Nantgavenny La NP7 ..95 E8
Nantsor Rd NP16 .....108 B3
Nantyglasdwr La HR3 ..88 F4
Napping La GL17 .....67 F6
Napping The GL17 ....67 F6
Narberth Cres NP44 ..107 B3
Narth La NP25 ....72 B1
Nash Cl Martley WR6 ..22 D6
Nash Dr NP19 ....120 B2
Nash Gn WR13 ....32 D5
Nash Gr NP19 ....120 B3
Nash Mead NP19 ....130 C8
Nash Rd NP19 ....130 C8
National Birds of Prey Ctr*
  GL18 ....59 E2
National Bldgs 10 NP20 119 C4
Naval Temple & Round House
  The* NP25 ....72 B7
Navigator* NP20 .....119 C3
Near Green Cl HR8 ...49 F8
Neath Cl NP44 ....106 A4
Neddern Ct NP26 ....124 F6
Neddern Way NP26 ..124 F7
Neerings NP44 ....106 A1
Nelson Dr NP19 .....120 E6
Nelson Mus & Local History
  Ctr* NP25 ....137 B2
Nelson St Chepstow NP16 116 F8
  Hereford HR1 ....136 C1
Nelsons Cl NP19 ......66 B7
Neston Rd NP19 .....120 E5
Nether Grange WR14 ..84 F1
Nethercourt NP44 ....106 B3
Netherhope La NP16 ..111 B5
Netherton Rd HR9 ....94 E8
Netherwent View NP26 123 A4
Netherwood Manor Cotts
  WR15 ....20 D8
Netherwood Rd HR2 ..93 D4
Nevern Wlk 3 NP44 ..107 B2
Nevill Hall Hospl NP7 ..95 B5
Nevill St NP7 ....95 D5
Nevill Terr NP4 ......101 D7
Neville Pk NP10 .....128 E1
Nevinson Pl HR1 .....93 E7
New Barn HR3 ....24 E4
New Barnfields HR4 ..37 A5
New Bldgs The NP10 ..104 B7
New Chapel Cl NP44 ..106 D1
New Cotts HR6 ....8 B1
New Court La NP7 ....61 E3
New House Bglws WR6 ..32 F7
New Inn Cl HR1 .....48 D5
New Inn Inf Sch NP4 ..105 B4
New James St NP4 ...101 D6
New Junction Cotts NP7 95 F7
New Market St
  Hereford HR4 ....136 B3
  Usk NP15 ....97 A4
New Mills Way HR8 ..89 C5
New Pastures NP20 ..119 A2
New Quay Rd NP19 ..129 E8
New Queen St NP4 ..101 C6
New Rank NP7 ....98 C5
New Rd Bromyard HR7 ..83 C6
  Caerleon NP18 ......114 C1
  Caldicot NP26 ......124 E5
  Crickhowell NP8 .....60 A5
  Kimbolton HR6 ......18 E8
  King's Thorn HR2 ....47 C2
  Lindridge WR15 ......22 D2
  Ludlow SY8 ....79 C5
  Mitcheldean GL17 ..66 C5
  Pontypool NP4 ......104 F3
  Welland WR13 ......42 E2
New Ruperra St NP20 ..119 C3
New St Cwmbran NP44 ..106 E5
  Ledbury HR8 ....89 D3

New St continued
  Leominster HR6 ......82 D5
  Ludlow SY8 ....79 C6
  Mitcheldean GL17 ..67 D5
  Newport NP20 ......119 D2
  Ross-on-W HR9 ......94 D5
New Terr NP4 ....104 A8
New Town GL14 ......67 B2
New William St 18 NP4 101 C6
Newbridge Farm Pk*
  HR8 ....50 A8
Newbury Ct HR4 ......90 C4
Newbury Pk HR8 ......89 D5
Newchurch Rd NP44 ..106 C3
Newchurch Rd HR3 ..25 C5
Newent Com Sch GL18 59 F4
Newgale Ho NP44 ....106 F3
Newgale Row NP44 ..106 F3
Newhouse Farm Ind Est
  NP16 ....116 F3
Newhouse Open Farm*
  HR2 ....92 D1
Newland Gn WR13 ....85 D7
Newland Way NP44 ..106 C3
Newlands HR1 ....91 A4
Newlands Cl 17 NP4 ..102 A1
Newlands Dr HR6 ....82 B4
Newlands Rd HR6 ....82 C4
Newlands The NP7 ....95 F8
Newman Cl
  Leominster HR6 ......82 C4
  Newport NP19 ......120 F5
Newman Ho HR6 ......82 C4
Newman Rd NP4 ......102 B1
Newmills Hill HR9 ....65 F5
Newnham Pl NP44 ....106 E3
Newport (Casnewydd) Sta
  NP20 ....119 B5
Newport Arc 3 NP20 ..119 B5
Newport Castle* NP20 119 C5
Newport Ctr(L Ctr)
  NP20 ....119 C4
Newport Mkt NP20 ..119 C5
Newport Mus & Art Gal*
  NP20 ....119 C4
Newport Nash Campus
  NP19 ....120 C2
Newport Rd
  Caldicot NP26 ......124 E5
  Chepstow NP16 ....116 D7
  Croesyceiliog NP44 107 B6
  Cwmbran NP44 ......113 A6
  Magor NP26 ....123 A3
  Pontypool NP4 ......105 A2
Newport Retail Pk
  NP19 ....120 D2
Newport St HR1 ......88 E4
Newstead Cl HR1 ....91 B3
Newton Cl HR8 ......89 E2
Newton Court La NP25 ..65 B1
Newton La Kington HR5 81 C7
  Norton LD8 ....6 D5
  Pen-y-Park HR3 ......34 B7
Newton Manor NP16 ..78 C4
Newton Way NP20 ....112 F2
Newton Wynd NP44 ..106 B1
Newtown La
  King's Thorn HR2 ....47 C3
  Newtown HR6 ....17 F4
Newtown Rd
  Cinderford GL14 ....67 B2
  Hereford HR4 ......136 C4
  Malvern WR14 ......84 E3
  Penperlleni NP4 ....103 F6
Neyland Path NP44 ..106 B2
Nicholas St NP4 ....104 C6
Nicholson Ct HR4 ....90 C6
Nidd Cl NP20 ....112 C1
Nidd Wlk NP20 ......112 C1
Nightingale Cl NP26 ..125 A4
Nightingale Ct NP10 ..128 E7
Nightingale Ho NP44 ..106 D5
Nightingale Rd WR14 ..85 C2
Nightingale Terr NP4 ..104 A8
Nimrod Dr HR1 ......119 A6
Ninewells Forest Wlk*
  NP16 ....76 B5
Noble View WR14 ....84 D3
Noden Dr HR9 ....67 C8
Noke La Kington HR5,HR6 ..15 F1
  Staunton on A HR4 ..16 A6
Nolan Rd HR4 ....136 B4
Nolton Pl NP44 ......106 A2
Nook The HR1 ....91 D2
Norbury Ho HR10 ....106 C2
Norbury Pl HR1 ......93 E7
Norfolk Cl NP44 ....106 A3
Norfolk Ho NP19 ....119 F6
Norman Cl NP26 ....124 F5
Norman St NP18 ....114 B2
Norman Way
  Caldicot NP26 ......125 C4
  Ruardean GL17 ......66 F4
Normandie Cl SY8 ....79 E4
Normands Ho NP44 ..112 C8
Normandy Way NP16 110 D1
Norrland Pl HR9 ......66 C8
Norse Way HR16 ....117 B7
North Ave GL17 ......67 B4
North End La WR13,WR14 84 E3
North Hill Gdns WR14 ..84 E3
North Lake Dr NP10 ..128 C6
North Malvern Ho WR14 ..84 F2
North Malvern Rd WR14 84 E2
North Pole La HR9 ..99 C7
North Rd Kingsland HR6 ..17 C8

North Rd continued
  Leominster HR6 ......82 C7
  Pontypool NP4 ......104 B6
  Ross-on-W HR9 ......94 F5
North Rd (Heol Y Gogledd)
  NP44 ....107 A5
North Row NP26 ......132 C6
North St Abergavenny NP7 ..95 C6
  Blaenavon NP4 ......101 B7
  Newport NP20 ......119 B4
North View NP7 ......99 F8
North Wlk
  Cwmbran NP44 ......106 E4
  Malvern WR14 ......84 E1
Northamfield 46 D8
Northdown Cl HR8 ....89 D5
Northern Way GL17 ..67 D5
Northfield Cl NP18 ..113 F4
Northfield Rd NP18 ..114 A4
Northleigh CE Prim Sch
  WR14 ....84 D4
Northmead HR8 ......89 D5
Northolme Rd HR2 ....92 C6
Northolt Dr HR4 ....36 F6
Northover Ct BS35 ..135 E6
Northside Pk HR6 ....28 A8
Northumberland Rd 2
  NP19 ....119 F6
Northway NP4 ....103 B2
Northwick Rd BS35 ..127 E1
Northwood Cl 22 GL14 ..67 C1
Norton Ave HR7 ......92 B6
Norton Cl HR9 ....65 D4
Nourse Pl GL17 ......67 D5
Nover Wood Dr HR1 ..48 E5
Nuffield Hospital Hereford
  HR1 ....91 C2
Nunwell Rd HR7 ......83 C5
Nupend Gdns GL17 ..67 F5
Nupend La GL17 ......67 F5
Nurdens The HR1 ....49 B7
Nurseries The NP18 ..121 D8
Nursery Dr HR4 ......37 F8
Nursery Rd Malvern WR14 ..84 E4
  Ross-on-W HR9 ......94 E6

O

O'Neal Ave NP19 ....130 A8
Oak Ave Hereford HR2 ..92 F6
  Madresfield WR13 ..85 F4
Oak Bridge Ct WR15 ..80 D3
Oak Cl Bromyard HR7 ..83 B5
  Chepstow NP16 ......116 F5
  Undy NP26 ....123 B3
Oak Cres Clehonger HR2 ..46 C8
  Hereford HR2 ....92 F6
  Malvern WR14 ......85 C1
Oak Ct HR1 ....102 A1
Oak Dr WR13 ....86 B2
Oak Field The 7 GL14 ..67 C1
Oak Gr NP25 ....64 D1
Oak La Burghill HR4 ..90 A7
  Llanellen NP7 ......68 D4
Oak Plock HR5 ....81 C6
Oak Rd Credenhill HR4 ..37 A6
  Ross-on-W HR9 ......94 E6
Oak St Cwmbran NP44 ..106 E2
Oak Tree Cl NP19 ....119 E8
Oak Tree
  Pontypool NP4 ......105 A5
  Tenbury Wells WR15 ..80 D6
Oak Tree Cl NP19 ....120 B5
Oak Tree La NP7 ....60 E2
Oak Tree Rise NP4 ..94 F7
Oak View NP4 ....101 E6
Oakdale La NP44 ....106 C2
Oakdale Path 6 NP44 ..106 C2
Oakdale Pl NP44 ....104 A8
Oakdean 7 GL14 ....67 C1
Oakdene Way NP7 ..60 D1
Oaker View NP7 ......17 F5
Oakfield NP18 ......113 F3
Oakfield Ave NP16 ..110 D1
Oakfield Gdns NP20 ..119 A4
Oakfield Prim Sch NP44 ..112 F8
Oakfield Rd
  Cwmbran NP44 ......106 F1
  Malvern WR14 ......85 A5
  Monmouth NP25 ....96 D7
Oakhill Pitch GL15 ..76 F3
Oakhill Rd GL17 ......67 D5
Oakland Dr HR8 ......89 D3
Oakland Rd GL17 ....67 B3
Oakland Terr
  Cwmbran NP44 ......112 E8
  Ross-on-W HR9 ......94 D3
Oakland Villas HR3 ..84 F1
Oaklands Cradley WR13 ..31 D1
Oaklands Cl HR4 ......86 F1
Oaklands Cotts HR9 ..57 D3
Oaklands Ct HR9 ....94 E6
Oaklands Pk NP26 ..125 D5
Oaklands Rd
  Newport NP19 ......119 F5
  Pontypool NP4 ......105 D8
Oaklands The
  Newtown HR8 ....39 E8
  Tenbury Wells WR15 ..80 D3
Oaklands View NP44 ..106 A3
Oakley Cl NP26 ......124 E6
Oakley St NP19 ......119 F3

Moo – Old 151

Oakley Way NP26 ....124 E6
Oaks Cl NP20 ....119 A2
Oaks La GL18 ....59 D2
Oaks The Clehonger HR2 ..37 E1
  Croesyceiliog NP44 ..107 B5
  Cwmbran NP44 ......121 E7
  Tenbury Wells WR15 ..11 F2
Oaksford NP44 ......106 A2
Oaktree Ct NP44 ....106 A2
Oakwood Cl 30 GL14 ..67 C1
Oatfield Cl HR4 ......90 C2
Oatlands HR4 ....90 C4
Oatleys Cres HR8 ....89 C5
Oatleys Rd HR8 ......89 D3
Oatleys Terr HR8 ....89 D4
Oban Way HR17 ......22 B3
Ochre Hill HR8 ......41 C3
Octagon The NP16 ..116 F5
Octavivs Cl NP10 ..128 E5
Offa St HR1 ....136 C2
Offa's Mead Prim Sch
  NP16 ....117 A8
Offas Cl NP16 ......117 A8
Offas Gn (Maes Offa) LD8 ..6 D6
Offway NP4 ....112 C1
Ogmore Cres NP20 ..112 C1
Ogmore Pl 8 NP44 ..107 B2
Ogwen Ho NP4 ......106 C2
Okell Dr HR9 ....94 E2
Olchon Valley HR2 ..44 B1
Old Abbey Pl NP8 ....60 C3
Old Abergavenny Rd
  Llanover NP7 ....68 E1
  Penperlleni NP4 ....103 B5
Old Barn 4 NP19 ....119 F8
Old Barn Ct Bircher HR6 ..9 C4
  Hereford HR1 ....91 B3
Old Barn Way NP7 ....95 E7
Old Bedstone Rd SY7 ..2 C4
Old Bell Chambers
  NP16 ....116 E8
Old Bowling Green Cl
  WR15 ....80 C6
Old Brickyard SY8 ..79 C5
Old Bulwark Rd NP16 116 E7
Old Cardiff Rd NP20 ..118 F1
Old Castle Cl NP10 ..128 E5
Old Chepstow Rd NP18 121 D8
Old Church Rd
  Colwall WR13 ....86 A2
  Colwall Stone WR13 ..41 F5
Old Coach Cl HR1 ....117 C2
Old Coach Rd HR14 ..117 C3
Old Dean Rd GL17 ..67 D6
Old Dixton Rd NP25 ..137 C3
Old Eign Hill HR1 ..93 D8
Old Estate Yd NP4 ..104 E5
Old Forge WR6 ......21 F3
Old Forge The HR1 ..136 A3
Old Forge The HR2 ..35 B2
Old Foundry The HR5 ..81 E6
Old Gloucester Rd NP44 ..94 E5
Old Green Intc NP20 ..119 C5
Old Hall Cl NP10 ....128 F7
Old Hall Cotts HR6 ..18 B2
Old Hereford Rd NP7 ..95 E7
Old High Town HR9 ..57 C3
Old High Town Gn HR9 ..57 C3
Old Hill NP18 ......120 C8
Old Hill Cres NP18 ..120 D7
Old Hill Rd NP18 ..120 D7
Old Hollow WR14 ..84 D4
Old House Mus The*
  HR1 ....136 C3
Old James St 16 NP4 ..101 C6
Old La HR9 ....57 C3
Old La (Simmonds La)
  HR9,GL18 ....59 C3
Old Langstone Court Rd
  NP18 ....121 B8
Old Maid's Wlk HR9 ..94 D4
Old Market Cl HR9 ..94 D6
Old Market St HR8 ..89 D4
Old Mill Cl HR4 ......136 B2
Old Monmouth Rd 10
  NP15 ....70 C2
Old Nursery Cl HR9 ..94 B5
Old Oak Cl NP16 ......32 C5
Old Orch WR13 ......32 C5
Old Orchard La WR14 ..84 E3
Old Pill Farm Ind Est
  NP26 ....125 B4
Old Queen St 2 NP4 ..101 C6
Old Rd Abersychan NP4 ..102 A3
  Bromyard HR7 ....83 C6
  Clifton u T WR6 ....22 A8
  Llantrisant NP15,NP10 ..77 D8
Old Rectory Cl NP7 ..102 A4
Old Rectory Gdns
  Bransford WR6 ......32 E7
  Much Birch HR2 ....47 C1
Old Ross Rd
  Abergavenny NP7 ....61 F2
  Llanvapley NP7 ......62 D4
Old Row NP25 ......125 F3
Old Sch Hill HR7 ....83 D6
Old School Ct HR7 ..83 D6
Old School Hill NP16 ..116 D7
Old School La
  Hereford HR1 ....91 A4
  Moccas HR2 ....37 F2
  Tenbury Wells WR15 ..80 D7
Old School Sarahs Tn
  HR2 ....44 D3

Old School The HR2 .... 56 B3
Old Shop La HR6 .... 8 A5
Old Shoppe Lands HR2 ....54 C7
Old St SY8 ....79 C3
Old Stables WR15 ....11 F2
Old Station Rd
  Bransford WR6 ....32 D8
  Newent GL18 ....59 F5
Old Stone La NP26 ....123 C3
Old Tay HR2 ....34 E1
Old Thatch CI HR2 ....35 F4
Old Tram Rd HR2 ....92 D6
Old Trap Rd NP7 ....60 D1
Old William St 12 NP4 ...101 C6
Old Wyche Rd WR14 ....86 E5
Oldbridge CI HR4 ....16 A5
Oldbury Bsns Ctr NP44 ...106 E2
Oldbury Ct 5 HR7 ....83 C6
Oldbury Rd NP44 ....106 E2
Oldfields CI HR6 ....82 C5
Oldwood Rd WR15 ....80 C2
Oliphant Circ NP20 ......112 F3
Oliver Rd NP19 ....120 A3
Olway CI NP44 ....107 A1
Ombersley La NP20 ....118 F4
Ombersley Rd NP20 ....118 F4
Ongar St Lingen SY7 ......7 F6
  Wigmore HR6,SY7 ....8 A6
Open Hearth CI NP4 .....104 E2
Orangery Wlk NP10 ......128 F7
Orchard Ave NP16 ....116 E5
Orchard Bsns Pk HR8 .....89 C7
Orchard CI
  Abergavenny NP7 ....95 C6
  Adforton SY7 ....3 A2
  Bodenham Moor HR1 ......28 D5
  Caldicot NP26 ....124 F4
  Clearwell GL16 ....72 F3
  Credenhill HR4 ....36 C6
  Dilwyn HR4 ....16 F1
  Eardisley HR3 ....34 A4
  English Bicknor GL16 ....66 A2
  Gilwern NP7 ....60 D1
  Hereford HR4 ....90 E5
  Kingsland HR6 ....17 C8
  Knighton HR2 ....46 A6
  Lea HR9 ....67 C8
  Mitcheldean GL17 ....67 D5
  Moreton-On-L HR4 ....37 F8
  Pontypool NP4 ....102 B1
  Presteigne LD8 ....6 E3
  11 Raglan NP15 ....70 C2
  Skenfrith NP7 ....64 A7
  Sutton St Nicholas HR1 ..38 C8
  Woodcroft NP16 ....111 A4
Orchard Ct
  Monmouth NP25 ....96 F3
  Newport NP19 ....119 D7
  Tenbury Wells WR15 ......80 C5
Orchard End NP25 ....96 F4
Orchard Farm CI NP16 ...117 B7
Orchard Farm Est NP4 ...102 C1
Orchard Gdns
  Chepstow NP16 ....110 F1
  Hereford HR2 ....93 A5
  Ludlow SY8 ....79 D5
  Portskewett NP26 ......125 D5
  Upper Sapey WR6 ....12 F2
Orchard Gn HR1 ....28 A2
Orchard Gr HR2 ....54 C7
Orchard La
  Crickhowell NP8 ....60 A5
  Cwmbran NP44 ....106 F4
  Ledbury HR8 ....89 D5
  Leominster HR6 ....82 B3
  Newport NP19 ....119 E7
Orchard Lea Alfrick WR6 ..31 F8
  Bitterley SY8 ....8 A5
Orchard Mews
  Abergavenny NP7 ....95 C6
  Newport NP19 ....119 D7
Orchard Pl
  Bredwardine HR3 ....35 A7
  Cwmbran NP44 ....106 D2
  Ledbury HR8 ....89 E2
  Peterchurch HR2 ....35 B1
Orchard Rd
  Caerleon NP18 ....114 A4
  Joy's Green GL17 ....66 D3
  Malvern WR14 ....86 F8
  Newent GL18 ....59 E5
Orchard Rise
  Chepstow NP16 ....116 B5
  Richard's Castle SY8 ....9 A7
  Shrewewton NP16 ....78 D4
Orchard St
  Abergavenny NP7 ....95 C6
  Newport NP19 ....119 D7
Orchard The
  Ponthir NP18 ....113 F6
  Ross-on-W HR7 ....94 F7
  Orchard View HR1 ....38 F5
  Orchard Way WR6 ....32 E7
Orchards The
  Hampton Bishop HR1 .....38 E1
  Longhope GL17 ....67 F6
  Newport NP20 ....78 D4
Orchid Ct
  Abergavenny NP7 ....95 C6
  Newport NP19 ....119 D7
Orchid Ct Cwmbran NP44 .106 A1
  Newport NP10 ....128 A7
Orchid Dr NP26 ....125 B4
Orchid Mdw NP16 ....116 B5
Ordnance CI HR4 ....37 F8
Orford Way WR14 ....85 C2
Oriel Ho WR14 ....84 F1
Oriel Rd NP19 ....119 E5

Orion Suite The NP20 ...119 D3
Orleton CE Prim Sch SY8 ..9 E6
Orleton CI WR13 ....42 E2
Park CI Abergavenny NP7 ..95 E6
  Hereford HR1 ....90 F5
  Malvern WR14 ....85 B4
  Newport NP20 ....118 E1
  St Briavels GL15 ....76 F7
Park Cres
  Abergavenny NP7 ....95 E6
  Clydach NP7 ....98 D7
  Newport NP20 ....118 E1
  Pontypool NP4 ....104 D7
Park Ct Abergavenny NP7 ..95 E6
  Undy NP26 ....123 D3
Park Dr Llangattock NP8 ..60 A4
  Newport NP20 ....118 F1
  Park End NP18 ....121 C8
Park Gdns
  Blaenavon NP4 ....101 C6
  Newport NP20 ....118 E1
  Pontypool NP4 ....104 C7
Park Glade NP16 ....76 B4
Park Gn HR5 ....81 C6
Park Hill La NP16,GL15 ...76 E2
Park House Flats NP4 ....95 E6
Park House La WR14 .....86 C6
  Leintwardine SY7 ....3 B5
  Upper Sapey WR6 ....13 B2
  Woofferton SY8 ....9 F8
Park Rd Abergavenny NP7 ..95 D6
  Caldicot NP26 ....124 E6
  Clydach NP7 ....98 D7
  Eardisley HR3 ....24 D3
  Kington HR5 ....81 C6
  Ludlow SY8 ....79 C3
  Malvern WR14 ....86 C8
  Pontypool NP4 ....104 C7
Park Side HR2 ....54 F4
Park Sq NP20 ....119 C4
Park St Abergavenny NP7 ..95 E6
  Blaenavon NP4 ....101 C6
  Hereford HR1 ....93 B7
  Pontypool NP4 ....104 C7
Park Stile Mill HR5 ......23 F8
Park Street Inf Sch NP7 ..95 C5
Park Ter NP4 ....102 A1
Park Terrace Prim Sch
  NP4 ....104 C6
Park The Blaenavon NP4 ..101 C7
  Hereford HR1 ....93 E7
Park View Bassaleg NP10 .118 B3
  Chepstow NP16 ....110 C1
  Cwmbran NP44 ....106 E6
  Kington HR5 ....81 C6
  1 Pontypool NP4 ....102 A1
  Ruardean GL17 ....66 F4
  Sedbury NP16 ....117 B8
  Weobley HR4 ....26 A6
Park View Gdns NP10 ...118 B3
Park Wlk HR9 ....94 E4
Park Wood CI NP18 .....113 E3
Park Y Brain La NP4 ....103 D7
Parke's La NP4 ....104 A6
Parkfield PI NP20 ......119 A5
Parklands NP4 ....103 F7
Parklands CI
  Chepstow NP16 ....116 B4
  Cwmbran NP44 ....106 E6
  Rogerstone NP10 ....118 C3
Parklawn CI NP44 ......106 E6
Parkmill HR9 ....65 C7
Parks Farm Rd HR3 .....34 B3
Parks Rd GL17 ....67 D5
Parks View The HR2 .....54 B8
Parkside Colwall WR13 ...86 B1
  Newport NP20 ....106 D2
Parkside Ct 15 NP4 .....102 A1
Parkview WR14 ....86 F8
Parkwall Hill NP16,NP26 .78 F1
Parkways SY8 ....79 C3
Parkwood Ct HR7 ....93 E4
Parragate Rd 14 GL14 ...67 C1
Parret CI NP20 ....112 F2
Parret Rd NP20 ....112 F2
Parret Wlk NP20 ....112 F2
Parry Dr NP19 ....120 C5
Parsons Croft HR9 ......94 F7
Parsons La GL17 ....51 F2
Parsons Wlk HR6 ....16 D5
Partridge Mead HR4 ....90 C2
Partridge Way NP10 ...128 F7
Parva Springs NP16 .....76 B4
Parys Rd SY8 ....79 E4
Passa La HR6 ....82 C2
Passey Ct HR5 ....81 D6
Pastures The
  Crow Hill HR9 ....58 D5
  Hereford HR2 ....93 B4
  Llanyrawon NP44 ....107 B3
Patches The GL17 ....66 F3
Paterson CI HR2 ....36 C1
Patterson Way NP25 ....96 B5
Patti CI NP19 ....120 C6
Paunton Cross WR6 .....30 E5
Pavement The HR3 ......88 D3
Pavilion Est NP4 ......104 A8
Pavilion Rd NP16 ......117 C2
Paxton Wlk NP10 ......118 A7
Paytoe Ind Est SY7 .....3 B4
Peachfield CI WR14 .....86 F5
Peachfield Rd WR14 ....86 F5
Pear Tree CI
  Bromyard HR7 ....83 B6
  Caerleon NP18 ....113 E2
  Malvern WR14 ....86 E4
Pear Tree Dr WR13 .....32 D5

Pear Tree La NP19 .....120 B3
Pegasus Ct NP7 ....95 E4
Pembridge CE Prim Sch
  HR6 ....16 C5
Pembridge CI HR2 ......92 E6
Pembroke Ave WR15 ....80 D5
Pembroke CI NP26 .....123 D3
Pembroke Ct
  Tenbury Wells WR15 .....80 D5
  Undy NP26 ....123 D3
Pembroke Gr NP19 .....120 A2
Pembroke PI NP44 .....107 B3
Pembroke Prim Sch
  NP16 ....116 E6
Pembroke Rd NP16 .....116 E6
Pembroke Terr NP4 ....101 E1
Pen Padrig NP7 ....99 E8
Pen-Y Parc Rd NP15 ....70 B3
Pen-Mynydd NP4 ......101 D7
Pen-Twyn La NP20 ......23 B3
Pen-Twyn La NP20 .....112 E2
Pen-Y-Bryn CI NP20 ...112 E2
Pen-Y-Graig Terr NP4 ..104 B8
Pen-Y-Llan La NP4 ....105 B8
Pen-y-Pound
  Abergavenny NP7 ....95 C7
Pen-Y-Pound Ct NP7 ....95 D7
Pen-Y-Rhiw NP7 ....60 F2
Pen-Y-Waun CI NP44 ...106 D2
Pen-Y-Waun Rd NP44 ...106 D2
Penallt NP7 ....98 D5
Penarth Ct NP44 ....107 B1
Penbailey HR2 ....55 D2
Penbedw NP44 ....107 B4
Pencarn Ave NP10 .....128 C6
Pencarn La NP10 ......128 D6
Pencarn Way NP10 ....128 D6
Pencoed La NP18 ......122 E2
Pencoed PI NP44 ......106 F6
Pencoed View NP18 ...122 B7
Pencombe CE Prim Sch
  HR7 ....29 D7
Pencombe Cross HR7 ...29 C7
Pencombe La HR7 ......83 A5
Pencraig View HR9 .....94 D7
Pencroft Rd HR2 ....92 F5
Penda PI NP19 ....117 A8
Pendant Pitch NP7 .....47 C3
Pendive Wlk NP44 .....106 E6
Pendoylan Wlk NP44 ...106 C1
Pendragon CI WR14 ....85 C4
Pengam La Llanover NP7 .73 B8
  Llanvair Kilgeddin NP7 ..69 B1
Penglaise Ct HR2 ......92 E6
Penhaligon Way HR4 ..136 B4
Penhow Castle* NP7 ....77 D1
Penhow Mews NP10 ...128 E5
Penkin CI NP19 ....120 D4
Penkin Hill NP19 .....120 D4
Penlan La HR3 ....24 A6
Penllyn Ave
  Cwmbran NP44 ....106 E6
  Newport NP20 ....118 F4
Penllyn La NP20 ......118 F4
Penmaes Rd HR4 ......106 A4
Penmoel La NP16 ......111 A3
Penmoyle Gdns NP16 ..111 A4
Penn Grove Rd HR1 ....91 B2
Penn Hall La WR6 ......13 C8
Pennine CI HR4 ....90 B3
Penny Cres NP20 ......112 C1
Pennyfarthing La NP26 .123 C3
Pennyfields 8 NP44 ...106 B3
Pennyplock HR2 ....36 C1
Penrice Gn 9 NP44 ....107 A2
Pensarn Way NP44 ....112 A8
Pensax Rd WR6 ....13 D6
Pentaloe CI HR1 ....48 D8
Penterry Pk NP16 ......116 C5
Pentland Gdns HR4 .....90 B3
Pentonville NP20 ......119 B5
Pentre CI NP44 ....112 B8
Pentre Farm La HR3 ...23 F4
Pentre Gr HR3 ....23 C3
Pentre La
  Abergavenny NP7 ....95 B7
  Bredwardine HR3 ....35 A6
  Cwmbran NP44 ....112 C5
  Llangwm NP15 ....74 D3
  Penperlleni NP4 ....103 C4
Pentre Rd NP7 ....95 B7
Pentre-Jack HR3 ....34 B5
Pentre-Poeth Rd NP10 .118 A2
Pentwyn NP7 ....92 E6
Pentwyn Ave HR2 ......92 E6
Pentwyn CI NP16 ......116 B6
Pentwyn Ct NP16 ......116 B6
Pentwyn La
  Coed-Cwnwr NP15 ......74 C2
  Govilon NP7 ....99 F7
Penyard Gdns HR9 .....58 D2
Penyard La HR9 ....94 E4
Penyard Villas WR9 ....94 F5
Penybont NP7 ....99 F8
Penybont Rd LD7 ....6 A6
Penyclawdd La NP7 .....61 E6
Penyfal Rd NP7 ....95 D6
Penyrgarn Inf & Jun Sch
  NP4 ....104 D8
Penyrgarn Rd NP44 ....104 D8
Penylog Rd NP18 ......108 B4
Penylan CI
  Bassaleg NP10 ....118 A3
  Pontypool NP4 ....105 B4

Penylan Ct NP44 ....112 B8
Penylan Rd NP19 ......120 A5
Penylan Way NP44 ....112 B8
Penyparc NP44 ....106 C6
Penyrheol Rd NP44 ....104 C3
Penyrhiwiau HR2 ......53 C7
Penywain La NP44 ....104 B6
Penywain St NP4 ......104 B7
Penywain Terr NP4 ....104 B7
Penywaun Row NP4 ....79 C4
Pepys Gr NP20 ....118 E2
Percival PI HR2 ....44 C5
Percival St HR4 ....90 D4
Percoed La NP10 ......128 C4
Percy Walton CI WR14 .87 A6
Peregrine CI HR2 ......93 A6
Peregrine Ct NP26 ....123 C3
Pergoed La NP4 ....105 F7
Perrins CI WR14 ....84 F4
Perry Ct NP44 ....104 A6
Perry's Court La GL17 ..66 E4
Perryfield HR2 ....56 F3
Perryfields HR1 ....49 B3
Perrystone La HR1 .....91 E1
Perseverance Rd
  Hereford HR4 ....90 F3
  Leominster HR6 ....82 B3
Perseverence CI HR5 ...81 E5
Perth-Bach La HR2 .....53 F5
Perthy CI NP44 ....112 B8
Perton La HR1 ....39 C3
Peterchurch Prim Sch
  HR2 ....35 B1
Peterson CI WR14 ......84 F1
Pettingale Rd NP44 ...107 B5
Petty Marsh GL17 ......51 C6
Pettycroft GL17 ....66 F4
Pheasant Rise HR9 .....65 F7
Phillip St NP19 ....119 E5
Phillip's Gro NP10 ....118 B4
Phillips Acre HR6 ....9 B3
Phillips La GL19 ....51 F2
Phillips St NP4 ....101 C7
Philsay Ho NP44 ......112 C8
Phoenix Dr NP16 ......117 A4
Piccadilly HR5 ....81 B3
Picked La NP18 ....130 C7
Pickersleigh Ave WR14 .85 B4
Pickersleigh CI WR14 ..85 B2
Pickersleigh Gr WR14 ..85 B2
Pickersleigh Rd WR14 ..85 B2
Picklenash Jun Sch GL18 .59 F5
Pict's Cross HR9 ......57 C5
Picton St NP4 ....104 E3
Picton Wlk
  Cwmbran NP44 ....106 B2
  Newport NP20 ....128 E5
Picwic Gn NP44 ....106 B2
Piercefield Ave NP16 ..110 C1
Piercefield Terr NP16 .110 B5
Pierrepont HR6 ....82 B5
Pierrepont Ct HR6 .....82 B5
Piers CI WR14 ....87 A5
Pig St HR4 ....25 D3
Pigs Cross GL18 ....59 D2
Pike Rd NP26 ....125 B4
Pill Row NP26 ....125 B4
Pill Way NP26 ....133 B7
Pilley Rd HR4 ....91 C1
Pillgwenlly Jun & Inf Sch
  NP20 ....119 C2
Pillmawr Circ NP20 ...113 B2
Pillmawr Rd
  Caerleon NP18 ....114 A3
  Newport NP18,NP20 ....113 D2
Pilning St BS35 ....135 F6
Pilning Sta BS35 ......135 F5
Pilton Vale NP20 .....113 B3
Pine Gdns HR4 ....104 A6
Pine Gr Hereford HR2 ..93 A6
  Newport NP20 ....128 F8
  Whitbourne WR6 ....22 B3
Pine Tree Rd NP44 ....105 A4
Pines The
  Abergavenny NP7 ....95 F8
  Wormelow HR2 ....47 B1
Pinetree CI HR7 ....83 C5
Pinewood CI
  1 Cinderford GL14 .....67 D1
  Newport NP20 ....113 B2
Pinford La HR9 ....58 F3
Pingry La GL16 ....72 F3
Pinnell PI 10 NP26 ...119 C3
Pinsley Rd HR6 ....82 D5
Pip Aston Barns SY8 ...24 B2
Piper CI NP19 ....38 E1
Pippin CI HR1 ....38 E1
Pippins Gn WR6 ....31 A5
Pippins The
  Clehonger HR2 ....37 B1
  Much Dewchurch HR2 ...47 A2
  Witton HR9 ....94 B5
Pitchard CI HR7 ....21 B8
Pitt Rd HR3 ....34 E1
Pixiefields WR13 ......31 D1
Pixley Wlk HR2 ....92 C4
Place Hill GL18 ....59 C4
Plaister's End HR8 ....89 D6
Plane Tree CI HR1 ....113 F2
Plantagenet St NP7 ....95 D5
Plantation Dr NP44 ...105 A4
Plantation The
  Presteigne LD8 ....6 F3
  Undy NP26 ....123 C3
Plas Bryn Gomer NP44 .107 A4

Plas Craig NP44 . . . . .106 F4
Plas Derwen NP44 . . . . . . .107 A4
Plas Derwen Cl NP7 . . . . . . .95 E3
Plas Derwen View NP7 . . . . .95 F3
Plas Derwen Way NP7 . . . . .95 F3
Plas Ebbw NP44 . . . . .106 F4
Plas Islwyn NP44 . . . . .106 E4
Plas Mawr NP15 . . . . .97 B4
Plas Trosnant [?] NP44 . . .106 E5
Plas Twyn NP44 . . . . .106 F5
Plas Ty-Coch NP44 . . . . . . .112 F5
Plasderwern NP8 . . . . .60 A4
Platform 88 HR9 . . . . .94 F5
Platts Row GL17 . . . . .67 D5
Players Ave WR14 . . . . .85 A5
Playford Cres NP19 . . . . . .120 F5
Pleasant Cl NP4 . . . . .102 A3
Pleasant Row HR2 . . . . .46 D8
Plough La HR4 . . . . .136 A3
Plough Rd
  Monkswood NP4,NP15 . . . .73 A6
  Penperlleni NP4 . . . . .103 F5
Ploughfields HR2 . . . . .35 F4
Plover Cl Hereford HR2 . . . .120 C1
  Newport NP19 . . . . .120 E1
Plover Cres NP26 . . . . .125 A4
Pludds Court Rd GL17 . . . . .66 E3
Plum Tree La NP26 . . . . . . .124 F4
Plumpton Ave HR4 . . . . .90 D5
Plym Wlk NP20 . . . . .112 E2
Point Pitch HR3 . . . . .25 C7
Pollard Cl NP18 . . . . .113 E2
Polo Ground Ind Est
NP4 . . . . .106 D5
Pomona Pl HR4 . . . . .136 A2
Pont Ap Hywell NP4 . . . . . .104 C7
Pont Faen Rd NP19 . . . . . .120 C3
Pont Y Weston HR3 . . . . . . .34 C4
Pont-Y-Felin Ave NP4 . . . . .105 A2
Pont-Y-Felin La NP4 . . . . . .105 A2
Pontfaen NP4 . . . . .60 C7
Ponthir Prim Sch NP18 . . .113 E7
Ponthir Rd NP18 . . . . .114 B4
Pontnewydd Prim Sch
NP44 . . . . .106 D5
Pontnewydd Wlk NP44 . . . .106 E4
Pontnewydd Wlk (Rhodfa
Pontnawydd) NP44 . . . . . .106 E4
Pontnewynydd Ind Est
NP4 . . . . .104 A8
Pontrhydyrun Ho NP4 . . . .107 A7
Pontrhydyrun Rd NP44 . . . .106 F7
Pontrilas Rd HR2 . . . . .54 D6
Pontyfelin Ind Est NP4 . . .105 A3
Pontllanfraith
NP4 . . . . .102 A2
Pontypool & Blaenavon Rly*
NP4 . . . . .100 E8
Pontypool & New Inn Sta
NP4 . . . . .105 B6
Pontypool Campus NP4 . .104 B5
Pontypool North Ind Est
NP4 . . . . .104 A8
Pontypool Street Mus*
NP4 . . . . .102 A2
Pool Cl NP4 . . . . .30 F3
Pool La North The NP25 . . .72 B1
  Newport NP19 . . . . .119 C7
Pool Mdw HR2 . . . . .46 F2
Poolbrook Prim Sch
WR14 . . . . .87 D7
Poolbrook Rd WR14 . . . . . .87 C6
Poole Cl HR2 . . . . .92 F6
Poole Ho HR2 . . . . .92 E6
Poolend Ctyd HR8 . . . . .40 B2
Poorscript Gdns NP7 . . . . . .54 E3
Poorscript La NP7 . . . . .54 E3
Poplar Ave NP44 . . . . .105 B5
Poplar Cl NP26 . . . . .124 C4
Poplar Rd Clehonger HR2 . . .46 C8
  Croesyceiliog NP44 . . . . . .107 A4
  Martley WR6 . . . . .22 F7
  Newport NP19 . . . . .120 B5
Poplar Terr NP44 . . . . .104 A8
Poplars Cl NP7 . . . . .61 D3
Poplars Ct NP18 . . . . .113 F3
Poplars Rd NP7 . . . . .61 D3
Port Mahon Cl NP25 . . . . .137 A1
Port Rd NP20 . . . . .119 B1
Port Wall* NP16 . . . . .116 F8
Portal Rd NP25 . . . . .96 D2
Portcullis La SY8 . . . . .79 C4
Porters Mill Cl HR6 . . . . . . .92 D6
Portfield St HR1 . . . . .93 B8
Porth Mawr Rd NP44 . . . .106 E4
Porthycarne Cl NP15 . . . . . .97 B5
Porthycarne Gate NP15 . . .97 A5
Porthycarne St NP15 . . . . . .97 B5
Portland Cl HR4 . . . . .26 B6
Portland Rd WR14 . . . . .84 F1
Portland St
  Hereford HR4 . . . . .136 B3
  Newport NP20 . . . . .119 D2
  Weobley HR4 . . . . .26 B6
Portna Way HR6 . . . . .17 F5
Porton Cnr NP18 . . . . .131 D4
Porton Rd NP18 . . . . .131 D3
Portskewett St NP19 . . . . .119 F3
Portwall Rd NP16 . . . . .116 E8
Post Office Cotts GL17 . . . .66 C2
Post Office La WR6 . . . . .32 E7
Postern [?] NP44 . . . . .106 B1
Potter Cl SY8 . . . . .79 D6
Potter St NP20 . . . . .119 D2
Potters Croft NP16 . . . . . . .117 B4

Pottery Rd NP20 . . . . .119 D2
Pottery Terr NP20 . . . . . . .119 C2
Pouk La WR6 . . . . .12 F4
Poultry La Hereford HR4 . . .90 C1
  Wellington HR4 . . . . .27 E2
Pound Bank Rd WR14 . . . . .87 C8
Pound Cl Ledbury HR8 . . . . .89 D3
  Tarrington HR1 . . . . .39 E3
Pound Comm WR14 . . . . . .87 C8
Pound Cvn Pk The HR3 . . . .23 F2
Pound Farm La HR9 . . . . . . .59 B5
Pound La Caerwent NP26 . . .78 B1
  Presteigne LD8 . . . . .6 E3
Pound Mdw HR8 . . . . .89 D3
Powell Croft HR9 . . . . .58 D5
Powell's Pl NP20 . . . . .119 D4
Power St NP20 . . . . .119 B7
Powis Cl NP10 . . . . .128 D5
Powys Wlk HR2 . . . . .92 D4
Poyner Cl SY8 . . . . .79 D5
Poyner Rd SY8 . . . . .79 D5
Preece Cl WR14 . . . . .84 F6
Presbytery Cl HR6 . . . . .82 B4
Prescoch La NP4 . . . . .104 D4
Prescood Hill NP4 . . . . .73 B1
Presteigne Ind Est LD8 . . . . .6 E3
Presteigne Prim Sch LD8 . . . .6 E3
Presteigne Rd HR6 . . . . .16 D8
Presteigne Wlk NP44 . . . . .106 C1
Preston Ave NP20 . . . . . . .118 C4
Preston Brook Cl HR8 . . . . .89 C5
Preston Cl NP16 . . . . .116 F4
Preston Cross HR8 . . . . .50 B6
Preston Cross NP16 . . . . . .116 F4
Preston Ct Madley HR2 . . . .36 A5
  Preston-On-W HR2 . . . . . . .35 F5
Price Cl Newport NP20 . . . .119 C2
  Pontypool NP4 . . . . .102 C1
Priestley Cl NP20 . . . . .118 F1
Prill Orch HR2 . . . . .54 C7
Prill Rd HR2 . . . . .54 C7
Primrose Cl Hereford HR2 . .92 E5
  Newport NP44 . . . . .106 A2
Primrose Gn [?] NP44 . . . .106 A2
Prince Charles Cl NP15 . . . .70 B2
Prince Charles Rd NP15 . . .70 C2
Prince Edward Rd NP4 . . . .92 D8
Prince of Wales Bsns Pk
  HR6 . . . . .82 C6
Prince Rupert Rd HR8 . . . . .89 C5
Prince St Blaenavon NP4 . .101 D6
  Newport NP19 . . . . .119 D6
  Pontypool NP4 . . . . .104 B7
Prince's St NP7 . . . . .95 D5
Prince's Wlk NP44 . . . . . . .105 B4
Princes Cl NP7 . . . . .95 D5
Princes Dnch HR2 . . . . .35 B1
Princess Ave HR1 . . . . .91 A3
Princess Margaret Ave
  WR14 . . . . .85 C5
Princess Way HR9 . . . . .94 E4
Prinknash Cl HR2 . . . . .92 C5
Prior St HR4 . . . . .136 B4
Prioress Mill La NP15 . . . . .73 D5
Priors Wlk HR2 . . . . .136 B1
Priorsfield HR2 . . . . .54 C7
Priory Cl Caerleon NP18 . . .113 E3
  Caldicot NP26 . . . . .124 F6
  Chepstow NP16 . . . . .110 D1
Priory Cres NP18 . . . . .121 B8
Priory Ct Abergavenny NP7 . .95 E5
  Malvern WR14 . . . . .86 F8
Priory Dr NP18 . . . . .121 B8
Priory Gdns
  Abergavenny NP7 . . . . .95 E5
  Langstone NP18 . . . . .115 B1
  Usk NP15 . . . . .97 B4
Priory La
  Abergavenny NP7 . . . . .95 D5
  Monmouth NP25 . . . . .96 E7
Priory Lea HR9 . . . . .66 C8
Priory Pl HR4 . . . . .90 F3
Priory Rd
  Abergavenny NP7 . . . . .95 E6
  Malvern WR14 . . . . .86 F8
  Priory St Monmouth NP25 .137 B3
  Usk NP15 . . . . .97 B4
Priory The Clifford HR3 . . . .33 E7
  Leominster HR6 . . . . .82 D5
Priory View HR2 . . . . .92 C6
Priory Way HR1 . . . . .121 B8
Priory Wood HR3 . . . . .33 F8
Probert Cl HR4 . . . . .82 C4
Probert Cres HR4 . . . . .16 F1
Probert Pl NP19 . . . . .119 E5
Probertsbarn La GL17 . . . . .66 C3
Progress Cl HR8 . . . . .89 C6
Prospect Cl BS35 . . . . .135 F2
Prospect Cotts SY8 . . . . . . .79 D4
Prospect Cres NP26 . . . . . .125 A6
Prospect La Kington HR5 . . .81 D6
  Llangrove HR9 . . . . .65 B6
Prospect Pl
  Cwmbran NP44 . . . . .106 E2
  Hereford HR2 . . . . .136 B1
  Kington HR5 . . . . .81 D6
  Pontypool NP4 . . . . .105 A4
Prospect Rd
  Abergavenny NP7 . . . . .95 C5
  Kington HR5 . . . . .81 D6
  Monmouth NP25 . . . . .96 D7
  Severn Beach BS35 . . . . . .135 E4
Prospect Row HR9 . . . . .59 B4
Prospect Terr HR9 . . . . .94 D6
Prospect Wlk HR1 . . . . .91 D2

Prosser La [?] NP20 . . . . . .118 F4
Pry Cl The WR15 . . . . .13 A8
Pudding St NP20 . . . . .54 B5
Pudford La WR6 . . . . .22 C8
Pugsley St NP20 . . . . .119 C6
Pulley Ave HR1 . . . . .36 F1
Pullings Mews HR1 . . . . . .136 C2
Pullmans Cl [?] HR1 . . . . . . .91 B2
Pullnogin Pool La HR9 . . . .62 C6
Pump Piece HR6 . . . . .82 C4
Pump St Bromyard HR7 . . . .83 C6
  Malvern WR14 . . . . .84 E3
  [?] Newport NP20 . . . . . . .119 B5
Purcell Sq NP19 . . . . .120 C5
Purland HR9 . . . . .94 D2
Purlieu The WR14 . . . . .86 D5
Putley Cl HR8 . . . . .49 E8
Putley Gn HR8 . . . . .49 F8
Putson Ave HR2 . . . . .93 B5
Pwllmeyric Cl NP16 . . . . . .116 B5
Pye Cnr HR10 . . . . .118 C3
Pye's Almshouses HR9 . . . .94 D5
Pyndar Ct WR13 . . . . .85 D5
Pynfold Gdns SY8 . . . . .79 C4
Pystol La GL15 . . . . .76 E7
Pytts Cotts WR15 . . . . .11 F2

Q

Quabbs La GL17 . . . . .67 B4
Quadrangle The WR13 . . . . .85 D5
Quality Sq SY8 . . . . .79 C4
Quantock Cl HR4 . . . . .90 B3
Quantock Dr NP19 . . . . . . .120 C6
Quarry Cl HR9 . . . . .94 E6
Quarry Gdns NP18 . . . . .79 C5
Quarry La HR1 . . . . .59 B4
Quarry Rd HR1 . . . . .93 D8
Quarry Rise NP26 . . . . .123 B4
Quay La HR1 . . . . .93 C7
Quay St HR1 . . . . .136 C2
Quayside NP16 . . . . .76 C4
Quebec Cl NP26 . . . . .118 D3
Queen Elizabeth High Sch
  HR7 . . . . .83 B5
Queen Elizabeth Rd
  WR14 . . . . .85 B5
Queen St
  Abergavenny NP7 . . . . .95 D5
  Newport NP20 . . . . .119 C3
Queen Victoria Meml
  Almshouses [?] NP19 . . .119 B4
Queen's Chambers [?]
  NP20 . . . . .119 B5
Queen's Cl Malvern WR14 . .84 E4
Queen's Croft NP19 . . . . . .119 B6
Queen's Ct HR8 . . . . .89 D4
Queen's Dr WR14 . . . . .84 E1
Queen's Hill
  Dingestow NP25 . . . . .71 A5
  Newport NP20 . . . . .119 B6
Queen's Hill Cres NP20 . . .119 B6
Queen's Rd
  Chepstow NP16 . . . . .116 C6
  Malvern WR14 . . . . .84 F4
Queen's Way Ledbury HR8 . .89 D4
  Llanwern NP19,NP26 . . . . .121 D1
Queens Gdns HR4 . . . . .90 C1
Queens Hill Gdns HR4 . . . . .90 D1
Queens Mews HR4 . . . . .90 D1
Queens Wood Forest Trails*
  HR9 . . . . .59 B7
Queensway Hereford HR1 . . .91 A3
  Newport NP20 . . . . .120 D1
Queensway Mdws NP19 . . .120 D1
Queensway Meadows Ind Est
  NP19 . . . . .120 D1
Queensway Cl HR4 . . . . . . .27 C3
Queensway Ctry Pk*
  HR6 . . . . .27 F6

R

Rabbit La HR2 . . . . .54 C7
Rachel Sq NP10 . . . . .128 E6
Radcliffe Ct HR1 . . . . .91 D2
Radnor Rd NP19 . . . . .119 F6
Radnor View HR6 . . . . .82 B5
Radnor Way NP44 . . . . . . .106 E3
Radstock Ct NP7 . . . . .95 D5
Radway Rd HR1 . . . . .38 E5
Raglan Cl
  Croesyceiliog NP44 . . . . . .106 F6
  Newport NP19 . . . . .119 C2
Raglan Ent Pk NP15 . . . . . .70 C2
Raglan Jun & Inf Sch
  NP15 . . . . .70 C2
Raglan Mews NP10 . . . . . .128 E7
Raglan Pl HR2 . . . . .92 D4
Raglan St NP19 . . . . .119 B5
Railway St NP19 . . . . .119 B5
Railway Terr
  Blaenavon NP4 . . . . .101 B6
  Colwall Stone WR13 . . . . . .42 A4
  Ewyas Harold HR2 . . . . . . .54 E6
  Pontypool NP4 . . . . .106 E8
  Rogiet NP26 . . . . .124 A4

Railway Terr continued
  Stretton Sugwas HR4 . . . . .37 B5
Railway View NP26 . . . . . .125 B4
Rainbow St HR6 . . . . .82 C5
Raleigh Ct HR4 . . . . .90 C2
Ramp The NP26 . . . . .123 D2
Ramsden Rd HR2 . . . . .93 D4
Ramsey Wlk
  Cwmbran NP44 . . . . .106 C5
  Newport NP19 . . . . .119 F7
Ramsons Cl HR4 . . . . .85 C3
Ranelagh Rd WR14 . . . . . . .85 C5
Ranelagh St HR4 . . . . .90 D2
Rankin Rd HR4 . . . . .90 C2
Rankine Cl NP20 . . . . .118 F1
Rannoch Ho [?] NP44 . . . .106 C2
Raphael Cl NP19 . . . . .120 A7
Raven La SY8 . . . . .79 C4
Raven Wlk HR2 . . . . .92 C4
Raven's Cswy HR4 . . . . .26 D3
Ravenscourt NP44 . . . . . . .106 B3
Ravenshill Woodland
  Reserve* WR6 . . . . .31 E8
Ravenswood Cl HR4 . . . . . .27 C3
Ravenswood Dr HR2 . . . . . .93 D4
Raycomb La HR8 . . . . .41 D4
Reade St NP25 . . . . .96 F3
Rectory Bglws WR6 . . . . . . .31 D7
Rectory Gdns NP26 . . . . . .123 D3
Rectory La HR13 . . . . .31 E2
  Madresfield WR13 . . . . .85 E3
  Malvern WR13 . . . . .87 F6
Rectory Mdw
  Eaton Bishop HR2 . . . . .36 F2
  Longhope GL17 . . . . .67 F6
Rectory Rd
  Crickhowell NP8 . . . . .60 A5
  Hampton Bishop HR1 . . . . .38 E1
  Llanvaches NP26 . . . . .77 E2
Red Barn Dr HR4 . . . . .90 C5
Red Ditch La GL19 . . . . .51 D1
Red Earl La WR14 . . . . .87 D8
Red Hill NP15 . . . . .97 C4
Red Hollow La HR2 . . . . . . .92 F5
Red House La NP16 . . . . . . .78 C4
Red La HR3 . . . . .23 B4
Red Lion Ct HR4 . . . . .136 B3
Redbrook CE Prim Sch
  NP25 . . . . .72 C4
Redbrook Ct HR4 . . . . .93 C5
Redbrook Ho NP44 . . . . . .106 F3
Redbrook Rd
  Monmouth NP25 . . . . .137 C1
  Newport NP20 . . . . .118 E4
Redbrook Way NP44 . . . . . .106 F3
Redcar Ave HR4 . . . . .90 C5
Reddings The NP16 . . . . . .116 F5
Rede Rd NP44 . . . . .106 B1
Redgate Ave WR15 . . . . . . .80 C4
Redham La BS35 . . . . .135 F8
Redhill Rd HR9 . . . . .94 D4
Redhouse La GL16 . . . . .66 A2
Redlake Mdw SY7 . . . . .2 A4
Redland Cl WR13 . . . . .86 A3
Redland Rd WR14 . . . . .85 A4
Redland St NP20 . . . . .119 B7
Redlands The NP19 . . . . . .120 C4
Redmarley CE Prim Sch
  GL19 . . . . .51 D2
Redmeadow Cres NP26 . . .125 B4
Redstone Rd HR4 . . . . .37 C7
Redvers St HR4 . . . . .119 F4
Redwick & Northwick CE
  Prim Sch BS35 . . . . .127 D2
Redwick Ct NP44 . . . . .106 F2
Redwick Gdns BS35 . . . . . .135 C2
Redwick Ho NP44 . . . . .106 F2
Redwick Rd BS35 . . . . .135 C8
Redwing Cl WR14 . . . . .84 D6
Redwing Wlk HR2 . . . . .92 C5
Redwood Cl
  Caerleon NP18 . . . . .113 E2
  Chepstow NP16 . . . . .116 E5
  Hereford HR2 . . . . .136 C1
Reece Ct NP19 . . . . .120 A3
Rees Cl NP20 . . . . .113 A3
Rees Rd NP44 . . . . .106 E3
Reeves La LD7 . . . . .2 B2
Reevesland Ind Est
  NP19 . . . . .120 A1
Regency Rd WR14 . . . . .85 B5
Regent Gdns HR1 . . . . .91 A2
Regent Sr NP7 . . . . .95 D5
Regent Way HR16 . . . . . . .118 E8
Reginald Terr NP10 . . . . . .118 B4
Rembrandt Way NP19 . . . .119 F7
Renoir Rd NP19 . . . . .120 A7
Reservoir Cl NP10 . . . . . . .118 B4
Rest Rd The HR3 . . . . .24 A5
Restway Cradley NP16 . . . .116 E8
Reynard Cl HR2 . . . . .93 F5
Reynolds Cl
  Newport NP19 . . . . .119 F7
  Welland WR13 . . . . .42 E3
Rhiw Melin HR4 . . . . .106 B6
Rhodri Pl [?] NP44 . . . . . . .107 B2
Rholben Rd NP7 . . . . .95 C7
Rhonos Rd NP7 . . . . .98 D7
Rhydd Cl WR14 . . . . .87 D4
Rhydwr Cl HR4 . . . . .35 D8
Rhydwern La
  Coed-Cwmwr NP15 . . . . . .74 C1
  Llantrisant NP15 . . . . .77 C8
Rhydnos St NP44 . . . . .101 C6
Rhymney St NP44 . . . . . . .106 A5
Rhyse La WR15 . . . . .80 F6

Rhystone La HR1 . . . . .38 E3
Ribble Sq NP20 . . . . .112 E2
Ribble Wlk NP20 . . . . .112 E2
Richard's Cl WR14 . . . . .84 E6
Richards Cl HR1 . . . . .91 C7
Richmond Cl NP44 . . . . . . .106 E5
Richmond Cres HR6 . . . . . . .82 A4
Richmond Pl NP44 . . . . . . .106 E5
Richmond Rd
  Abergavenny NP7 . . . . .95 F6
  Cwmbran NP44 . . . . .106 E5
  Malvern WR14 . . . . .85 A4
  Newport NP19 . . . . .119 E7
  Pontypool NP4 . . . . .104 E1
Richmond St
  [?] Cwmbran NP44 . . . . . .106 E5
  Hereford HR4 . . . . .136 B3
Richmonds Pitch WR14 . . . .42 C4
Rickfield The NP25 . . . . .96 E8
Riddiemore Ave HR2 . . . . . .92 F5
Riddings Mdw SY8 . . . . .79 E4
Riddings Rd SY8 . . . . .79 E5
Ridge Pl GL17 . . . . .66 D1
Ridgebourne Rd NP25 . . . . .81 A6
Ridgemoor Rd HR6 . . . . . . .82 D6
Ridgeway
  Colwall Stone WR13 . . . . . .41 F1
  Easthor HR8 . . . . .51 B8
  Monmouth NP25 . . . . . . .137 C1
  Newport NP19 . . . . .118 D4
  Pontypool NP4 . . . . .102 D1
Ridgeway Ave
  Hereford HR2 . . . . .93 A5
  Newport NP19 . . . . .118 E5
Ridgeway Cl NP20 . . . . . . .118 E4
Ridgeway Cres
  Newport NP20 . . . . .118 E4
  Whitchurch HR9 . . . . .65 D4
Ridgeway Ct NP20 . . . . . . .118 E4
Ridgeway Dr NP20 . . . . . . .118 F4
Ridgeway Gr NP20 . . . . . . .118 E4
Ridgeway Hill NP20 . . . . . .118 E5
Ridgeway Park Rd NP20 . .118 E5
Ridgeway Rd HR2 . . . . .38 D7
Rifle Gn NP44 . . . . .101 C7
Rifle St NP44 . . . . .101 C7
Ringfield Dr HR1 . . . . .48 E5
Ringland Circ NP19 . . . . . .120 D6
Ringland Ctr NP19 . . . . . . .120 F6
Ringland Ind Sch NP19 . . .120 F6
Ringland Jun Sch NP19 . . .120 E6
Ringland Way NP18,
  NP19 . . . . .121 A6
Ringwood Ave NP19 . . . . . .120 D6
Ringwood Hill NP20 . . . . . .118 D5
Ringwood Pl NP19 . . . . . . .120 D6
Ripon Wlk HR4 . . . . .90 D4
Risca Rd NP20 . . . . .118 B4
River La NP44 . . . . .106 C5
River Row NP44 . . . . .104 A8
River View
  Chepstow NP16 . . . . .116 E8
  Hereford HR2 . . . . .93 B5
  Ross-on-W HR9 . . . . .94 E6
River View Cl HR2 . . . . .48 B6
Riverdale Pk HR2 . . . . .45 C3
Riverside Newport NP19 . .120 D2
  Pontypool NP4 . . . . .104 C7
  Tenbury Wells WR15 . . . . . .80 C5
Riverside Ct
  Hereford HR4 . . . . .136 B2
  Pontypool NP4 . . . . .104 C7
Riverside Dr NP4 . . . . .101 C5
Riverside Mill NP16 . . . . . .110 F1
Riverside Pk
  Monmouth NP25 . . . . .137 C2
  Severn Beach BS35 . . . . . .134 F6
Rivermead NP44 . . . . .107 A2
Road Two BS10 . . . . .135 A3
Roath Ct NP44 . . . . .107 A3
Robbin's La [?] NP20 . . . . .119 C2
Robert Cl NP20 . . . . .119 C2
Robert's Row NP13 . . . . . .100 B1
Roberts Cl NP10 . . . . .118 A7
Robertson Way NP20 . . . . .113 A4
Robin Hood La NP18 . . . . .115 E2
Robins Terr [?] HR1 . . . . . . .91 B2
Robinson Rd HR4 . . . . .37 A6
Robinson La GL17 . . . . .66 D2
Robinsons Mdw HR8 . . . . . .89 D5
Rochdale Terr [?] NP44 . . .102 A1
Rochester Ct HR2 . . . . .92 D6
Rochester Rd NP19 . . . . . .119 F5
Rock Green Terr SY8 . . . . . .79 E6
Rock La Ludlow SY8 . . . . . . .79 D4
  Upper Sapey WR6 . . . . .13 B2
Rock Rd SY8 . . . . .64 B4
Rock Terr SY8 . . . . .79 D6
Rock Villa La HR10 . . . . . . .110 F1
Rockbridge Pk LD8 . . . . .6 C4
Rockfield Ave NP25 . . . . . .137 A2
Rockfield Cl NP26 . . . . .77 B2
Rockfield Cres NP26 . . . . .123 D3
Rockfield Glade NP26 . . . . .77 B2
Rockfield Ho NP26 . . . . . . .104 B8
Rockfield Rd
  Hereford HR1 . . . . .91 B1
  Monmouth NP25 . . . . .96 B5
Rockfield Rise NP26 . . . . . .123 D3
Rockfield St NP19 . . . . .119 D7
Rockfield View (Trem Maes
  y-Graig) NP26 . . . . .123 C4

Rockfield Way (Trem Mab y-Graig) NP26 ...123 D4
Rockhill Rd NP4 ...104 D5
Rocklea NP25 ...71 E4
Rocks Cl The NP16 ...75 F6
Rocks Gn SY8 ...79 D7
Rocks Rd GL17 ...66 D3
Rockwood Cl NP25 ...137 A1
Rockwood Rd NP16 ...116 E7
Roding Cl NP20 ...112 D1
Rodney Par NP19 ...119 C5
Rodney Rd NP19 ...119 C5
Roebuck Mdws GL17 ...66 F3
Rogers Ave HR2 ...136 A1
Rogiet Jun & Inf Sch NP26 ...124 B4
Rogiet Pool NP26 ...124 B4
Rogiet Rd NP6 ...124 D5
Rogiet Terr NP26 ...124 B4
Rolls Ave NP25 ...96 B5
Rolls Cl NP44 ...106 A2
Rolls Wlk NP10 ...118 A6
Roman Baths Mus* NP18 ...114 C2
Roman Gates NP18 ...114 C2
Roman Legionary Mus* NP18 ...114 B2
Roman Park View NP25 ...75 E8
Roman Rd HR4 ...37 A5
Roman Reach HR8 ...113 F2
Roman Way
  Caerleon NP18 ...114 A3
  Malvern WR14 ...85 C5
  Ross-on-W HR9 ...94 C3
  Stretton Sugwas HR4 ...37 B5
  Trellech NP25 ...75 E8
Roman Wlk 16 HR7 ...83 C6
Romany Way HR2 ...92 F4
Romney Cl NP19 ...120 B7
Romney Huts HR2 ...93 F5
Romsey Dr HR2 ...92 C6
Romsley Ct 9 NP44 ...106 C2
Ronald Rd NP19 ...119 E6
Rookery La GL15 ...72 F2
Ropewalk Ave HR6 ...82 B4
Rosamund Cl NP10 ...128 F5
Rosary The NP16 ...110 D1
Rose Bank HR7 ...83 C6
Rose Gdns NP44 ...107 B4
Rose St NP20 ...119 B6
Rosebery Cl HR4 ...136 B4
Rosebery St NP4 ...104 E3
Rosecroft Dr NP18 ...121 C8
Rosedale WR6 ...13 F6
Rosedale Cl HR2 ...92 B5
Rosegarden The NP20 ...118 F5
Rosemary SY7 ...3 B4
Rosemary Gdns HR1 ...93 E8
Rosemary La
  Leintwardine SY7 ...1 B4
  Madley HR2 ...36 C1
  Tibenham Chapel HR6 ...76 F1
Rosemund Dr HR1 ...28 F2
Rosendale Ct 5 NP19 ...119 F5
Roseville Terr HR6 ...8 B1
Roslins The HR9 ...94 D3
Ross Com Hospl HR9 ...94 D4
Ross Ho NP44 ...106 F2
Ross La NP20 ...119 F3
Ross Rd Abergavenny NP7 ...95 E6
  Hereford HR2 ...92 F5
  Mitcheldean GL17 ...67 D6
  Newent GL18 ...59 F5
  Ross-on-W HR9 ...94 E8
Ross Road (Red Hill) HR2 ...92 C5
Ross St NP20 ...119 B8
Rossees La WR6 ...22 E8
Rosser St NP4 ...104 A7
Rosslyn Rd NP19 ...119 F5
Rother Ave NP7 ...95 D7
Rother Cl NP20 ...112 D3
Rotherwas Chapel* HR2 93 F5
Rotherwas Cl HR2 ...93 C5
Rotherwas Ind Est HR1 ...93 D5
Rothesay Mead HR2 ...92 C5
Rothesay Rd NP19 ...119 F5
Rothwell Rd WR14 ...86 F1
Rougemont Gr NP16 ...116 F4
Rough Leasow WR6 ...31 D5
Round Oak View HR4 ...37 B8
Roundwood Cl NP26 ...77 C2
Routs View NP18 ...121 B5
Row The
  Shirenewton NP16 ...78 C4
  St Arvans NP16 ...110 A8
Rowan Cl Ross-on-W HR9 ...94 C3
  Undy NP26 ...123 C4
Rowan Cres NP4 ...104 D2
Rowan Dr NP16 ...116 E5
Rowan Ho 1 NP44 ...106 B1
Rowan Way NP20 ...113 B3
Rowandean 6 GL14 ...67 C1
Rowans The HR9 ...67 B8
Rowantree Cl HR2 ...92 C5
Rowberry St HR7 ...83 C6
Rowden House Sch HR7 ...20 D3
Rowland Cl HR1 ...93 E7
Royal George NP25 ...137 B3
Royal Gwent General Hospl NP20 ...119 B3
Royal National Coll for the Blind HR1 ...91 B3
Royal Oak Dr NP18 ...120 E7

Royal Oak Gdns WR14 ...85 B5
Royal Oak Gn NP44 ...107 B4
Royal Oak Hill NP18 ...120 E7
Royal Oak Rd GL17 ...66 E3
Royal Par HR9 ...94 D5
Royce Wlk NP10 ...118 A6
Royston Cres NP19 ...120 B4
Ruardean CE Prim Sch GL17 ...66 E4
Ruardean Garden Pottery* GL17 ...66 E4
Ruardean Rd GL17 ...66 E3
Rubens Cl NP19 ...119 F7
Rubins Way NP25 ...72 B1
Rudge Gr HR1 ...28 B2
Rudhall Cl HR9 ...94 E6
Rudhall Mdw HR9 ...94 E6
Rudhall View HR9 ...67 D8
Rudry St NP19 ...119 C6
Ruff La NP25 ...47 D1
Ruffet's Cl NP16 ...116 D8
Ruffitt The GL14 ...67 D1
Rugby Rd NP19 ...119 D5
Rugg The HR6 ...82 B5
Rumble St NP11 ...73 A6
Rumney Wlk NP44 ...107 B3
Rundlemead WR13 ...41 E8
Runston Chapel* NP16 ...78 E2
Runton Cl NP20 ...118 B3
Rupera La NP20 ...119 C3
Ruperra La NP20 ...119 C3
Rupert Brooke Dr NP20 ...118 F2
Rush Wall Magor NP26 ...122 C1
Rushby Mdw NP25 ...96 B5
Rushock HR5 ...14 F5
Rushock Bank HR5 ...15 A5
Ruskin Ave NP10 ...118 A7
Ruskin Cl NP44 ...106 A2
Ruskin Rise NP20 ...118 E2
Russel Cl NP44 ...106 A2
Russell Cl Hereford HR1 ...91 B3
  Malvern WR14 ...85 B3
Russell Dr Malvern WR14 ...85 B3
  Newport NP20 ...113 A2
Russell Drive Gdns NP20 ...113 A2
Russell St 4 NP44 ...106 C5
Russet Cl
  Langstone NP18 ...121 C8
  Ledbury HR8 ...89 D2
Ruth Rd NP4 ...104 F5
Rutherford Hill NP20 ...113 A2
Rutland Pl 10 NP20 ...119 C3
Ryder Cl HR1 ...93 E7
Ryders The HR8 ...40 B4
Ryefield Rd HR9 ...94 F5
Ryelands Gr HR5 ...82 B3
Ryelands Orch HR8 ...82 C3
Ryelands Rd HR6 ...82 C4
Ryelands St HR4 ...136 A2
Ryley Row HR9 ...94 F4

S

St Alban's RC High Sch NP4 ...104 C6
St Alban's RC Prim Sch NP4 ...104 B7
St Andrew's Ave NP16 ...116 F4
St Andrew's Cl HR4 ...37 F8
St Andrew's Inf Sch NP19 ...119 F3
St Andrew's Jun Sch NP19 ...119 F3
St Andrew's Rd WR14 ...87 A6
St Andrew's Wlk NP15 ...109 E2
St Ann St NP10 ...110 F1
St Ann's Rd WR14 ...84 E1
St Ann's Well* WR14 ...86 E8
St Anne's Cl
  Cwmbran NP44 ...106 E5
  Rogerstone NP10 ...118 B4
St Anne's Cres NP19 ...119 F7
St Annes Cres NP25 ...123 D3
St Annes Way GL15 ...76 E7
St Anthony's Cl NP44 ...104 D2
St Arvans NP44 ...106 F7
St Arvans Cres NP7 ...95 F7
St Augustine Rd NP44 ...104 D2
St Augustine's Ct HR2 ...92 C5
St Barnabas Cl HR1 ...93 B3
St Basil's Cres NP20 ...118 A3
St Basil's Stores NP10 ...118 A3
St Beckets Mews HR2 ...92 D6
St Benedict Cl NP44 ...104 D2
St Benedict Ct NP10 ...118 A2
St Bernard Dr WR14 ...87 A5
St Botolphs Gn HR6 ...82 B5
St Briavels Castle* GL15 76 E7
St Briavels CE Prim Sch GL15 ...76 E7
St Briavels Mews NP10 ...128 E5
St Bride's Cl NP26 ...123 A4
St Bride's Cl NP25 ...123 A5
St Brides Cl NP44 ...107 A2
St Brides Cres NP20 ...128 F8
St Brides Gdns NP20 ...128 F8
St Bruel's Cl GL15 ...76 F7
St Cadoc's Cl NP18 ...114 A3
St Cadoc's Hospl NP18 ...114 A3
St Cadoc's Hospl NP18 ...113 F2
St Cadoc's Rd NP4 ...102 D1

St Cadocs Ct NP15 ...70 B2
St Catwg's Cl NP8 ...60 A4
St Charles Cl HR2 ...93 C5
St Charles Flats HR2 ...93 C5
St Clares Ct NP26 ...93 B5
St Crispin Cl NP25 ...137 B1
St Cybi Ave NP15 ...109 C6
St Cybi Dr NP15 ...109 C6
St Cybi Rise NP15 ...109 B6
St David Lewis RC Jun & Inf Sch NP20 ...112 F2
St David's Cl
  Chepstow NP16 ...116 E7
  Pontypool NP4 ...104 C2
St David's Cres NP7 ...69 C8
St David's Ct NP26 ...123 B3
St David's Dr NP7 ...95 F8
St David's RC Jun & Inf Sch NP20 ...118 E1
St David's Rd
  Abergavenny NP7 ...95 F8
  Cwmbran NP44 ...106 F3
St David's Rise HR2 ...47 F2
St David's St LD8 ...6 E3
St Davids Ct NP7 ...95 F8
St Davids Cres NP20 ...118 F1
St Davids RC Prim Sch NP44 ...106 F5
St Davids Rd HR4 ...37 A6
St Dial's Cl NP25 ...96 B3
St Dials Ct NP44 ...106 E2
St Dials St NP44 ...106 D3
St Dominics Retreat
  Redwick NP26 ...122 E1
  NP26 ...123 C8
St Donats Pl 7 NP44 ...107 B2
St Dubricius Gdns NP26 ...123 D3
St Dunstan's La WR15 ...12 A6
St Edward St NP20 ...119 B4
St Ethelbert Cl HR1 ...38 C8
St Ethelbert St HR1 ...136 C2
St Ethelbert's Hospl HR1 ...136 C2
St Ewens Rd NP16 ...116 E6
St Faith's Cl NP7 ...95 C3
St Francis Cl NP7 ...95 F7
St Francis Xavier's Prim Sch HR1 ...91 B3
St Gabriel's RC Jun & Inf Sch NP19 ...119 E7
St George Rd NP16 ...116 E7
St George's Cres
  Abergavenny NP7 ...95 F7
  Newport NP19 ...119 F7
  Orleton SY8 ...9 E6
St Georges Way NP44 ...117 B4
St Gile's Hospl 4 HR1 ...93 B8
St Gregory's Ct NP4 ...92 C6
St Guthlac St HR1 ...93 B8
St Helen's Cl
  Abergavenny NP7 ...95 C5
  Llanellen NP7 ...68 C5
St Helen's Cres NP7 ...68 C5
St Helen's Rd NP7 ...95 C5
St Hilda's Rd NP44 ...104 E2
St James CE Prim Sch
  Hereford HR1 ...136 C1
  Malvern WR14 ...84 C1
St James Cl HR1 ...38 F4
St James Mews NP25 ...137 C2
St James Rd HR1 ...93 B8
St James Terr HR1 ...136 C1
St James' Field NP44 ...104 D2
St James' Sch NP25 ...137 C2
St James' St NP25 ...137 C2
St James's Dr WR14 ...84 F2
St James's Rd WR14 ...84 F2
St James's St NP44 ...84 C1
St John Kemble Ct NP2 ...92 D5
St John Mediaeval Mus* HR1 ...136 C3
St John St HR1 ...136 C2
St John's Cres NP4 ...104 A7
St John's Gdns NP16 ...110 D1
St John's La NP7 ...95 D5
St John's La SY8 ...79 C3
St John's Rd Ludlow SY8 ...79 C3
  Ruardean GL17 ...66 F4
St John's St NP7 ...95 D5
St Johns Ct NP25 ...137 B2
St John's-on-the-hill Sch NP16 ...110 F2
St Johns Cl NP4 ...104 A7
St Johns Rd NP19 ...119 F5
St Joseph Pl NP44 ...113 B6
St Joseph's Private Hospl NP20 ...113 B4
St Joseph's RC High Sch NP10 ...128 E7
St Joseph's RC Jun & Inf Sch WR14 ...84 E3
St Josephs Cl NP26 ...123 D3
St Julian St NP20 ...119 B4
St Julian's Ave
  Ludlow SY8 ...79 D4
  Newport NP19 ...119 F7
St Julian's Comp Sch NP19 ...120 A7
St Julian's Inf Sch NP19 ...120 A7
St Julian's Jun Sch NP19 ...120 A7
St Julian's Rd NP19 ...119 F7

St Julian's Well SY8 ...79 D5
St Julians Ct NP19 ...119 E7
St Julians Rd NP19 ...119 E7
St Kellens SY8 ...79 E3
St Kingsmark Ave NP16 ...110 D1
St Kitts Cl WR14 ...84 F5
St Laurence CE Prim Sch SY8 ...79 D3
St Lawrence La NP16 ...116 C7
St Lawrence Pk NP16 ...116 C7
St Lawrence Rd NP16 ...116 C8
St Luke's Rd NP4 ...102 A1
St Mableys Cl NP7 ...62 D1
St Margaret Rd SY8 ...79 E5
St Margaret's Rd
  Hereford HR1 ...93 C7
  Ruardean GL17 ...66 F4
St Margarets Gillach HR2 ...44 F5
  3 Malvern WR14 ...85 A4
St Margarets Cl HR4 ...27 E3
St Mark's Cres NP20 ...119 B5
St Martin's Ave HR2 ...136 B1
St Martin's Prim Sch HR2 ...92 F6
St Martin's St NP20 ...119 B4
St Martins Ct NP20 ...118 F3
St Mary St
  Chepstow NP16 ...116 E8
  Newport NP20 ...119 B4
  Pontypool NP4 ...104 D3
St Mary Street Arc NP16 ...116 E8
St Mary's CE Prim Sch
  Bromesberrow Heath HR8 ...51 C5
  Bucknell SY7 ...2 C4
  Credenhill HR4 ...37 A6
St Mary's CE Prim Sch HR1 ...48 D5
St Mary's Cl
  Llanvair Kilgeddin NP7 ...69 B2
  Pontypool NP4 ...104 D3
  Tenbury Wells WR15 ...80 C5
St Mary's Cres Alfrick WR6 ...31 F7
  Rogiet NP26 ...124 B4
St Mary's Ct Hereford HR4 ...90 E3
  7 Newport NP20 ...119 B4
St Mary's La SY8 ...79 C5
St Mary's Mews SY8 ...79 C5
St Mary's of Hope CE Prim Sch HR6 ...28 A7
St Mary's Pl NP26 ...125 D5
St Mary's RC High Sch HR1 ...38 D3
St Mary's Rc Jun & Inf Sch NP20 ...119 B6
St Mary's RC Prim Sch NP16 ...116 E7
St Mary's Rd
  Monmouth NP25 ...137 B2
  Nash NP18 ...130 C4
St Mary's St
  Monmouth NP25 ...137 B2
  Ross-on-W HR9 ...94 D5
St Mary's Way NP15 ...97 B4
St Mary's Wlk HR6 ...14 F5
St Marys Yd NP7 ...69 B1
St Marys Cl GL18 ...50 D2
St Marys La HR4 ...90 A7
St Marys Rd NP7 ...95 E6
St Matthew's Rd NP4 ...104 D5
St Maur Gdns NP16 ...110 D1
St Melions Cl NP25 ...96 B5
St Michael Gr NP44 ...113 B7
St Michael St NP20 ...119 D2
St Michaels RC Jun & Inf Sch NP20 ...119 C2
St Milborough CE Prim Sch SY8 ...79 E5
St Nicholas Ho WR14 ...84 D3
St Nicholas St NP44 ...136 B2
St Oswalds Cl NP4 ...104 E1
St Owen Almshouses 5 HR1 ...93 B8
St Owen Gate HR1 ...136 C2
St Owen Pl HR1 ...136 C2
St Owen's St HR1 ...136 C2
St Patrick's RC Jun & Inf Sch NP19 ...120 A4
St Paul Rd HR1 ...93 D8
St Paul's CE Prim Sch HR1 ...93 E8
St Peter's Cl NP8 ...60 C7
St Peter's Dr WR6 ...22 D6
St Peter's Gdns HR7 ...83 B6
St Peter's Prim Sch NP4 ...101 C6
St Peter's Sq
  Hereford HR1 ...136 C2
  Lucton HR6 ...8 E3
St Peter's St HR1 ...136 C3

St Peter's Terr 2 HR7 ...83 C6
St Peters Cl
  Lugwardine HR1 ...38 E4
  Malvern WR14 ...42 C4
  Moreton-on-L HR4 ...37 F8
St Peters Cl Clos Sant Pedr NP44 ...106 B2
St Peters Mews SY8 ...79 C5
St Philips NP19 ...119 F4
St Richard's Sch HR7 ...20 B2
St Ronans NP7 ...95 E3
St Stephen's Cl
  Caerwent NP26 ...78 C1
  Ludlow SY8 ...79 C4
St Stephen's Rd NP19 ...119 D2
St Stephens Ct NP26 ...123 B3
St Tathan's Pl NP26 ...78 C1
St Tecla Rd NP16 ...116 E6
St Teilo Ct NP26 ...123 D3
St Teilo's Rd NP7 ...95 F7
St Tewdric Rd NP16 ...116 F7
St Tewdrics Pl NP16 ...116 F7
St Theodor's Ct HR2 ...92 D6
St Thomas Cantilupe CE Prim Sch HR1 ...136 C3
St Thomas Rd HR4 ...136 A3
St Thomas's Sq NP25 ...137 A1
St Tysoi Cl NP15 ...74 F5
St Vincent's Cl HR2 ...93 C5
St Vincents Ct NP19 ...119 D5
St Vincents Dr HR2 ...96 A5
St Weonards Prim Sch HR2 ...56 B3
St Woolos Cl 3 NP20 ...119 B6
St Woolos Gn 2 NP44 ...106 E4
St Woolos Hospl (General) NP20 ...119 B3
St Woolos Jun & Inf Sch NP20 ...119 B4
St Woolos Pl NP20 ...119 B4
St Woolos Rd NP20 ...119 B4
St Woolos' Cath NP20 ...119 B4
St Wulstans Dr WR14 ...42 C4
Salisbury Ave HR1 ...91 E1
Salisbury Cl 2 NP20 ...119 C3
Salisbury Ct HR4 ...106 C3
Salisbury Rd HR4 ...37 A6
Salisbury Terr NP4 ...101 E1
Salmon Cl BS35 ...135 A6
Saltbox La WR15 ...80 D2
Saltmarsh La HR2 ...130 E2
Samuel Salter Cl NP7 ...95 C3
Sand Pits HR6 ...82 C4
Sandfields HR8 ...51 B3
Sandford Rd SY8 ...79 E4
Sandiford Ploc HR6 ...16 C5
Sandown Dr HR4 ...90 A4
Sandpiper Cres WR14 ...84 E6
Sandpiper Way NP10 ...128 E6
Sandpits Ave SY8 ...79 D4
Sandpits Cl Ludlow SY8 ...79 D4
  Martley WR6 ...22 D6
Sandpits Rd SY8 ...79 D5
Sandringham Cl
  Malvern WR14 ...85 C6
  Ross-on-W HR9 ...94 C4
Sandy Cross HR7 ...21 B3
Sandy La Caldicot NP26 ...124 F7
  Caldicot, Caerwent Brook NP26 ...124 F7
  Cradley WR13 ...31 D1
  Hewelsfield GL15 ...76 E5
  Newport NP10 ...128 F8
Sandy's Rd WR14 ...85 C3
Sandybrook Cl NP44 ...106 C1
Sandys Cl HR1 ...93 C3
Sandyway La HR9 ...65 D3
Sargent's La HR9,GL18 ...59 B4
Saron Rd HR4 ...103 C8
Saunders Cl HR9 ...67 D8
Savage Hill GL16 ...72 E4
Sawpits La HR9 ...65 E4
Saxon Cl WR6 ...21 E8
Saxon Pl HR2 ...117 A7
Saxon Way HR8 ...89 C6
Sayers Ave HR4 ...90 B4
Scar La
  Staunton-on-W HR3,HR4 ...35 C7
  Woolhope HR1 ...49 A7
Scar The HR1 ...34 D6
Scarborough Rd 1 NP19 ...119 E8
Scard St 5 NP20 ...119 C3
Sch of Nursing & Midwifery Studies HR1 ...114 A2
Schallenge HR7 ...83 C6
School Cl Pontypool NP4 ...104 B8
  Kington HR5 ...81 C6
School Cres
  Joy's Green GL17 ...66 D3
  Pontypool NP4 ...104 C1
School Ct Cwmbran NP44 ...106 F2
  Llanvaches NP16 ...77 F3
School Hill NP16 ...116 E8
School Hill Ind Est HR1 ...116 E8
School La Abbey Dore HR2 ...45 C1
  Brimfield SY8 ...10 A2
  Clehonger HR2 ...46 D8
  Gilwern NP7 ...60 D1
  Govilon NP7 ...99 E8
  King's Thorn HR2 ...47 D3
  Kinnersley HR3 ...15 C6
  3 Leominster HR6 ...82 C4
  Longhope GL17 ...67 A6
  Narth The NP25 ...72 B1

School La *continued*
Newport NP20 ....119 C4
Norton LD8 ....6 D6
Penperlleni NP4 ....103 E6
Pontypool NP4 ....104 B7
5 Ross-on-W HR9 ....94 E5
Stauntton-on-W HR4 .....35 D8
Wigmore HR6 ....8 C8
School Lane (Lon Yr Ysgol)
LD8 ....6 D6
School Mews SY8 ....79 D5
School Rd
Ewyas Harold HR2 ....54 C7
Joy's Green GL17 ....66 D3
4 Leominster HR6 ....82 D5
Ruardean GL17 ....66 F4
Tarrington HR1 ....39 E3
Upper Lydbrook GL17 .....66 B4
School Rd The HR3 ....23 D7
School View NP4 ....104 D5
School Way BS35 ....135 A6
Scot's Cl HR1 ....93 B7
Scotch Firs HR1 ....48 D5
Scotland Pl WR15 ....80 D5
Scott Cl NP20 ....118 E1
Scott Wlk NP10 ....118 A6
Scottleton St LD8 ....6 A7
Scowles Rd GL16 ....72 F6
Scudamore Cl HR2 ....54 D6
Scudamore Comm HR3 ....33 E5
Scudamore St HR4 ....90 D1
Sea Bridge Mdws SY7 ....2 B5
Sea Street La NP26 ....132 E4
Sea View NP26 ....125 E4
Sea View Terr NP26 ....124 B4
Seabrook Pl HR9 ....58 D2
Seasons Cl HR7 ....123 A3
Seaton Ave HR1 ....91 D1
Second Ave HR9 ....94 D7
Second St NP19 ....130 B8
Sedbury Bsns Pk NP16 ...117 B8
Sedbury La NP16 ....111 A1
Sedgefield Rd HR1 ....93 C7
Sedgemoor Ct NP20 ....119 A6
Sedley Cl NP44 ....107 B2
Serpentine Rd NP20 ....119 B5
Seven Stars Rd **1** GL14 ...67 C1
Seven Stiles Ave NP19 ....120 D2
Severn Ave NP16 ....111 A1
Severn Beach Prim Sch
BS35 ....135 A6
Severn Beach Sta BS35 ...135 A6
Severn Bridge Ind Est
NP26 ....125 C4
Severn Cres NP16 ....116 F7
Severn Dr WR14 ....87 D8
Severn Rd BS35 ....134 F3
Severn Terr **12** NP26 ....119 B4
Severn Tunnel Junction Sta
NP26 ....124 C4
Severn View
Caldicot NP26 ....124 E4
6 Cinderford GL14 ....67 D1
Cwmbran NP44 ....106 A6
Severnwood Gdns BS35 ...135 A5
Seymour Ave NP26 ....77 B2
Seymour Ct WR14 ....85 B6
Seymour Rise NP26 ....77 B2
Shaft St HR8 ....135 A8
Shaftesbury Ct NP20 .....119 C6
Shaftesbury Wlk **5**
NP20 ....119 C6
Shakespeare Cl NP20 .....124 E5
Shakespeare Cres NP20 ..118 E2
Shakespeare Dr NP26 .....124 E5
Shakespeare Rd
Cwmbran NP44 ....106 C2
Hereford HR4 ....90 C1
Shakespeare Row NP26 ..124 E5
Shannon Rd NP20 ....112 F2
Sharman Pitch NP4 ....66 C7
Sharps Way NP16 ....116 F5
Shaw Gr NP20 ....118 E2
Shaw Wlk WR14 ....85 C2
Shawley Ct NP44 ....106 C2
Shawls Farm La HR4 ....44 A4
Shaymoor La BS35 ....135 F4
Shea Gdns **24** NP20 .....119 C3
Sheaf La NP19 ....119 B4
Shearman Rd SY8 ....79 E4
Sheepcote The HR8 ....40 B1
Sheet Ho SY8 ....5 C5
Sheet Rd Ludlow SY8 ....79 E3
Sheet SY8 ....5 C5
Shelburns Terr WR14 ....84 F4
Shellard Wlk HR2 ....92 E5
Shelley Cl NP26 ....124 E5
Shelley Cres NP25 ....96 B5
Shelley Gn NP44 ....106 C2
Shelley Rd NP19 ....119 F5
Shellingham Way HR2 .....92 C6
Shelsley Dr WR13 ....86 D3
Shenmore Batchy Hill
HR2 ....45 D8
Shenstone Cl WR14 ....97 D8
Shepherd Dr NP18 ....115 E1
Shepherd's Hill Caravan Site
NP4 ....102 B5
Shepherds Cl HR8 ....89 D2
Sherborne Cl HR2 ....92 E5
Sherbourne Ct NP4 ....104 E1
Sherbourne Rd NP4 ....104 E1
Sherford St HR7 ....83 D6
Sheridan Cl NP20 ....119 C2
Sheridan Rd HR4 ....90 C2
Sherrard's Green Rd
WR14 ....85 C1

Sherridge Rd WR13 ....32 C6
Sherrington Dr HR4 ....90 D2
Shetland Cl NP19 ....119 F7
Shetland Wlk NP19 ....119 F7
Shinwell Rd HR4 ....136 B3
Shipton Cl HR4 ....90 B3
Shire Hall NP25 ....137 B2
Shirenewton Old Rd
NP26 ....78 D1
Shirenewton Prim Sch
NP16 ....78 C5
Shires The Gilwern NP7 ....60 D7
Hereford HR2 ....93 B4
Shirley Cl WR14 ....85 B1
Shobdon Airfield HR6 ....16 D7
Shobdon Loop Wlk* HR6 ..8 B1
Shobdon Prim Sch HR6 ...16 D8
Shop Rd NP4 ....101 F1
Shortwood Family Farm*
HR7 ....29 C5
Shotts La GL18 ....59 C3
Shrewsbury Cl **8** NP20 ..119 C6
Shropshire Way SY8 ....79 E4
Shrubbery The HR9 ....94 C3
Shuttlefast La
Malvern WR14 ....87 A1
Malvern Wells WR14 ....42 D4
Sickert Cl NP19 ....120 A6
Siddons Rd HR1 ....93 E7
Sidney Box Dr HR4 ....90 D3
Sidney Rd NP26 ....124 E5
Sidney St NP20 ....119 B4
Silk Mill La SY8 ....79 C3
Silley's Cl NP16 ....110 F2
Silure Way NP18 ....121 B8
Silurian Cl HR4 ....82 D3
Silver Birch Cl NP18 ....113 E2
Silver Fir Cl HR2 ....92 C5
Silver Fir Sq NP10 ....118 B3
Silver La NP8 ....60 A5
Silver St Colwall WR13 .....86 B2
Mitcheldean GL17 ....67 D5
Simpson Cl NP20 ....113 A3
Sims Sq NP19 ....120 D5
Sinclair Dr HR1 ....93 E7
Singleton Court Bsns Pk
NP25 ....96 A5
Sir Charles Cres NP10 ....128 F5
Sir Charles Sq NP10 ......128 F5
Sirhowy Ct NP44 ....106 B4
Siskin Cres NP26 ....124 B4
Sitwell Cl SY7 ....2 C4
Sitwell Terr SY7 ....2 C4
Siward James Cl HR1 ......28 D5
Six Ways Ind Est WR14 ....87 B8
Sixth Ave HR9 ....94 D7
Sixth Avenue Cl NP4 ......94 D7
Sixth St NP19 ....119 F7
Skenfrith Castle* NP7 .....64 A7
Skenfrith Mews NP10 .....128 E5
Skenfrith Wlk HR4 ....92 D5
Skillion Bsns Ctr NP19 ...119 F1
Skinner La **4** NP20 .....119 C5
Skinner St NP20 ....119 C5
Skippe Cl HR8 ....89 C5
Skirrid Ct NP7 ....61 F7
Skirrid Rd NP7 ....95 D6
Skirrid View NP7 ....95 E8
Skyrrold Rd WR14 ....87 C8
Slade St NP19 ....119 F3
Slade View NP26 ....124 B4
Sling La WR14 ....85 A1
Sling Orch HR7 ....83 B6
Slough Rd LD8 ....6 D3
Sluvad Rd NP4 ....105 C3
Small Breeds Farm Park &
Owl Ctr The* HR5 ....81 D2
Smallbrook La NP44 ......106 F3
Smallbrook Gdns HR9 .....94 F5
Smallbrook Rd HR9 ....94 E5
Smithville Cl GL15 ....76 F7
Smithville Pl GL15 ....76 F7
Smithy Cl GL16 ....66 A2
Smithy The NP16 ....75 D1
Smoke Alley HR8 ....89 E4
Smooth Stones NP16 ......116 A7
Snail's Bank WR6 ....30 E3
Snitton La SY8 ....5 E6
Snodhill Dorstone HR3 .....34 E3
Snodhill Old Tay HR2,HR3 .34 E2
Snowdon Ct NP44 ....107 A5
Soane Cl NP10 ....118 A7
Soar Cl NP44 ....107 B6
Sohn St NP19 ....119 B5
Soliars Cl HR4 ....90 D1
Somers Cl WR13 ....32 C5
Somers Ct WR14 ....84 F4
Somers Park Ave WR14 ...84 F4
Somers Park Prim Sch
WR14 ....84 F4
Somerset Cl NP44 ....89 E4
Somerset Cotts NP18 .....110 F1
Somerset Dr **6** NP15 ....70 C2
Somerset Ind Est NP44 ...106 F5
Somerset Rd
Cwmbran NP44 ....106 F4
Monmouth NP25 ....137 A1
Newport NP19 ....119 E7
Somerset Way NP16 ....116 F4
Somerset Cres NP19 ......120 B5
Somerton Cl NP18 ....120 B3
Somerton **1** NP18 ....120 B3
Somerton Jun & Inf Sch
NP19 ....120 A4
Somerton La NP19 ....120 A4
Somerton Pk NP19 ....120 A3
Somerton Rd NP20 ....120 A3

Sor Brook Picnic Site*
NP44 ....107 E8
Sorrel Dr NP20 ....119 A6
Sorrel Way WR14 ....87 C7
South Ave NP4 ....104 D1
South Cl NP44 ....107 B1
South Ct NP4 ....104 D1
South End La WR13 ....43 F7
South Gr NP26 ....124 C4
South Lake Dr NP10 ......128 D5
South Lawn WR14 ....86 E5
South Market St NP20 ....119 D3
South Par HR1 ....89 E3
South Pontypool Ind Pk
NP4 ....104 F4
South Rd NP44 ....112 F8
South Row Redwick NP26 .132 F5
Summerleaze NP26 ....133 A6
South St Leominster HR6 ..82 D4
Pontypool NP4 ....104 E1
South View
Llanvaches NP26 ....77 E2
Pontypool NP4 ....104 B7
South Wlk
Cwmbran NP44 ....106 E3
Mitcheldean GL17 ....67 D5
Southall Terr GL18 ....59 E2
Southbank Cl 38 F5
Southbank Rd HR1 ....91 B1
Southbank St HR1 ....91 C1
Southbrook View NP26 ...125 C4
Southend The HR8 ....89 E3
Southern Ave HR6 ....82 E3
Southgate Cl HR2 ....136 B1
Southholme Rd HR2 ....92 C5
Southview Terr **15** NP4 ..101 C6
Southville Rd **8** NP20 ...118 F4
Southway NP4 ....103 E5
Southwell Cl HR2 ....64 C8
Southwood Cl GL16 ....66 C1
Sovereign Arc **4** NP20 ..119 C4
Spaniorum View BS35 ....135 F3
Sparrington Cotts HR7 .....19 D1
Sparrow Cl WR14 ....85 C4
Sparrowhawk Cl WR14 ....85 C5
Sparrows La HR9,GL18 .....59 B4
Speke St NP19 ....119 F3
Speculation Rd GL14 ......67 B2
Spencer Dr WR14 ....87 A7
Spencer Rd NP20 ....119 A4
Spindle Rd NP44 ....85 C3
Spinks Ct NP7 ....95 E7
Spinney Gr HR1 ....93 F8
Spinney The NP44 ....113 B2
Spoon La HR3 ....34 E5
Spout Hill NP16 ....78 D4
Spout La Drybrook GL17 ...67 A4
Shirl Heath HR6 ....17 B6
Spring Cl Colwall WR13 ....86 B2
Malvern WR14 ....85 B4
Spring Ct WR14 ....86 E5
Spring Gdns Hereford HR4 .85 B5
Newport NP20 ....119 C2
Tenbury Wells WR15 ....80 B6
Spring Gr Cwmbran NP44 .106 A3
Ledbury HR8 ....89 E2
Spring Grove La WR15 .....80 C2
Spring La
Croesyceiliog NP44 ....107 A5
Malvern WR14 ....85 B4
Newport NP20 ....85 B4
Spring La N WR14 ....85 C4
Spring La S WR14 ....85 C3
Spring Lane Ind Est
WR14 ....85 C4
Spring Mdw HR9 ....58 E5
Spring Pl GL17 ....66 E4
Spring St NP19 ....119 B7
Spring Terr NP4 ....104 D2
Springbank WR14 ....84 F1
Springdale HR9 ....59 B4
Springetts La
Ewyas Harold HR2 ....54 D8
Weston u P HR9 ....58 C2
Springfield Pencombe HR7 .27 C7
Richard's Castle SY8 ....9 E8
Springfield Ave HR2 ....136 A1
Springfield Cl
Croesyceiliog NP44 ....107 A6
Ludlow SY8 ....79 D4
Marden HR1 ....28 B2
Springfield Dr
Cinderford GL14 ....67 C1
Newport NP20 ....120 D6
Springfield Glade 84 F5
Springfield Pl HR1 ....136 C2
Springfield Rd
Abergavenny NP7 ....95 E6
Pontypool NP4 ....104 D1
Ross-on-W HR9 ....94 E7
Withington HR1 ....38 F5
Springfield Terr NP4 ......105 A3
Springvale NP26 ....106 C4
Springvale Ind Est
NP26 ....106 C4
Springwells NP7 ....95 F7
Spytty Rd NP19 ....120 C2
Square The
Cwmbran NP44 ....106 A6
Goodrich HR9 ....66 A6
Kington HR5 ....81 D6
Magor HR9 ....123 B3
Ruardean GL17 ....66 E4
St Briavels GL15 ....76 E7
Squires Cl NP20 ....118 B6
Squires Gate NP10 ....118 A6

Squirrel La SY8 ....5 D5
Squirrel View SY8 ....5 C5
Stable Row NP4 ....101 C7
Stack Sq NP4 ....101 C7
Stafford Rd
Caldicot NP26 ....124 F4
Newport NP19 ....119 E7
Pontypool NP4 ....104 E4
Stage Coach Lo HR4 ......136 B2
Stallard Ct **3** HR1 ....91 B2
Stallard's Cl HR7 ....83 B5
Stallards La HR2 ....47 D3
Stamford Ct NP20 ....119 A6
Stanberrow Rd HR4 ....92 E5
Stanbrook Rd
Hereford HR2 ....92 B5
Tenbury Wells WR15 ....80 D6
Standale Rd HR2 ....92 E5
Standard Signs Est
NP19 ....119 D7
Standard St NP8 ....60 B5
Stanfield HR1 ....39 B4
Stanford Ct Abberley WR6 .13 F5
Newport NP20 ....120 D5
Stanhope St
Abergavenny NP7 ....95 C6
Hereford HR4 ....136 A3
Staniers Way HR1 ....91 C4
Stanley Cl **2** NP20 ....119 B5
Stanley Pl **7** NP20 ....119 B5
Stanley Rd Malvern WR14 .85 B1
Newport NP20 ....119 B5
Stanton Cl SY8 ....79 C6
Stanton Dr SY8 ....79 C6
Stanton Rd SY8 ....79 D6
Stapleton Pl HR4 ....136 A2
Staplow HR8 ....41 A1
Star La NP4 ....104 B8
Star Rd Llanover NP7 ....73 A8
Star St NP44 ....106 E2
Star Trad Est NP18 ....114 A5
Star Villas NP18 ....114 A5
Starling Cl NP20 ....124 B4
Stars Pitch GL17 ....67 D5
Station App
Bassaleg NP10 ....118 B3
Hereford HR1 ....91 B1
Station Bglws WR13 ....86 B1
Station Cl NP26 ....124 E4
Station Ct NP18 ....124 A3
Station Dr SY8 ....79 C5
Station Ent NP7 ....95 F4
Station Farm NP4 ....106 F5
Station La GL17 ....67 F5
Station Rd
Abergavenny NP7 ....95 E4
Caerleon NP18 ....114 B3
Caldicot NP26 ....124 F4
Chepstow NP16 ....116 F8
Clydach NP7 ....98 E7
Credenhill HR4 ....90 D6
Cwmbran NP44 ....106 F5
Govilon NP7 ....99 E8
Hereford HR4 ....136 A2
Llanwern NP18 ....121 B4
Moorhampton HR4 ....25 F2
Pilning BS35 ....135 F4
Ponthir NP18 ....113 F6
Portskewett NP26 ....125 E5
Presteigne LD8 ....6 E3
Raglan NP15 ....70 C2
Rogiet NP26 ....124 B4
Severn Beach BS35 ....135 A6
Woofferton SY8 ....10 A7
Station St
Abersychan NP4 ....102 A4
Cinderford GL14 ....67 C1
8 Newport NP20 ....119 B5
Ross-on-W HR9 ....94 E5
Station Terr
3 Cwmbran NP44 .....106 E5
Dymock GL18 ....50 D2
Station Trad Est HR7 ....83 D6
Station Yard Ind Est
NP16 ....116 F8
Staunton Ho GL16 ....72 D7
Staunton on Wye Prim Sch
HR4 ....35 D8
Staunton Rd GL16,NP25 ..72 C7
Steam Mills GL14 ....67 B2
Steam Mills Prim Sch
GL14 ....67 B2
Steam Mills Rd GL14 ....67 B2
Steamer Point WR14 ....85 B2
Steel Wave* NP20 ....119 C5
Steep St NP16 ....116 E8
Steepfield NP4 ....107 A6
Steer Cres NP19 ....120 D2
Stelvio Park Ave NP20 ....118 F3
Stelvio Park Cres NP20 ...118 F3
Stelvio Park Dr NP20 ......118 E3
Stenders Ct GL17 ....67 D5
Stenders Rd GL17 ....67 D5
Stenders The GL17 ....67 C5
Stepaside NP16 ....116 A7
Stephen's Cl HR4 ....90 B1
Stephen's Ct NP7 ....95 F8
Stephenson St NP19 ......119 E1
Stepping Stones The
NP19 ....103 E7
Stepstile HR5 ....15 D2
Sterndale Bennett Rd
NP19 ....120 F5
Sterrys Cnr HR9 ....59 C4
Sterrys Rd HR9 ....59 C4

Stevelee NP44 ....106 C1
Stevenson Cl NP10 ....118 A6
Stevenson Ct NP10 ....118 A6
Stevenson Street Ind Est
NP19 ....129 F8
Steventon Cres SY8 ....79 D3
Steventon Gdns SY8 ....79 D3
Steventon New Rd SY8 ....79 E3
Steventon Rd SY8 ....79 E2
Steynton Path NP44 ......106 C2
Stiels HR4 ....113 B8
Stockenhill Rd HR6 ....82 B4
Stockholm Pl HR9 ....67 C8
Stockley Cross HR6 ....16 B8
Stocks La Almeley HR3 ....25 B7
Malvern WR13 ....32 A3
Stocks Rd WR6 ....31 F6
Stockton Bury Gdns*
HR6 ....18 D7
Stockton Cl **9** NP19 ....119 E8
Stockton Cross HR6 ....18 D7
Stockton Grange WR6 .....13 C6
Stockton Rd
Abberley WR6 ....13 D6
Newport NP19 ....119 D8
Stockton Rock SY8 ....13 F5
Stockwood Cl NP18 ....115 B1
Stockwood Way NP18 ....121 B8
Stoke Cross HR7 ....29 F5
Stoke Dr SY8 ....5 E1
Stoke Edith HR1 ....39 D3
Stoke La
Bishops Frome HR7 ....30 A5
Bromyard HR7 ....30 B5
Little Cowarne HR7 ....29 F5
Stoke Prior Prim Sch
HR6 ....18 E3
Stoke Prior Rd HR6 ....18 D4
Stokes Cotts NP18 ....113 F6
Stokes Dr NP18 ....113 E6
Stone Cl WR13 ....86 A2
Stone Cotts NP26 ....125 F4
Stone Ct WR13 ....86 B2
Stone Dr WR13 ....86 A2
Stone St Kingstone HR2 ...46 A8
Madley HR2 ....36 E2
Stonebarrow Pl GL18 ....50 D2
Stonebow Rd HR1 ....91 B1
Stonehill Cl HR7 ....83 C5
Stonehill Dr HR7 ....83 C5
Stoneleigh Dr HR4 ....92 B5
Stoney Rd GL18 ....50 E2
Stoneyhills Ind Est HR9 ...65 D4
Stony St Ind Est HR7 ....83 D7
Stopford Cl HR1 ....93 D7
Storer Ct WR14 ....87 B7
Stores Row HR5 ....15 D2
Stoulgrove La NP16 ....111 A4
Stour Cl NP44 ....106 C1
Stow Hill NP20 ....119 B4
Stow Park Ave NP20 ....119 A3
Stow Park Circ NP20 ......119 A3
Stow Park Cres NP20 ......119 A3
Stow Park Dr NP20 ....119 A3
Stow Pk Ave NP20 ....119 A3
Stowe La
Colwall Stone WR13 ....42 A4
St Briavels GL15 ....72 E1
Stowe Path **4** NP44 ....107 B2
Stowe Rd GL15 ....76 D8
Straight Mile The HR2 .....93 E4
Straits La NP18 ....130 E5
Strand The NP44 ....106 E4
Stratford Ho NP20 ....118 E3
Stratford Rd HR4 ....90 C5
Strawberry Field HR9 ......57 C3
Streatley Mews SY8 ....79 C4
Stretton Cl HR4 ....90 B2
Stride Cl BS35 ....135 A6
Striguil Rd NP16 ....116 E6
Stroud Cl HR8 ....89 B4
Stroncken Way HR4 ....90 E5
Stuart Cl NP16 ....110 D1
Stud La WR6 ....13 E6
Suckley La HR6 ....16 C5
Suckley Prim Sch WR6 ....31 D6
Suckley Rd WR6,WR13 ....32 D7
Sudbrook Rd NP26 ....125 D4
Sudbury Ave HR1 ....93 E7
Sudbury Wlk **8** NP20 ...118 F4
Sudeley Cl WR14 ....84 F6
Suffield Cl WR6 ....32 D6
Suffolk La WR6 ....32 D6
Sufton La HR1 ....39 A1
Sufton Rise HR1 ....39 A1
Sugar Tump HR7 ....59 B4
Sugarloaf Vineyard*
NP7 ....95 A8
Sullivan Circ NP19 ....120 D1
Summer Pool WR6 ....30 D3
Summerfield Rd
Abergavenny NP7 ....95 E6
Malvern WR14 ....85 E5
Summerfields NP19 ......120 D6
Summerhill Ave HR9 ......119 E6
Summerhill Ho **9** NP19 .119 F7
Summerhouse La NP16 ..116 F4
Sun La HR5 ....81 D6
Sundale HR9 ....59 B4
Sunlea Cres NP4 ....104 F6
Sunningdale Hereford HR1 .90 F5
Leominster HR6 ....82 C5
Sunningdale Cl NP19 .....120 D6

Sunny Bank
Abergavenny NP7 ....95 C5
Lower Maes-coed HR2 ....44 D2
Sunny Croft NP26 ......125 F5
Sunny Side NP15 ....97 C5
Sunnybank Ct NP4 ....104 E3
Sunnybank Rd NP4 ....104 D2
Sunnybank Way NP4 ..104 D2
Sunnymead Cl GL17 ....67 B4
Sunnyside NP7 ....98 C4
Sunnyvale NP15 ....70 B2
Sunrise WR14 ....85 B1
Sunset Row HR5 ....81 E6
Sunshine Cl HR8 ....89 C5
Surrey Pl NP19 ....119 E7
Sussex Ave HR9 ....94 D4
Sussex Cl NP19 ....119 E7
Sutherland Cres NP19 ..120 A7
Sutton Prim Sch HR1 ....38 D8
Sutton Rd NP19 ....119 D8
Swagwater La HR9 ......59 C5
Swallow Dr NP26 ......125 A4
Swallow Way NP10 ....128 E8
Swan Bank HR3 ....88 D3
Swan Cl Caldicot NP26 ..125 A4
Tenbury Wells WR15 ......80 D6
Swan Ct Ross-on-W HR9 ..94 D5
Tenbury Wells WR15 ......80 D6
Swan La WR15 ....80 D6
Swan Orch WR6 ....32 A8
Sward Cl NP10 ....118 A7
Sweetman's Yd HR4 ..136 A4
Swinburne Cl NP19 ....120 A5
Swiss La GL17 ....67 A4
Swiss Wlk HR4 ....90 A2
Sycamore Ave
Caldicot NP26 ....124 E6
Chepstow NP16 ....116 E5
Newport NP19 ....120 B4
Sycamore Cl
Bodenham Moor HR1 ......28 D5
Cradley WR13 ....31 D1
Ludlow SY8 ....79 D6
Malvern WR14 ....85 A5
Ross-on-W HR9 ....94 C3
Sycamore Croft HR2 ....36 C1
Sycamore Ct NP16 ....110 B5
Sycamore La HR4 ....90 A7
Sycamore Pl NP44 ....106 B6
Sycamore Rd
Harrow Hill GL17 ....67 B3
Pontypool NP4 ....104 D2
Sycamore Rd S NP4 ....104 E3
Sycamore Terr NP26 ..123 B3
Sydwall Rd HR2 ....92 D6
Syers Croft HR2 ....46 C8
Sylvan Cl NP20 ....113 B3
Sylvan View NP16 ......76 B4
Symonds St HR1 ......136 C2
Symondscliff Way NP26 .125 C4

T

Tabernacle Rd NP26 ....77 E2
Taberness Cl WR6 ......22 E2
Tabor Gdns WR14 ......85 A3
Taff Ct NP44 ....106 A5
Taff Rd NP26 ....125 A6
Talbot La NP20 ....119 C4
Talfaen Cl NP4 ....102 C1
Talgarth Cl NP44 ......106 E4
Taliesin NP44 ....106 E4
Taliesin Cl NP10 ......118 B6
Taliesin Dr NP10 ......118 B6
Tallard's Pl NP16 ......117 A8
Tallis Cl NP19 ....120 E5
Talybont La HR9 ....65 C3
Tamar Cl NP20 ....112 E2
Tan House Cl NP16 ......78 D4
Tan House Dr NP18 ....114 C2
Tan House Mdws HR5 ....31 A7
Tanglewood Cl NP7 ......95 E6
Tanglewood Hts WR14 ..84 E3
Tanhouse La
Cradley WR13 ....31 C1
Malvern WR14 ....84 F6
Tannery Ct NP15 ....80 C4
Tanyard La Kington HR5 ..31 A7
Ross-on-W HR9 ....94 E6
Target Cl HR8 ....89 C5
Tarsmill Ct HR2 ....93 D4
Tatton Rd NP19 ....130 D8
Taunton Way HR4 ......90 C5
Tavern La WR15 ....12 B8
Tavern Mdw HR6 ....27 F7
Tavistock Dr HR2 ......92 D6
Taylors Cl HR2 ....136 B1
Tayson Way WR14 ......85 A5
Tea Shed Crossroads
NP26 ....123 D5
Teal Cl NP26 ....123 C3
Tech Way NP25 ....36 F6
Tedder Ave HR4 ....36 F6
Teddy Bears of Bromyard
Mus* HR7 ....83 D6
Tees Cl NP20 ....112 F2
Televillages The NP8 ..60 B5
Telford Cl NP10 ....118 B6
Telford St NP19 ......119 C5
Teme Ave Ludlow SY8 ....79 D3
Malvern WR14 ....87 D8
Teme Cl HR7 ....83 C6
Teme Ct WR6 ....22 B3
Teme La WR6 ....32 C8

Teme St WR15 ....80 D5
Teme Way HR8 ....89 C5
Temes Gn SY8 ....5 B1
Temeside SY8 ....79 D4
Temeside Cl WR15 ......80 D6
Temeside Ct SY8 ....79 D3
Temeside Est SY8 ......79 D3
Temeside Gdns SY8 ......79 D3
Tempest Dr NP16 ......116 D8
Templars La HR1 ....93 B8
Temple Ave WR13 ......85 F4
Temple Ct HR2 ....54 C7
Temple Mdw SY8 ....10 D7
Temple St NP20 ......119 D2
Tenbury CE Prim Sch
WR15 ....80 D4
Tenbury Com Hospl
Tenbury High Sch WR15 ..80 C3
Tenbury Rd HR4 ....90 A1
Tenbury Wells Bsns Pk
WR15 ....11 D6
Tenbury Wells Bsns Pk
Clarkes Mdw WR15 ......80 E3
Tenbury Wells Mus*
WR15 ....80 D5
Tenby Cl
Llanyravon NP44 ....107 A3
Newport NP20 ....128 E5
Tenison Rd HR4 ....102 D1
Tennyson Ave NP18 ..121 A4
Tennyson Cl
Caldicot NP26 ....124 E5
Hereford HR4 ....90 C1
Tennyson Dr WR14 ......85 A2
Tennyson Rd
Caldicot NP26 ....124 E5
Newport NP20 ....120 A5
Tensing Cl HR4 ....90 B3
Tern Ct NP44 ....106 A5
Terrace The NP26 ......125 E4
Terrills La WR15 ....80 D3
Tetbury Cl NP20 ......119 C7
Tewdric Ct NP44 ......107 B5
Tewends [12] NP44 ....106 E1
Tewkesbury Wlk [6]
NP20 ....119 C6
Teynes NP44 ....106 B1
Thames Cl NP20 ......112 E1
Third Ave HR9 ....94 D7
Third St NP19 ....130 B8
Thirlmere Pl [6] NP19 .119 F8
Thirlstane Rd WR14 ....86 F6
Thirsk Ave HR4 ....90 D5
Thistledown Gr HR1 ....93 F8
Thomas Cl Hereford HR2 ..93 C5
Ledbury HR8 ....89 C5
Thomas Ct HR6 ....82 C5
Thomas Row HR9 ....94 F5
Thomas St NP16 ......116 E8
Thompson Ave NP19 ..120 B3
Thompson Cl NP19 ....120 C3
Thompson Pl HR4 ....90 D1
Thorn Bsns Pk HR1 ......93 D5
Thorn The HR2 ....47 B3
Thorn Tree Dr NP14 ....87 B4
NP10 ....118 B4
Thornbury Pk NP10 ....118 B4
Thornbury Park Sh Ctr
Thorncliff Ct [11] NP44 .106 C2
Thorngrove Rd WR14 ....87 A8
Thornhill Cl NP44 ......106 B6
Thornhill Rd NP44 ....106 B6
Thornwell Prim Sch
NP16 ....116 E5
Thornwell Rd NP16 ....116 F5
Three Choirs Vineyard*
GL18 ....59 F7
Three Counties
Showground* WR13 ......87 B2
Three Crosses Cl HR9 ..94 E6
Three Crosses Rd HR9 ..94 E6
Three Elms Rd HR4 ......90 C3
Three Elms Trad Est HR4 ..90 C4
Three Mills Trad Est HR7 ..83 C7
Three Owls HR6 ....17 C8
Thrift Ct WR6 ....21 E6
Tibberton Grange [1]
WR14 ....87 A8
Tibberton Rd WR14 ....87 A8
Tick Bridge La HR6 ....18 E5
Tidnor La HR1 ....38 E2
Till Gr NP18 ....113 F3
Tilley's Alley HR8 ......89 E4
Tillington Rd HR4 ......90 A6
Tillis View GL16 ....72 D7
Tillsland NP44 ....112 C8
Tinglebrook Cl HR2 ....36 C1
Tinkers La NP25 ....75 F8
Tinmans Gn NP25 ......72 F2
Tintern Abbey* NP16 ..76 C2
Tintern Cl Cwmbran NP44 .106 F2
Ross-on-W HR9 ....94 D3
Tintern Cross NP16 ....75 F3
Tintern Hts NP16 ......76 A5
Tintern Old Sta* NP16 ..76 C3
Tippett Cl NP17 ......120 E5
Tipton's La SY7 ....9 D7
Tollgate Rd SY8 ....79 F3
Tollstone Way NP7 ......54 E3
Tolpath NP44 ....106 A1
Tom Mann Cl NP19 ......120 E7
Tomkyn's La HR3 ....34 A4
Ton Rd Cwmbran NP44 ..106 C1
Cwmbran, Fairwater NP44 ..106 B2
Llangybi NP15 ....109 B5
Ton-Bach St NP4 ......101 D6
Ton-Mawr Ave NP4 ....101 D6

Ton-Mawr Rd NP4 ....101 D6
Ton-Mawr St [17] NP4 ..101 C6
Tone Cl NP20 ....112 D2
Tone Rd NP20 ....112 D2
Tone Sq NP20 ....112 D2
Torfaen Bsns Ctr NP4 ..104 F4
Torfaen Terr [2] NP4 ..102 A1
Toronto Cl NP44 ......118 D3
Torridge Rd NP20 ......112 C3
Torvale Ind Est HR6 ....16 D7
Tower Hill HR7 ....83 C5
Tower House Dr GL19 ..51 F2
Tower Rd HR4 ....92 D8
Tower St Crickhowell NP8 ..60 A5
Ludlow SY8 ....79 C4
Tower The HR3 ....34 C3
Tower View NP25 ....96 B4
Towers The NP44 ......106 F3
Town Bridge Bldgs NP4 .104 C7
Town Reach NP20 ......119 C5
Townend LD8 ....6 E3
Townsend
Mitcheldean GL17 ....67 D5
Ruardean GL17 ....66 E4
Townsend Cl
Leominster HR6 ....82 C5
St Briavels GL15 ....76 F7
Townsend Ct HR6 ......82 C5
Townsend Rd NP19 ....119 D6
Townsend Way WR14 ..85 D4
Towtree La HR4 ....37 C5
Toynbee Cl NP25 ......137 B4
Trafalgar Cl NP25 ......72 F6
Traherne Cl Ledbury HR8 .89 E2
Traherne Pl HR1 ....41 B8
Lugwardine HR1 ....38 D4
Tram La NP44 ....113 D7
Tram Rd Caerleon NP18 ..114 C2
Cwmbran NP44 ....106 B6
Tramway Cl NP44 ......106 A1
Tranch Rd NP4 ....104 A6
Trannon Ct NP44 ......106 A4
Tranquil Pl NP44 ......106 E1
Traston La Newport NP19 .120 B1
Newport NP19 ....120 B1
Traston La NP19 ......120 B1
Traston Rd NP19 ......130 A8
Traveller's Seat NP25 ..63 D5
Traverner Trad Est
NP18 ....114 B3
Trawsmawr La NP26 ....112 C4
Tre Essey Cross HR9 ....64 F8
Tre Honddu NP7 ....61 F7
Tre-Elidyr NP7 ....68 E3
Tre-Herbert Rd
Croesyceiliog NP44 ......107 D6
Llandegveth NP18 ......108 A3
Treago Gr NP44 ....92 C4
Trebat St NP19 ....120 C6
Tredegar Ct NP20 ......119 C2
Tredegar Dr NP26 ......123 D3
Tredegar House Ctry Pk*
NP10 ....128 D7
Tredegar House Dr
NP10 ....128 E6
Tredegar Park View
NP10 ....118 C4
Tredegar St NP19 ......120 C3
Tredillion Rd NP7 ......95 F6
Treetops NP26 ....125 D5
Trefoil Cl WR14 ....87 D7
Tregare St NP19 ......119 D6
Tregarn Cl NP18 ......115 E2
Tregarn Ct NP18 ......115 F2
Tregarn Rd NP18 ......115 F2
Tregate Cl NP25 ....96 C7
Tregwilym Cl NP10 ....118 A4
Tregwilym Ind Est NP10 .118 A4
Tregwilym Rd NP10 ....118 A4
Tregwilym Wlk NP10 ..118 B4
Trelawny Cl NP15 ......97 C5
Trelay Rd NP15 ....74 C1
Trelech Cl NP44 ......106 C6
Trellech Prim Sch NP25 ..75 F8
Trelleck Cross NP25 ....75 E7
Trelleck Rd NP44 ......76 B4
Trem Twynbarlwm
NP44 ....106 D1
Trem-y-Mynydd NP4 ..101 D6
Tremlett Cl HR4 ....90 D2
Tremorithic Rd
Abbey Dore HR2 ....45 A1
Lower Maes-coed HR2 ....44 F2
Trenchard Ave HR4 ....36 F6
Trenchard St HR9 ......94 D5
Trent Rd NP20 ....112 D3
Tretower Ct NP44 ......107 B3
Trevethin Com Sch NP4 .104 C2
Trevine Path NP44 ....106 C2
Trevithick Cl NP20 ....112 F3
Trewern Rd NP44 ....78 A1
Trewern Rd HR4 ....44 C2
Triangle The GL15 ......76 D4
Trilleck Ave HR4 ....92 D5
Trinity Ct Hereford HR4 ..90 D1
Newport NP20 ....119 D1
Trinity Dr HR9 ....94 B3
Trinity Pl NP20 ....119 D2
Trinity Pl NP20 ....119 D2
Trinity Prim Sch HR4 ....90 C3
Trinity Rd
Cwmbran NP44 ....106 D5
Harrow Hill GL17 ....67 B3
Hereford HR4 ....90 C2
Malvern WR14 ....84 F7
Trinity Sq HR1 ....136 C5
Trinity St NP7 ....95 D5
Trinity Terr NP7 ....95 D5

Trinity View NP18 ......113 E3
Trinity Way [24] GL14 ..67 C1
Tristram Ct HR1 ....93 F7
Tronddi Cl NP26 ......124 F6
Trosnant St NP4 ......104 C6
Trosnant Villa NP4 ....104 C6
Trostrey NP44 ....112 C8
Trostrey Cl NP44 ......105 B4
Trostrey St NP19 ......119 D6
Trostry La NP16,NP20 ..77 E3
Trothy Way NP7 ....63 A1
Troy Gardens / Gerod Troddi
NP25 ....96 D2
Troy Way NP25 ....96 C2
Trussel Rd (Heol Trussel)
NP25 ....96 D2
Tubular Cotts NP16 ....111 A1
Tudor Cres NP10 ......118 B4
Tudor Cres NP10 ......118 B4
Tudor Dr NP16 ....110 C1
Tudor Gdns NP16 ....75 D1
Tudor Pl HR6 ....17 C8
Tudor Rd Cwmbran NP44 .106 E3
Monmouth NP25 ....72 B7
Newport NP19 ....119 E8
Tudor Rise HR9 ....94 D2
Tudor St Abergavenny NP7 .95 C4
Ross-on-W HR9 ....94 D2
Tudor Woods NP44 ....107 B2
Tudorville Pl HR9 ......94 D3
Tump La Undy NP26 ....123 C3
Tunnel La
Middleton on t H HR6 ....10 A3
Orleton SY8 ....9 F5
Tunnel Terr NP20 ......119 B4
Turberville Rd NP44 ..106 E4
Turkey Tump La HR2 ..56 C7
Turnant Longtown HR2 .53 B8
Turnberry Dr HR1 ......91 A5
Turner Ct HR8 ....89 E4
Turner St Hereford HR1 .93 B8
Newport NP19 ....119 D6
Turners End NP44 ......106 B1
Turnpike Cl
Chepstow NP16 ....110 C1
Pontypool NP4 ....104 F6
Turnpike End NP16 ....117 B4
Turnpike Rd NP44 ......107 B1
Turnstiles The NP20 ..119 C7
Tuscidum Way GL17 ....67 D5
Tutshill Gdns NP16 ......111 A1
Tweedy La NP19 ....119 F5
Twinberrow Ct WR14 ..84 F5
Twinings The [6] NP44 .106 B3
Twissell's Rd NP44 ....106 A6
Twm Barlwm View
NP44 ....107 B2
Twmpath Gdns NP44 ..112 E8
Two Locks Rd NP44 ..106 D1
Twyford Rd HR2 ....93 C4
Twympath Rd NP44 ....104 B6
Twyn Allwys Rd NP7 ..99 E8
Twyn La NP4 ....73 A4
Twyn Oaks NP18 ......114 D3
Twyn Sq NP25 ....97 B4
Twyning St HR7 ....83 B6
Ty Bach HR2 ....44 B1
Ty Box Cl NP44 ......106 D5
Ty Box Rd NP44 ......106 D5
Ty Brith Gdns NP15 ....97 B4
Ty Canol Way NP44 ..106 A2
Ty Coch Distribution Ctr
NP44 ....112 C4
Ty Coch La NP44 ......112 E8
Ty Cradoc Shawls HR2 ..44 A4
Ty Draw La NP15 ......103 E3
Ty Fry Cl NP7 ....101 D7
Ty Gwyn Rd
Cwmbran NP44 ....106 B3
Penperlleni NP4 ....103 C3
Ty Gwyn Way NP44 ....106 C5
Ty Mynydd
Blaenavon NP4 ....101 D6
Cwmbran NP44 ....106 C5
Ty Tudor NP44 ....106 D2
Ty-n-y-coed NP4 ....96 D2
Ty-Brith NP25 ....71 A5
Ty-canol Ct NP44 ....106 A1
Ty-Canol Row NP44 ..106 A1
Ty-Clyd Cl NP7 ....60 F1
Ty-Coch La
Cwmbran NP44 ....106 A4
Cwmbran, Ty Coch NP44 ..112 E8
Ty-Coch Terr NP44 ....112 E8
Ty-Coed NP44 ....106 C5
Ty-Dan-y-Wal NP13 ..100 B1
Ty-Draw NP4 ....103 E3
Ty-Freeman Rd NP15 ..74 A6
Ty-Gwyn NP44 ....106 A2
Ty-Gwyn Way NP44 ....106 C5
Ty-Newydd Rd NP15 ..74 A6
Ty-Newydd Way NP44 .106 C5
Tydies NP44 ....112 B8
Tydu View NP10 ......118 B4
Tylers Way NP16 ......117 B8
Tyllwyd Rd NP7 ....118 F4
Tyndings The SY7 ......22 B5
Tyne Cl NP20 ....112 D1
Tyne Rd NP20 ....112 D1
Tynewydd Ave NP44 ..106 E6
Tynewydd Farm Cl
NP44 ....106 E6
Tynewydd Gn NP44 ....106 E6

Tynewydd North Cl
NP44 ....106 E6
Tynewydd South Cl
NP44 ....106 D2
Tythings Cres GL18 ....59 F4
Tythings Mews GL18 ..59 F4
Tythings The GL18 ......59 F4

U

Underhill NP16 ....76 C4
Underhill Cres NP7 ......95 D7
Underhill Rd HR1 ....93 C8
Underwood Est NP25 ..96 F4
Undy Prim Sch NP26 ....123 C3
Unicorn Ct HR4 ....26 B6
Union La HR7 ....21 B1
Union Mews HR3 ....88 D3
Union St NP7 ....95 C5
Union Rd W NP7 ....95 C5
Union Road Ind Est NP7 ..95 B5
Union St HR1 ....136 C3
Union Wlk HR1 ....136 C3
Univ of Wales Coll
NP18 ....114 A3
Univ of Wales Coll Newport
(Allt-yr-yn Campus)
NP20 ....118 F5
Upcott La HR4 ....24 F6
Uphill Rd GL17 ....66 D2
Upland Dr NP4 ....102 B1
Uplands WR6 ....30 F1
Uplands Ct [3] NP19 ..119 F6
Uplands Rd
Gaer-llawr NP15 ....74 F1
Llantrisant NP15 ....77 E8
Uplands Terr NP44 ....106 C3
Upper Bilson Rd [2] GL14 .67 C1
Upper Bridge St NP4 ..104 C6
Upper Chase Rd WR14 ..87 B8
Upper Chilstone HR2 ..36 A2
Upper Church St NP16 .116 E8
Upper Coedcae Rd NP4 .101 D7
Upper Court Rd HR8 ....41 A6
Upper Cross HR8 ....89 E4
Upper Ct Colwall WR13 ..86 B2
Luston HR6 ....9 D1
Upper Cwmbran Inf Sch
NP44 ....106 B6
Upper Cwmbran Rd
NP44 ....106 B6
Upper Dock St NP20 ..119 C5
Upper Fee SY8 ....79 C3
Upper Galdeford SY8 ..79 C4
Upper Garn Terr NP4 ..100 F8
Upper Hall Cl HR8 ......89 E4
Upper Hardwick La HR7 .83 A6
Upper Hengoed HR5 ....23 C2
Upper Hergest HR5 ....14 D2
Upper Hill HR8 ....49 D8
Upper Hill St NP44 ....101 D6
Upper Hos WR6 ....31 F7
Upper Howsell Rd WR14 .84 F5
Upper Linney SY8 ......79 C4
Upper Maes Coed HR4 ..44 D5
Upper Nelson St NP16 .116 E8
Upper Park Terr NP20 ..104 C6
Upper Power St NP19 ..119 B7
Upper Ruels St HR8 ....51 B8
Upper Southfield Rd GL17 .66 C4
Upper Tennyson St
NP19 ....104 A5
Upper Trosnant St NP4 .104 C6
Upper Waun St NP4 ....101 C7
Upper Welland Rd WR14 .42 C3
Upper Welson HR3 ......24 D8
Upper Woodland St
NP4 ....101 D7
Upper Wrigglebrook La
HR2 ....47 C2
Upperfields HR8 ....89 E5
Upton La NP20 ....118 F4
Upton Rd NP20 ....118 F4
Urishay Comm
Craswall HR2 ....43 E8
Michaelchurch Escley HR2 ..34 D1
Urishay Ct HR2 ....44 B8
Urishay Villa
Michaelchurch Escley HR2 ..44 B8
Snodhill HR2 ....34 D1
Usk Bridge Mews NP15 ..97 A4
Usk Cl Caldicot NP26 ..125 A7
Hereford HR4 ....92 E5
Usk Ct NP44 ....106 B4
Usk Dr NP7 ....60 C2
Usk Prim Sch NP15 ......97 C5
Usk Rd Caerleon NP18 ..114 C3
Llandewaugh NP15,NP16,
NP26 ....77 F4
Pontypool NP4 ....104 F6
Pontypool, Little Mill NP4 .103 D3
Raglan NP15 ....70 B2
Shirenewton NP16 ......78 C5
Usk Vale Cl NP19 ......119 D6
Usk Vale Ct NP18 ......104 A4
Usk Vale Dr NP18 ......104 F6
Usk Vale Mews NP18 ..114 B3
Usk View Llanfoist NP7 ..68 A3
Newport NP19 ....120 A8
Usk Way NP20 ....119 D1

V

Vaga Cl HR2 ......92 D7
Vaga Cres HR9 ......94 D6
Vaga St HR2 ......92 D7
Vale Veiw NP19 ......120 A7
Vale View NP7 ......95 E8
Valentine Cl NP16 ......117 A4
Valentine Rd NP4 ......102 A3
Valley Inheritance Mus The* NP4 ......104 C2
Valley Rd GL17 ......66 D1
Valley View HR7 ......20 A3
Van Dyke Cl NP19 ......119 F7
Vanbrugh Cl NP19 ......118 B6
Vanbrugh Gdns NP20 ......118 E1
Vancouver Dr NP20 ......118 D3
Vandra Cl WR14 ......85 B5
Vantage Point Bsns Village GL17 ......67 D6
Varnister La GL17 ......66 F4
Varnister Rd GL17 ......66 F4
Varteg Rd NP4 ......101 E3
Vashon Cl SY8 ......79 E5
Vaughan La HR2 ......47 C3
Vaughan St HR4 ......136 C3
Vaughan Williams Dr NP19 ......120 C5
Vauxhall GL18 ......59 F4
Vauxhall La NP16 ......116 D8
Vauxhall Rd NP16 ......116 D8
Vauxhall Way NP25 ......96 F7
Vectis Cl HR9 ......94 D3
Veldo La HR1 ......110 A6
Veldt House Barns HR8 ......50 B5
Venn's Cl HR1 ......136 C3
Venn's Ct HR1 ......91 B3
Venn's La HR1 ......91 B3
Venta Silurum Roman Town* NP16 ......78 C1
Vention La GL17 ......66 D3
Ventnor Rd NP44 ......106 E2
Vermeer Cres NP19 ......120 A7
Vernon Cl WR6 ......22 D6
Vernon Williams Cl HR2 ......92 C4
Veronica Cl NP10 ......118 B3
Verschoyle Gdns HR9 ......94 F7
Viaduct Rd NP4 ......104 D5
Vicarage Cl
  Bassaleg NP10 ......118 B2
  Ewyas Harold HR2 ......54 C7
Vicarage Gdns NP26 ......78 C1
Vicarage Hill NP20 ......119 B4
Vicarage Rd
  Hereford HR1 ......136 C1
  Pilning BS35 ......135 C7
Vicarage St HR6 ......82 D5
Vicarage Terr NP4 ......102 A5
Victoria Ave
  Bromyard HR7 ......83 D5
  Newport NP19 ......119 F6
Victoria St **7** NP4 ......119 C4
Victoria Cres
  Newport NP4 ......119 B4
  Severn Beach BS35 ......135 A6
Victoria Cl
  Abergavenny NP7 ......95 E6
  Kington HR5 ......81 E6
  Newport NP19 ......119 E5
Victoria Est NP25 ......137 A1
Victoria La NP19 ......119 F6
Victoria Mews HR5 ......81 E6
Victoria Park Rd WR14 ......136 A5
Victoria Pl **6** NP20 ......119 C4
Victoria Prim Sch NP4 ......102 A4
Victoria Rd
  Chepstow NP16 ......116 F5
  Kington HR5 ......81 E6
  Ledbury HR8 ......89 C3
  Malvern WR14 ......84 E1
  8 Newport NP20 ......119 C4
  Pontypool NP4 ......104 D5
Victoria St
  Abergavenny NP7 ......95 D5
  Cwmbran NP44 ......106 E2
  Hereford HR4 ......136 B2
  Leominster HR6 ......82 D5
  Pontypool NP4 ......104 E3
Victoria Terr
  Crickhowell NP8 ......60 A6
  Cusop HR3 ......88 E3
Victoria Way HR4 ......123 C3
Victoria Wlk
  Malvern WR14 ......84 F1
  Malvern, North Malvern WR14 ......84 E3
Viking Way HR4 ......89 C5
Vilberie Way HR4 ......90 D2
Villa St HR2 ......92 C4
Villa The SY8 ......79 C6
Villa Way HR8 ......89 D2
Village The WR6 ......26 A7
Villas The NP4 ......125 F4
Vimpennys La BS35 ......135 E1
Vincent St HR4 ......101 C7
Vine Acre NP25 ......96 D7
Vine Cotts NP16 ......116 E8
Vine Ct NP25 ......137 B4
Vine La WR15 ......11 E3
Vine Pl **9** NP19 ......119 E6
Vine Tree Cl HR1 ......38 F6
Vine Tree Pk HR9 ......94 D2
Vinegar Hill NP26 ......123 C3
Vines The HR4 ......90 E3
Vinesend La WR13 ......31 F2
Vineyard Rd HR1 ......93 D7

Vineyard The
  Monmouth NP25 ......137 B4
  Walterstone HR2 ......53 F4
Vineyards The HR3 ......24 C1
Virdi Mews HR4 ......36 F6
Viscount Cobham Ct WR14 ......85 B2
Viscount Evan Dr NP10 ......128 F7
Vivian Rd NP19 ......119 E4
Vowles Cl HR4 ......90 D1
Vroe The HR2 ......54 C5

W

Wades The **14** NP44 ......106 B1
Wainbridge Cres BS35 ......135 D7
Wainfelin Ave NP4 ......104 B7
Wainfelin Rd NP4 ......104 B7
Wainland Pl GL16 ......72 F3
Waldbronn Cl NP25 ......137 A1
Walden Grange Cl NP19 ......120 B5
Walford Ave HR9 ......94 D2
Walford Davies Dr NP19 ......120 C5
Walford Prim Sch HR9 ......66 C7
Walford Rd HR9 ......94 D3
Walford St NP20 ......119 B7
Walk The NP4 ......105 A4
Walkdens **3** NP44 ......106 B1
Walker's Gn HR1 ......28 B2
Walker's La GL17 ......66 F4
Walkmill SY8 ......79 F7
Wall St HR4 ......136 B3
Wallace Cl NP15 ......97 C5
Wallace Hall Row **5** HR9 ......94 E5
Wallbrook Ct HR2 ......93 E4
Wallhouse Rd HR9 ......94 E7
Wallis Ave HR2 ......136 A1
Wallis Cl NP25 ......137 B4
Wallsend HR1 ......28 A1
Wallvern Wood NP16 ......110 C1
Walmer Rd NP19 ......119 F5
Walmer St HR4 ......136 B3
Walney La HR1 ......91 C3
Walnut Cres WR14 ......86 F5
Walnut Dr NP18 ......113 E2
Walnut Gdns HR5 ......81 D6
Walnut Gr NP26 ......79 C1
Walnut Tree Ave HR2 ......92 E6
Walnut Tree Cl HR9 ......94 D2
Walsall St NP19 ......119 E4
Walterstone Comm HR2 ......53 F4
Walton Cl Hereford HR2 ......93 A5
  Newport NP19 ......120 C4
Waltwood Park Dr NP18 ......121 F7
Waltwood Rd NP18 ......121 E6
Walwyn Cl GL17 ......66 F5
Walwyn Rd Colwall WR13 ......86 B2
  Colwall Stone WR13 ......41 F4
Wapley Hill Forest Walks* 7 D1
Ward Cl NP19 ......120 A7
Warden Cl LD8 ......6 C3
Warden Rd LD8 ......6 C3
Warlock Cl NP19 ......120 F5
Warncombe Link HR4 ......90 C3
Warren Cl HR3 ......88 C3
Warren Dr HR8 ......89 E3
Warren La King's Thorn HR2 ......47 C3
  Longhope HR9 ......59 A1
Warren Slade NP10 ......116 F5
Warren's Rd NP25 ......71 F1
Warrendale NP44 ......106 B1
Warth La BS35 ......127 D3
Warwick Cl
  Chepstow NP16 ......116 D6
  Cwmbran NP44 ......106 A3
  Pontypool NP4 ......105 A2
Warwick Ho WR14 ......86 F8
Warwick La **2** NP20 ......120 A5
  Newport NP19 ......120 A5
Warwick Rd Hereford HR2 ......93 B5
Warwick Wlk HR4 ......90 C5
Washing's La NP25 ......72 C5
Waste Rd NP25 ......70 E6
Watch House Par NP20 ......119 C1
Waterfield Rd HR2 ......92 D5
Waterloo **1** HR6 ......82 D5
Waterloo Cl WR13 ......85 E4
Waterloo Ct NP44 ......104 E1
Waterloo La HR1 ......91 C4
Waterloo Rd Kington HR5 ......81 F7
  Newport NP20 ......119 A3
Watermeadow HR1 ......91 C2
Watermill HR4 ......27 D3
Waters La NP20 ......119 C5
Waters Way NP16 ......116 E7
Waterside
  Abergavenny NP7 ......95 E5
  Hereford HR6 ......36 F6
  Ross-on-Wye HR9 ......94 E4
Waterside Cl NP10 ......118 A7
Waterside Ct
  Cwmbran NP44 ......106 A2
  Newport NP20 ......119 D1
Waterside Wlk W NP10 ......118 A6
Waterworks La
  Aberystwan NP4 ......102 A5
  Leominster HR6 ......82 E4
Waterworks Mus* NP4 ......92 D7
Watery La
  Bodenham Moor HR1 ......28 E5
  Cusop HR3 ......33 F5

Watery La continued
  Hereford HR2 ......93 C4
  Lea HR9 ......67 C8
  Madley HR2 ......36 A2
  Malvern WR14 ......42 C3
  Much Marcle HR8 ......49 F4
  Newent GL18 ......59 F4
  Tarrington HR1 ......39 E6
  Tyberton HR2 ......35 F1
  Walton LD8 ......14 C7
Watery Lane / Lon Dyfriog NP25 ......96 A4
Watkins Ct HR4 ......136 B2
Watkins La **2** NP20 ......118 F4
Watkins' Way WR14 ......87 C7
Watling St Leintwardine SY7 ......3 B5
  Ross-on-Wye HR7 ......83 C5
Watts Cl NP10 ......118 B6
Waun Hywel Rd NP44 ......106 C6
Waun Rd NP44 ......106 C1
Waunfield La NP15 ......73 F7
Waunllapria NP7 ......98 C5
Wavell Dr NP20 ......113 A3
Waveney Cl NP20 ......112 C2
Wayfield Cres NP44 ......106 F5
Wayne Cl NP16 ......75 C6
Weare Cl NP20 ......112 C2
Weavers Orch HR4 ......35 D8
Web Tree Ave HR2 ......92 F5
Web's Orch HR8 ......40 B4
Webley Cl NP18 ......114 A4
Webley Gdns NP18 ......114 A4
Webley Rd GL17 ......66 F7
Wedderburn Rd WR14 ......87 C8
Wedgwood Dr NP20 ......125 E5
Wednesbury St NP19 ......119 F4
Weeping Cross La SY8 ......79 D3
Wegnalls Way HR6 ......82 A4
Weir Garden The* HR4 ......36 E4
Welbeck Ave HR1 ......91 D1
Weldon Cl NP44 ......106 A4
Welford Gn HR4 ......90 C3
Well Cl NP16 ......116 F4
Well La GL17 ......67 A4
Well Vale HR9 ......65 D3
Welland Circ NP20 ......112 C2
Welland Cres NP20 ......112 C2
Welland Gdns WR13 ......42 E2
Welland Prim Sch WR13 ......42 C7
Wellbrook Cl HR1 ......91 B4
Wellbrookside HR2 ......35 B1
Wellfield NP7 ......54 E3
Wellfield Cl
  Abergavenny NP7 ......95 D7
  Coed-y-paen NP4 ......73 A1
Wellfield La NP4 ......104 D1
Wellington Barns HR4 ......27 D1
Wellington Dr NP44 ......106 A3
Wellington La NP4 ......27 D1
Wellington Pl HR1 ......93 D8
Wellington Prim Sch HR4 ......27 E3
Wellman Rd HR6 ......58 A5
Wellmeadow GL16 ......72 D7
Wells Cl Malvern WR14 ......42 C4
  Newport NP20 ......118 E1
Wells La WR13 ......31 C2
Wells Rd Credenhill HR4 ......37 A6
  Malvern WR14 ......86 E4
Welsh Court Rd HR8 ......49 E1
Welsh House La GL18 ......59 F8
Welsh St NP16 ......113 D8
Wend The GL17 ......67 F5
Wenlock Cl HR2 ......92 B5
Wentloog Cl NP44 ......106 E3
Wentsland Cres NP44 ......104 A6
Wentsland Rd NP44 ......104 A6
Wentwood Cl NP44 ......106 C6
Wentwood Dr NP26 ......77 E2
Wentwood Forest Walks* NP26 ......77 D5
Wentwood Rd NP18 ......113 E2
Wentwood View NP26 ......124 F7
Wentworth Rd HR1 ......91 A5
Weobley Cl HR2 ......92 D5
Weobley High Sch HR4 ......26 B6
Weobley Prim Sch HR4 ......26 B6
Wern Ddu
  Ewyas Harold HR2 ......54 B7
  Longtown HR2 ......53 F7
Wern Hill NP4 ......104 B6
Wern Ind Est NP10 ......118 A5
Wern La NP4 ......73 A4
Wern Rd NP4 ......104 E1
Wern School Cl NP4 ......104 E1
Wern Terr NP4 ......104 B6
Werngifford HR2 ......62 A8
Werstan Cl WR14 ......87 C7
Wesley Cl NP44 ......106 D2
Wesley Gdns NP16 ......75 D1
Wesley Rd
  Cinderford GL14 ......67 C1
  Leominster HR6 ......82 B5
Wesley St NP44 ......106 E2
Wesley Way NP16 ......75 D1
Wessington Dr HR1 ......91 B4
West Adam St NP16 ......78 B2
West Ave Drybrook GL17 ......67 B4
  Pontypool NP4 ......104 D1
West Bank NP44 ......107 B2
West Bank Ct **8** NP4 ......119 C4
West End Mapor NP20 ......123 A2
  Ruardean GL17 ......66 E4
  Undy NP26 ......123 C4
West End Gdns NP26 ......123 C4
West End St NP16 ......78 B3
West Floyd St NP16 ......78 C3
West Hill HR2 ......83 B5

West Hill Rd NP4 ......102 B1
West Jefferson St NP16 ......78 C2
West Lea **3** NP15 ......70 C2
West Malvern Rd WR14 ......86 D6
West Market St NP20 ......119 D3
West Monmouth Comp Sch NP4 ......104 B5
West Nash Rd NP44 ......130 C4
West Park La **1** NP20 ......118 F4
West Park Rd NP20 ......118 F4
West Penn St NP16 ......78 C2
West Rd NP15 ......73 B5
West Roedin NP44 ......112 C8
West St Hereford HR4 ......136 B2
  Leominster HR6 ......82 D5
  Newport NP20 ......119 B4
  Pembridge HR6 ......16 C1
West View Almeley HR3 ......25 A6
  Joy's Green GL17 ......66 D3
  Newent GL18 ......59 F4
West View Terr NP4 ......101 B7
West Wall LD8 ......6 E3
West Way Rd NP20 ......119 B1
Westbury HR7 ......29 F5
Westbury Cl WR14 ......93 C5
Westbury St HR6 ......82 D4
Westcroft HR6 ......82 B4
Western Approach Distribution Pk BS35 ......135 C4
Western Ave
  Chepstow NP16 ......116 F5
  Hereford HR4 ......90 A2
  Mitcheldean GL17 ......67 D5
  Newport NP20 ......118 C3
Western Cl HR6 ......82 D5
Western Ind Est NP18 ......114 B4
Western Rd NP7 ......95 B7
Western Valley Rd NP10 ......118 C3
Western Way GL18 ......59 F4
Westfaling St HR4 ......90 C1
Westfield Caldicot NP26 ......124 E5
  Llangrove HR9 ......65 B6
Westfield Ave
  Caldicot NP26 ......124 E5
  Newport NP20 ......113 A2
Westfield Cl
  Bromyard HR7 ......83 C5
  Caerleon NP18 ......113 F4
Westfield Ct **2** GL14 ......67 C1
Westfield Dr NP20 ......113 A2
Westfield Lower Specl Sch NP20 ......113 A2
Westfield Rd
  Caerleon NP18 ......113 F3
  27 Cinderford GL14 ......67 C1
  Monmouth NP25 ......96 C7
  Newport NP20 ......119 A5
Westfield Sch HR6 ......82 C4
Westfield Way NP20 ......113 A2
Westfield Wlk HR6 ......82 C4
Westfields Trad Est WR4 ......90 D2
Westgate HR6 ......81 F6
Westgate Ct NP18 ......114 B2
Westhill Gdns HR7 ......83 B5
Westholme Rd HR1 ......92 C5
Westland View HR6 ......9 D2
Westlyn Cl WR14 ......85 B3
Westminster Ave HR1 ......91 D1
Westminster Bank WR14 ......84 C1
Westminster Rd WR14 ......86 E4
Westmoor Cl NP18 ......113 F4
Weston Beggard La
  Bartestree HR1 ......38 F4
  Weston Beggard HR1 ......39 B4
Weston Gr HR1 ......91 D1
Weston Gr HR9 ......94 F5
Weston Hill WR6 ......22 E2
Weston Rd SY7 ......2 C4
Weston under Penyard CE Prim Sch HR9 ......58 D2
Westray Cl NP19 ......119 F7
Westview SY8 ......5 D8
Westville Rd **9** NP20 ......118 F4
Westward Rd WR14 ......84 E6
Westway NP16 ......124 C4
Westwood Ind Est HR2 ......90 A6
Wetherby Dr HR4 ......90 C5
Wetmore La
  Leintwardine SY7,SY8 ......3 F7
  Ludlow SY8 ......4 A7
Wettons The HR6 ......25 D8
Weyloed La NP16 ......79 D6
Weyman Rd SY8 ......79 D6
Weymore La SY7 ......2 E4
Wharf La NP19 ......119 E5
Wharf Rd NP19 ......119 E5
Wharton La HR4 ......18 C2
Wheat Field Cl NP25 ......96 B4
Wheatcommon La
  Ashford Carbonell SY8 ......5 A2
  Richards Castle SY8 ......4 F1
Wheathill Cl WR13 ......79 E5
Wheatridge Rd HR4 ......90 C5
Wheatsheaf Ct NP26 ......123 B3
Wheeler Orch WR15 ......80 C3
Wheeler Rd SY8 ......79 E5
Wheeler St NP20 ......119 C5
Whimsey Rd GL14 ......67 E2
Whippingtton's Cnr GL16 ......72 E7
Whistle Halt Sta NP4 ......98 D1
Whistle Rd NP44 ......107 B4
Whistler Cl NP19 ......120 A7
Whitbatch Cl SY8 ......79 C6
Whitborn Cl WR14 ......87 C8
Whitborn End WR14 ......87 C8

Vag – Wil   157

Whitbourne CE Prim Sch WR6 ......21 F3
Whitbread Rd SY8 ......79 D5
Whitby Pl NP19 ......119 D6
Whitchurch CE Prim Sch HR9 ......65 E4
Whitcliffe Rd SY8 ......79 B3
White Ash Glade NP18 ......113 F2
White Ave NP10 ......128 E5
White Castle* NP7 ......62 E3
White Cross Rd HR4 ......90 C2
White Friars SY8 ......79 D5
White Hall La NP44 ......107 B1
White Horse Sq HR4 ......90 C1
White Horse St HR4 ......90 C1
White House Cl HR1 ......28 B2
White House Ct WR6 ......21 E3
White House Rd NP44 ......107 A5
White's Cl HR7 ......29 F5
Whitebrook Way NP44 ......106 F2
Whitecastle Cl HR2 ......92 D4
Whitechapel Wlk NP26 ......124 C5
Whitecross Cotts HR9 ......57 D3
Whitecross St NP25 ......137 B2
Whitecross High Sch HR4 ......90 D2
Whitecross Rd HR4 ......90 D1
Whitecross St NP25 ......137 B2
Whitefriars Rd HR4 ......92 D6
Whitehall Gdns NP26 ......123 C2
Whitehall Rd
  Hampton Bishop HR1 ......48 B8
  Mordiford HR1 ......39 A1
Whitehart La NP18 ......114 C1
Whitehill Cl NP15 ......96 B4
Whitehill La
  Drybrook GL17 ......67 B4
  Rockfield NP25 ......64 C2
Whitehill Park Ind Est HR4 ......26 A7
Whitehorse Cl HR4 ......90 D1
Whitehouse Dr HR2 ......46 A6
Whitehouse La HR9,GL18 ......59 C5
Whitehouse Rd BS35 ......135 C7
Whitehouse Way HR1 ......91 D1
Whitemores La HR7 ......95 D5
Whitestone Bsns Pk HR1 ......38 F5
Whitethorn Gr WR14 ......85 C3
Whitewall NP26 ......123 C1
Whitney Court Rd HR3 ......23 F3
Whitney Village Rd HR3 ......23 F2
Whitson Common Rd NP18 ......131 C4
Whitstone NP19 ......120 B6
Whittern Way NP4 ......91 D2
Whittle Ct NP20 ......113 A3
Whittle Dr NP20 ......113 A3
Whyle La HR6 ......19 B7
Wick Rd BS35 ......135 C2
Widemarsh St HR4 ......136 C4
Wiesenthal St NP19 ......125 A6
Wigga The HR2 ......54 A6
Wigmore Castle* HR6 ......8 B8
Wigmore High Sch HR6 ......8 B7
Wigmore Primary Sch HR6 ......8 B7
Wilcae Terr **1** NP15 ......70 C2
Wilcroft Pk HR1 ......38 E4
Wilden Bank HR1 ......29 B4
Wildings The SY8 ......79 E6
Will Paynter Wlk NP19 ......120 D7
Will's View LD8 ......6 E3
Willenhall St NP19 ......119 E4
William Brown Cl NP44 ......113 A7
William Lovett Gdns **1** NP20 ......119 B4
William Morris Dr **1** NP19 ......120 D6
William's Hospl **3** HR1 ......93 B8
William's Mead HR1 ......38 E4
Williams Cl **2** NP20 ......119 C3
Williams Field La NP25 ......137 A2
Willins NP44 ......112 B8
Willow Cl
  Abergavenny NP7 ......95 E4
  Bromyard HR7 ......83 B5
  Caldicot NP26 ......124 E5
  Chepstow NP16 ......37 A6
  Credenhill HR4 ......37 A6
  Newport NP19 ......120 B2
Willow Dr NP18 ......121 E6
Willow Gn NP18 ......113 F2
Willow Gr Hereford HR2 ......93 A6
  Malvern WR14 ......22 E5
Willow Rise HR1 ......38 C8
Willowbrook HR4 ......54 D7
Willowdean **3** GL14 ......67 C1
Willowfields HR1 ......38 F5
Willows The
  Croesyceiliog NP44 ......107 A5
  Dymock GL18 ......50 D2
  Hereford HR2 ......93 A5
  Longhope GL17 ......67 F5
  Raglan NP15 ......96 A3
  Redwick NP26 ......132 E5
  Undy NP26 ......123 B3
Wills Row NP10 ......118 B4
Wilmot Rd WR14 ......87 B8
Wilson Rd NP19 ......120 A7

Wilson St NP20 ....119 D2
Wilson Terr LD8 ....6 D3
Wilton Ave HR2 ....92 D5
Wilton Cotts HR9 ....94 B5
Wilton La HR9 ....94 B5
Wilton Rd Malvern WR14 ..87 B8
Ross-on-W HR9 ....94 C5
Wilton View HR9 ....94 D7
Wimborne Rise NP44 ...106 C5
Wincanton Cl HR4 ....90 C4
Winchecombe Ho HR2 ...92 D6
Winchester Ave HR1 ....91 D1
Winchester Cl NP20 ...119 A1
Windermere Rd HR4 ....90 D3
Windermere Sq 4
  NP19 ....119 E8
Windmill La NP26 .....124 B5
Windmill Rd NP26 ......77 E3
Windmill Sq 7 NP20 .119 C3
Windrush Cr NP20 .....112 E2
Windrush Cres WR14 ...87 D8
Windsor Cl Magor NP26 .123 A3
  Malvern WR14 ....85 C6
  Ross-on-W HR9 ....94 F7
Windsor Dr NP26 ......123 A3
Windsor Gdns NP26 ...123 A3
Windsor Pk NP26 ......123 A3
Windsor Pl NP10 ......118 B4
Windsor Rd
  Abergavenny NP7 ......95 B7
  Cwmbran NP44 ....106 C2
  Hereford HR2 ....93 B5
  Newport NP19 ....119 F5
  Pontypool NP4 ....104 E3
Windsor St HR4 ....90 D1
Windsor Terr 2 NP20 .119 B4
Winfield GL18 ....59 F4
Winforton Common Rd
  HR3 ....24 C2
Wingate St NP20 ......119 C1
Winnington Cl WR6 .....21 F8
Winsford Gr NP7 ....60 D1
Winsgrave Bglws WR6 ..32 B8
Winslow Rd HR7 ....83 B6
Winston Cl HR8 ....89 E2
Winston Rd HR2 ....93 A5
Winstone Rd NP4 ......102 B1
Winter's Cross HR9 ....57 B4
Wintles Cl GL17 ....67 D5
Wintour Cl NP16 ......110 D1
Wirewood Cl NP16 .....111 A2
Wirewood Cres NP16 ..111 A2
Wishlade's Row HR5 ...81 D6
Wistaria Cl NP20 .....113 B3
Wiston Path NP44 ....106 B2
Witham St NP19 ......119 E4
Withies Cl HR1 ....38 F6
Withies Rd HR1 ....38 F6
Withington Prim Sch
  HR1 ....38 F6
Withy Cl NP26 ....123 A3
Withy La NP25 ....96 D8
Withy Wlk NP26 ......123 A3
Withybrook Cl HR2 .....93 C5
Withypool HR2 ....92 E4

Woburn Cl HR9 ....94 F7
Wolf Bsns Pk HR9 .....94 F5
Wolseley St NP20 .....119 C1
Wonastow Cl NP25 .....96 B3
Wonastow Rd NP25 ....96 B3
Wonders The HR8 ......49 D7
Wood Cl Llanyravon NP44 .107 B1
  Rogerstone NP10 ....118 A7
Wood Cres NP10 ......118 A7
Wood Edge HR9 ....94 D2
Wood End St HR8 ......51 B4
Wood Farm Rd WR14 ...86 F2
Wood La Bromyard HR7 ..20 D5
  Gorsley GL18 ....59 D4
Wood Path NP44 ......107 A6
Wood Rd The HR3 .....24 A3
Wood Terr HR4 ....37 A4
Wood View La HR9 .....94 E5
Woodbine Gdns NP26 .123 B3
Woodbury La HR2 ......35 C5
Woodbury Rise WR14 ..84 E4
Woodcroft Cl NP16 ...111 A4
Woodcroft La NP16 ...111 A4
Woodcroft Terr NP16 .111 B4
Woodend La Gorsley HR9 .59 A4
  Little Cowarne HR7 ....29 E5
Woodend Lane Bsns Pk
  HR7 ....29 F5
Woodend Rd GL17 ......67 B3
Woodfarm Rd WR14 ....86 F2
Wooden Cres HR6 ......82 B4
Woodfield HR2 ....56 E5
Woodfield Rd
  Ledbury HR8 ....89 D2
  Pontypool NP4 ....105 A4
Woodgate Rd GL14 .....67 C1
Woodgreen Cl HR1 .....28 B2
Woodhouse La Orleton SY8 .9 C7
  Richards Castle SY8 ....4 D1
  Whitton LD7 ....6 A8
Woodhouse Way HR2 ...93 A5
Woodhouses SY8 ....4 C7
Woodland Cres NP7 ....95 B3
Woodland Ct NP44 ....107 A4
Woodland Dr NP10 ...118 A3
Woodland Park Rd
  NP19 ....119 F6
Woodland Park View 5
  NP19 ....119 F6
Woodland Rd
  Abergavenny NP7 ......95 E6
  Coleford GL16 ....72 F8
  Croesyceiliog NP44 ..107 A4
  Drybrook GL17 ....67 B4
  Llanmartin NP18 .....121 E6
  Newport NP19 ....119 F6
  Suckley WR6 ....31 D6
Woodland St
  Blaenavon NP4 ....101 D7
  Cwmbran NP44 ....106 D4
Woodland View
  Caldicot NP26 ....124 F6
  Croesyceiliog NP44 ..107 A5
  Joy's Green GL17 .....66 D3
  Monmouth NP25 ......96 F3
  Pontypool NP4 ....104 B8
  Rogiet NP26 ....124 C4
  Ross-on-W HR9 ....94 E4

Woodland Way LD8 ......6 C5
Woodland Wlk NP18 ...121 C4
Woodlands NP25 ....72 B1
Woodlands Cl
  Malvern WR14 ....42 C4
  St Arvans NP16 ......110 B6
Woodlands Dr NP20 ...113 A4
Woodlands Jun & Inf Schs
  NP44 ....106 B5
Woodlands The
  Llandogo NP25 ....76 B7
  Pontypool NP4 ....104 D7
Woodleigh Cl HR8 ......89 C4
Woodleigh Rd HR8 .....89 D4
Woodmeadow Rd HR9 ..94 D2
Woodpecker Cl NP26 .124 B4
Woodshears Dr WR14 ..87 A7
Woodshears Rd WR14 ..87 A7
Woodside Newport NP10 .128 E7
Woodside Rd
  Cwmbran NP44 ......106 E4
  Pontypool NP4 ......102 B2
Woodside Trad Est NP15 .97 A4
Woodside Way NP44 ..106 C4
Woodstock Cl NP26 ..124 F4
Woodstock St NP26 ..124 F4
Woodstock Way NP26 .124 F5
Woodview GL18 ....59 D7
Woodview Ct NP4 ....104 B6
Woodview Terr NP4 ...104 B6
Woodville Gr HR1 ......38 C8
Woodville Rd NP20 ...118 F4
Woodyatt Ct WR14 ....87 A7
Woodyatt's Cross HR2 ..36 D1
Woolhope Rd HR1 ......48 D5
Woolpitch NP44 ......106 B3
Woolpitch Wood NP16 .116 C8
Wootton La HR3 ....25 A7
Worcester Cl NP44 ...107 A3
Worcester Cres NP19 .120 A8
Worcester Path NP44 .107 A3
Worcester Rd
  Bromyard HR7 ....20 B2
  6 Cinderford GL14 ...67 D1
  Ledbury HR8 ....89 F5
  Leominster HR6 ....18 E4
  Leominster HR6 ....82 E4
  Malvern WR13,WR14 ...85 D6
  Risbury HR6,HR7 ....19 D4
Worcester St NP25 ...137 B2
Wordsworth Cl
  Caldicot NP26 ....124 E4
  Cwmbran NP44 ....106 D2
Wordsworth Gn WR14 ..85 A2
Wordsworth Rd
  Hereford HR4 ....90 C2
  Newport NP19 ....120 A5
Wren Ave WR14 ....85 C2
Wrenford Ct NP20 ....119 C4
Wrigglebrook La HR2 ..47 C2
Wrigglebrook Pitch HR2 .47 C2
Wright Cl NP19 ....120 B3
Wrights Ct 4 HR6 ....82 D4
Wyatt Cl NP25 ....96 C2
Wyatt Rd HR1 ....38 E7

Wych The HR5 ....81 C6
Wyche Rd WR14 ....86 E5
Wye Ave Bromyard HR7 ..83 C6
  Malvern WR14 ....87 D8
Wye Bridge* NP25 ...137 C2
Wye Cres Bettws NP20 .112 E2
  Chepstow NP16 ......116 E7
Wye Ct NP44 ....106 B4
Wye End Rd HR3 ....88 E4
Wye Ford Rd HR3 ......88 D4
Wye Rapids Cotts HR9 ..65 E2
Wye St Hereford HR2 .136 B2
  Ross-on-W HR9 ....94 D5
Wye Terr HR4 ....136 B2
Wye Valley Bsns Pk HR3 .88 C2
Wye Valley Link Rd
  NP16 ....116 E5
Wye View HR8 ....89 C5
Wye View Ho NP16 ...117 A7
Wye View La HR9 ......65 E3
Wye View Terr NP25 ...72 C4
Wye's Gn NP25 ....72 C4
Wyebank Ave NP16 ...111 A1
Wyebank Cl NP16 ....117 A8
Wyebank Cres NP16 ..117 A8
Wyebank Dr NP16 ....111 A1
Wyebank Pl NP16 ....117 A8
Wyebank Rd NP16 ....117 A8
Wyebank Rise NP16 ..117 A8
Wyebank View NP16 ..117 A8
Wyebank Way NP16 ..117 A7
Wyebridge St NP25 ..137 C2
Wyecliffe Terr HR1 ...136 C3
Wyedean Rise HR2 ....92 C6
Wyedean Sch NP16 ...117 A8
Wyefield Ct NP25 .....96 C2
Wyelands HR2 ....48 B6
Wyelands Cl HR2 ......93 A6
Wyelands View NP16 .116 B4
Wyesham Ave NP25 ...96 F3
Wyesham Inf Sch NP25 .96 F3
Wyesham Jun Sch NP25 .96 F3
Wyesham La NP25 .....72 B7
Wyesham Rd NP25 ....96 F3
Wyeside Commercial Ctr
  NP25 ....96 F4
Wyeside Gdns HR3 ....88 C2
Wyeside Pk HR9 ....66 C5
Wyeverne Rd 1 NP19 .120 A5
Wykewane WR14 ....87 D7
Wyndbrook La GL19 ...51 F4
Wyndcliffe View NP16 .110 B5
Wyndecliffe Ho NP16 .117 A7
Wyndham Rd NP7 ......95 F6
Wyndham St NP20 ...119 C6
Wynniattes Way WR6 ..13 F6
Wyntour Ho NP16 ....117 A8
Wynyard Cl HR6 ....82 B4
Wyrebrook Gdns WR15 .12 A8
Wyrebrook Orch WR15 .12 A8
Wyson Ave SY8 ....10 B7
Wyson Cl SY8 ....10 B6
Wyson La SY8 ....10 A6
Wyson Terr SY8 ....10 B7
Wyvern Rd NP16 .....117 B1

Y

Y Dolydd-Meadows The
  HR3 ....88 C2
Yarlington Mill HR2 ...92 C5
Yates Hay Rd WR14 ....84 F5
Yazor Rd HR4 ....90 D2
Yeld La HR5 ....81 A6
Yeo Cl NP20 ....112 E1
Yeo Rd NP20 ....112 E1
Yeoman Cl HR8 ....89 C6
Yetts The NP16 ......117 B8
Yew Tree Cl
  Colwall Stone WR13 ...41 F4
  Kingstone HR2 ....46 A6
  Undy NP26 ....123 C2
Yew Tree Ct NP26 ...124 F4
Yew Tree Gdns HR4 ....37 B4
Yew Tree La
  Caerleon NP18 ....114 B3
  Malvern WR14 ....42 C4
Yew Tree Rise NP26 ..124 D4
Yew Tree Terr
  Croesyceiliog NP44 ..107 A5
  Cwmbran NP44 ......106 D2
Yewberry Cl NP20 ....113 B2
Yewberry La NP20 ....113 B2
Ynys La NP44 ....107 A5
York Cl Cwmbran NP44 .106 A3
  Hereford HR4 ....90 C5
  Malvern WR14 ....85 C6
  Monmouth NP25 .....137 A1
York Pl NP20 ....119 B4
York Rd Bromyard HR7 ..83 B6
  Cinderford GL14 ......67 D1
  Newport NP19 ......119 E7
Ysgol Gyfun Gwynllyw
  NP4 ....102 C1
Ysgol Gymraeg Casnewydd
  NP18 ....120 E4
Ysgol Gymraeg Cwmbran Jun
  & Inf Sch NP44 .....106 D2
Ysgol Pil NP44 ......106 C6
Ysgol Y Ffin NP26 ...125 F3
Ysguborwen NP7 ....95 E7

Z

Zetland Rd WR14 .....84 F2

Any feature in this atlas can be given a unique reference to help you find the same feature on other Ordnance Survey maps of the area, or to help someone else locate you if they do not have a Street Atlas.

The grid squares in this atlas match the Ordnance Survey National Grid and are at 500 metre intervals. The small figures at the bottom and sides of every other grid line are the National Grid kilometre values (**00** to **99** km) and are repeated across the country every 100 km (see left).

To give a unique National Grid reference you need to locate where in the country you are. The country is divided into 100 km squares with each square given a unique two-letter reference. Use the administrative map to determine in which 100 km square a particular page of this atlas falls.

The bold letters and numbers between each grid line (**A** to **F**, **1** to **8**) are for use within a specific Street Atlas only, and when used with the page number, are a convenient way of referencing these grid squares.

Example The railway bridge over DARLEY GREEN RD in grid square B1

Step 1: Identify the two-letter reference, in this example the page is in **SP**

Step 2: Identify the 1 km square in which the railway bridge falls. Use the figures in the southwest corner of this square: Eastings **17**, Northings **74**. This gives a unique reference: **SP 17 74**, accurate to 1 km.

Step 3: To give a more precise reference accurate to 100 m you need to estimate how many tenths along and how many tenths up this 1 km square the feature is (to help with this the 1 km square is divided into four 500 m squares). This makes the bridge about **8** tenths along and about **1** tenth up from the southwest corner.

This gives a unique reference: **SP 178 741**, accurate to 100 m.

Eastings (read from left to right along the bottom) come before Northings (read from bottom to top). If you have trouble remembering say to yourself "Along the hall, THEN up the stairs"!

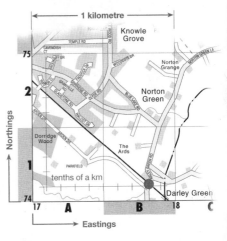